MW01114430

NEW
CONCISE
HANDBOOK

Second Edition

Hans P. Guth

San Jose State University

Wadsworth Publishing Company
Belmont, California
A Division of Wadsworth, Inc.

English Editor: Angela Gantner
Editorial Assistant: Julie Johnson
Production Editor: Vicki Friedberg
Managing Designer: Cynthia Schultz
Print Buyer: Randy Hurst
Permissions Editor: Jeanne Bosschart
Designer: James Chadwick
Copy Editor: Denise Cook-Clampert
Compositor: Thompson Type, San Diego
Cover: Cynthia Schultz

Credits

Printed in the United States of America   34

1 2 3 4 5 6 7 8 9 10 — 95 94 93 92 91

Library of Congress Cataloging-in-Publication Data

Guth, Hans Paul, 1926–
    New concise handbook / Hans P. Guth. — 2nd ed.
       p.   cm.
    Includes index.
    ISBN 0-534-15024-1
    1. English language — Usage — Handbooks, manuals, etc.   2. English language — Grammar — 1950– — Handbooks, manuals, etc.   3. English language — Rhetoric — Handbooks, manuals, etc.   I. Title.
PE1460.G78   1991
808'.042 — dc20   90-49334

PREFACE:
TO THE INSTRUCTOR

New Concise Handbook, Second Edition, is a compact guide to written composition. It is realistically focused on the needs of today's classrooms and provides

- balanced treatment of the larger elements of composition (purpose, audience, content, organization) and the standards of written English
- graphic demonstration of how prewriting, organizing, and revision techniques pay off in better student writing
- an exceptionally accessible writer's grammar with the plain-English explanations and concrete clues students need to grasp essential grammatical concepts
- a treatment of punctuation that stresses the functions punctuation marks serve in a sentence
- an exceptionally clear and comprehensive guide to the mysteries of documentation (MLA and APA), with an MLA Directory giving both the Works Cited entry and parenthetical documentation for over forty citations
- a word processing section with instructions and exercises for the beginner

Special Features of the Second Edition

MINIMUM PROFICIENCIES Each chapter starts with a quick rundown of minimum proficiencies, focusing on basic "survival skills" for the student while making it clear that there is more to good writing than meeting minimum standards.

WRITING WORKSHOPS Writing workshops show students how to work at their writing while interacting in class work or working in small groups.

DISCOURSE EXERCISES Lively and informative discourse exercises illustrate principles of grammar or punctuation by placing exercise sentences in the context of mini-compositions.

PEER EDITOR EXERCISES A second major exercise strand presents realistic student-written sentences for individual editing or peer review.

Additional Support for the Instructor

■ More than a routine more-of-same workbook, *New Concise Workbook*, Second Edition, provides backup explanations and follow-up exercises for students with inadequate preparation or special needs. Worksheets are formatted for quick scoring by the instructor or peer-marking by members of the class.

■ The *Wadsworth English Proficiency Test* (Forms A and B) is a 100-item multiple choice test that stresses simplicity of format and can be administered during one conventional class period. It includes instructions for a writing sample.

■ *New Concise Manual*, Second Edition, provides a complete answer key for the handbook as well as teaching hints for new and experienced faculty.

A WORD OF THANKS For assistance in preparing this second edition, I would like to thank the following reviewers: Toni-Lee Capossela, Boston University; Peggy Jolly, University of Alabama; Philip Korth, Michigan State University; Roy Lambert, University of Florida; Peter F. Neumeyer, San Diego State University; and Robert C. Peterson, Middle Tennessee State University.

H. Guth

ABOUT THE AUTHOR

Hans P. Guth is Professor of English at San Jose State University, where he has been honored as Outstanding Professor and Professor of the Year. He wrote his doctoral dissertation at the University of Michigan on Kenneth Burke and other moderns. He has worked with composition faculties in workshops and institutes in most of the 50 states, and has been a visiting professor at Stanford University, the University of Illinois, and the University of Hawaii.

His articles on Spenser, Kafka, and other literary subjects have appeared in *PMLA*, *Anglia*, and *Symposium*; his articles on rhetoric and composition include "The Politics of Rhetoric" (1972), "Composition Then and Now" (*Rhetoric Quarterly*, 1980), and "How I Write: Five Ways of Looking at the Blackbird" in Tom Waldrep's *Writers on Writing* (1985). Guth's writing texts and professional books include *Words and Ideas, English Today and Tomorrow, English for a New Generation, The Writer's Agenda*, and *Essay: Reading with the Writer's Eye*.

Guth is co-director and program chair of the Young Rhetoricians' Conference sponsored by San Jose State University, which each year brings together composition teachers from around the country for a lively festival of the art of rhetoric.

BRIEF

CONTENTS

CONTENTS

4 Sentence Basics 134

5 Grammar for Writers 176

11 The Research Paper 388

NEW
CONCISE
HANDBOOK

1

PREWRITING AND WRITING

Note: The following is a quick rundown of minimum proficiencies in the area covered in this chapter. Remember that there is much more to good writing than meeting minimum standards. However, if you fail to meet the standards summarized here, your message may not reach the reader and you may not get credit for what you do well.

Some basic requirements appear again and again in descriptions of successful papers:

(1) Good writing has a purpose. We write to give directions or advice. We write to explain something difficult. We write to set the record straight or air a grievance. We write to expose neglect or promote a good cause. In an effective piece of writing, the writer has focused on an issue or a need, has sized up the audience, and has accomplished something that made the paper worth writing and reading.

(2) Good writing has substance. Good writers know where to turn for material. They are alert observers who notice revealing details and register quotable quotations. They use techniques like brainstorming to bring to mind memories that are to the point. When they work up a subject, they read what experts and pundits have to say. They listen to people with the inside story — whether in informal conversation or in a structured interview.

(3) Good writing has a point. It satisfies the reader who wants to know: "What are you trying to tell me? What are you trying to prove?" Effective writers push toward a thesis — a key statement that sums up what they are trying to say or what their evidence shows. They bring together related details and relevant evidence and funnel it into a general conclusion.

(4) Good writing has a plan. The writer has worked out a pattern of organization that the reader can follow. The writing has a master plan that the writer can chart or outline for the reader — setting up a contrast between then and now, or examining in order of importance key causes of homelessness, or weighing the pro and con on a current issue.

(5) Good writing supports general ideas with specific examples. It moves in for a closer look at places, people, and events. The opinions presented do not remain vague secondhand ideas; the writer follows them up with convincing specifics and authentic details. Key terms, from *freedom of speech* to *computer literacy* and *rust belt*, come to life as the writer shows what they mean in practice.

(6) Good writing reaches the reader. It explains what is difficult and new. It honors the readers' standards for serious written English: the right word, sentences that say clearly what they mean, punctuation and spelling that help carry the message instead of getting in the way.

OVERVIEW   How do experienced writers move from the preliminary (or **prewriting**) stage to the finished product? Think of your writing as a creative process that moves through five intermeshing stages:

TRIGGERING   Why are you writing this paper? What are you trying to do? Who is the audience? What will this piece of writing do for the writer and for the reader?

GATHERING Where are you going to turn for material? What do you already know, and how can you learn more? What opportunities will you have for drawing on personal experience, taking a first-hand look, talking to insiders, or consulting authoritative sources?

SHAPING How are you going to lay out your material? How does it add up — what is the point? How are you going to proceed — what is your strategy?

REVISING As you read your first draft, where does it say what you are trying to say, and where does it fall short? Can the reader follow your train of thought, or do you need to reshuffle parts of your paper? Do you need to do more to show connections between ideas?

EDITING Where should the wording be more pointed or more vivid? Which sentences are wordy, roundabout, or confused? Did you check spelling and punctuation to make sure your writing is ready-to-print?

1a A REASON TO WRITE

Make sure you have a reason to write.

Good writing has a purpose. When we read a successful paper, we sense that the writer set out to accomplish something. People write best when they tackle a topic that they care about, that they can get involved in personally. For instance, you are likely to write with conviction when you

- share your expertise about cars, Mexican cooking, or computers
- prove a point about student loans or about the homeless that has been overlooked

---

REASONS FOR WRITING

to give directions	to sound a warning
to give instructions	to enlist support
to give advice	to clear someone's name
	to champion a cause
to clarify confusion	to correct abuses
to correct misconceptions	
to set the record straight	to promote a product
to register a grievance	to advance a policy
to come to terms with the past	to gain employment
to report events	to entertain
to share data	to inspire
to present a theory	to build morale
to argue a position	

- challenge a stereotype about a group to which you belong (Italians, Southerners, Mormons, jocks)
- enlist support for a cause

Even when you write on an assigned subject, try to find the tie-in with your own experience or convictions. Here are motives that may activate different kinds of papers:

■ People often write eloquently when they write to *register a grievance* or to come to terms with a problem. In writing an autobiographical paper, you may be telling your story *to bear witness:* You may have been present at the arrest of a friend, getting into trouble for what the officers considered interference. By giving a faithful account of the events, you may be trying to show what you learned about police procedures.

■ Much informative writing is set in motion by a need *to clear up confusion* or *to correct misunderstanding*. On a subject you know well — sports, diets, country music, child custody — you may listen to other people and finally say: "No, that is not the way it is at all!" You will feel the urge to set the record straight.

■ The writer's aim may be to persuade us *to correct abuses* (fleecing of the elderly, overcrowding in prisons); *to condemn evildoers* (as in an exposé of bribes in high places); or *to support a good cause* (a peace initiative, opportunities for the disabled).

Study the following *student editorial* as an example of purposeful writing. What was the author's purpose? Where does she state her main point? What are major stages in her argument? How effectively does she reach a student audience?

The Press Pass and Compassion

Journalists are hard of heart, nose, and head, according to many people. They worship bylines and headlines, clambering over people's feelings and lives to make it to the top.

"It's the press," the secretary whispers, hand covering the phone. "Should I say you're not in?" The pesticide industry executive ponders for a moment, then winks and says, "I'm gone for the day." After the secretary hangs up the receiver, the boss says, "Doesn't matter anyway. Those damn scribblers will put whatever they want."

Across town, a man lies on the ground, groaning in agony, his life's blood forming in pools on the gravel. His wife, uninjured by the now-dead sniper, stands nearby, screaming at reporters to stand back.

In the state capital, a defeated politician sits in his office, wandering the path to the polls over and over again in his mind, while a reporter conducts an interview. The reporter asks questions that seem to imply the politician's very hopes and dreams belong in another era.

In each situation the reporter seemed an enemy or an intruder to the people involved. It's not surprising. Journalists prod, probe, and pry for a living. They are salaried tellers of tales, but unfortunately, much news is unhappy, and those stories often hurt the subjects.

However, journalists also feel bad when they must ask the hard questions of the injured, the bereaved, and the defeated. Reporters see more than most human beings' share of certain things: mangled cars and airplanes, drowned children, young ambition slain by the assassin's bullet, to name but a few.

At such scenes, journalists often wear their hearts on their sleeves. Tear-stained notes mark the print reporter's feelings, while a radio announcer on the scene may sound his concern via a husky voice during the newscast.

Compassion and empathy do not forestall the journalist's duty to record current events for all to know. Reporters must provide readers the history of today so they'll be aware of what's going on in the world, but also so they can share the feelings of others. Knowing what another mother feels like, whether she's two states or two continents away, helps to foster an understanding of other people, whether it's joy over a child's recovery from illness or shared sorrow in the child's death.

When a tot drowns in a backyard pool, it's rough to ask the parents how long they left the boy or girl alone, why there was no enclosure around the swimming area, and whether the child knew how to swim. But it has to be done. It is news, and it may well prevent another drowning by alerting other parents to the dangers involved when toddlers and water mix.

Less tragic but still difficult circumstances also present challenges for reporters, who serve as the public's representative in places the public cannot or does not go. When something's amiss, whether in city hall, student government, or the church business office, journalists serve as surrogate eyes and ears for other citizens. It's a professional and civic duty to study the situation and report on it, no matter how reticent officials are to discuss the matter, and reticent is a true understatement.

To go where few ever go, to report the facts and to keep one's sanity—that's the duty of all reporters, and it's one few would willingly relinquish, despite the lousy pay, fierce competition, and ulcer-producing environment.

There's no better feeling than to find out and expose fraud, to tell a story of smile-invoking good times, or to write of a life well lived. It makes up by far for the sleepless election nights and ambulance chasing.

Maria J. Gunter, *Spartan Daily*

WRITING WORKSHOP 1 In the following *planning reports*, student writers explain what they are trying to do in a paper in progress. What is each trying to do? What kind of paper does the planning report make you expect? What kind of reader would make a good audience for the paper?

1.   **Farmers in White Coats**

New varieties of crops are being engineered in sterile laboratories by biochemists and chemical engineers instead of being developed by years of planting and selective breeding in the fields. A new kind of "farmer" in a white coat and surgical gloves is replacing the one in overalls and boots. I will point out the tremendous advantages of the new plant varieties with such features as increased resistance to disease and a sharply reduced need for the use of herbicides and pesticides that damage the environment.

2.   **The Endangered Middle Class**

Is the traditional middle class on the way down? Are high-paying jobs in steel or auto manufacturing being replaced by low-status, low-pay work like hamburger flipping? Will the next generation of young Americans have jobs sweeping up in factories owned and run by the Japanese? I am going to present and explain statistics showing that the gloomy picture of tomorrow's job prospects familiar to newspaper readers may be wrong.

3.   **Fitness as a Way of Life**

Fitness has been a way of life for me for years. The benefits have always been obvious to me—improved health and an improved sense of well-being. This in turn leads to a certain self-assurance in other, unrelated endeavors. I have played competitive tennis and have been and still am an avid jogger and hiker. I jog every morning before 6 a.m. My family has a poor health and physical fitness record. My mother, a non-athlete, chain smoker, and heavy coffee drinker most of her life, died at age 54. My older brother, also a non-athlete, has been a heavy drinker and "drug dabbler" and has had a heart attack. In my essay, I will explain this background as the motivation for my lifetime commitment to physical fitness.

4.   **A Special Day**

I want to describe the ridiculous Valentine's Day phenomenon. It is unfortunate that we need to set aside a special day to tell others that we care about them. I want to tell the people who every year dart frantically from card shops to candy stores that this annual behavior is absurd. We should find better ways to show others that we care about them. I want to give my supporting arguments first and then finish with my key point. I believe this will be a better approach than to start with my main point, which might at the beginning sound preachy or sugary and lose some of the audience immediately. If I save the main point for the last, readers may at least be ready to consider it.

1b   THE AUDIENCE PROFILE

Keep your audience in mind as you write.

Who is your intended reader? How you size up the needs and expectations of your target audience will help shape what you do and how you proceed.

THE EDUCATED READER Much of your writing will aim at an imaginary educated reader. Ideally, educated readers are thinking readers; they look for a thoughtful, well-worked-out piece of writing rather than glib talk. They care about issues of public interest and are open to new ideas. They frown on name-calling (*redneck, bleeding-heart liberal*), sexist language (*just like a woman*), and cheap shots of all kinds.

THE LAY AUDIENCE In informative writing, we play the role of the expert explaining specialized information to a lay audience. We shed light on matters that interest our readers but that they lack time to research on their own: security systems for cars, new treatments for mental illness. Our responsibility is to show patience with the needs of the outsider: We provide necessary background, explain technical terms, and present new ideas one step at a time.

THE IN-GROUP AUDIENCE An in-group is a limited audience that shares a common interest or believes in a common cause. Groups that share a common purpose include unions, Rotarians, *Star Trek* aficionados, Elvis Presley fan clubs, and the like. Writers will find such a group a willing audience if they know the history and the lore of the group, if they can show their commitment to its shared values.

SPECIAL AUDIENCES Much writing targets a special audience identified by age, sex, occupation, religion, or ethnic background (or by a combination of these). Much advertising, for instance, singles out a particular range of customers and works on their special needs or vulnerability.

Your relationship with the audience will help set the **tone** of your writing. If your audience expects you to take it and the subject seriously, you will write a fairly formal kind of English. If your audience expects to be entertained, you will move toward a more informal style. For most of your writing in a composition class, the right level is between two extremes — neither hyperformal nor disrespectful and slangy. The best modern prose is *moderately formal* — formal without being stiff or pompous. The following passage is an example of effective modern prose that is never too far removed from plain talk. (Note words and phrases like *picture phone, whisked, cheap, come and gone*.)

Looking Back at the Future

The future was to have been a wondrous time, with a picture phone in every home and an atomic-powered car or a personal airplane in every garage. Conveyor-belt sidewalks were to have whisked us through space-age cities while atomic power plants generated clean energy so cheap there would be no need to meter it. But the future, as envisioned a generation ago, has come and gone. Picture phones, atomic cars, and moving sidewalks have all died on the drawing board. Nuclear energy is here, but it has not exactly lived up to its expectations.

John Flinn, *San Francisco Examiner*

WRITING WORKSHOP 2   Work alone or with a group to prepare an *audience profile*. Study closely one recent issue of a publication that aims at a distinct audience. Prepare a portrait of the imaginary ideal reader for a publication like the following: *Sports Illustrated, Popular Science, The Wall Street Journal, The New Yorker, Ms., McCall's, New York, The New Republic, Rolling Stone.* What common background or shared interests do the editors assume? Do they cater to shared likes and dislikes? Do they appeal to shared values? The following is a sample passage from one student's report:

> Increasingly, the advertisements in *McCall's* are designed to catch the eye of a woman who has a career as well as a home. A perfect example is the back cover, featuring a woman telling about her first day at a new job. The woman looks like a housewife who has decided, for whatever reason, to go to work after twelve years. We don't know if she's married, divorced, separated, widowed, or what, so a woman in any of these circumstances could easily identify with her. New York Life Insurance has an ad on page 95 with the woman behind the desk with pictures of kids and husband. (Is he dead? Or is it a boyfriend?) The headline says "for people with big responsibilities." Obviously New York Life thinks enough career women read *McCall's* for it to be worth its money to advertise in the magazine. On page 211 is an ad promoting nuclear power plants with a woman being the spokesperson, billed as a Nuclear Cost Accountant.

1c	PREWRITING TECHNIQUES

Work up a rich fund of material for your paper.

Writers develop their own ways of working up a subject. They jot down rough ideas, prepare a scratch outline, or start a preliminary file on their word processors. They collect clippings or photocopies, and they take systematic notes on their reading.

JOURNAL WRITING Many professional writers use **journals**, diaries, or logs to record ideas and impressions from day to day. The entries in your journal or writer's log might deal with family occasions, jobs, childhood memories, friendships, or personal problems. You might devote entries to current reading, public events, or TV shows and movies. Use such entries as raw materials for more formal, more structured kinds of writing. Example:

> When I was sixteen years old, I worked for the Pope, in a manner of speaking. My first job was that of a part-time receptionist at the St. John rectory. The rectory, a Spanish-style building, white-washed and topped with a red tile roof, was the nerve center of the parish. As one of three part-time receptionists, I needed tact and courtesy, decent communication skills, and a basically friendly outlook toward the rest of humanity. My duties included answering the telephone and writing messages; stuffing, sealing, and organizing mountains of envelopes; running errands; closing the church at night; and often helping with the dishes. It wasn't a bad job for a sixteen-year-old. I also had free access to the refrigerator and baked goods. I performed my job with a happy-go-lucky attitude, but I was often troubled and surprised by the number of people who were in need of food and shelter. Before I worked at the rectory, I thought I had been living in a prosperous middle-class parish.

WRITING PRACTICE 3   Start a *journal*. Write in it regularly to record observations, thoughts, memories, or notes on current viewing and reading. Include detail that would provide promising material for future papers:

- graphic details on a *setting* where events take place
- capsule portraits of *people*
- dramatic highlights of *events*
- striking *quotations:* what people actually said
- your candid *reactions* or feelings (*how* you reacted, and also *why*)

13

Brainstorming **Brainstorming** is the process of jotting down, in rough unsorted form, the ideas and associations that a topic brings to mind. Jog your memory for relevant observations, incidents, data, slogans, headlines, remarks.

(1) Keep moving. Put down anything that might possibly be useful. Leave the sorting out and any second thoughts for later.

(2) Let one thing lead to another. Often one remembered incident will jog your memory and bring to mind other related events or details from the memory banks of the brain.

(3) Push toward specifics. Include scenes we can visualize, snatches of dialogue we can hear.

Develop your own format for your preliminary brainstorming on a topic. The following examples show some common varieties:

■ IDEA INVENTORY — listing possibly relevant points:

(American business)

> failing in the world market
> unable to compete
> unable to produce quality goods — VCRs, televisions, digital watches
> moving production overseas
> employer vs. employee
> employee apathy
> Atari: moving production overseas, eliminating American jobs
> Dow: people exposed to chemical contamination
> the bigger we are the harder we fall
> violating personal freedoms: mandatory drug testing, required polygraph tests
> Ivan Boesky and insider trading — anything to make a buck

■ THINKING OUT LOUD — ranging over the subject, recording preliminary thoughts as they come to mind:

(The macho male)

Macho: Big, muscular, unfeeling, rough — harsh, moves to kill. (Sylvester Stallone: I hate what he promotes.) Negative impression. Hard craggy faces with mean eyes that bore holes in you.

Men who have to prove themselves through acts of violence. The man who is disconnected from his feelings, insensitive to women's needs — cannot express himself in a feeling manner.

The word seems to have negative connotations for me because I work part-time in a bar. I am forever seeing these perfectly tanned types who come on to a woman. As a child, macho meant a strong male type who would take care of me — paternal, warmth in eyes. John Wayne: gruff, yet you feel secure knowing someone like this was around.

Crude, huge — the body, not the heart — tendency to violence always seems close to the surface. Looks are very important. Craggy face. Bloodshed excites them. Arnold Schwarzenegger muscles, gross.

Tend to dominate in relationships — desire for control. "Me Tarzan — you Jane."

In the following paper, the author of the brainstorming sample has sorted out the material and formulated the conclusions it suggests. Compare the paper with the brainstorming notes.

Misconceptions of Macho

"Macho" — the word makes me see yet another prototype of the muscular tanned male walk through the doors of the establishment where I work. He glides past me, lean and smooth. Dressed to kill, not a hair out of place, he lets his eyes dart this way and that, trying to zero in on his female prey of the evening. Suddenly, some woman catches his eye. He saunters over, makes some unintelligible remark, and the courting dance has begun.

The stereotype of the macho is the tough man who proves his maleness through acts of violence or through dominant behavior. Sylvester Stallone as Rambo creates the stereotypical image, complete with mayhem, blood, guts, and brute strength. The price the macho pays is that he is incapable of expressing himself in a caring, feeling manner. He is insensitive to a woman's needs. He may be the strongest, toughest, most handsome, and best-at-everything kind of person in the world, but he lacks emotional qualities that would link him with the rest of humanity.

Macho is as much a state of mind as a matter of physical appearance. A macho male can be a five-foot-tall, ninety-eight pound weakling and still have that condescending attitude toward a woman, looking down on her as if she were nothing more than a vehicle put here by God for his own pleasure. As a woman who works in the bar and restaurant business, I have seen this scenario played out many times: A lone woman comes into a bar, perhaps to meet a friend, and finds that she is fair game. The macho male will invade her space immediately; he will not be put off even with a blunt "Get lost!" He thinks all women are little Barbie dolls equipped to satisfy his every whim. This man operates from a "Me Tarzan, you Jane" mentality. His desire to dominate and control is too great to allow any real intimacy to develop.

Yet I remember that when I was a child the image of the strong male held different associations for me. The macho ideal of my childhood was more of a gentle giant. Though tall, strong, and gruff in his John Wayne manner, he was not afraid to show emotion in his "manly" way. Yes, he was tough. But he was never openly condescending towards women, because roles were still definitely defined. He took charge of his wife and family, but he was paternal and at the same time respectful. He had that Jimmy Stewart twinkle of warmth that I remember seeing in the old movies. He represented security, he inspired trust, and he seemed open and genuine. These qualities are missing in today's macho male.

WRITING WORKSHOP 4   As a *brainstorming* exercise, jot down any ideas, memories, observations, or associations that come to mind on one of the following topics. Keep writing—leave the sorting out of material for a later stage. Share the result with a group of your peers. What kind of paper might come out of this exercise? Choose one:

fitness	Disneyland	evangelists
diets	vandals	game shows
guns	the police	dress for success
charity	drunk drivers	long hair
celebrities	ex-friends	the aged

CLUSTERING **Clustering** is a kind of free-association writing taught by Gabriele Rico in her book *Writing the Natural Way*. When clustering, a writer starts with a central stimulus word that becomes the core of the cluster. Different lines of association then branch out from the center. A network of images and thoughts takes shape that the writer then turns into a finished piece of writing. Here is a sample cluster and the writing sample based on it:

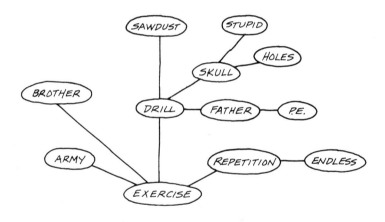

Drill

Drill to me is a nightmare. I never minded arithmetic or grammar drills in school; I could do them, and they gave me a sense of security. But I can't think of those drills without a crowd of images bursting forth. I see my father bending close to my face saying with horrible enunciation: "Can't-you-drill-that-into-your-thick-skull?" At the same time I see an overlaid image of a real drill, drilling into plywood and showering sawdust everywhere. And I see, too, my brother in green, marching endlessly, with the drill sergeant barking orders at him. For good reason, the word *drill* rhymes with *kill*.

WRITING WORKSHOP 5   From the list that follows, choose a word or phrase that is rich in meaning for you. Make sure it calls up memories or starts a train of thought. First, get your ideas down on paper by *clustering*, letting your ideas branch out from the word as a central core. Then write a paragraph or longer passage in which you arrange your material in an order or pattern that makes sense to you. Choose one:

rivals	home	chance
divorce	veteran	alone
the team	free	addiction
bullies	being close	loyal
cheating	losing	success

INTERVIEWS   Experienced writers listen to witnesses, experts, and insiders. They often draw on informal interviews with people whose background or special commitments qualify them to speak with authority on a topic.

(1) Get people to talk. Good interviewers know how to put people at their ease. They build trust, getting people to talk freely and confidentially.

(2) Structure your interview. Sometimes an interviewer will start with safe, nonthreatening factual questions and then push on to questions close to the other person's heart. Sometimes an interviewer will use more aggressive tactics to goad people into revealing what at first they were perhaps not ready to say. If you are writing on the problems of the elderly, you may approach the interview with a prepared set of questions like the following:

- What did you do before you retired?
- How or why did you retire?

- What do you like most about retirement?
- What do you like least about retirement?
- What do you think about mandatory retirement?
- How is retirement different from what you expected?
- If you could turn the clock back twenty years, what would you do differently?

(3) Be an attentive listener. Use written notes (or your tape recorder) to capture key facts, revealing personal statements, and shades of opinion. Sometimes you may write up the results of an interview in a *question-and-answer* format.

Question: What is the best part of the job for you?

Answer: The best part is the people. I get to interact with a lot of people. We get to talk with them. I walk around a lot and meet new people. My last job was in the kitchen, in the back at McDonald's, making hamburgers and cheeseburgers. I like this job better.

Question: When you were younger, what did you think work would be like?

Answer: I don't think my father enjoyed working very much. He used to come home tired. I mean, he didn't usually say, "I really had a great day at work today." So I thought work was going to be very unpleasant.

Question: Was your father right?

Answer: I guess he was right in a way. Most people wouldn't work without pay. I think it's a great incentive to pay people. But I need to do something I can enjoy. I want to be able to say, "I enjoy work."

You will often draw on interviews in papers using other sources as well. However, you may also devote a whole paper to the results of a fruitful interview. Study the following *interview paper* as a model:

Picking Up Garbage

Gabriel was born the youngest of thirteen children. He grew up in the old country and has been in the United States for three years. Every morning he goes to his job in the waste landfill area. When I ask him about his work, he says: "I used to pick up papers in the area. Everybody starts out with that job. Some people are able to save some money that way. Then they go back to the old country, drink and relax for a few months, and then, when they run out of money, come back here. They will always be picking up papers. I don't want to go back. I drive a truck now, and I crush the garbage. I save money."

I ask him about the place where he lives. He is not living with family. "It is a small place with fifteen people living there. I feel bad because we all sleep together in two rooms. I am the first one to go to work in the morning. So when my alarm goes off at 5:30 A.M., everybody is disturbed. I feel bad that everybody wakes up because of the noise from my alarm. But what can I do? I have to work."

Gabriel spends little time at the place where he "lives." He usually works more than five days and goes to school four evenings a week. What does he like least about his job? He says that he does a lot of thinking while he drives the truck. "You know that the American people throw out many things. Much of it is good stuff. I see toys that are brand new. I see radios that are not broken. I see many things that I would like to send to people in my own country. But I cannot pick up any of the things. There is a rule. The driver is not allowed to get out of the truck."

I assume that the company is trying to protect the drivers' health by not letting them handle items from the garbage cans. But Gabriel says that the rule is intended for the driver's safety: Once a driver who climbed out of the truck to pick up something was run over by another driver who did not see him.

"A few times," Gabriel says, "I have taken the chance of losing my job. I got out and picked up a tape recorder once. I brought it home, and it worked perfectly. The Americans throw away so many things like that. It's like throwing away money. Americans are very rich. The people in my country are very poor. Every day I see good things thrown away, and it breaks my heart to crush them. I am destroying what my people could use."

I am looking at the job of the garbage collector from a different perspective since I talked to Gabriel. I used to think that the filth and the smell would bother me most about the job. I found that what bothers Gabriel most is the idea of looking at "waste" all day.

WRITING WORKSHOP 6   Prepare a set of questions for an *interview* and try to get feedback or suggestions from a group. Conduct the interview and present the results first in a question-and-answer format. After discussion and feedback, write a paper interpreting the results of the interview. Make good use of brief, revealing quotations. Interview a person *outside* your own familiar world. For instance, interview

- a police officer working in a high-crime neighborhood
- a security guard for a posh apartment complex
- the owners of a mom-and-pop grocery store
- an illegal immigrant
- a member of a religious cult
- a guard in a correctional institution

READING NOTES   Many professional writers keep a file of clippings (and photocopies) that stores information, statistics, provocative comments, and revealing sidelights on topics in which they have a tentative interest. Suppose you are working on a paper that will explore the cult of the star athlete. You should be able to glean material like the following from a few days' reading of current newspapers and magazines:

Inflated salaries

- A *Time* article listed players signed to million-dollar-a-year contracts during the last year. Even such figures pale compared with the earnings of athletic superstars like quarterback Steve Young, who garnered a $40 million lifetime contract from the now defunct USFL and then went on to sign another $5 million contract in the NFL.

The other side of the star system

- Arthur Ashe, first male black athlete to win the Wimbledon tennis tournament said in a widely quoted article in the *New York Times:* "For every star earning millions there are six or seven others making $20,000 or $30,000." Many others have their careers cut short by injuries. Most high school athletes never make it to the pros.

Parallel patterns in college athletics

- G. Ann Uhlir, dean at Texas Woman's University, says about women in college sports: "Opportunities for elite women athletes have improved, but total participation slots available for women have declined."

With notes such as these, you are well on the way toward a paper that will contrast the glamorous image of the star athlete with the realities facing the rank and file.

WRITING WORKSHOP 7   Examine several issues of newspapers and newsmagazines to study the coverage of a topic currently in the news. Take *detailed notes:* Summarize information, jot down striking details, condense key statistics, quote provocative comments by experts or insiders. Choose a topic like the following:

1. *The Congested Future:* traffic problems and solutions
2. *Women's Sports:* toward equality?
3. *Health Alert:* a health hazard currently in the news
4. *Call the Police:* police work in today's communities
5. *Troubled Youth:* young people in trouble with the law
6. *Domestic Violence:* battered wives or abused children
7. *Red Tape:* regulation and deregulation
8. *Crisis Coverage:* a crisis currently in the news

Work out a general conclusion (or conclusions), and write a paper in which you use the material from your notes to support your general point (or points). Clearly identify each author and publication; put all directly quoted material in quotation marks. Hand in your reading notes with your paper.

DISCOVERY FRAMES   Experienced writers ask themselves questions that help them cover an event or explore an issue. We can often ask: What do I already know about this from *experience*? How is this issue covered in the *media*? Are there any popular stereotypes or *misunderstandings* that might have to be cleared up? What are some of the underlying *causes* of the current situation? What *authorities* could I turn to to confirm my tentative conclusions? We call such a set of questions for the systematic exploration of a topic a **discovery frame** — a framework or program for fruitful investigation.

Suppose you want to alert your readers to a current issue. Perhaps you are aiming at an audience apathetic about the homeless, junk food, high dropout rates, or violence in TV programming for children. A set of questions like the following could guide you to material that would make the issue real for your readers:

I. *What is the issue?* What striking event, example, or statistic would best dramatize the issue for your reader?

II. *How are the media dealing with the issue?* What are some striking recent examples of media coverage? Has the issue recently been the subject of newspaper articles, television shows or documentaries, interviews, talk show patter, movies, editorials in the campus daily, cartoons? What questions or points come up again and again?

III. *What popular misconceptions or prejudices cloud the issue?* Is the problem lack of information or traditional ways of thinking?

IV. *What are the experts saying?* Who *are* the experts? Do they agree, or are they divided?

V. *Where has the issue touched your own experience?* What do you know from firsthand observation? How has it touched the lives of people you know well?

VI. *What does the future hold?* What are the plans for action? Are there promising alternatives? Is the outlook good or discouraging?

WRITING WORKSHOP 8   The high points of much autobiographical writing are events that changed the writer's outlook or thinking — a first encounter, a turning point, a traumatic disappointment, a painful separation. Focus on an important incident or event in your own life. Work up material that will answer the five *storyteller's questions*:

I.   THE SETTING — Where are we? What will it take to make your readers visualize the setting, the scene?

II. THE PEOPLE — Who are the key players in the drama? What do they look like; how do they talk and act?

III. THE SITUATION — What led up to the event? What background or context do you need to fill in for your readers?

IV. THE EVENT — What happened? How did things come to a head? How can you dramatize the high point of the story?

V.   THE POINT — What did you learn from the event? How did it change your thinking or your attitude? Why is it worth remembering?

WRITING WORKSHOP 9   Prepare to write a paper analyzing a *current trend*. Is it a passing development or does it represent some significant lasting change? Use a discovery frame like the following as a guide to material for a paper that would start with surface symptoms but go beyond them. If possible, arrange for feedback from a group.

The Fitness Fad

1. *Surface Symptoms:* Where do you see telltale signs of the current fitness craze? What signs do you see in your neighborhood or on campus? How is it reflected in current advertising and, more generally, in the media? (For instance, how aware are you of runners on streets and highways, of ads for exercise bikes and rowing machines and running shoes, of health clubs and aerobics classes?)

2. *Firsthand Exposure:* Are you yourself a participant or merely an observer? Have you had a chance to take a close-up view at people seriously involved? (For instance, do you have close friends or family members who have taken up running, weight lifting, or aerobic dancing? What do they do? What do they say?)

3. *Background Facts:* In your studies or reading, what facts have you encountered concerning the physical benefits of popular kinds of activity or exercise? What do the experts say about such benefits as weight control, stress reduction, or the prevention of heart disease?

What are the comparative advantages of different kinds of activity? (For instance, is it true that one hour of running produces the same health benefits as three hours of walking?)

4. *Deeper Causes:* What are some of the underlying causes of the cult of physical fitness? What are revealing slogans, or what are key ideas in the mystique that surrounds it? (For instance, what is a "natural high"? Are we observing a reaction against a mechanized and plastic culture and a return to physical and biological basics? Is keeping in shape a natural ideal for the me generation?)

5. *Doubts or Second Thoughts:* What warnings by medical authorities have you read about the dangers of the fitness craze? What do doctors say about the need for stress tests and for medical supervision in general?

WRITING TOPICS 1

On which of the following topics do you have something to say? Choose a topic for which you can work up material from a *range of sources:* observation, experience, viewing, listening, or reading.

1. Have you ever felt the need to correct misinformation or to clear up a *misunderstanding*? What was the problem? Why did you care? What did you say, or what should you have said?

2. Have you ever felt the need to alert others to the significance of something that is often overlooked or *ignored*? Why is it important?

3. Have you ever felt like a *whistleblower*— knowing that something highly touted does not work or is badly flawed? Or wanting to expose incompetence or deception? What could or should have been your report to those in charge?

4. Have you ever wanted to pay tribute to *unsung heroes*? What men or women do you think deserve more recognition than they receive? Why is their contribution overlooked? What can you say to right the balance?

5. Have you been involved in promoting a *good cause?* Who is your target audience? What could you say to break through the crust of apathy?

6. Have you ever reacted negatively to being *stereotyped?* Have you ever felt put down not as an individual but as a member of an ethnic, racial, religious, or other similar group? What is the stereotype? What would you say to counteract the stereotype?

7. Does our society neglect the *disabled?* What is it like to be disabled in today's world? What difference have recent changes in attitudes, facilities, and opportunities made? Write for the concerned citizen and voter.

8. Does our society still have assumptions about *women's work?* What new challenges are women taking on? Where have they been especially successful? What barriers are especially serious? Decide whether to write mainly for a male or a female audience.

---

2   **ORGANIZING AND DRAFTING**

OVERVIEW How does a paper take shape? How do you move from scattered notes to a first draft? Keep in mind three questions that will help give shape and direction to your writing:

■ **What is your focus?** A writer has to learn how to focus attention on one limited topic or one major point. In practice, we do not write about birds in general or about welfare as a large umbrella topic. We write because some part of our subject is not well known, and we want to fill the gap. We write because an issue has come up, and we want to take a stand.

■ **What is your point?** Your reader will want to know: "What are you trying to tell me?" Push toward a central **thesis:** The thesis of your paper sums up what the paper as a whole is trying to show. It summarizes the message of the paper or its central point.

■ **What is your plan?** A well-planned paper moves through steps that the reader can follow. Many writers start with a rough **trial outline** and then scratch it to do another. Some writers work out a fairly detailed working outline to follow in their first draft.

Bring your subject into focus.

Our reader wants to know: "What are you trying to accomplish? What are you trying to say?" This kind of question helps us bring a paper into **focus**. The more clearly focused a paper, the better the chance that our point will sink in or that our information will be put to use.

(1) Limit the area you are going to cover. No one can write a paper on a large sprawling subject like "Education in America." You will often have to narrow a broad general subject until you arrive at a topic that will allow you to take a closer look. With topics like the following, you are moving closer to issues that you could make real for your reader:

How Computers Teach
Math and the Woman Student
Busing: The Long Way to School
Prayer in the Public School

Look at how the following general issue has been scaled down. The more specific topics make possible a paper that becomes specific enough to become real or convincing to your reader:

VERY GENERAL: Improving the Quality of Life

LESS GENERAL: Cleaning Up the Environment
Transportation Fit for Human Beings

SPECIFIC: Bottles vs. Cans: A Problem in Ecology
            Plastics That Decompose
            The Psychology of Litterbugs

(2) Concentrate on a key question that your paper will answer. The more specific the key question you choose, the more likely your paper is to have a clear focus. "How do crime comics shape their readers' attitudes?" is a very *general* question. Try to point your question at a more limited issue.

- Is it true that the heroes look white, Anglo-Saxon, and Protestant, while villains look Latin or Asian?
- Is it true that in crime comics people are either all good or all bad?
- Do crime comics reveal the political sympathies of their authors?

Avoid questions like "What are some of the causes of adolescent crime?" The "What-are-some" kind of question may lead to a paper in which many different things are mentioned but few of them studied in detail. Try a "What-is-the-most" or "What-is-the-best" kind of question:

KEY QUESTION: What is the most serious obstacle to communication between teenagers and their parents?
KEY QUESTION: What are three key features shared by successful television comedians?
KEY QUESTION: What is the best source of alternative energy?

PEER EDITOR 10   Suppose the topics listed below had been suggested by your classmates as possible topics for short papers. Help *narrow* these to more specific topics that would allow the writer to zero in on a limited issue and do it justice. Suggest *one or more* manageable specific topics for each of the following:

Computers
The Plight of the City

The Future of Marriage
Educational Opportunities for Minorities
Jobs for the Class of 2001
Freedom of the Press
Protecting the Consumer
Sexism

PEER EDITOR 11   Suppose your classmates had been given a choice of the topics listed below. For each formulate one *pointed question* that might provide a take-off point for a focused paper:

  student government
  sexual harassment
  welfare reform
  abortion laws
  urban renewal
  the homeless
  media stereotypes
  comic strips

2b | PUSHING TOWARD A THESIS

Use a strong thesis to help unify your paper.

When you state a **thesis**, you take a stand; you commit yourself to a point of view. You answer the central question your paper raises, or you sum up your solution to the problem it has identified. Your thesis tells your readers: "This is what I have found. This is what I mean to show."

Practice summing up in a single sentence what you are trying to tell your readers:

THESIS: The huge sales of Valentine's cards and gifts testify to a need for romance that most people do not openly admit.

THESIS:	Lottery funds for schools allow people to feel virtuous about helping education, but almost none of the money is spent on classroom instruction.
THESIS:	Colleges should shift the emphasis from spectator sports to active participation.

A thesis does not merely map out a topic; it sums up what you have to say:

TOPIC:	The treatment of youth in American advertising
THESIS:	American advertising promotes a cult of youth that makes older people seem irrelevant and unwanted.

A good thesis pulls together materials that at first might have seemed to point in different directions. Suppose you are taking stock of what you have seen of the current fitness craze. You remember a workout program that became a drain on your pocketbook. You know a woman obsessed with the "model look." You have taken a close look at fitness magazines, with their endless stream of advertisements. You have read about anorexia and bulimia. On the next page is a rough chart of how these observations might feed into a general conclusion. Look especially at how the thesis emerges from the materials that feed into it.

In a well-focused paper, the thesis will often appear at the end of a brief introduction that raises the issue:

The Fitness Drain

The bill for my spa payment came in the mail again this month. When I signed up, First Lady Spa promised me that I could use their first-class weight-lifting machines and attend an endless number of aerobic classes for only $21.40 a month. I was handed a 20% discount card for Leotard World, and I was on my way to perfect fitness. I soon discovered that the more I went to the spa, the more items I was expected to buy. First of all, I needed special aerobic shoes, which cost about $45.00. *In the name of looking good, women everywhere seem to be sacrificing their hard-earned money—and jeopardizing their health.*

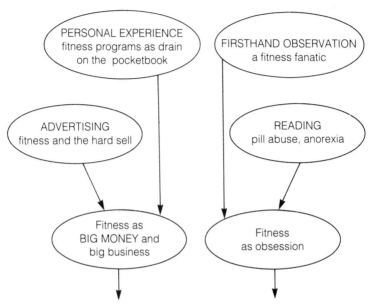

THESIS: In the name of looking good, women everywhere seem to be sacrificing their hard-earned money and jeopardizing their health.

The body of the paper will then offer the evidence needed to support this charge. (Often the conclusion will reinforce the initial thesis.) Remember:

(1) Whenever you can, sum up your thesis in a single sentence. A well-written thesis is a clear statement of a limited point.

TOPIC: Urban redevelopment
THESIS: Redeveloped neighborhoods lack the varied life of the grown neighborhoods they replace.

TOPIC: Violence in movies
THESIS: Too many of today's movies make killing seem quick and easy.

(2) Revise a vague or open-ended thesis. A strong thesis points a definite direction. Revise thesis statements that are too open-ended, that do not take a stand:

WEAK: Many today are searching for the perfect prescription for a happy family. There are **several necessary ingredients** if this prescription is to be filled.

REVISED: A happy family needs a firm basis in love and affection, constantly strengthened by shared joy and sorrow.

(3) Make your thesis hint at the overall plan of the paper. Experiment with making your thesis a preview of your overall plan:

THESIS: Contrary to the stereotype of student apathy, political opinion on campus is a three-ring circus featuring the aggressive young conservative, the well-meaning liberal, and the activist radical left.

(Comment: The reader will expect key sections illustrating each of these three categories.)

Note: Avoid the *misleading* thesis, which mentions points at the beginning of a paper that are not taken up later. If your initial pre-scription for a happy family mentions affection, joy, and sorrow, your reader expects that all three of these will be taken up in your paper, to be illustrated and discussed.

WRITING WORKSHOP 12   Choose *three* of the following topics. Select topics that allow you to draw on relevant observation, experience, reading, or viewing. For each topic, formulate a *trial thesis* that you could support in a short paper. For each tentative thesis, write a paragraph to explain how you would support or defend the stand you take.

1. Parents in current situation comedy
2. Toys as a reflection of American values
3. Changing images of women in current American movies
4. The family in current television commercials

5. Newspaper coverage of crime
6. Teachers' attitudes toward minority students
7. Idealism on campus — passé or alive
8. The decline of good manners
9. Beauty pageants
10. Guns for self-defense

PEER EDITOR 13   Study and evaluate each of the following statements as the possible thesis for a short paper. Answer the following questions about each:

■   What kind of support does the thesis need? What kind of follow-up does it make you expect?

■   If you were writing on the same subject, would you change the thesis to make it reflect your own point of view?

1. The self-service gas station points toward a future where service to the customer will be increasingly hard to find.
2. Fear of violence restricts the activities of many Americans.
3. The typical amusement park has become an artificial wonderland of plastic smiles, faked nostalgic settings, and regimented crowds.
4. Most young Americans today are cynical about politicians and apathetic about elections.
5. Much of the current cult of health foods and healthful living is faddish and overdone.

| **2c** | ORGANIZING YOUR PAPER | *plan* |

Work out an organizing strategy for your paper.

What will guide you in working out a ground plan for a paper? You will often be adapting basic organizing strategies that reflect the way our minds take in and process information. The following may help you shape all or part of a paper:

CHRONOLOGY When we use **chronological order**, we follow events as they happen in time. In much how-to writing — directions, instructions — we focus on telling the reader what to do next. For example, we may move from the choice of flour and other ingredients through the necessary steps in the process that produces good pasta. The following excerpts present, in chronological order, major stages in the writer's growing up:

Sports, Anyone?

Looking back, we sometimes find that our attitudes on something important have changed drastically over the years; we find ourselves in a different place. . . .

As a child, I had a marked disdain for sports. This was probably the result of my being very bad at them. While my grade school peers played Pop Warner football and Little League baseball, I went to art and music camp. This was no real problem until junior high school. There, adolescents were socially made or broken in gym class. People who were good at sports were cool. People who had the misfortune of having a pair of hands like masonry were seriously not cool. . . .

I cowered my way through seventh grade, my self-confidence plummeting as I was picked last for every sport. That summer I grew a few inches and wondered how I would survive. One way was to become a fan of sports. I took up basketball. I rooted hard, studied statistics daily, and learned about jump shots and layups. Eventually, my basketball prowess enabled teams to pick me second or first. The real status leap occurred in the ninth grade when I became a gym helper, assisting the gym teachers with the lowly seventh graders. . . .

Since, I have graduated from basketball, soccer, and stickball in high school to volleyball, bicycling, and jogging in college. Today I enjoy sports for the physical pleasure of doing something well with my body, of feeling healthy, of learning the limits of my physical capabilities. I have moved beyond the kind of jock mentality that knows sports only for winning, for dominating the other side.

EXEMPLIFICATION Often our basic strategy is to lay down a barrage of convincing examples to support a point. We group together parallel examples — instances that all point in the same direction. We can then funnel these into a thesis that sums up a pattern or a trend.

One student wrote about the gentrification of a quiet rural riverfront. He complained that for the new owners the small creatures living in this habitat were not wildlife to be cherished but the target of "pest control." In the body of the paper, the writer furnished the examples backing up the indictment. Different sections of the paper described the new residents' warfare against the beavers (who might damage trees), the muskrats (who might nest in the styrofoam used to float boat docks), the groundhogs (who might burrow in the high-priced riverfront), and the owls (whose hoots might disturb the new residents in their slumber).

Problem to Solution   We often move from problem to solution, from an urgent question to a needed answer. In the following overview, note the boldfaced links, or **transitions**, that lead the reader from one step to the next.

Overworked and Underpaid

Day-care workers will remain underpaid unless not only parents but also government agencies and employers assume their part of the responsibility.

Day-care workers who care for preschoolers in a good program do much the same work as kindergarten teachers but are likely to be paid much less. . . .

Contrary to what one might expect, substandard salaries are not limited to financially strapped centers in poor neighborhoods. In the brightly painted, profit-making centers that dot suburban highways the pay can be just as low. . . .

Why are the wages of day-care workers so low? **For one thing**, the job has traditionally been considered woman's work. **In the past**, older women seeking only to supplement their husbands' incomes were not deterred by the paltry wages. . . .

Today, the basic economics of running a center put the squeeze on wages. **In the first place**, many centers must meet state-mandated teacher-student ratios and still charge fees that parents can afford. . . .

In the second place, large day-care chains attract customers by clean classrooms, cheery decor, and impressive toys and playground equipment. Their ability to provide these attractions depends on their ability to keep wages very low. . . .

What is the answer? To raise salaries, day-care centers need higher fees from parents, or increased state aid, or contributions from corporations helping pay for day care for the children of their employees.

Certainly, some parents could afford to pay higher fees. . . .

However, in most families the cost of child care takes an enormous chunk out of the family income. . . .

As a result, parents have concentrated their efforts on getting state legislatures to provide increased support. . . .

Only recently have large corporations faced the need of helping their employees provide for satisfactory care. . . .

LEAST TO MOST We often move from least to most, or from worst to best, or from unlikely to most probable. Suppose a baseball fan is trying to champion his favorite sport. He places different kinds of popular sports on a scale, from the most to the least violent:

The National Pastime

I. Boxing is an extreme example of a **violent sport**. Although sportswriters talk about a boxer's skill, spectators come to see a slugger; they want to see the knockout.

II. Football is a violent sport **masked as a contest of skill**. Although it is called a contact sport, it is really a collision sport.

III. Baseball is the **most civilized** of the major spectator sports. Although there are injuries in baseball, the spectator's attention is focused on the skill, the strategy, the beauty of the sport.

WRITING WORKSHOP 14 Our personal experience seems miscellaneous as it happens from day to day. But often when we look back years later, we notice a pattern. For instance, have you gone through several *stages or phases* in your attitude toward parents, school, relatives, church, police, sports, camping, or immigrants? Choose one of these or a similar topic. Write a planning report sketching out how a paper tracing several stages or phases would shape up.

WRITING WORKSHOP 15   From the following topics, choose one that has a special meaning for you. Work up detailed material, relating the topic to your own observation, experience, and viewing or reading. Structure your material and prepare a detailed *working outline:*

- Include a thesis that sums up your general conclusion and sets a general direction for the paper.
- Set up major divisions or categories. (If you wish, include hints of details or examples to be used, putting them in parentheses.)
- After you revise your outline as necessary in response to your classmates' or your instructor's comments, use your revised outline as a guide in writing a first draft.

1. *O What a Feeling:* how car commercials sell cars
2. *You've Come a Long Way:* career opportunities for women
3. *Details at Eleven:* the predictable television news
4. *The Computer Invasion:* how computers are changing our lives
5. *The Throw-It-Away Society:* how products become obsolete
6. *I Know the Type:* victims of prejudice
7. *A Tale of More Than Two Cities:* different faces of the city
8. *The Fractured Family:* sources of friction in the modern family

---

2d　　　USING OUTLINES　　　*plan*

Work out an outline that fits your subject and serves your purpose.

Outlines range from scribbled working outlines to the detailed formal outlines often required with major writing projects.

(1) Use an informal working outline to chart your course. Think of your working outline as a **trial outline** — a first rough sketch that helps you see how things fit together and how they might have to be shifted around. Suppose you are writing a paper on the roots of the regulations that ensnarl us in our overregulated society.

Your first trial outline may focus on the role of government and Big Brother agencies:

> regulation by legislation:
>> speed limit
>> seat belts/air bag
> regulation by government agencies:
>> sexual imbalance in college sports
>> special traffic lanes

As you explore the subject further, you may decide to add a third category that is sometimes overlooked:

> regulation as the result of citizen initiatives:
>> nonsmoking sections in restaurants

(2) Use a formal outline as a final check on organization and as a guide to the reader. A **final outline** is often a well-worked-out chart, a detailed guide to the organization of a finished paper. The more substantial your paper, or the more ambitious your project, the more you may need a detailed outline that allows you to check the flow of your discussion or argument.

■ **Use the topic outline to present, in logical order, the topics and subtopics that a paper covers.** Like other outlines, the **topic outline** often starts with a thesis sentence summarizing the central idea of the paper. Notice the use and placement of Roman numerals (for the major categories) and of capital letters (for the subdivisions) in the following outline. *Sub-subdivisions* are marked by Arabic numerals.

Generations in Conflict

THESIS: The traditional conflict between parents and their teenage children is still with us.

I. The traditional generation gap
    A. Authoritarian fathers and rebellious sons
    B. Conformist mothers and independent daughters

OUTLINE FORMAT

Your Title

THESIS: Your thesis sentence appears here.

I. Roman numeral for first major section
  A. Capital for first subdivision
  B. Capital for second subdivision
    1. Arabic numeral for third-level subhead
      a. lowercase for fourth-level subhead
      b. lowercase for fourth-level subhead
    2. Arabic numeral for third-level subhead
  C. Capital for third subdivision
    1. Arabic numeral again
    2. Arabic numeral again
II. Roman numeral for second major section (and so on)

II. Modern causes of conflict
  A. Freedom to be yourself
    1. Dress
    2. Hairstyle
  B. Unchaperoned outings
  C. Choice of part-time jobs
  D. Choice of friends and associates

■ **Use a sentence outline to sum up, in one complete sentence each, what you have to say on each topic and subtopic.** The **sentence outline** forces us to think through our material more thoroughly than the topic outline, which merely indicates the ground to be covered. The following is a sentence outline for a paper that systematically surveys the factors that have helped or hindered women in their struggle for equal pay.

Why Women Earn Less Than Men

THESIS: While some traditional causes of women's low earning power are becoming less important, current patterns of professional advancement will have to change before true progress can take place.

I. Some traditional causes for the low earning power of women are becoming less important as a result of social change.
    A. Traditional prejudices about "men's work" and "women's work" are weakening.
    B. Large differences in educational opportunities for men and women have slowly disappeared.
    C. Traditional conceptions of women as short-term employees are changing as many women spend most of their adult lives in the labor force.

II. Current patterns of economic success and professional advancement continue to work against women, nevertheless.
    A. In most occupations, the years between age 25 and 35 are crucial to future success.
        1. Blue-collar workers discover the job openings and training opportunities that lead to highly paid skills.
        2. Corporations identify promising candidates for advancement in management.
        3. Professionals finish advanced degrees and compete for promising jobs.
    B. The years between age 25 and 35 are the most likely years for many women to be absent from the labor force or work part time because of family responsibilities.

III. For women to achieve more nearly equal earning power, society must revise its patterns of promotion and advancement to provide greater opportunities for mature women reentering the labor force.

Check your finished outlines against the following guidelines:

■ **Make your headings serve your purpose.** Writing about campus social life, you might divide students into Greeks, dorm dwellers, rent sharers, and loners. Writing about students' academic lives, you might divide them into grinds, crammers, prevaricators, and ad-libbers (who make up answers to exam questions as they go along).

■ **Avoid a confusing mixture of criteria.** What is the point of dividing students into graduates of local high schools, low-income students, and Catholics? Your readers can see the point of your categories if there is some common principle of selection, for example, geographic origin (local, rest of the state, out of state, foreign) or religious belief (Catholics, Protestants, Jews, Muslims, agnostics).

■ **Avoid single subdivisions.** Where there is a section A, you will need a section B; where there is a subdivision 1, you will need a subdivision 2. If in a paper on campus dress styles your section D ("Religious garb of the mysterious East") has only one subdivision ("Hare Krishna"), leave the section undivided.

■ **Reconsider a too-long sequence of parallel entries.** If you have eight or nine divisions under a single heading, see if you can set up subdivisions with two or three entries each.

■ **Use parallel wording to point up the relation between parallel ideas.** Your original wording might have been "I. Breaking the ice II. How to get acquainted III. A lasting relationship" and additional headings similarly mismatched. Try making each entry run along similar grammatical lines:

    I.   Breaking the ice
   II.   Getting acquainted
  III.   Cementing a relationship
  IV.   Cooling off
   V.   Drifting away

WRITING WORKSHOP 16 The following interest inventory was adapted from a student paper. Arrange the items in a *topic outline*. Set up major headings and arrange them in an order that will make sense to the reader.

1. contact sports
2. coffee dates
3. religious retreats
4. taking a friend to the movies
5. work for worldwide disarmament
6. long hikes
7. beach barbecues
8. vacation trips
9. fellowship meetings
10. swimming
11. social work
12. student government

WRITING WORKSHOP 17   A student paper listed the following points as guidelines for parents. Prepare a *sentence outline* grouping these points under major headings.

1. Parents should avoid swearing or vulgarity.
2. Parents should not contradict each other in the presence of children.
3. Parents should provide encouragement when children do something constructive.
4. Punishment should be impartial when there are several children.
5. Parents should not shower their children with gifts.
6. One parent should not overrule the other in matters of discipline.
7. Parents should show affection, whether by a pat on the back or a good word.
8. Parents should respect children as individuals, letting them develop their own likes and dislikes.
9. Parents should not be overprotective.
10. Children should be allowed to learn from their own mistakes.
11. Parents should refrain from quarreling in the presence of their children.
12. Parents should teach good manners by example.
13. Parents should allow their children to choose their own friends.
14. Parents should not give vent to their frustrations or irritations by punishing their children.
15. Parents should not take notice of children only when they do something wrong.

WRITING WORKSHOP 18   Prepare both a *topic outline* and a *sentence outline* of a paper you have recently written. Observe conventional outline form.

WRITING TOPICS 2

Choose a topic that allows you to focus on a limited part of a larger subject. Work out an overall plan. Sum up your central idea or thesis early in your paper and support it with specific details and examples.

1. Have you ever had to play a role that required you to change your behavior or assume a different personality? What did you learn from the experience? For instance, focus on playing the role of supervisor, camp counselor, scout, college athlete, poor relation, best friend, parent, or spouse.

2. Focus on a turning point in your life. Choose an event that had a lasting effect on you, a decision that made the difference, or an unexpected change for better or for worse. What did the event or the change mean for you?

3. Have you ever had to revise a stereotype about a group of people? (Or have you found a stereotype to be in part true?) Focus on a stereotype like the marine, the jock, the authoritarian father, or the housewife.

4. Support as fully as you can one limited statement about one of the following. Write to provide guidance for a concerned audience: parents, fellow media watchers, people working in advertising, or the like.

    - toys as a reflection of American society
    - the role of women in current American movies
    - images of blacks or Hispanics in American advertising
    - the image of the native American in American Westerns
    - the treatment of conflict or violence in science fiction
    - guidance from teachers and counselors concerning jobs for women

5. Focus on a specific campus or community issue about which you have been concerned. Present and support a concrete proposal for change or improvement. Write for the campus community or the larger local community.

OVERVIEW You write exposition whenever you share information or clarify ideas. For instance, you write exposition when you show your fellow students how to convert to a vegetarian diet. A psychologist writes exposition when analyzing our response to serious illness, tracing it through three major stages: denial, anger, acceptance. Here are key questions that guide us when we organize expository writing:

THESIS AND EXAMPLES "What does this mean in practice?"

CLASSIFICATION "What goes with what?"

PROCESS "How does it work?"

COMPARISON AND CONTRAST "How are two things similar? How do they differ?"

CAUSE AND EFFECT "What caused the present situation? What will be the consequences of different courses of action?"

PRO AND CON "What are the arguments in favor, and what are the arguments against?"

DEFINITION "What territory does a key term cover — what does it include, and what does it leave out?"

Sometimes, one of these organizing strategies will give shape to a paper as a whole. Especially in a larger piece, however, they are likely to work in combination.

Support your thesis with detailed examples.

Much effective writing starts with a strong **thesis** and then presents an array of authentic examples. These show what a theory or proposal means in practice. To make an idea meaningful, we provide **illustration** — one or more examples that show the principle in action.

A paper following the *thesis-and-examples* pattern might proceed like this:

A National Disgrace

THESIS: How bad are our jails? **Critics of American prisons have found that concern for the physical and mental health of the inmates is often substandard. . . .**

first set of examples   Facilities are often primitive. One observer found thirty men confined in a cell with a single toilet. . . .

second set of examples   Health care is often totally inadequate. In a lawsuit filed in Alabama, an inmate reported what happened after prison doctors set her broken legs in a cast. After she repeatedly complained about excessive itching, doctors reluctantly removed the cast; they found roaches inside, eating her leg. . . .

third set of examples   Woe betide the prisoner having severe emotional problems or suffering from mental illness. In Colorado, a depressed prisoner who requested an appointment with the prison psychologist received a note asking: "What the hell do you want me to do?" . . .

Remember the following guidelines for an effective thesis-and-examples paper:

(1) Avoid a mere catalog effect. Suppose you are trying to show why many young people are disillusioned with political leaders. Do not merely list (and lump together) Presidents from Johnson and Nixon to Carter and Reagan. Discuss at least one or two of these examples *in detail*—to show what young people might have expected of them and where and how they fell short.

(2) Look for convincing representative examples. When we report on the lifestyles of a campus, our eye is tempted to rest on some of the most conspicuous (and eccentric) people we observe. Help your reader feel that the people you discuss as examples are indeed representative of different groups that make up the campus population.

(3) Arrange your examples in an effective order. One familiar strategy is to start with familiar examples (to put the reader in an assenting mood) and then go on to important less familiar ones. A writer discussing the menace from toxic chemicals might start by reminding us of familiar spectacular examples but might then go on to lesser known everyday examples to convince us that the problem is of urgent concern.

PEER REVIEW 19   Study the following *thesis-and-examples* paper. Answer the following questions:

- How does the writer lead up to the *thesis*? What is it?
- Take stock of the *examples* the writer uses to support the thesis. Are they skimpy or ample? Which seem fairly general? Which are most striking or convincing?
- Chart the *categories* the writer has set up to group the examples. What explains the order in which they appear?
- Is the *conclusion* expected or unexpected? Is it tagged on or well earned?

A Life of Crime

"Lawlessness" and the "breakdown of law and order" have long been clichés of conservative political oratory. Candidates to the right of the political spectrum have often run against "crime in the streets." Today many Americans find that reality has caught up with rhetoric. Crime is everywhere becoming a familiar facet of everyday life.

According to police statistics, professional crime is steadily increasing. Burglaries are now an everyday occurrence in what used to be "nice quiet neighborhoods." In spite of television cameras and other safety precautions, bank holdups have tripled in number during the last ten years in many parts of the country. Increasingly, major robberies are planned commando-style and executed with military precision and ruthlessness.

Just as disturbing is the steady growth in personal moral laxity on the part of ordinary people: petty pilfering, routine stealing, "ripping off" the employer or the customer. Dresses put on the clothesline to dry disappear. Watches and wallets disappear from high school locker rooms. Recently a principal was caught stealing petty change from vending machines.

In many areas of our lives, we see a steady increase of personal aggressiveness and vindictiveness. Students threaten and bully teachers. Customers settle an argument with the bartender by fire-bombing the establishment. People taken to court vow to "get" witnesses who testify against them.

We see the same trend toward more lawlessness on the political scene, where it is projected onto a larger screen. Newspaper readers and television viewers have become accustomed to assassinations, bombings, and reprisals as part of the daily news. For many years, terrorism has been a major unsolved political problem in places like Northern Ireland, Italy, and the Near East. People are not allowed on airplanes until they have been searched for deadly weapons. High government officials drive to work surrounded by bodyguards.

As the result of these and similar trends, many ordinary citizens are losing faith in traditional law enforcement. People are ready to join vigilante groups and to "take the law in their own hands." Can you blame them?

WRITING TOPICS 3

Write a *thesis-and-examples* paper. Formulate a strong thesis. Provide detailed and convincing examples or case histories. Choose one of the following:

1. Trend watchers are fond of charting trends that are *reversals* of what was once fashionable. Document such a reverse trend — a return to ceremonies, to formal dress, to patriotism, or to monogamous relationships.

2. Some of our most successful journalists practice the art of the *exposé*. They expose the shortcomings or wrongdoings of people in positions of trust or authority — politicians, television evangelists, Supreme Court justices. Provide and discuss striking examples of this tendency in the media.

3. Have *public manners* deteriorated? Is it true that everywhere we see examples of boorish, hostile, aggressive behavior? Formulate your own thesis, and support it with striking instances.

4. Politicians like to invoke *traditional American virtues* — neighborliness, tolerance, sympathy for the underdog, and the like. Are they prospering, or are they becoming extinct? Focus on one of these, and support your thesis with detailed examples.

CLASSIFICATION

Sort things out by establishing workable categories.

Much of the organizing we do for a short paper fits under the heading of **classification**. We sort things out to group together those that belong together. Remember the following guidelines:

(1) Start with established categories if appropriate, but modify or reject them as necessary. A subject may divide along established lines. For instance, people who have come to this country from abroad differ in legal status:

The Stranger in Our Midst

I. Temporary visitors (usually not allowed to work here and expected to return home)

II. Illegal aliens (who live and work here but have no valid papers)

III. Resident aliens (allowed to work here and often planning to
become citizens)

IV. Naturalized U.S. citizens

This division is useful in a debate on immigration policy. A different set of categories may be relevant in an argument over bilingual
education:

I. Unassimilated (immigrants who live in foreign-speaking en-
claves, where children hear little English)

II. Bicultural (bilingual immigrants who want their children to be
equally at ease in both languages)

III. Assimilated (fully Americanized immigrants whose children
may know only snatches of the parents' first language)

(2) Set up a consistent principle of classification. Are you
applying the same basic question (or questions) as you set up each
category? For instance, in classifying sports in contemporary life, you
may ask, "What is the nature of the *competition*?" This way, you would
focus on the underlying motives of the participants, setting up a
scheme like the following. Notice that the thesis of the paper serves
as a preview of the writer's major categories:

Meeting the Competition

THESIS: Sports offer us a means of testing ourselves by facing and
overcoming opposition, whether human competitors, the
forces of nature, animals, or our own human limits.

I. Competing with other human competitors
   A. football
   B. racquetball
   C. wrestling

   II.   Competing with the forces of nature
       A.   rock climbing
       B.   skiing
       C.   sailing
  III.   Competing against animals
       A.   rodeos
       B.   bullfights
  IV.   Competing with ourselves
       A.   marathon running
       B.   body building
       C.   golf, bowling

(3) Arrange your major categories in a meaningful sequence. The following scheme for male stereotypes in popular entertainment starts with one extreme, then looks at in-between types, and finally arrives at the opposite end of the scale:

    I.   The outdoor macho type
   II.   The male authority figure (doctor, professor, expert)
  III.   The harassed, well-meaning father
  IV.   The wimp

(4) Develop each category with detailed, convincing examples. As in other writing, one key example treated in convincing detail and supported by several briefer examples may provide the most effective mix as you treat each category.

WRITING WORKSHOP 20 From among the following, choose one set of familiar or established categories that seem useful or instructive. (Revise or modify the categories if necessary.) For each category in your chosen set, fill in related material that would help flesh it out: observations that give it meaning, associations that cluster around it, images that it brings to mind.

- urban — suburban — rural
- child — adolescent — adult
- unskilled — semiskilled — skilled

- exclusive neighborhood — middle-class neighborhood — low-income neighborhood
- science fiction — fantasy — horror
- honor student — average student — dropout

WRITING TOPICS 4

Write a *classification paper* that sets up workable categories, supported by convincing examples. Your instructor may ask you to prepare a trial outline for group discussion. Choose a topic in one of the following categories:

1. Set up a system of classification that could serve as a shopper's guide for a *concerned consumer*. (Your instructor may ask you to prepare a trial outline for class discussion.) Set up three or more major categories for one of the following:

   - kinds of restaurants
   - places to live (in your area or more generally)
   - major options in buying a car
   - types of television shows for children
   - kinds of exercise
   - major choices in selecting a college

2. Set up a system of classification that would help a trend watcher understand *current trends*. (Your instructor may ask you to prepare a trial outline for class discussion.) Select an area like the following. Make sure your principle of classification becomes clear to your readers:

   - male stereotypes in commercial television
   - criminals in current crime shows
   - sports as symbols of social status
   - kinds of work open to women today
   - kinds of marriages
   - sports popular with young adults
   - levels of sophistication in local entertainment offerings

Trace essential steps in the right order.

To make a reader see how something works or how it came about, we often have to trace a **process**. We follow a process through its major stages, paying careful attention to how one thing leads to another. What we learn from the process paper has many applications. We apply it when we

- explain a *scientific* process:
  How energy of motion converts into electricity
  How a translation machine scans a sentence
- give *directions*:
  How to plant a lawn
  How to make pottery
- trace a *historical* chain of events:
  How nomads became villagers
  How the railroad transformed rural America

The following instructions will help you write process papers:

(1) Explain the why as well as the how. Start by explaining the purpose or the benefits of the process:

The Natural Way to Eat Bread

Much of the bread we see on supermarket shelves is filled with preservatives so that it can stay on the shelves longer without spoiling. Much of it has an unnatural bleached appearance. It often has the consistency and the taste of a sponge. **To reduce the amount of dubious chemicals in our diet, we can learn to bake our own bread from natural ingredients**. . . .

(2) Pay patient attention to detail. Include the details that are needed to make things work. Provide necessary information about materials, tools, or procedures:

Yeast is composed of minute organisms that grow when exposed to moisture and heat. After the yeast has been dissolved in hot water and milk, mix it with the other ingredients of the dough. Turn the dough out on a lightly floured pastry cloth and knead it for about five minutes until it is smooth and elastic. The bread is now ready to rise, with the entire process taking about four or five hours. Place the dough in a lightly greased bowl, cover it with a damp cloth, and let it rise to about double its original bulk. Make sure the temperature is about 80 degrees: A higher temperature will produce a dry bread. If the room is too cold, put the dough in the oven with a pan of hot water under it. After the dough has risen to about double bulk, turn the dough out on a lightly floured cloth and knead it again for about five minutes. . . .

(3) Divide the process into major stages. Dividing a process clearly into steps will build your readers' confidence, assuring them that they will be able to understand or master one step at a time. The following might be the major stages for the paper on how to bake bread:

    I.   Assembling the ingredients
    II. Mixing the dough
    III. Letting the dough rise
    IV. Baking the bread

(4) Do justice to one major stage at a time. The following might be a selection from safety instructions for drivers. The writer's task would be to fix steps like the following firmly in the reader's mind:

first step   To bring a skidding car back under control, you have to know how to use three different ways of controlling the movement of your car. **First**, turn the steering wheel as hard and fast as necessary. Use it to make your wheels point in the direction of the skid. Work your wheel rapidly if the skidding car keeps changing its direction. . . .

second step   **Second**, make use of your gas pedal to help you control the car. Ease your foot off the pedal when the car first begins to skid, but keep your foot hovering over it. Press down on the pedal lightly when your front wheels seem to be pointing in the direction of the skid. . . .

(5) Clarify technical terms. In writing about navigation in space, have you taken for granted terms like *zero gravity, guidance system,* and *ecliptic plane?*

DISCOURSE EXERCISE 21 Study the following sample paragraph introducing the reader to essential technical terms for a manufacturing process. What does the writer do to make key terms intelligible to the newcomer or the outsider?

The Cheese Process

The first step in producing processed cheese is to sterilize the milk in a large metal vat, usually about the size of a Volkswagen bug. The milk is heated under pressure in order to destroy unwanted bacteria. It is then allowed to cool to about 70 to 78 degrees. The milk is now ready for the addition of the "starter" organism. The starter organism is a bacterial culture added to the sterilized milk to start the production of lactic acids — acids that form when milk sours. Like the starter used to produce sourdough bread, this culture is specifically nurtured to stimulate a spoiling of the milk that will not prove harmful to the health of the consumer. Once the desired acid level is attained, the solution is said to be "ripe." This is the time to add rennet, an enzyme that causes the milk to coagulate, forming curds. Curds are large clumps of solidified milk from which the cheese will be eventually made; whey is the watery part of the solution that is left behind.

■■■■■■■■
| **WRITING TOPICS 5** |

Among the following topics, choose one that allows you to draw on close observation or detailed investigation.

1. Help your readers recover a lost art or skill: baking their own bread, growing their own vegetables, making their own clothes,

doing their own woodwork or cabinet work, making their own pottery, producing their own honey.

2. Many synthetic products have over the years taken the place of natural or homemade ones. Investigate the process that produces one such substitute or "improvement." Possible topics: processed cheese, soybean burgers, imitation ice cream, imitation crabmeat, decaffeinated coffee. Write for consumers who like to know what they are eating or using.

3. Investigate and explain some new or advanced process or technology. Possible topics: using robots on an assembly line, solar energy to heat a house, a computer to produce graphics, lasers in surgery. Explain what is difficult to the newcomer or outsider.

3d   COMPARISON AND CONTRAST   *plan*

Bring out similarities and differences.

A writer often has to look at several related things and show how they are similar or how they differ. Effective **comparison or contrast** lays out the relevant details in such a way that the reader can follow the cross-references and take in the overall picture that emerges. Remember the following guidelines:

(1) Discover your purpose. Why are you setting up the comparison or contrast the way you do? Perhaps you are trying to guide readers in a current crisis by tracing parallels with a similar situation in the past. Perhaps you want to warn customers of an innovation that has serious disadvantages.

(2) Explore similarities and differences. Brainstorm; take notes. Writing about traditional and modern marriages, you might line up distinct features in two columns:

TRADITIONAL	MODERN
church wedding	live together first
till death do us part	high divorce rate
virgin bride	family planning
subservient wife	both work
husband works	backyard weddings
take the good with the bad	equal relationships
husband handles finances	supportive, caring male
housewife cleans and cooks	share chores
wait on the husband	mixed marriages
sex on demand	marriage contract
talk about sex is taboo	mutual sex
marry your own kind	discuss problems
feminine wife	

(3) Consider tracing the comparison or contrast point by point. You look at the safety record, say, or the maintenance needs of a domestic car to see how that record compares with that of its Japanese counterpart. You then go through your set of major criteria or major features, asking for each: "*On this point*, what is the record of Car A? What is the record of Car B?"

Follow the Leader

THESIS: It is becoming harder to tell a best-selling imported car apart from its closest domestic competitor.

I. Economy
   A. Initial cost (data for both cars)
   B. Cost of operation (data for both cars)
   C. Resale value (data for both cars)
II. Comfort and convenience
   A. Space for passengers and luggage (data for both cars)
   B. Maneuverability (data for both cars)
III. Performance
   A. Acceleration and speed (data for both cars)
   B. Durability (data for both cars)
IV. Maintenance (data for both cars)

(4) Consider taking up two things separately — but covering the same points in the same order. Such a **parallel-order comparison** gives a coherent picture of each of the two things being compared. The following is an outline for a parallel-order comparison of two famous heroes of classical antiquity: Odysseus (or Ulysses) and Achilles. The writer starts with a basic similarity but then goes on to important differences:

The Fox and the Lion

THESIS: Odysseus and Achilles are both great warriors, but they differ in the other qualities that make an epic hero admirable.

I. Odysseus as epic hero
  A. Great warrior (unsurpassed in archery, etc.)
  B. Accomplished orator (successful in pleading his own cause)
  C. Shrewd counselor (carefully weighing facts and situations)
  D. Very human character (loves good food and wine)
II. Achilles as epic hero
  A. Great warrior (triumphs over Hector)
  B. Not a great speaker (tends to be haughty and insolent)
  C. Impulsive person (quick to yield to resentment)
  D. Half divine (indifferent to food)

(5) Group similarities and differences together if that seems the best strategy. In comparing the traditional Western with its modern offspring, you might first want to show the similarities: the setting, the familiar cast of characters, the gunslingers intimidating the townspeople, the strong silent hero, the climactic shootout. Then you might go on to what makes a Clint Eastwood Western different.

(6) Mark the transition from point to point. As necessary, steer the reader toward similarities by using words and phrases such as *like, similarly, exact counterpart,* and *along similar lines.* Signal contrasts by words and phrases such as *however, by contrast, on the other hand, nearly opposite,* and *as a counterpoint.*

WRITING WORKSHOP 22   Find a recent newspaper or magazine article focused on a *difference or contrast* of current interest. Summarize the contrast, pinpointing essential differences. Include key points, essential explanations, and selected examples. Choose a subject like the following:

- right brain and left brain
- Japanese and American work ethics
- word processor and typewriter
- agribusiness and family farm
- natural foods and imitation foods

PEER REVIEW 23   Study the following example of a *comparison-and-contrast* paper. What is the *purpose* of this comparison? What is the *plan*? What are effective or striking *details*? How do you react as the reader?

Your Personality May Be Harmful to Your Health

In a famous study, cardiologist Meyer Friedman and Ray Rosenman linked cardiovascular disease to what they called the Type A personality. David Jenkins, an expert on the subject, describes the Type A person as marked by "competitiveness, striving for achievement, aggressiveness, haste, impatience, restlessness, and feelings of being under the pressure of time and under the challenge of responsibility." The Type B person is everything Type A is not: relatively passive, relaxed, noncompetitive, more patient, and quick to find time for recreation. A barrage of studies by psychologists and physicians has found connections between Type A behavior and ulcers, heart disease, headaches, asthma, and even cancer. My own experience with Type B people, however, tends to show that they suffer from just as many and similar health problems as their Type A counterparts.

One reason doctors find more wrong with Type A people may be that instead of going to a doctor a Type B person talks to a bartender. If a Type A person gets sick enough that her work is affected, she will take some money out of the bank and go to the doctor. A Type B person may want to see a doctor, but the chances are he has just spent his last hundred dollars on a triangular box kite or a pocket-size television set.

Type A people are known for pursuing money at the expense of their health, so it is not surprising that my mother, an upholsterer, has chronic back problems. My father, on the other hand, got his bad back and limp in a motorcycle accident. Type B personalities like my father tend to match in recreational injuries the damage Type A persons suffer from overexertion.

Many Type A problems are the result of substance abuse. The aspirin taken three at a time for tension headaches causes ulcers. The coffee that gets them through the day is hard on the digestive tract. They may drink to ease tension. But though these habits cause problems, they are at least kept in check by the need to perform. Type B people often have nothing to stop them from destroying their innards. The bar often is the focal point of what matters to them: conversation, friendship, laughter.

Type A ailments not shared by Type B people are balanced by unique Type B problems. Type A people at least tend to feed themselves and their families. Even during the hardest times there was always a gallon of milk, a loaf of bread, a block of cheese, and a sack of vegetables in my mother's refrigerator. While an upholsterer's wages usually keep her kitchen stocked like a bomb shelter, her ex-husband, my father, never has enough for groceries. His refrigerator is like half of a jigsaw puzzle. It holds hot sauce (no tortillas), pancake syrup (no flour or eggs), three bottles of imported mustard, the cardboard container from a six-pack, and a wedge of French cheese.

WRITING TOPICS 6

As you write on one of the following topics, make sure your comparison or contrast serves a purpose and meets the needs of the intended reader.

1. With pairs like the following, we are sometimes told the two things being compared are very different. At other times, we are told the two overlap — they are more alike than they seem. What

do *you* think? Choose a pair like the following for a detailed comparison and contrast:

- city and suburb
- drinking and drugs
- army life and civilian life
- married life and life after divorce
- commercial and public television

2. Pairs like the following present options or *alternatives* in many people's lives. Prepare a detailed comparison and contrast that could help guide the reader's choice. Choose a pair like the following:

- a factory job and a service job
- immigrant tradition and the American way
- private school and public school
- marriage and the single life

3. The following pairs represent *opposite poles* in arguments over public issues or public policy. Prepare a detailed comparison and contrast that could guide a voter's or an official's choices:

- private transportation and public transit
- American and Japanese attitudes toward work
- downtown: pedestrian malls or street traffic
- wilderness areas or open parks

3e　| CAUSE AND EFFECT　　　　*plan*

Explain things by tracing causes and their effects.

In analyzing a problem, we often try to identify the causes that helped create it. We ask: "What brought this on? What caused the present situation?" Once we sort out the major causes (or identify the main cause), our readers might be ready to listen to a possible solution. The following might be preliminary notes for a **cause-and-effect** paper that examines underlying causes and suggests possible remedies:

Hotheads and Short Fuses

Symptoms

A professor drives his car back to campus in the evening to pick up papers at his office. He is unable to avoid hitting a jaywalker who suddenly appears in front of his car. The incensed jaywalker drags the driver out of the car while the car careens wildly across the street. . . .

After a narrow victory over a traditional rival in a championship football game, the celebrating fans rock and overturn cars driven by supporters of the visiting team; one car is set afire; dozens of people are hurt. . . .

Causes

According to zoologists, primates mark their territories by scent or visual display; humans similarly "leave their mark" on territory they are otherwise unable to control.

Gangs that vandalize schools or public property as a group effort reinforce their sense of mutual loyalty, producing a stronger degree of "social bonding."

An oppressive or frustrating environment produces pent-up anger. Anger causes people to lash out, often at the wrong target. People who feel thwarted or hemmed in strike back at others who they rightly or wrongly feel are invading their turf.

Cures

Traditional Response: We try to discourage misbehavior by public outcry, threats of punishment — with dubious results.

Modern Behavior Modification: Psychologists ask us to think about the underlying psychological mechanisms that precipitate (or prevent) violent and destructive behavior. One landscape architect in Seattle wraps newly planted trees in gauze. The gauze bandage, suggesting something wounded or vulnerable, is designed to produce a caring rather than a destructive response.

Note: Be prepared to recognize *several* major causes. We would often like to find one root cause (and thereby simplify the matter). But in many situations, we have to recognize that several major factors may have contributed to a combined result.

WRITING WORKSHOP 24 Choose a subject like acid rain, erosion, lowered groundwater levels, or the deteriorating infrastructure. Find a one-page or two-page excerpt from an article (or textbook) that seems a model for informative and helpful analysis of causes and effects. Present your find to members of a small group or to your class as a whole.

WRITING TOPICS 7

Write a paper in which you *analyze major causes* (or one single major cause) for one of the following. (Make a list of possible or alleged causes for preliminary class discussion.)

- unsafe city streets
- long-lasting marriages
- depression among young people
- sexual discrimination
- high divorce rates
- the success of recent blockbuster movies
- popularity of television personalities

3f | PRO AND CON *log*

Weigh the pro and con to reach a balanced conclusion.

To help readers make up their minds, we often line up the arguments on two sides of an issue. We first discuss the advantages of a proposal or a program and then the disadvantages. We first present arguments in support of a new method or approach; then we look at possible objections. Ideally, a balanced conclusion will emerge at the end.

A **pro-and-con** paper often follows an exceptionally clear overall pattern. Often the arguments in the first half of the paper will all point in the same direction. Roughly halfway into the paper, a link like *however* or *nevertheless* or *on the other hand* will signal that it is time to turn to the arguments on the other side. Here is how you might line up arguments in a paper that moves from *on the one hand* to *on the other hand*:

Motorcycle Helmets

The Issue: Should helmets be required by law for all riders and passengers of motorcycles?

Pros	Cons
1. Most motorcycle deaths are caused by injuries to the head. It is estimated that 20,000 lives could be saved if all motorcycle drivers and passengers wore proper head protection.	1. Motorcycle riding in the open air is one of our last personal freedoms.
2. 86% of the cost of treating motorcycle injuries is ultimately borne by the State as motorcyclists typically don't have the insurance or resources to pay their own care.	2. Helmets make it difficult to hear sirens and other road noises and would actually make riding less safe.
3. Insurance rates could be reduced if costly medical care and legal assistance could be reduced.	3. Many motorcyclists are free spirits who enjoy the elements--the wind in their hair--too much to accept such a restrictive device.
4. California auto drivers are required by law to wear seatbelts-- why not protective devices for motorcyclists?	4. Helmets are hot, sweaty contraptions that are tight, ill-fitting, and plain uncomfortable.
5. Auto drivers need to be spared the lifelong responsibility for injury or death that could have been prevented by adequate protection.	5. A good quality helmet costs $60 or more. Many young people and students can't afford such an expense.
	6. Storing a helmet when not riding is a problem. Few motorcycles have a lockable storage area sufficient to hold a helmet.

Conclusion: All the reasons against requiring motorcycle helmets combined aren't worth the risk of a single life or the hurt and emotional pain of one

auto driver who must live forever with the death or
injury of another on his mind. The State has a
vested interest in motorcycle safety since so many
state dollars go for medical costs associated with
accident injuries that are largely preventable.

In writing a pro-and-con paper you may anticipate the outcome by stating your conclusion as your thesis early in the paper. Or you may leave the issue open, involving your reader in the conflicting claims, leading up to a balanced conclusion at the end.

Remember the following advice: Give roughly equal space to both sides. Even if you favor one side, show that you know and respect the arguments on the other side. Try not to condemn or denounce; do not advertise the views you favor as those of all right-thinking Americans.

WRITING WORKSHOP 25   Working with a group or your class as a whole, explore the *pros and cons* of a current controversy. Have one team present the arguments on the one side. Have a second team present the arguments on the other side. Use the results as material for a group report or as background for your individual pro-and-con paper. Choose a topic like the following:

- Is compulsory drug testing compatible with American traditions of privacy?
- Are AIDS victims entitled to protection of their privacy? Should they be obligated to tell employers (or insurance companies) of the state of their health? Are doctors and journalists justified in revealing the cause of death of prominent AIDS victims?
- Are the institutions of American democracy incompatible with secret intelligence activities, or "covert operations"?

WRITING TOPICS 8

Write a pro-and-con paper about an issue on which there is something to be said on both sides. Do justice to arguments for and against. Aim at a balanced conclusion that will persuade a reasonable, well-informed reader. Choose a topic like the following:

- Should citizens have the right to use arms in defending themselves against attackers or intruders?
- Should a major aim of instruction in the public schools be to promote one common national language?
- Should expressways and freeways have special lanes reserved for buses and cars carrying several passengers?
- Should government agencies be barred from damming the last remaining wild rivers?
- Should government agencies be barred from helping finance abortions for the poor?
- Should drug testing be compulsory for people holding sensitive jobs?

3g | DEFINITION | *def*

Trace the meaning of an important term.

A **definition** can help the reader see the common element in different and confusing uses of the same word. Or it can make the reader see the different uses that make a word vague or confusing. Your major purpose in defining a term may help you shape the organization of a paper:

(1) Show the common denominator in different uses or meanings. For instance, what basic common element is present when we hear the label *permissive* applied in different areas of our society? You could sum up the common element early in your paper. You could then devote major sections to the application of the word in several areas of American life.

(2) Analyze key elements that together determine the meaning of a term. Sometimes a single criterion furnishes the central clue. More often, several key requirements combine to help us stake out the full meaning. The following excerpts from a magazine article explain key ingredients of the conservative temperament:

The True Conservatism

One autumn Saturday afternoon I was listening to the radio when the station switched to the Dartmouth-Harvard game. The game had not begun, and the announcer was rambling on about the nip in the air, the autumn colors, past games, this year's players, their names and hometowns. . . . Autumn, a new crop of players, New England: The world was **on a steady keel** after all.

That morning, anyway, I felt like a conservative. . . .

Two elementary attitudes underlie the conservative tradition. **The first** is a passionate sense of the need to conserve — the land, the culture, the institutions, codes of behavior. . . .

The second attitude is a cautious view of raw democracy, or direct representational government. The conservative believes firmly in the rights of minorities and those institutions that protect minorities from the whims of the majority, such as the Supreme Court — an elite, appointed body — and the Constitution, particularly the First Amendment. . . .

An outgrowth of these attitudes — and one with particular value — is the humor that the skeptical turn of the conservative mind can bring to bear on confused, disaster-prone but unreservedly grand schemes for the betterment of mankind. . . .   Susannah Lessard, "Civility, Community, Humor: The Conservatism We Need," *The Washington Monthly*

(3) Clarify an important term by marking it off from terms that cover similar ground. In the following excerpt, the student writer defines a controversial new term by contrasting it with a more familiar idea:

Calibrating the Wage Scales

Pay equity, the system under which employment law currently functions, guarantees equal pay for equal work, and it is protected by existing antitrust and civil rights legislation. As long as female and male cashiers or truck drivers or supervisors are paid the same, employers have obeyed the law. . . .

Comparable worth, on the other hand, would require equal pay for work of equal value. In the words of Jane Bryant Quinn, writing in *Newsweek*, it would require "equal pay for jobs that, although different from those held by men, call for a comparable amount of knowledge, skill, effort, and responsibility." Every study indicates that the more an occupation, no matter how valuable or important to society, is dominated by women, the less it tends to pay. . . .

Legally, pay equity is much more clear-cut than comparable worth. What is the relative value of brains and brawn, education and experience, indoor work and outdoor work? How do we compare the value of a secretary's work with that of a garbage collector?. . .

Nevertheless, women need ways to advance economically without taking on "men's work." Like many others, I have tried taking on "different" jobs with unpromising results. For five months during the rainy season, I lifted fifty-pound bundles of newspapers and threw the Sunday edition. . . .

(4) Show how the history of a term helps explain its current uses. The following outline shows three stages in the development of the word *democracy*:

We the People

THESIS: Over the centuries, the term *democracy* has moved away from its original Greek meaning of direct rule by the people.

I. Ideally, democracy gives people a direct voice and vote in the common business of the community.
   A. The Greek beginnings
   B. Early town meetings
II. In practice, participation in the political process is often indirect and ineffectual.
   A. Parliamentary democracy
   B. Checks and balances
III. In modern "popular democracies," an authoritarian leadership claims to exercise power in the name of the people.

Note: In practice, an **extended definition** will often require a combination of approaches.

(5) Try to sum up the meaning of a key term in a one-sentence definition. A **formal definition** first places a term in a larger class and then spells out distinctive features:

TERM	CLASS	FEATURES
Oligarchy	is a form of government	in which power lies in the hands of a few.
A martyr	suffers persecution	for refusing to renounce his or her faith.

If the general class is too shapeless, it will not start focusing your reader's attention. (Classifying an epic as "a type of literature" is less helpful than classifying it as "a long narrative poem.") The specific qualities you list may not be specific enough. (A patriot is "a person who promotes the best interests of the country," but we more specifically apply the term to those who do so *unselfishly* — not for gain or personal glory.) Finally, your definition may not make allowance for important exceptions. (A senator is "an elected representative of a state" — but some senators are not elected but appointed to fill a vacant seat.)

PEER EDITOR 26 Which of the following student-written sentences are good examples of *formal definitions*? What makes them accurate, informative, or useful? Which of the definitions fall short, and why?

1. Privacy is the privilege of having one's personal belongings, space, and thoughts free from intrusion.
2. Islam is the religion of the Muslims and is widely practiced in the Near East.
3. A referendum is a method of giving the public a voice in political decisions.
4. A sorority is a private association that provides separate dormitory facilities with a distinct Greek letter name for selected female college students.
5. Ecology is the study of the closely webbed interrelationships between organisms and their environment.
6. Initiative is a personal quality that makes people attempt new and difficult things.
7. Pacifism is the belief that disputes between nations can and should be settled without war.

8. Due process is a traditional set of legal procedures that protect us against swift and arbitrary punishment.

WRITING PRACTICE 27 Write formal *one-sentence definitions* for five of the following terms:

censorship	human rights	expediency	primaries
dictatorship	avant-garde	jury trial	pollution
soap opera	Peace Corps	Puritanism	bigotry

WRITING TOPICS 9

1. Write a *two-paragraph paper* in which you draw the line between two overlapping terms. Devote one paragraph to each term. Choose a pair like the following:
   - dissent and disobedience
   - justified force and violence
   - authoritarian and totalitarian
   - justice and getting even
   - love and a relationship

2. Write an *extended definition* that would initiate a newcomer or outsider. Choose a term like the following: *high tech, aerobics, human rights, environmentalism, vegetarian, punk.*

3. Which of the following is for you more than just a cliché? Write an *extended definition* that shows your readers why the term is important.

consumerism	born-again Christians	computer literacy
pluralism	equal opportunity	privacy
permissiveness	law and order	bigotry
the work ethic	bureaucracy	police brutality

2

WRITING AND REVISING

Note: The following is a quick rundown of minimum proficiencies in the area covered in this chapter. Remember that there is much more to good writing than meeting minimum standards. However, if you fail to meet the standards summarized here, your message may not reach the reader and you may not get credit for what you do well.

The following guidelines for minimum revision will help you produce a stronger final draft:

(1) Revise for a strong beginning. Dramatize the issue. Use a striking example or a provocative statistic to bring the issue to life for your readers.

COLORLESS: It is an accepted fact at most workplaces that unions and management should be at odds. A new view of management/employee relations must be taken for the business to reach greater levels of success.

DRAMATIZED: In many American corporations, union and management are bickering over coffee breaks and toilet privileges while a Japanese company is already making the product that will put them both out of business.

(2) Strengthen your thesis. Spell out your main point. Make your introduction lead into a thesis that provides a true *preview* or *overview* of what you are trying to show.

VAGUE: There are *certain traditional attitudes* that prevent management and union from working together for the good of all. (What *are* these traditional attitudes?)

71

POINTED: **Two ingrained attitudes** keep management and union from working together for the good of all: the **management's** shortsighted **preoccupation with raising profitability** at the expense of morale, and the **union's** shortsighted **insistence on raising employee benefits** regardless of cost.

(3) Streamline your overall plan. Make your readers see the organizing strategy that gives shape to your paper. If necessary, reshuffle major parts so that your readers will see a strong overall pattern like the following:

- the *major stages* in the life cycle of the salmon as it leaves the spawning grounds for the sea and finally battles its way back upstream
- the *contrast* between yesterday's mom-and-pop neighborhood stores and the plastic, muzak-filled shopping malls of today

(4) Move in for the closer look. A first draft often stays on a general level and moves on too fast. Try to answer the questions sure to arise in the reader's mind: Are these real people? What do they look like? Where does this kind of thing happen? What does it take to make this work? Fill in details to make your readers see real people, visualize real-life situations.

CLICHÉ: Ceremonies are not empty gestures but are full of special meaning. As the music announces her arrival, the bride all in white steps down the aisle supported by her father. . . .

CLOSE-UP: Ceremonies are not empty gestures but are full of special meaning. Once a year, Jewish families gather to celebrate Passover and share this ceremony with a Seder dinner. The ceremony commemorates **the Hebrews' being set free by Pharaoh** as told in the 12th chapter of Exodus. Foods like **unleavened bread and bitter herbs** are symbolic of the feast. The unleavened bread reminds us that the Jews had to leave Egypt in a hurry — there was no time for the bread to rise. The bitter herbs symbolize the hard and bitter lives of the slaves. . . .

(5) Fill in the missing links. Show the connections between parts of your paper. As needed, supply transitional phrases — directional signals that let your readers know where they are going. Use links like *for instance, for example,* or *to illustrate* to alert readers to supporting examples. Use links like *however, nevertheless,* or *on the other hand* to signal a turning point in the argument.

(6) End on a strong note. Do not just repeat. Spell out what your story means to you or what it should mean to the reader. Restate your main idea pointedly and graphically, so that your readers will remember.

4 **REVISING AND EDITING**

OVERVIEW Writing and revising are not separate activities, since writers shape and reshape their material from the moment they jot down their first notes. However, you will naturally concentrate on getting something down on paper first and then become increasingly concerned with getting it into final shape. Effective writers know they are not finished when they have finished a first draft. They have learned to look at their writing through the reader's eye, noticing weaknesses that need work. They have learned to profit from feedback from peers, editors, teachers, or reviewers.

When reworking a paper, make sure to go beyond the most obvious editing needs: dangling modifiers and missing commas, wrong words and sentences missing a verb. To profit from criticism, learn how to respond to comments on the *larger elements* of a paper. Act on comments on the purpose, substance, organization, and overall effectiveness of a paper.

Learn to do more than a cosmetic revision.

Remember instructions like the following when revising for the larger elements — purpose, substance, structure, and style:

(1) Strengthen your beginning. Is there a vivid introduction of the issue? Is there a pointed statement of a central thesis? Is there a helpful preview of what the paper is going to do? Study the following revision of an introduction in response to a reader's comments:

ORIGINAL: South of the Border

Many times I have watched commercials and television shows that supposedly show the lifestyle of
Mexicans south of the border. My friends have often
asked me if the way Mexicans are portrayed there is
true, and I have to say "no." Mexicans aren't as
old-fashioned as they are portrayed on television
and in movies; they are like any other modern
people.

COMMENT: Let us have a look at *one* striking commercial to give
us a vivid picture of what you have in mind. Then spell
out the central point for the rest of your paper more fully.
Make your thesis more of a preview of what your paper is
going to cover.

REVISION: South of the Border

When people think of Mexico, they usually remember a "Fly Mexicana" airline commercial and picture a brown-skinned, black-haired person wearing a
white suit, sandals, and a sombrero. I often have
to tell my friends that the picture they get of Mexico from commercials and television shows is not
true. Mexicans are not as old-fashioned as they are
made to look on our television screens or in movies.
Most people in Mexico are like any modern people.
They work, study, eat, have a social life, and dress
as Americans do; but then again, some of their customs may differ somewhat from the American style.

(2) Strengthen your overall plan. It is not too late to *rethink* your overall plan — to shuffle major sections for a more logical or more natural sequence. Suppose you have started a paper on ethnic humor by explaining the new etiquette for the telling of ethnic jokes: People should not tell jokes to put down others; they should tell jokes only about their own ethnic group. People of British extraction will tell British jokes; people of German extraction will tell German jokes. In your second section, you have contrasted the new etiquette with the offensive Polish jokes or Italian jokes of the past. In a third section, however, you have claimed that some ethnic jokes are meant to be affectionate rather than cutting or demeaning.

On second thought, you decide that the order of your paper is anticlimactic — it presents a new idea first and then seems to backtrack and lose its punch. In your revision, you reshuffle your major sections to *lead up* to the main point, going from the undesirable to the desirable:

REVISED: **Humor Is No Laughing Matter**

   I. Truly offensive jokes about other ethnic groups
  II. Affectionate jokes about other ethnic groups
 III. The new etiquette: jokes about one's own nationality

(3) Provide a stronger follow-through for key points. In a first draft, you will often move on too fast — broaching one general idea and then going on to the next. Look for important points that lack striking detailed examples:

ORIGINAL: Television presents a constant stream of commercials promising to make us more attractive and to
make our lives more glamorous. Advertisers seem to
think that viewers are naive enough to expect a new
toothpaste or a new shampoo to transform their love
lives. . . .

REVISED: Television presents a constant stream of commercials promising to make us more attractive and to
make our lives more glamorous. The man in a new
compact picks up a woman on a street corner. She
likes his sun roof. A woman hunting for a lost ear-
ring under a table is joined by an admirer. He
likes her fresh breath; she mentions her brand of

```
toothpaste; they live happily ever after.  And, of
course, whenever a commercial for clothes or makeup
is presented, the gorgeous face of a famous model
hints that Ultima II or Maybelline or Chardon jeans
will transform the population at large into
beauties.
```

(4) Clarify connections and strengthen transitions between points. Show connections; provide a bridge or transition from point to point. The following excerpts are from a paper with poorly marked turns:

Stereotypical Males

Can you give more of a PREVIEW?

The reruns of serials that in my youth filled television screens during the daytime mirrored perfectly the traditional ways of stereotyping the American male. **This stereotyping started in childhood**. From *The Little Rascals* to *Dennis the Menace*, it was always the boys (and never the girls) who got into mischief (and who had all the fun). . . .

prepare reader for CONTRAST

These bad boys had to grow up to be men. From *I Love Lucy* to *The Dick Van Dyke Show*, the man was the stereotypical breadwinner who worked outside the home, while the housewife stayed home to cook and care for the children. . . .

weak link show LOGICAL connection?

Another favorite of the old serials was the professional man—the doctor, lawyer, or teacher giving everyone sage advice. . . .

Another old standby was the kindly old grandfather or uncle who was grouchy on the surface at times but who really has a heart of gold. . . .

Look at the way the revised version provides the missing links:

The Cartoon Male

The reruns of serials that in my youth filled television screens during the daytime mirrored perfectly the traditional ways of stereotyping the American male. **This stereotyping started in childhood and followed the male into manhood and old age**. From *The Little Rascals* to *Dennis the Menace*, it was always the boys (and never the girls) who got into mischief (and who had all the fun). . . .

Paradoxically, these bad boys grew up to be the men **who were the traditional providers and heads of their households**. From *I Love Lucy* to *The Dick Van Dyke Show*, the man was the stereotypical breadwinner who worked outside the home, while the housewife stayed home to cook and care for the children. . . .

Closely related to the father responsible for the well-being of the family was the wise professional who represented a father image. He was the doctor, lawyer, or teacher giving everyone sage advice. . . .

At the end of his career, we would see the stereotypical male as the kindly old grandfather or uncle who under a sometimes grouchy surface carried a heart of gold. . . .

(5) Leave your reader with a strong final impression. A first draft often simply seems to run down, without a strong summing up or final pulling together of important points. Sometimes the writer at the end backs away from the issue ("Will there be stricter gun control laws, or will we all eventually own a gun?"). Replace a weak ending with a conclusion that has the courage of your convictions:

REVISED: Perhaps it is true that we only hear what we
    want to hear, but I yet have to find an argument
    to counter the statistics showing 200 gun-related
    deaths in this country for every similar death in
    a country like England. Slogans that claim "Guns
    don't kill people" are not my idea of a strong argu-
    ment. We need to strengthen current laws concerning
    gun control because the number of lives lost through
    the use of handguns in this country is appalling.

WRITING WORKSHOP 1   Share a *first draft* of a paper with a group of your classmates for peer review. Ask them for candid oral or written comments. Write a summary and evaluation of the feedback you received. Ask the group to answer questions like the following:

- In their opinion, what is your paper trying to do, and how successful is it?
- What are strong points of the paper?
- What are weak points?

- What specific suggestions for improvement do your readers have?
- How did they personally react to your paper, and why?
- What kind of audience do they think would react best? What kind is likely to react negatively, and why?

WRITING TOPICS 10

Take a paper through a cycle of successive revisions in response to feedback from your instructor and to peer review. Aim at more than token revision of the larger elements: purpose, substance, organization, tone, and style. Choose one of the following topics:

1. Much biography focuses on how people rise to a challenge. Has a major challenge, issue, or obstacle played a role in your own life? How did it affect you? How did you cope with it?

2. Traditionally, home has meant to many people a central place in their lives that shaped their outlook and personalities and offered them a safe harbor to which to return. In the modern world, many people feel that this idea of "home" is extinct. People feel they are isolated or cast-off individuals; and home is simply a place where they find themselves at sundown. Which of these views is closest to your own? Describe your own concept of home, using detailed illustrations from your personal experience and observation.

3. The traditional American work ethic encouraged people to do their work with a sense of pride and satisfaction. In recent years, well-known authors have claimed that many Americans are dissatisfied with their work. Many Americans, we are told, hate their jobs. To judge from what you have seen of the world of work, how true are these charges? Draw on your own observation or experience.

4. Do you consider the police your friend or your enemy? In an emergency or in a difficult situation, would you expect the police to be on your side?

5. Does current popular entertainment glorify youth and create an unfavorable image of age? Are older people made to seem irrelevant or unwanted?

4b | FINAL EDITING

Recognize high-priority items for final editing.

Many writers and editors have checklists or style sheets for a last-minute check of usage and mechanics. To flag editing problems for you in your papers, your instructor may use the numerical handbook key or the correction symbols employed throughout this handbook. Suppose you are carrying over to the written page the sentence fragments of stop-and-go conversation. (Fragments like this one.) The abbreviation *frag* or the guide number **9a** will guide you to the section of this handbook that describes fragments and offers guidelines for correcting them.

Here is a sampling of high-priority items that you should look for in final editing and proofreading of your papers:

KEY   SYMBOL

9c   *CS*   **(1) Correct comma splices.** A comma splice uses only a comma to splice together two related statements. (Where the two statements join, there is no coordinator like *and* or *but*, no subordinator like *if* or *whereas*.) Use a semicolon instead of the comma:

COMMA SPLICE: We scratched the dog act, the poodle was ill.
SEMICOLON: We scratched the dog act; the poodle was ill.

Comma splices also result when only a comma appears between two statements joined by *therefore* or *however*. These and similar conjunctive adverbs require a semicolon:

COMMA SPLICE:	Peking seemed drab and bureaucratic, Shanghai **however** seemed lively and sophisticated.
SEMICOLON:	Peking seemed drab and bureaucratic**;** Shanghai, **however**, seemed lively and sophisticated.

11d   *agr*   **(2) Correct faulty agreement.** Agreement requires matching forms for subject and verb: The *train stops* here (singular); the *trains stop* here (plural). Blind agreement results when the verb agrees with part of a wedge that came between it and the subject:

> FAULTY: The credibility of these **witnesses are** open to question.
>
> REVISED: The **credibility** of these witnesses **is** open to question. (What is open to question? Their credibility **is**.)

12   *ref*   **(3) Correct vague or confusing pronoun reference.** Pronouns like *she* or *they* or *this* serve as shorthand references to people and things, but they need to point clearly to what they stand for. Avoid loose pronoun reference; especially, avoid shifts in the way you refer to a typical or representative person:

> SHIFT: **The typical woman** today does not expect Prince Charming to take care of **their** every need. (We are looking at *one* typical woman.)
>
> REVISED: The typical woman today does not expect Prince Charming to take care of **her** every need.

36a   *cap*   **(4) Check for missing capital letters.** Capital letters, like apostrophes, do not show in speech and are therefore easily overlooked. Capitalize names of days, months, places, states, ships, schools. Especially, capitalize the names of nationalities and languages: *Mexican, Spanish, Italian, Canadian, Australian, Japanese, American.*

35b   *ap*   **(5) Use the apostrophe for the possessive of nouns.** The possessive tells us *whose:* my *brother's* keeper, the *world's* safest airport; the *coach's* unexpired contract, the *cat's* meow. Remember the basic rule: apostrophe and *s* if you are talking about one; *s* and apostrophe if you are talking about several:

SINGULAR	PLURAL
Whose? a **friend's** BMW	the **tenants'** cars
my **brother's** nose	my **brothers'** noses
one **country's** history	other **countries'** problems
a **week's** wage	two **months'** salary

A final word: PROOFREAD. Never hand in a paper without giving it a slow, careful final reading. If at all possible, wait — half an hour, a day. (If you merely go over a paper quickly after you finish it, you will tend to see what you *meant* to write rather than what you actually did.)

4c | A PAPER WITH COMMENTS

Study — and act on — comments on your papers.

You will be doing much of your revising and final editing in response to your instructor's comments on your papers. Look for reinforcement of what you are doing right and for help with what needs work. Pay special attention to problems that come up several times in the same paper. Here is a sample student paper with correction symbols and instructor's comments:

#98869 *wrong form?*

As a consequence of our ~~strive~~ for better technology and efficiency, Americans are becoming severely di**sp**atisfied with their <u>job environment and organiza-</u>

clarify what you mean? <u>tion</u>. This businesslike drive for profit and spee**d** causes three serious problems *in or for?* <u>in</u> the American worker: lack of loyalty, <u>lack</u> of praise, and lack of knowing you**'re** *ap* needed.

Lack of loyalty is caused primarily by the very impersonal interaction that

---

good revealing detail — but give additional evidence?

goes on between employee and boss. I started a job at a company where I <u>was referred</u> to as only "98869." I stayed for only a short while and quit. I felt no loss at leaving anybody behind, because they were just faces with numbers written on them. No one ever bothered you. It was more efficient that way!

shift from I to you?
17b

Another major problem that <u>causes dissatisfaction</u> is the lack of praise for a job well done. After I quit my first job, I got a job as an assistant legal secretary. Each day I had to prepare wills, depositions, <u>and basically run the office</u>. Little by little I became more annoyed by my constant lack of any kind of praise. Then one day it hit me all at once. The lawyer called me from a phone in the city courtroom. He needed me to prepare some things and bring them to him in court. He gave me half an hour. He proceeded to tell me all the things he needed. I had one hand on the typewriter, one on the copier, and one in my briefcase looking for my car keys! When I got downtown with one minute to spare, he said: "I wish I could have looked this over before I got in there. Was there a lot of traffic or something?" Not once did he ever thank me for my help. I felt that no matter what I did it wouldn't be appreciated.

FP 17d

nice exaggeration (this whole paragraph is better developed)

In my next job, as a bookkeeper/organizer, I realized what the lack of knowing that you are needed could do. When I began this job I enjoyed each day. I could use my organizing skills and keep the company and its employees

sf 17b

SINGULAR

p   all on schedule. Each one had their own
section and I would organize it the best
way possible. I received a lot of
praise from these employees and was told
they couldn't do without me.

redundant?   Sure! About ⑥ months later I was 39b
introduced to my new replacement. He

nice image   sat there with his lights blinking and
little typed words flowing across the

hy   screen. He had a rainbow colored apple
sf   (with a bite taken out of it) on its
front. "It's our new computor," said

good use of direct quotation   the lady I knew only as "the computor
lady." "It can do everything. Everyone
will be able to write and read messages
on it and it organizes things beauti-
fully." Well, it wasn't long before I
felt very inadequate. The computer
could do what used to take me an hour in

MM ⑭b   30 seconds. These feelings of inade-
sp   quacy really effected my sense of self-
confidence.

These three problems cause many

p   workers like me to keep looking hoping
that someday a job that offers a chance
of personal loyalty, accomplishment and
pride, and the feeling of being valued

awk   (will come along.)

*your paper uses personal experience well to
show what the thesis means. The organization is clear, and the transitions are
smooth. The style is sometimes awkward
(see the specific pointers above).*
REVIEW REFERENCE OF PRONOUNS AND SHIFTS
IN PRONOUN REFERENCE - 12 and 17b.

EDITING PRACTICE 2 Rewrite each of the following sentences to correct a common editing problem. If you need help, turn to the appropriate section of this book.

KEY	SYMBOL	
11d	*agr* agreement	**1.** The typical diet article in newspapers and magazines *treat* food as if it were a foreign agent.
36a	*cap* capitals	**2.** Alice Walker's *The Color Purple* was read by millions of *americans*.
9a	*frag* fragment	**3.** The press chronicled his misadventures. *With great glee.*
33b	*sp* spelling	**4.** Changes in our laws have not *detered* people from *commiting* crimes.
35b	*ap* apostrophe	**5.** Stations use enticing "newsbriefs" to catch the *viewers* attention.
9c	*CS* comma splice	**6.** Blue jeans recognize no *classes, they* are merely American.
13b	*ca* case	**7.** Children may not know *who* to trust.
14b	*DM* dangling modifier	**8.** *Sitting on top of an animal filled with furious energy,* the gate opens and the bronco dashes for the other side of the stadium.
17d	*90* or // faulty parallelism	**9.** We went to the apartment to pick up the bills, financial statements, and *finally clean out the refrigerator.*
12d	*ref* pronoun reference	**10.** Although the study of techniques is helpful to an artist, *they* do not need a degree to paint.

| WRITING WITH A WORD PROCESSOR |

Make use of the full potential of your word processor.

Many writers today use word processors that allow them to draft and revise on a monitor screen, to store documents on disks, and to print out finished copy. Many students do most or all of their writing on a personal computer (PC) with word processing capability; others have access to workstations hooked up to large **mainframe** computers.

(1) Try brainstorming on the computer. The following might be your first jottings for a paper on the world mirrored in television commercials:

```
diet drinks: bouncy kids on beach, plastic smiles
(great teeth)
designer jeans: child prodigy celebrity models
"spend, spend; consume, consume"
happy wife-mother, cute all-American kids, a
shaggy dog
Bill "I'm-so-sensitive" Cosby
look and smell the best we can
```

On further thought, you might rearrange these notes and add to them as follows:

```
diet drinks, bouncy kids on beach, plastic smiles
(great teeth)
designer jeans: child prodigy celebrity models
look and smell the best we can
woman in slinky black dress selling vodka
thin is in
Diet Brew won't go to your waist
happy wife-mother, cute all-American kids
Bill "I'm-so-sensitive" Cosby
beaming white-haired Mom gets long-distance call
from young executive
```

(2) Store promising material for future use. Set up a file for anecdotes, statistics, and quotations that may prove useful for a planned writing project. A file of promising material for your paper on commercials might include the following. Note the **retrieval code** that keys stored material to a writing assignment or to a subdivision of a project.

```
commercial minidramas

      In the small elegant apartment, the lights
are dimming, music is playing softly, and a young
woman sits by the telephone.  "Tom?" she says in
a provocative voice.  "This is Julie . . . I have
a bottle of Stanley's Bristol Cream Sherry and
. . . you would? . . . great . . . 8:00."

      Two teenagers are obviously attracted to
each other, but things are still very uncomfort-
able.  The boy comes to the rescue by bringing
the girl an XYZ root beer.  The commercial ends
as the two walk away together singing "Nothing's
so smooth and easy as XYZ root beer."
```

(3) Draw on stored material while writing your first draft. Transfer and adapt stored material for use in your paper. Suppose you have stored a quotation from a personal interview with a police officer. Here is how this passage might look after you have transferred it to your first draft, adding the necessary connecting links:

```
      Sergeant Jason said, "We see people at their
worst all the time.  The general public just
isn't exposed to the violent situations and peo-
ple out of control."  Most people don't know any
police officers personally, "and when they have
contact with one, it is usually negative:  They
are getting a ticket, or their house has been
robbed.  They are frustrated, and they take their
frustrations out on the officer."  As a result,
"it is easy for police officers to become cyni-
cal.  They risk their lives and know that what
they do is not appreciated."
```

(4) Use the full potential of your word processor for revision. Add, delete, and reshuffle material as you rewrite your first draft. Rereading a passage in your first draft, you might decide that it badly needs real-life detail. Here is how the passage might read with some lifelike detail inserted:

```
      Two of my brothers studied Karate and Ai-
kido. Often, I was called upon to act as the
"live dummy" for the prescribed movements my
brothers performed. For instance, one of my
brothers would ask me to throw a punch at him.
As soon as I extended my arm, and before I could
blink, I found my limb precariously twisted be-
hind my back with my body twisting in wretched
pain. This early introduction to the martial
arts has remained etched in my memory.
```

(5) Edit with special care. In final editing of your work, you can correct many spelling errors and punctuation problems with the stroke of a key. You may also be able to instruct the computer to find and correct *all* occurrences of a misspelled word (like *mideval*) in your text. If a spelling check is part of your software, it will identify clear-cut misspellings like *identified* and *should of* and query possible confusions (*to* or *too? there* or *their?*).

CAUTION: **Proofread.** Do not be fooled by the finished appearance of word-processed text. The speed and ease of typing on an electronic keyboard often multiply transposed letters (*wrtier*), run-together words (*taggedon*), random misspellings, and miscellaneous glitches. Whenever you can, *double*-proof all text: Proofread it first when it is still on the screen, then again when you print out a trial copy.

WRITING PRACTICE 3   Enter the following passage on your screen. Then go on typing, writing your reactions, comments, examples or counterexamples, arguments or counterarguments.

> A history instructor found that an increasing number of her students could not understand what Hitler had done wrong. One student described Hitler as "a kid with a dream" who enjoyed "a pretty good run at the top of the charts."

REVISION PRACTICE 4   How are the sentences in the following paragraph related? Enter the paragraph on your screen. Then, at the beginning of as many sentences as you can, *insert* a missing link. Choose a transition like *also, for instance, similarly, finally, however, but, in fact, it is true that,* or *on the other hand*.

> Our history textbooks have often pictured the Spaniards as a haughty and fanatical people. Every school child used to read about the cruelties of the Spanish Inquisition in hunting down the enemies of the true faith. Anglo historians have often blamed the Spanish conquistadores for wholesale massacres of the native populations of Mexico and Peru. Recently historians have asked us to revise this negative picture. Millions of Indians died in the fifty years after the Spanish conquest. Most of them died as victims of Old World diseases like smallpox, against which they had no immunity. Prominent leaders in the Spanish church argued that the Indians were not savages but had immortal souls and deserved our love as fellow human beings. More than other colonial nations, the Spaniards intermarried with the conquered peoples.

REVISION PRACTICE 5   Study the following passage and enter it on your screen. Assume that you are the author and that you have decided to make two major changes. Move the second sentence to the end as a clincher sentence. Rearrange the order of the examples so that there will be a better flow from the least to the most serious.

> Professionals often face a familiar dilemma: whether to reveal to others dark secrets that their clients have told them in the strictest confidence. Often the choice is to tell and feel like a rat or to keep

silent and become an accomplice. Should a psychiatrist warn an ex-spouse that a patient is planning to "get even"? Should a priest tell the authorities that a parishioner has committed murder? Should a journalist go to jail for contempt of court rather than reveal to a judge the source for information about organized crime? Should a teacher tell parents about teenagers planning to elope?

---

5 COHERENCE

OVERVIEW Effective writing moves ahead purposefully, taking us along. It has **coherence**; it "hangs together." The writer brings a topic into focus — and stays on the topic. The readers feel they know where the paper is headed. The turns in the road are well marked.

5a TITLES

Use your title to attract the reader.

Effective titles stake out the subject. Increasingly, writers include in their titles a key word that helps a computer retrieve publications relevant to a particular topic. Ask yourself about your own tentative title: Is it likely to be noticed and remembered? A good title often has a satisfying pattern; it may use a striking image or play on words:

Aerodynamics: Cheating the Wind
The Art of Teaching Science
Looking for a Job Is a Job
Questioning Quotas
Good News for Bad Backs

Make sure that your title sounds like your personal choice, not a colorless general category. Avoid titles that give no hint of your personal point of view:

WEAK:	Urban Decay
BETTER:	Neighborhood or Turf?
	No One Is Safe
	The Uncertainties of Gentrification

WRITING WORKSHOP 6   With a group of your fellow students, discuss your reactions to the following *book titles*. How effective is each title? What kind of book does it seem to promise? Who do you think would be a good audience or an ideal reader for each book?

Strategies for Women at Work
Easy Basics for Good Cooking
Our Bodies, Ourselves
Computer Programing for the Compleat Idiot
Number: The Language of Science
Make Your Money Grow
A Place Called School
Nuclear War, Nuclear Peace
Lost Worlds of Africa
The Marital Arts

5b	**INTRODUCTIONS**

Make your introduction lead up to your central idea.

An effective introduction sketches out the territory to be covered and sets the tone for the rest of the essay. Study the following examples of effective introductions. Look at how each writer dramatizes the issue and leads directly to the **thesis** or central idea of the paper.

(1) Start with a striking example. Select one vivid example to catch the attention or arouse the indignation of the reader:

Test-Tube Food

Extrusion is the method of chopping or powdering foodstuffs and then reforming them to make them look whole. A striking example of extruded products is a foot-long rod of hard-cooked egg used by many caterers, restaurants, and institutions that want to bypass the cost of shelling real eggs. One of these rods enables a busy chef to cut seventy-five perfect center slices. Amazingly, the yolks of these high-tech eggs do not slip out of their white rims. Unfortunately, the slices have a rubbery texture and a vaguely sulfurous aftertaste. **Everywhere today, we encounter processed foods that have been adapted to give them eternal shelf life, to make them more profitable, and to destroy their original texture and taste.**

(2) Start with an event currently in the news. Relate your subject to events of current public concern:

Programed for Failure

A few weeks ago, Malcolm Hyde, a graduate of Oakmont High School, sued the Oakmont Unified School District for having failed to teach him to read and write. Malcolm had been one of the estimated 20 to 30 percent of the students in our public schools who "mark time or drop out." For the parents of such children, it is not enough to be content when a student "passes" and "stays out of trouble." **Parents of educationally deprived youngsters must start taking a direct interest in what happens in the classroom from day to day.**

(3) Relate your subject to firsthand personal experience. Show that your subject has a personal meaning for you:

A Thicket of Regulations

Shortly after my eighteenth birthday, my father died of hypertension. At that time, medication that would have controlled his illness was available in Canada but banned in the United States by the Federal Drug Administration. Less than one year after his death it was made available through a belated clearance by the agency. **Every year, promising experimental drugs are delayed because of a maze of bureaucratic regulations and the horrendous cost of extensive testing and trial use.**

(4) Use a striking quotation as the keynote for the rest of your paper. Quote an eyewitness, authority, or insider:

Be Happy in Your Work

"64,000 hours are at stake!" That is what Richard Bolles, author of *What Color Is Your Parachute?*, tells readers trying to choose a profession. His figure represents the number of hours that an average person will work during a lifetime. **In spite of such warnings, many people drift into kinds of work that they dislike.**

(5) Use a striking contrast to lead up to your key point. For instance, use a *then-and-now* contrast to point up a change:

We Are What We Wear

The late sixties was the height of the love affair between the media and youth. Movies, magazines, pop music, and advertising extolled the teenage girl — a long-haired, blank-faced disco-dancing adolescent wearing a mini-skirt and thin as a stick. Today, most women no longer want to look like teenagers. The new ideal is the woman with both a career and a family. She's in her thirties or forties; she has character — you can see it in her face. **The media are struggling toward a new image of the mature woman, wearing a classic suit.**

(6) Use striking statistics to dramatize the issue:

Growing Up a Little Faster

According to one recent survey, seven out of ten children of divorced parents had not seen their real father in more than a year. **The traditional practice of awarding custody of children to the mother left a whole generation of children of divorce without the natural father as a model and a guide.**

Avoid weak or ineffective introductions:

- *Repeating the assignment* (often word for word).
- *A dictionary definition* (unless you turn to a dictionary definition to bring out something important that is often overlooked).
- *Puffing up the subject:* "Bird-watching is a wonderful hobby. I have spent countless hours of untold pleasure watching birds. . . ."
- *Complaints or apologies:* "Many contradictory opinions abound on the subject of the perfect interview. I find it hard to give a candidate for a job meaningful advice in a paper of 500 words. . . ."

WRITING WORKSHOP 7 Find three recent magazine articles whose *titles* and *introductions* you consider exceptionally effective. Explain how they attract the reader's attention and what strategy they use to lead the reader into the subject.

PEER EDITOR 8 Study the following *titles* and *introductions*. Which are effective, and how? Which are weak, and why?

1.   **Dangerous Books**

Any list of the books most frequently banned in American schools is sure to strike a chord in the reader's mind. One title I recently saw listed took me back to my junior year in high school. An English teacher who trusted me took me to the storage room to give me a brand-new copy of Kurt Vonnegut's *Slaughterhouse-Five*. There on the shelves were two hundred more brand-new copies that had never been given to students. The principal had decided these books were "unsuitable" for young minds. It seems that often the books that are censored are the ones students would be most likely to read on their own, as "unrequired" reading.

2.   **Job Dissatisfaction**

In this day and age, Americans feel that the benefits they receive from their occupation are not quite in accord with the efforts they expend. Why do Americans feel this way? The answer probably lies in the American culture. Job dissatisfaction is in part due to the way Americans live at the present time.

3. **Television Shows**

Many of my friends watch the music shows that are popular on television. There are also exercise shows, the news, situation comedies, specials, children's shows. The list could go on and on. What I am trying to show is that there are different types of shows on television, and I will try to describe a few of them in the following pages.

4. **Freeze!**

The average police officer fires a gun at a criminal perhaps once in a lifetime of service. In the typical crime show on television, there is hardly an episode without a climactic shootout, with police officers' guns blazing away. The net results of these programs is not to promote respect for the law but to make the viewer accept guns and gunplay as an ever-present fact of city life.

5c | CONCLUSIONS

Use your conclusion to reinforce your central message.

Avoid conclusions that are merely lame restatements of points already clear. Make sure your conclusion *adds* something to the effectiveness of your paper. Here are some examples of effective conclusions:

(1) Use a final anecdote to reinforce the central idea. Close with an incident that dramatizes your main point:

(*From an article on the growing pains of Third-World countries*)

. . . My Nigerian friend looked out over the congested traffic as we sat in the stalled car. "Money," he said suddenly. "When we don't have it, it bothers you. When you get it, it worries you." He had summed up the story of his country, caught between ancient poverty and sudden wealth.

(2) Make striking details serve as symbols of a trend. For example, hobbies or styles of dress may symbolize attitudes:

(*From a paper on prevailing conservative trends on campus*)

. . . In the shopping area across from the main entrance to the campus, head shops have been replaced by stores that sell roller skates and running shoes. Conservative styles of dress are coming back: tweed sports jackets and skirts. Some of the students dress up to go to the library.

(3) Use a strong final quotation to reinforce your main point. Quote an authority or insider:

(*From a paper on commercialism and the artist*)

. . . Some of the world's leading artists and performers have managed to solve this age-old dilemma: how to reach a large audience without pandering to popular taste. Toward the end of her career, the great gospel singer Mahalia Jackson was asked about several albums she had done for a "commercial" label. She said: "All my life, I have sung for my supper as well as for the Lord."

(4) Conclude with a suggestion for remedial action. Tell your readers what they can *do*:

(*From an article on prison reform*)

. . . If the leading citizens in a community would make it a point to visit their state prison, talk with the warden, then return to their communities with a better understanding of actual down-to-earth prison problems, they would have taken one of the most important and most effective steps toward a solution of our crime problem.   Erle Stanley Gardner, "Parole and the Prisons — An Opportunity Wasted," *Atlantic*

Avoid ineffective conclusions like the following:

- The well-meaning *platitude:* "Making our neighborhoods safe will require the vigilance of every concerned citizen."
- The *silver lining:* "Humanity in the past has survived earthquakes, famines, and the plague. And after all, we have already lived with the threat of nuclear war almost half a century."
- The *sidestepped question:* "Death is sometimes more merciful than a life of suffering. But who decides, and on what grounds? These are moral questions, and, as with all moral questions, the answers will have to come with time."
- The *lame afterthought:* "Of course, if we burn more coal rather than rely on nuclear power, we will further pollute our atmosphere. This is a problem for the engineers of the future to resolve."

PEER EDITOR 9   Study the following *conclusions*. Which seem like a strong summing up or wrapping up, and why? Which are weak, and why?

1. *From a paper on trade barriers American businesses encounter in Japan:*

    . . . Americans as well as Japanese know the pleasures of pointing the finger at someone else. It is frustrating for us Americans to have to think about matters that are our own responsibility, such as balancing our federal accounts or adapting to changing foreign markets. It is much easier to point the finger at our trading partners and shout "foul."

2. *From a paper warning against excessive emphasis on careers in a college education:*

    . . . Students today have an almost hypnotic fascination with the subject of careers. They eat, drink, sleep, and, above all, sweat jobs. As a dean of students said at a Midwestern school, "I sometimes think that if I stopped one of these students on the street and asked, 'Who are you?' the answer would be 'I'm prelaw.'"

3. *From a paper on appeals used by American advertisers:*

    . . . Advertisers know how to exploit our love of gadgets and our desire for a more glamorous life. They exploit the customer's yearning to be attractive, upwardly mobile, and forever young. Moral lectures will not stop advertisers from using methods that work. If we object to being exploited, we as consumers must learn to take a good look at what we really want. We must decide whether we want trendiness and surface glamor or value for the dollar.

4. *From a paper on test-tube babies:*

    . . . Do doctors have a right to produce life in a laboratory? Nobody knows who is right or wrong on this issue, but what is important is that humanity still has the desire to learn more and to explore this field of unknowns, trying to find answers in our never-ending quest for knowledge.

WRITING TOPICS 11

Choose a topic that you can relate to your own observation, experience, viewing, or reading. Pay special attention to beginning and ending. Provide an attractive but also informative *title*. Write an effective *introduction*. Write a strong *conclusion* that does not merely repeat but instead reinforces your key point.

1. Thomas Carlyle, a nineteenth-century British writer, wrote about the role of outstanding personalities in history. He once said, "Hero worship exists, has existed, and will forever exist, among mankind." What kinds of heroes do young Americans look for today?

2. Some people claim that differences in dress, hair length, and other matters of outward appearance are merely superficial. However, other people claim that such outward signs often show something important about the attitudes or values of a person. What is *your* opinion? Support or defend your point of view.

3. In the seventies, about 50 percent of college freshmen felt "there is too much concern in the courts for the rights of criminals." Ten years later, the proportion had grown to 65 percent. What explains this shift in attitude? Where do *you* stand? Back up your point of view.

5d   SYNONYMS AND RECURRENT TERMS *coh*

Use key terms and their synonyms to focus attention.

Often, the coherence of a paper shows in a network of closely related terms. **Synonyms** — words that mean almost the same — keep our attention focused on the same issue: *crime, lawlessness, transgression, felony*. Other related terms may reassure us that the writer is sticking to the subject: *violence, enforcement, gunplay*. Suppose you are reading an article on the psychological effects that *overcrowding* has on people in modern cities. In a well-focused article, other terms and phrases will echo the central term: "overpopulation," "penned up," "massive congestion," "great numbers," "rush-hour crush," "cramped quarters," and the like. Such synonyms or closely related terms show that the writer is never straying far from the central point.

DISCOURSE EXERCISE 10   Study the following passage. Trace the *network of related terms* or expressions that refer in some way to the sending or reception of signals.

Satellite Television

The transmission of television and other signals by satellite has become a technological commonplace. Communications satellites now ring the globe. They have made possible improved navigation and flight control, worldwide high-speed data transmission, business teleconferencing, and increased telephone service. (The annoying little delay in most international and many domestic phone calls is the time it takes a microwave, traveling at the speed of light, to zip back and forth between Earth and a satellite.) They have also brought about the rapid expansion of cable television, the wild proliferation of new programming, and in the past four or five years a brand-new industry aimed at enabling people to receive satellite signals in their homes. Perhaps a million Americans own satellite antennas of varying shapes and sizes. They use them to receive as many as a hundred different television channels bearing everything from X-rated movies to unedited network news stories to Russian weather reports to talk shows whose hosts are nuns.

Ten years ago no regular American television programming was transmitted by satellite. Today almost every viewer, whether or not he owns a satellite antenna, watches shows that have spent at least part of their lives bouncing through outer space.   David Owen, *Atlantic*

Provide a bridge from one point to the next.

Effective writing provides smooth **transitions** — signals that help the reader move on from one part of a paper to the next. **Transitional phrases** are directional signals that help the reader move along without stumbling. Words like *similarly, moreover,* and *furthermore* signal that an additional example or a further reason is about to reinforce the same point. *Admittedly* and *granted* tell the reader that we are about to recognize a legitimate objection; we are ready to grant or concede a point. Links like *nevertheless* or *however* show that we are ready to take on or refute the objection.

Weak transitions, often using *also* or *another*, merely add without showing why. If you can, show the logical connection with what went before:

WEAK LINK: **Another** misleading image created by television is that of the typical married male. . . .

BETTER: **After marriage**, the carefree young male of televisionland turns into the stereotypical middle-aged television male worried about insurance. . . .

COMMON TRANSITIONAL PHRASES

ILLUSTRATION:	for example, for instance, to illustrate
ADDITION:	similarly, furthermore, moreover, too, besides
EXPLANATION:	that is, in other words
REINFORCEMENT:	indeed, in fact, above all
LOGICAL RESULT:	so, therefore, thus, accordingly, consequently, as a result, hence
CONTRAST OR OBJECTION:	but, yet, however, nevertheless, on the other hand, conversely, on the contrary
CONCESSION:	granted, admittedly, to be sure, no doubt, it is true that
SUMMARY:	in short, in brief, to sum up
CONCLUSION:	finally, in conclusion, to conclude
CHRONOLOGY:	first, next, later, soon, meanwhile, in the end

DISCOURSE EXERCISE 11 Study the two following passages from a discussion of sexual stereotypes. Find all the *transitional phrases*. Explain how they are used — how they steer the attention of the reader.

Less Than a Person

When people respond to one of the many stereotypes of women, they are reacting to an idea rather than to the real person. Therefore, their impressions are often wrong, and their behavior is often inappropriate. For example, if people think a woman is a soft and delicate creature incapable of reason, they may defend, protect, and think for her. They may substitute their reality for hers and deny her own experience its validity. But worse than having her individuality denied by others, is the way she herself may identify with the stereotypes, treating herself as less than a person. . . .

Women have traditionally had their roles and their worth defined for them by their usefulness in the family. The woman who pours great energy and talent into the task of rearing children and making a home for her family fulfills a role which is vital to society's survival. However, she is unlikely to be paid or given any positive public recognition. Instead, she is known as "just a housewife," a label which belittles all her dedication and effort as well as the vital role she performs.   James Hall, Nancy J. Jones, and Janet R. Sutherland, *Women: Portraits*

WRITING TOPICS 12

In writing on one of the following topics, pay special attention to the overall *coherence* of your paper. Focus your discussion on a unifying key term. Give special thought to the pattern you set up. Provide the signals that will steer your readers' attention.

1. Write a paper in which a central term, with its synonyms and related terms, helps focus the readers' attention. Write to answer (or to agree with) critics of current American life or society. Choose one:

   ■ the myth of American goodwill
   ■ the computerization of America
   ■ the tradition of being a good neighbor
   ■ the lost war on poverty
   ■ the feminization of poverty

2. Write a paper in which you lead your reader from the familiar to the unexpected, or from the least important to the most important. Write for readers looking for advice. Choose one:

   ■ the secret of a happy marriage
   ■ how to keep a job
   ■ how to enjoy the outdoors
   ■ how to improve relations between police and community
   ■ how to fight depression

3. Write a paper in which you go from problem to solution. Write for readers skeptical of the "quick fix." Choose a problem like the following:

   ■ peer pressure and drugs
   ■ graffiti
   ■ dropouts
   ■ managing on a tight budget
   ■ recruiting scandals

3

WRITING BETTER PARAGRAPHS

Note: The following is a quick rundown of minimum proficiencies in the area covered in this chapter. Remember that there is much more to good writing than meeting minimum standards. However, if you fail to meet the standards summarized here, your message may not reach the reader and you may not get credit for what you do well.

If your paper is a sequence of short two-or-three-sentence paragraphs, it will seem choppy and disorganized. If you write a page without a paragraph break, your readers will think that you have not sorted out your material.

(1) Focus your paragraph on one limited part of your topic. In the following paragraph, a famous science writer focuses on one striking natural phenomenon — the fact that many fish in the deep sea generate their own light:

> **The deep sea has its stars, and perhaps here and there an eerie and transient equivalent of moonlight, for the mysterious phenomenon of luminescence is displayed by perhaps half of all the fishes that live in dimly lit or darkened waters, and by many of the lower forms as well.** Many fishes carry **luminous torches** that can be turned on or off at will, presumably helping them find or pursue their prey. Others have **rows of lights** over their bodies, in patterns that vary from species to species and may be a sort of recognition mark or badge by which the bearer can be known as friend or enemy. The deep-sea squid ejects a spurt of fluid that becomes a **luminous cloud,** the counterpart of the "ink" of his shallow-water relative.   Rachel Carson, *The Sea Around Us*

(2) Try summing up your central idea in a topic sentence. What is the point of your paragraph? What is it supposed to show or to prove? A topic sentence early in your paragraph spells out the unifying idea that the rest of the paragraph will support. In the following paragraph, a historian makes an important point about the civilization of ancient Greece:

TOPIC SENTENCE: **Greeks enslaved foreigners and other Greeks.** Anyone captured in war was dragged back as a slave, even if he was a Greek of a neighboring polis. In Athens slaves, *evidence* especially women, were often domestic servants, but of 150,000 adult male slaves, 20,000 were set to work in the silver mines, in ten-hour shifts, in tunnels three feet high, shackled and lashed; the forehead of a retrieved runaway was branded with a hot iron. Aristotle called slaves "animate tools," forever indispensable, he thought, unless you were a utopian who believed in some future invention of automatic machinery. In Athens it was understood that the most efficient administrator of many slaves was someone who had himself been born into slavery and then freed; such a man would know, out of his own oppressive experience with severity, how to bear down hard. Cynthia Ozick, "The Moral Necessity of Metaphor," *Harper's*

(3) Support your main point with graphic details or examples. Go to the *for example* or *for instance*. Show what an idea means in practice. Look at the following topic sentence and the array of examples designed to make the reader say: "I see what you mean."

TOPIC SENTENCE: **Everywhere we look today, we see city people wearing cowboy fashions.**

first example People who have never been on a horse spend hundreds of dollars for elaborately decorated Texas-style boots.

second example They buy crafted leather belts with richly decorated silver buckles.

third example Passengers march onto airplanes wearing broad-brimmed cowboy hats.

fourth example	Shirtmakers cultivate the urban-cowboy look.
fifth example	Blue jeans, once worn mostly by ranch hands, are now the national uniform of the young.

(4) Help your reader see how your paragraph is laid out. Use transitional expressions, or directional signals, to steer the reader: the *for example* that introduces an illustration, the *however* that brings in an objection, the *therefore* that draws a logical conclusion. Show clearly that your paragraph contrasts the old and the new, or that it weighs the pro and con.

6　WRITING THE PARAGRAPH

OVERVIEW Paragraphs enable us to cover a subject one step at a time. Each well-written paragraph is a group of related sentences that focus on one part of a subject and do it justice. It is true that in some kinds of writing a paragraph merely gives us a convenient break:

- In much *newspaper writing*, paragraphs are very short. There may be a paragraph break after every two or three sentences.
- In *dialogue*, a paragraph break signals a change from one speaker to another.

Nevertheless, in writing that explains, informs, or argues with the reader, the basic unit is a solidly developed paragraph that answers basic questions in the reader's mind:

- It focuses on one limited point or issue. (What are we talking about?)
- It presents an overall idea or conclusion. (What is the point?)
- It backs up the main point with examples or other supporting material. (What makes you think so?)
- It provides signals that help the reader see how you have arranged your material. (How is your paragraph laid out?)

Use a paragraph to group together related material.

The raw material for a paragraph is a group of related data or observations. Reading about sharks, for instance, we may notice several things that explain how sharks appear mysteriously whenever there is a chance of food:

first observation	Sharks can smell blood from a quarter of a mile away, and they follow the faint scent to their prey.
second observation	Sharks sense motion in the water with special sense organs. Something thrashing about in the water is for sharks a signal of food.
third observation	Sharks are sensitive to bright light. They are attracted to bright and shiny objects, and to contrast between light and dark.

These observations add up to a general conclusion: Sharks are well equipped for tracking down food. In the finished paragraph, this conclusion will serve as the central idea that holds the paragraph together. We usually put such a central idea early in the paragraph as a **topic sentence**:

> **Sharks, known as voracious eaters, are well equipped for identifying and tracking down food**. As they prowl the water, they seem to sense the presence of unsuspecting prey from a considerable distance. There are several reasons why sharks are efficient at hunting down their prey. They can smell blood from a quarter of a mile away, and they follow the faint scent to a wounded creature. Sharks sense motion in the water with special sense organs; something thrashing about in the water is for them a signal of food. Finally, sharks are sensitive to bright light. Light reflected from something moving in the water alerts them, especially if it is the reflection from the shiny scaly surface of large fish.

PARAGRAPH WORK 1 For each passage, write a sentence that could be used as the topic sentence of the complete paragraph.

1. _____ . The spines of cactuses are actually vestigial leaves. The bulb of an onion is a cluster of specialized leaves. Thorns of spiny plants and tendrils of climbing plants are often modified leaves, as are the needles of pine trees. The hard, woody sheathing of palm trees is a modified leaf, so large in one Amazonian plant that local tribes use it as a makeshift canoe.

2. _____ . People trying to protect whales have steered their small boats between the hunted whales and the sailors of catcher boats attempting to harpoon the animals. Other volunteers have harassed sealers on the harp seal breeding grounds on the ice of the Magdalen Islands. They have sprayed baby seals with organic dye that would make their pelts worthless for the hunters who club the defenseless cubs and then strip them of their fur. In one widely reported incident, an American released dolphins caught and penned up for slaughter by crews of Japanese fishing boats as threats to their catch.

3. _____ . Many companies now employ private security guards to protect business property. The sales of burglar alarms and other security equipment for private homes have increased steadily over the years. Locksmiths do a booming business fitting entrance doors with multiple locks, dead bolts, and the like. Increasing numbers of private citizens buy handguns intended as last-ditch protection of their families and their property.

6b | THE TOPIC SENTENCE |

Use a topic sentence to sum up the major point.

In most well-written paragraphs, we include a statement that tells our readers: "This is what I am trying to show. This is what I am trying to prove." A **topic sentence** is a sentence that sums up the main point or key idea of a paragraph. Often the topic sentence is the very first sentence:

TOPIC SENTENCE: **Some of the job areas most popular with students are very small**. No more than 1,000 foresters will be hired this year, although perhaps twice as many students may get forestry degrees. Only 2,700 new architects will be needed to design all the buildings sprouting on the landscape, and almost twice that number graduated in a recent year. Everyone wants to design things, but, according to the Department of Labor, only about 300 industrial designers are added to the labor force during an average year. Landscape architecture is appealing, too, because it combines creativity with outdoor work, but only 600 are expected to find jobs in the field this year.

Look at some common ways we vary the basic pattern of **statement and support**:

■ A topic sentence may call for some *explanation*: A second and perhaps a third sentence may restate the main idea, explaining a key term, spelling out how, when, or where. Then the paragraph may go on to *illustration*: The main point gets needed support from the examples or details that back it up:

TOPIC SENTENCE: **I always wished to be famous.** As other people have
explanation   an imagination for disaster, I have had an imagination for fame. I can remember as a boy of nine or ten returning home alone from the playground in the early evening
illustration   after dinner, dodging, cutting, stiff-arming imaginary tacklers on my way to scoring imaginary touchdowns before enormous imaginary throngs who chanted my name. Practicing free throws alone in my backyard I would pretend that I was shooting them at a crucial moment in a big game at Madison Square Garden. Later, as a boy tennis player, before falling off to sleep, I imagined the Duchess of Kent presenting me with the winner's trophy on the center court at Wimbledon.   Aristides, "A Mere Journalist," *The American Scholar*

■ After providing illustration, the writer may decide to remind us of the point in a **clincher sentence**:

TOPIC SENTENCE: **The new trend toward vocationalism is particularly counterproductive in an uncertain economy, when jobs are both scarce and changeable.** It makes slim indeed

explanation the chances of picking the right specialization years in advance of actual entry into the labor market. The writer of an article in the *New York Times Magazine* extrava-

illustration gantly extolling the virtues of New York's Aviation High School appeared unaware of its own ultimate contradiction: only 6 members of that year's 515-member graduating class reported that they had found jobs in the

restatement aviation industry. **The primary reason for youth unemployment is not lack of training but lack of jobs.**   Fred M. Hechinger, "Murder in Academe," *Saturday Review*

■ Sometimes we delay the topic sentence *till the end* of the paragraph. We take our readers along, making them look at our evidence or examples, steering them toward a conclusion very similar to our own:

examples first The shops of the border town are filled with many souvenirs, "pinatas," pottery, bullhorns, and "serapes," all made from cheap material and decorated in a gaudy manner that the tourist thinks represents true Mexican folk art. Tourists are everywhere, haggling with the shopkeepers, eager to get something for nothing, carrying huge packages and boxes filled with the treasures bought at the many shops. Car horns blare at the people who are too entranced with the sights to watch where they are going. Raucous tunes pour from the nightclubs, open in broad daylight. Few children are seen in the town, but some boys swim in the Rio Grande and dive to retrieve the coins that tourists throw as they cross the bridge above. People come for a cheap thrill or cheap liquor. **A border town is the tourist's Mexico, a gaudy caricature of the real country.**

Remember what a good topic sentence does for the reader:

(1) A good topic sentence is like a promise to your readers. It gives them a sense of what to expect. In each of the following examples, the topic sentence steers the paragraph in a different direction:

TOPIC SENTENCE 1: **Daytime TV commercials are increasingly bizarre.** They offer car insurance for even the most reckless and Visa cards for the most delinquent. Then there's the ad featuring a young fellow waiting for his friends to come and watch the Big Game on his new TV. How did he get the money? Well, Pharmakinetics will pay ambitious young men up to $1,000 to test the absorption rates of new drugs—on themselves. . . .

TOPIC SENTENCE 2: **Like the sitcoms of the 50s, daytime TV commercials are far from gender-blind.** Men learn to be mechanics; women train to be nurses' aids. Men have a career in data entry; women attend the Washington School for Secretaries. Men worry about hair loss, women about weight gain. . . .

(2) A good topic sentence often hints at how the paragraph is going to be organized. It gives the reader a preview of points to be covered. Look at the program implied in each of the following topic sentences:

TOPIC SENTENCE: Just as traffic lights may be red, amber, or green, so job interviews may be classified according to their probable results as hopeless, undecided, or promising. (We now expect a description of the **three kinds**.)

TOPIC SENTENCE: During my high school years, I saw a major change in the way schools treated bilingual students. (We now expect an account of the situation first **before** and then **after** the change.)

PARAGRAPH WORK 2   Study the following topic sentences. What is the author's point or intention? What details, examples, statistics, or the like could you provide to help develop the rest of the paragraph?

1.   It is becoming harder for the average high school graduate to get into and to stay in college.
2.   Americans increasingly run into the ever-present computer during the business of an ordinary day.
3.   A major industry can shape the quality of life of a whole town.
4.   Violence in movies is getting more brutal.
5.   Many young people have negative attitudes toward the police.
6.   Corporations ceaselessly develop marketing strategies designed to make what we already own obsolete.
7.   At one time or another, most people's lives are touched or changed by divorce.
8.   Terrorism, like auto accidents, has become a standard part of the news.

6c   DEVELOPING THE PARAGRAPH   *dev*

Build up your paragraph with a solid array of relevant detail.

In a well-developed paragraph, the topic sentence is backed up by details or examples. Following through with specific examples or details is second nature for experienced writers; after making a point, they naturally go on to the "for example" or the "for instance":

> **Latin American culture has been and is a dynamic element in the development of our own.** It has, **for example,** furnished more than 2,000 place names to the United States postal directory. Its languages have influenced American English, as such simple examples as "rodeo" and "vamoose" indicate. Its customs are part of our

"Westerns" on television. Its housing, its music, its dances, its scenery, its ruins, and its romance have been imitated and admired in the United States. One third of the continental area of this republic was for a long period, as modern history goes, under the governance of Spanish viceroys or of Mexico. The largest single Christian church in the United States is identical with the dominant church in Latin America.   Howard Mumford Jones, "Goals for Americans," *Saturday Evening Post*

If you chart the material in this paragraph, you see a solid array of details that point in the same direction: Much in our culture has roots or parallels in Latin American culture and history:

LATIN AMERICAN CULTURE AND OUR OWN

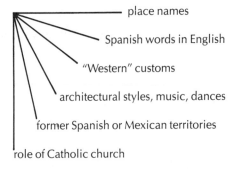

place names

Spanish words in English

"Western" customs

architectural styles, music, dances

former Spanish or Mexican territories

role of Catholic church

Try other typical ways of backing up a topic sentence with convincing detail:

(1) Use one exceptionally detailed example to drive home a point. Sometimes one striking example or summarized case history is remembered where more routine examples would be forgotten:

TOPIC SENTENCE: **As more and more clerical workers use computers, they increasingly find that their work is monitored from afar.** For example, computerization changed the working conditions in the accounting department of a large airline. The company hired a computer consultant to observe the work of clerks sifting through flight coupons and tabulating revenues. The consultant then devised a

key example

computerized system that enabled supervisors to keep exact count of how many tickets each clerk was processing each day. The system also identified periods during the day when productivity would dip while workers socialized or took breaks. The system enabled supervisors to set work quotas and to identify electronically those employees who fell short. Like the chickens on a computerized chicken farm, the workers were no longer allowed to waste the company's time.

(2) Choose one of several examples for especially detailed treatment. After giving more general examples, push toward specifics; move in for the closer look. In such a paragraph, you **downshift** — you move into a slower gear to allow the reader to take a closer look at one part of the scenery. To help you visualize the downshifting that occurs in this kind of paragraph, imagine the paragraph laid out in a step pattern like the following:

1 GENERAL: **We constantly expect more of computers.** Our tests for the artificial intelligence we build into electronic computers are constantly becoming more demanding. ————————————————➤

2 INTERMEDIATE: When machines first performed simple calculations, people were amazed to see a collection of gears and levers add 2 and 2. ————————————➤

2 INTERMEDIATE: Early computers amazed people by winning a game of tic-tac-toe. Today we are no longer surprised to see computers play chess, challenging world champions. ————————————————➤

3 SPECIFIC: Current tests of computer intelligence ask a human subject to type questions and comments on a communication typewriter and then to judge which responses are being returned by another human being and which by a computer. For instance, a computer program called DOCTOR simulates the responses of a human therapist. According to a recent article on artificial intelligence, "some of the individuals interacting with DOCTOR thought they were getting typed responses from a real therapist."

PARAGRAPH WORK 3   How would you complete each of the following paragraphs? For each, *downshift* to one or more striking examples developed in detail. Modify or adapt the opening sentences if you wish.

1. *The fitness craze shows no signs of abating.* Sportswear stores carry twenty different kinds of running shoes, with the price of each pair representing three days' wages for the person working at Mac-Donald's or Burger King. . . .

2. *It is hard for young people to find heroes in the political arena.* Several recent Presidents have started in office with much popular support, only to be discredited or disgraced before they finished their duties. What Waterloo was to Napoleon, Watergate was to Richard Nixon, who resigned in disgrace when his White House "plumbers" were caught breaking and entering. . . .

3. *In our modern society, what cannot be counted does not count.* Numbers are the very models of modern facts. We expect to be served our customary diet of statistics — to be kept up to date with the latest swing in the unemployment rate, the consumer price index, or the President's standing in the polls. . . .

4. *Moviegoers and television viewers are fascinated by the possibility of extraterrestrial life.* Several years ago, the hit of the movie season was a spindly-fingered, child-size extraterrestrial who looked like an intelligent lizard. . . .

PARAGRAPH REVIEW 4   Study the way a central idea or main point is developed in the following paragraphs. Answer the following questions about each:

- What is the main point? Is it stated in a topic sentence? Where in the paragraph?
- Is any part of the paragraph a restatement or explanation of the main idea?
- What is the nature of the supporting material — multiple examples, one key example, downshifting to a more detailed example? (What is the source of the supporting material?)

1.   The influx of women into the corporate world has generated its own small industry of advice and inspiration. Magazines like *Savvy* and *Working Woman* offer tips on everything from sex to software, plus the occasional instructive tale about a woman who rises effortlessly from managing a boutique to being the CEO of a multinational corporation. Scores of books published since the mid-1970s have told the aspiring managerial woman what to wear, how to flatter superiors, and, when necessary, fire subordinates. Even old-fashioned radicals like myself, for whom "CD" still means civil disobedience rather than an eight percent interest rate, can expect to receive a volume of second-class mail inviting them to join their corporate sisters at a "networking brunch" or to share the privileges available to the female frequent flier.   Barbara Ehrenreich, "Strategies of Corporate Women," *The New Republic*

2.   When I was in grade school, I had many friends. They often invited me over to their houses. My parents would let me go if I asked politely. They sent me off with the usual warnings about not riding my bike in the middle of the street or being back in time for supper. One year my mother and I were looking at my class picture, and I pointed out a good friend of mine whose house I had often visited. Looking at his picture, my mother realized he was of a different race. I was never given permission to visit his family again. When I complained, I was told my friend was not a desirable influence. I believe that we are born with no natural instinct for prejudice but that we learn prejudices later in life from others.

3.   Commercial fishing around the world can barely keep up with the growing demand for scarce protein. In a recent year, the total catch amounted to 74 million tons, which works out to 16 kilograms per person for the world, or almost a quarter of all animal protein consumed. More than a hundred species of finfish and shellfish are harvested commercially around the world, and 22 species provide 100,000 tons or more. However, per capita catches have been slowly dropping during the last decade. At least eleven major fisheries have been depleted to the point of collapse, ranging from the anchovy in Peru to the Alaska crab. In fact, only squid and the Antarctic krill are still underfished, since harvesters find it hard to make them palatable to new consumers.

| **6d** | TRANSITION | *trans* |

Use transitional expressions to help your reader follow.

A transition helps a reader "travel across" or move on from one point to the next. It provides a bridge from one idea or detail to another. **Transitional phrases** help your reader see how your paragraph is laid out; they help the reader follow from point to point. (See also **5e**.)

Trace the transitional expressions that guide the reader through the following paragraph:

TOPIC SENTENCE:	**Doctors have found that the way a drug is given can be important.** The commonly prescribed antibiotic
example	tetracycline is **one example**. It is completely absorbed when injected in a vein or muscle and fairly well ab-
caution	sorbed in pill form on an empty stomach. **But** because the presence of food in the stomach interferes with ab- sorption, patients are advised to take tetracycline before
additional point	meals. **Further**, drugs are not absorbed equally after in-
result	jection into different muscles. **Therefore**, doctors now pay more attention to the site at which drugs are in-
example	jected. **For example**, in the case of a drug called lido- caine, which is used in the treatment of heart rhythm abnormalities, studies have shown that it was absorbed faster following its injection into the deltoid muscle in the arm than into a muscle in the leg. Lawrence K. Altman, "Drugs — How Much Is Enough?" *New York Times*

PARAGRAPH WORK 5   Fill in the missing transition that will steer the reader in the right direction.

The search for new sources of energy has often proved disappointing. _____ , the extracting of oil from shale rock has proved less viable than its promoters had hoped. Companies looking for alter- native sources of oil started to mine shale, heat it to 900 degrees F, and draw off the raw shale oil, to be refined and made into petroleum. One ton of rock can yield 35 gallons of oil. One project was designed to produce as much oil as a medium-size oil field in Oklahoma. _____ , oil prices failed to rise as predicted, and development costs shot through the roof. _____ , oil companies put their shale projects on hold.

6e | COHERENCE | *coh*

Know how to improve coherence in a paragraph.

When a paragraph has **coherence**, it "hangs together." The material in it is relevant — it helps the writer make the point. In addition to clear transitions, use the following to strengthen coherence in your paragraphs:

(1) Use recurrent or related terms to help hold a paragraph together. In many paragraphs, a network of related terms makes for coherence and keeps the reader's attention focused on the point at issue. In the following paragraph, note the many words and phrases that echo the idea of purity: *naked — nude — pure — elemental — beyond corruption — natural — basic.*

<table>
<tr><td></td><td>To the Greeks, who get the credit for inventing it, gymnastics was "the **naked** sport" (the word *gymnos* means "**nude**"), and the phrase manages to be both evoc-</td></tr>
<tr><td>TOPIC SENTENCE:</td><td>ative and correct. There is something **pure about gymnastics**, something **so elemental** that the sport seems **beyond** either **corruption or adornment**. The athletes do not work against an opponent or against some arithmetical measure of time, distance, or weight. The gymnast works, instead, against the body's **natural** limits, with little protective clothing or equipment to help when courage or talent fails. The apparatuses of gymnastics are **basic** and symbolic, nothing more than artificial tree limbs, level tumbling lawns, and imitation saddles. Geoffrey Norman, "The Naked Sport," *Esquire*</td></tr>
</table>

(2) Use parallel structure to line up ideas of equal importance. In the following paragraph, the repetition of similar sentence openings signals that the writer is continuing the same trend of thought:

> With a few splendid exceptions, professional reviewers do not really read books. **They are** in the book business. And that makes a big difference. **They are** so bored and so jaded with the sheer volume of books that pass through their hands that if they manage to respond freshly to one, it's nothing short of a miracle. **They tend** to regard all books as guilty until proven innocent. But readers are different. **They regard** each book with optimism. **They expect** their lives to be changed — and often write to tell me that they were.

PARAGRAPH REVIEW 6   Study the devices that make for coherence in the following paragraphs.

1.   All the evidence indicates that the population upsurge in the underdeveloped countries is not helping them to advance economically. On the contrary, it may well be interfering with their economic growth. A surplus of labor on the farms holds back the mechanization of agriculture. A rapid rise in the number of people to be maintained uses up income that might otherwise be utilized for long-term investment in education, equipment, and other capital needs. To put it in concrete terms, it is difficult to give a child the basic education it needs to become an engineer when it is one of eight children of an illiterate farmer who must support the family with the produce of two acres of ground.   Kingsley Davis, "Population," *Scientific American*

2.   Most often the male role in advertising is that of the strong, silent outdoorsman, athlete, or adventurer. The archetypal male figure in advertising is, of course, the Marlboro Man. This famous mythic figure was the product of an intensive campaign which transformed a poorly selling cigarette, originally aimed at women smokers, into the biggest selling filter-tip on the market. At the same time, it promoted an attitude about male roles still being sold in almost every cigarette ad currently in print. Commercials for beer also push the

take-charge male image, showing men, generally in groups, participating in active, physically demanding sports or jobs and being re-
warded with a cool bottle of beer. Rarely are women seen in these
commercials other than as silent companions to these he-men. The
Marlboro Man and his descendants exemplify the self-sufficient,
highly individualistic male who provides the complement to
the sexy, empty-headed female of toiletry commercials.   David
Burmester, "The Myths of Madison Avenue," *English Journal*

| REVISING PARAGRAPHS   *foc, dev*

Refocus and bolster weak paragraphs.

Revise weak paragraphs by highlighting the key idea, by
strengthening the network of supporting details, and by streamlining
the pattern that gives the paragraph direction and shape.

(1) Spell out your key idea. Look over your shoulder at the
reader who wants to know: "What does this show?" The following
revision of a weak paragraph adds the topic sentence that spells out
the point:

IMPLIED: The Lone Ranger—what a man! Fearless and brave,
he rides in on his white horse, sending the bad guys running for cover. After rescuing the heroine and saving the
town, he rides off into the sunset, alone. How about Tarzan, Lord of the Jungle, or Dirty Harry Callahan with his
.44 Magnum ablazing? My favorite heroes were the
mountain men—rugged solitary men fighting Indians,
wrestling bears, and discovering the only safe route
through the mountains. . . .

SPELLED OUT: **When I was growing up, I was totally taken in by**
movies and books that glorified the rugged outdoors
type. The Lone Ranger—there was a man! Fearless and

brave on his white horse, he sent the bad guys scrambling for cover. After rescuing the heroine and saving the town, he rode off into the sunset alone. Tarzan, Lord of the Jungle, another loner, single-handedly thwarted the evil designs of poachers or thieves of tribal treasure. My favorite reading was books about the mountain men — rugged solitary men fighting Indians, wrestling bears, and discovering the only safe route through the mountains, all in one day. I read every book I could find about such giants as Jedediah Smith and Joseph Walker. These men spent months, even years, in the mountains trapping beavers and living off the land, completely alone.

(2) Build up the supporting material in weak paragraphs. Readers need more than a general idea; they need things they can visualize and imagine. Get down to specifics:

GENERAL:

Images of blacks in the media have certainly changed. They now sell deodorant and toothpaste and light beer, just like other people. Bill Cosby's show, which became a top-rated program on television, presents a comfortable middle-class family and its everyday problems. . . .

SPECIFIC:

Blacks at one time were hardly visible in the media except as stereotypes (the field hand, the porter, the maid). That certainly has changed. Blacks now sell deodorant and toothpaste and light beer. Bill Cosby's show, which became a top-rated program, shows a comfortable middle-class family and its everyday problems. Some black viewers have complained that Cosby's Dr. Huxtable doesn't represent the average black person. It is true that the average black family is not headed by a doctor father and a lawyer mother. On the other hand, neither is the average white family. But when Cosby identifies his son's room as "the room where clothes go to die," we don't think about whether this is a black family. We know it is a real family. And this seems to be the heart of the matter. When whites grow accustomed to the idea that blacks

differ very little from them, it becomes more and more
difficult to keep prejudice alive.

(3) **Fit your supporting details into a pattern that the
reader can follow.** The following paragraph answers questions about
comets in the order in which these questions might arise in the
reader's mind:

TOPIC SENTENCE:	**Comets strew debris behind them in interplanetary space.** Some of it is seen from the earth as the zodiacal
where observed	light, which is visible as a glow in the eastern sky before sunrise and in the western sky after sunset. (It is brightest
how produced	in the tropics.) Much of the zodiacal light near the plane of the earth's orbit is sunlight scattered by fine dust left behind by comets. Under ideal observing conditions, cometary dust also appears as the Gegenschein, or counterglow: a faint luminous patch in the night sky in a direction opposite that of the sun. Comets need to contribute about 10 tons of dust per second to the inner solar system in order to maintain this level of illumination.
how ended	Over a period of several thousand years, the particles are gradually broken down by collisions with other particles, or are blown away by solar radiation. Fred L. Whipple, "The Nature of Comets," *Scientific American*

(4) **Strengthen the transitional signals that will guide your
reader.** The signals in the following paragraph nudge the reader in
the right direction:

then	**Some of us are old enough to recall when** the stereotype of a "liberated woman" was a disheveled radical, notoriously braless, and usually hoarse from denouncing
now	the twin evils of capitalism and patriarchy. **Today** the stereotype is more likely to be a tidy executive who carries an attaché case and is skilled in discussing market shares
emphatic reinforcement	and leveraged buy-outs. **In fact**, thanks in no small part to the anger of the earlier, radical feminists, women have gained a real toehold in the corporate world: about 30

> percent of managerial employees are women, as are 40
> percent of the current MBA graduates.   Barbara Ehren-
> reich, "Strategies of Corporate Women," *The New Republic*

PARAGRAPH WORK 7   For each of the following paragraphs, do a rewrite that would strongly present and support a central point.

1.   Many parents think that once their children are at school any-thing they do is the responsibility of the school. Parents blame schools for not maintaining strict supervision on campus. However, although most schools have strong policies, these can also be bro-ken. The staff cannot possibly watch all of the students all of the time. Parents should teach their children to have more respect for others.

2.   Let us look at the average worker in an average American fac-tory. Henry, an assembly worker, punches in at eight in the morning. On the line, he does the same repetitive job all day. At five o'clock, he punches out and heads home.

3.   In many of my classes, teachers have asked me about my Irish heritage. Without my telling them that my father is Irish, they assume I am Irish from merely looking at my name. Many people admire the "fighting Irish" of the Notre Dame football team. On Irish holidays like St. Patrick's Day, many Americans share in the nostalgia for old customs and the old songs. Newspaper articles about the Irish often dwell fondly on their folklore and their love of song and story.

PARAGRAPH TOPICS 1

1.   Write a paragraph that traces *one strand* in your growing up. Select an issue or important concern that will help your class-mates know you better as a person. Show in vivid detail why it mattered to you.

2.   Write a paragraph that follows up a key idea with *three or four well-chosen examples*. Choose one of the following topics:

   a.   Choose three or four examples of animals (other than do-mestic animals or pets) that have survived well *in spite of* the onslaught of human civilization. Start with a topic sentence that makes a general point about the examples you have chosen. Then follow through with your examples.

b. New inventions or technological breakthroughs gradually become old-fashioned and finally lose their usefulness. Choose three or four examples. Present them in a paragraph, using them to back up your topic sentence.

3. Write a paragraph that explains a characteristic attitude or emotion of the young (frustration, rebellion, ambition) to older people — or that explains a characteristic attitude or emotion of the old to the young. Provide *an exceptionally detailed example* that will bring your key term to life for your reader.

4. Write a *details-first* paragraph that creates a setting or a mood likely to be unfamiliar to your readers. First, fill in striking, characteristic details. Then, at the end, fill in the meaning the place or the mood has for you.

---

7   KINDS OF PARAGRAPHS

OVERVIEW The basic expository paragraph launches a main idea and then follows it up with examples or details. Other paragraphs follow a somewhat different pattern. Their organization mirrors their function: to trace a step in a process, to compare two related things, or to choose between alternatives.

7a   NARRATION, DESCRIPTION, PROCESS *coh*

Follow a pattern appropriate to your subject.

In a narrative, in description, in explanations, or in instructions, a paragraph often traces a pattern that is built into the subject matter.

(1) Make a paragraph follow a pattern in time. In telling the story of something that happened, present major stages or key developments in **chronological** order — the way they followed one another in time. The following paragraph about opening day at Disneyland takes us from the beginnings (the glut of cars on the freeway) to the morning-after newspaper report:

TOPIC SENTENCE:

getting in

early snafus

high noon

morning after

> Disneyland was capitalism with a human face — or a smiling rodent's — and its opening day was set for July 17, 1955. **Even the mastermind recalled it as "Black Sunday"; everything went wrong.** The glut of visitors turned the Santa Ana Freeway into a seven-mile parking lot. Refreshment stands ran out of food and drink for the nearly 30,000 invited guests and thousands more ticket counterfeiters who stormed the gates. Rides broke down immediately. A gas leak forced the shuttering of Fantasyland. The day's corrosive heat sent women's spiked heels sinking into the asphalt on Main Street. Nor was this debacle to be covered over with Tinkerbell dust: the whole sorry spectacle was broadcast on a live TV special co-hosted by Ronald Reagan. WALT'S DREAM A NIGHTMARE, proclaimed the Los Angeles *Tidings*.
> *Time*

(2) Make a paragraph follow a pattern in space. The following model paragraph makes the eye travel gradually from what is close by (the house and its garden) to the far distance (the tropical forest):

TOPIC SENTENCE:

this side of gorge

river at bottom

opposite bank

distant forest

> **The house stood in what was certainly the best position in Mamfe.** It was perched on top of a conical hill, one side of which formed part of the gorge through which the Cross River ran. From the edge of the garden, fringed with the hedge of the inevitable hibiscus bushes, I could **look down** four hundred feet into the gorge, to where a tangle of low growth and taller trees perched precariously on thirty-foot cliffs. Round gleaming white sandbanks and strange, ribbed slabs of rock, the river wound its way like a brown sinuous muscle. **On the opposite bank**, there were small patches of farmland along the edge of the river, and **after that** the forest reared up in a multitude of colors and textures, spreading endlessly back until it was turned into a dim, quiver-

ing, frothy green sea by distance and heat haze.   Gerald
M. Durrell, *A Zoo in My Luggage*

(3) Make a paragraph trace a process. To help us understand
how something works, a paragraph may trace a process step by step.
The following paragraph traces the stages in a natural cycle. Notice
the transitional expressions that take us a step forward in time:

TOPIC SENTENCE:	**Beavers often create forest ponds that for a time become the home of insects, reptiles, fish, otters, herons, and other animals.** Beavers can transform a pine forest
initial cause	into an entirely new habitat by damming a stream. The pond will flourish for a short time — perhaps a few decades. The pond's creatures adapt to seasonal changes. **In**
seasonal pattern	**the winter**, the pace slows beneath the frozen surface. Frogs and turtles bury themselves in the mud. **But soon after the ice thaws**, the natural rhythms accelerate. Dragonflies breed, fish spawn, and soon all the energies
reason for change	begin to prepare for another winter. **But when the food supply is exhausted**, the beavers will leave. Without their hard work and constant maintenance, the dam falls into disrepair and the water runs out. The area reverts to a
end of cycle	swamp, **then** a marsh, a meadow, and **finally** a forest once again in this never-ending natural cycle.

PARAGRAPH WORK 8   Write a paragraph that traces a central theme
or recurring idea through several sections of a movie or book. Make your
paragraph follow a rough *chronological order*.

7b | COMPARISON AND CONTRAST   *coh*

Use a paragraph to develop a comparison or contrast.

We often use a paragraph to line up two things for comparison.
Comparison can help a reader understand something difficult or new

by showing how it is similar to something familiar. Contrast can alert the reader to important differences. Often comparison or contrast helps us make a choice.

(1) Line up similarities and differences. The following paragraph illustrates a common pattern for combined **comparison and contrast,** showing first similarities and then differences. Note the *however* that signals the turning point:

TOPIC SENTENCE: **People riding a moped should remember that it is not really a motorcycle but only a bicycle with a small motor attached.** The moped may look like a lightweight

similarities   motorcycle, and it can weave through stalled traffic and crowded places like a motorcycle. Like a motorcycle, it is cheaper and easier to maintain than the bulky, gas-

differences   guzzling family car. **However**, the moped creates a real safety problem for people who ride it in ordinary traffic. It has much less weight and power than a real motorcycle. The driver depends on a very small, underpowered engine. The wind caused by a passing truck or bus can make the lightweight moped impossible to control.

(2) Trace a detailed analogy. An **analogy** is a comparison that traces a close parallel through several specifics. The two things being compared have to be alike in basic and instructive ways, not just superficially similar.

TOPIC SENTENCE: **We are not unlike a particularly hardy crustacean.** The lobster grows by developing and shedding a series of hard, protective shells. Each time it expands from within, the confining shell must be sloughed off. It is left exposed and vulnerable until, in time, a new covering grows to replace the old. With each passage from one stage of human growth to the next we, too, must shed a protective structure. We are left exposed and vulnerable — but also yeasty and embryonic again, capable of stretching in ways we hadn't known before. These sheddings may take several years or more. Coming out of each passage, though, we enter a longer and more stable period in which we can expect relative tranquility and a sense of equilibrium regained.   Gail Sheehy, *Passages*

PARAGRAPH WORK 9   Write a *then-and-now* paragraph that traces a contrast between old and new customs or patterns of behavior. Study the following paragraph as a possible model:

We have lost contact with many of our traditional rites of grieving. In rural America everybody had a role in the rites of death. Farm women dressed the body while the men built the casket. The body was buried on the family's land or in a nearby cemetery, by community members. Mourners wore black, or black armbands, for a long time — often a full year. The black would say, "I'm grieving; be gentle with me." Now, mourners are invisible. If a bank teller is short with me, there's no way to know that he is upset because his mother just died. For most of this society, grieving is set aside after a few days. Companies give three days bereavement leave for the death of an immediate family member, no time for the death of a friend. After three days, we are supposed to come back and perform as usual.

7c | ARGUMENT | *coh*

Write a paragraph that can serve as a step in an argument.

When we reason with a reader, we try to present our points in such a way that a reasonable or objective reader would have to agree. Here are several kinds of paragraphs that follow familiar logical patterns:

(1) Write a paragraph that supports your point with convincing reasons. In the following paragraph, the student writer presents reasons showing that her attitude toward convenience foods is more than a personal dislike:

TOPIC SENTENCE: **I object to convenience foods because they do not serve the cause of good nutrition.** These expensive,
reasons   elaborately packaged, highly processed products are usually a combination of many ingredients, some of which have nothing to do with nutrition. Often the extra ingredients are there to provide long-term preservation and to improve coloring, texture, or taste. Refined sugar is one example of an often unnecessary ingredient. We eat too much sugar without realizing that much of the sugar we consume is hidden sugar. Almost every processed foodstuff contains sugar in some form: honey, molasses, sucrose, corn syrup, dextrose, and the like. Too much sugar plays a role as a cause of heart disease, diabetes, and high blood pressure. Salt is also abundantly used in processing beyond what is necessary for good health. The biggest argument against processed convenience foods is that during processing and packaging many of the original nutrients are lost and then artificially replaced by "enriching."

(2) **Trace a pattern from cause to effect.** We often explain something by first taking a look at its causes. Then we look at the results these causes have produced. In the following paragraph, a crucial *therefore* takes us from cause to effect:

cause   Japan is a nation that, lacking natural resources, must live by its wits, by social discipline, and by plain hard work. It is not surprising, **therefore**, to discover that dur-
effect   ing the last twenty years Japan has quietly been establishing a new, higher set of educational standards for the world. On a whole raft of international tests of achievement in science and math, Japanese students outperform all others. Japan's newspaper readership level is the world's highest. A considerably larger percentage of Japanese (90 percent) than Americans (75 percent) or Euro-

peans (mostly below 50 percent) finish the twelfth grade, and a greater proportion of males complete university B.A. degrees in Japan than in other countries. Japanese children attend school about fifty more days each year than American students, which means that, by high-school graduation, they have been in school somewhere between three and four more years than their American counterparts.   Thomas P. Rohlen, "Japanese Education — If They Can Do It, Should We?" *The American Scholar*

(3) Use a paragraph to weigh the pro and con. The following example lines up advantages and disadvantages in an exceptionally well-balanced way. Note the transitions that take us from the pro to the con in each set of examples:

TOPIC SENTENCE: **Like other modern inventions, computers have a capacity for use and abuse, a potential for good and bad.** Computers allow people to fly safely and quickly across continents, **but** they also make it possible to send missiles from one country to another. Computers can speed credit cards to us and help us use them with ease, **but** they can also be used to compile records that invade a citizen's privacy. Computers serve as electronic tutors; pocket-size electronic calculators can solve compli-cated problems with amazing speed. **However**, the stu-dents who start early to rely on calculators may see their own math abilities remain underdeveloped. The same computers that help administrators and accountants can ruin a student's class schedule or bill the wrong person for a thousand dollars' worth of merchandise.

(4) Use a paragraph to define an important term. The fol-lowing paragraph defines the term *conjunction* as used by astronomers and then illustrates its use:

explanation   In addition to Venus, there are four other planets visible to the naked eye — Mercury, Mars, Jupiter, and Sat-urn. During their movements across the sky, two planets

key term

may sometimes appear to pass very close to one another — though in reality, of course, they are millions of miles apart. **Such occurrences are called conjunctions**; on occasion they may be so close that the planets cannot be separated by the naked eye. This happened for Mars and Venus on October 4, 1953, when for a short while

examples

the two planets appeared to be fused together to give a single star. Such a spectacle is rare enough to be very striking, and the great astronomer Johannes Kepler devoted much time to proving that the Star of Bethlehem was a special conjunction of Jupiter and Saturn.   Arthur C. Clarke, *Report on Planet Three*

PARAGRAPH REVIEW 10   Study the following *sample paragraphs*. What is the purpose of each paragraph? What is the main point, and where is it stated? How is the paragraph organized? What transitions help steer the reader?

1.   Three fourths of the world's people receive very little attention from American reporters. They are the peasants, the three billion people who are still traditional subsistence cultivators of the land. There should be no doubt that these people are worth our attention: all the major contemporary revolutions — in Mexico, Russia, Cuba, Angola — have involved peasant societies. In almost every case, the revolution was preceded by cultural breakdown out in the villages, because the old peasant ways and views of life no longer worked. The 450 or so American foreign correspondents only rarely report on these billions, because the peasants live in the world's two million villages, while the governments, wealth, and power — as well as telephones, cable offices, files, and typewriters — are in the cities.   Richard Critchfield, *Columbia Journalism Review*

2.   The most disquieting aspect of the silicon chip is not that it distances us from nature; even before the Industrial Revolution, man was trying to do that. The more troubling fact is that electronic developments distance us from understanding. Any child of fifty years ago looking inside a household clock, with its escapement and

weights or spring, could see in a few minutes how it worked. A child of today peering at a digital watch can learn nothing. Yesterday's children could appreciate that pushing a switch on a television set meant completing a circuit. Today's children, using remote control devices based on ultrasound or infrared radiation, can scarcely comprehend what they are doing. The real danger of the microelectronic era is posed by what was called, even in the days of macroelectronics, the black box mentality: passive acceptance of the idea that more and more areas of life will be taken over by little black boxes whose mysterious workings are beyond our comprehension. Bernard Dixon, "Black Box Blues," *The Sciences*

3.　　When a beachcomber discovers a marooned marine mammal, center volunteers jump into their rescue truck to collect it. This can be a tricky business, because the arrival of humans is likely to excite the animal enough to stimulate his instinct to attack. The rescuers approach small seals and sea lions behind a "herding board" that protects the people and guides the animal into the rescue truck. They may briefly pop a blanket over the animal's head, says Schramm, "so they can't see where to bite." The uninitiated might be tempted to pet a young seal or sea lion with its invitingly thick coat and big cow eyes. But the animals are not as adorable as they look. Even the youngsters have very sharp teeth, and they're not afraid to use them. A larger elephant seal or sea lion is a bigger challenge and must be approached "with great caution," Schramm says. To collect the larger animals, rescuers use a "bull pull," a long pole with a rope on the end that is slipped over a large pinniped's neck to keep the biting end a safe distance from the people herding it into the truck.　Linda Currey Post, "Shelter from the Storm," *San Francisco Focus*

PARAGRAPH TOPICS 2

1. Write a paragraph that traces a clear pattern in *space or time* for the confused newcomer or outsider. Start with a topic sentence that sums up or previews what you describe. Choose a topic like the following:

- the layout of a baseball field
- building the foundation for a house
- disassembling the engine of a car
- the layout of your favorite park

2. Write a paragraph that develops a *comparison or contrast* to help guide the choices of an undecided reader. Start with a topic sentence that sums up the comparison. Choose a topic like the following:

- driving a car and riding a motorcycle
- organic and ordinary food
- downhill and cross-country skiing
- jogging and walking

3. Develop an *analogy* as a guide to the curious. Complete one of the following statements and use it as a topic sentence for a paragraph that fills in the details or examples needed to follow up the analogy. (Or develop an analogy of your own choice.)

- Love is like ——————— .
- Failure is like ——————— .
- The army is like ——————— .
- Marriage is like ——————— .

4. Write a paragraph in which you take a stand and then *give reasons* for the position you have taken. Keep in mind the unconverted or hostile reader. Choose a topic like the following:

- large families
- stricter speed limits
- health foods
- financial aid to minority students
- more financial support for women's sports
- calculators in math classes

5. Write a paragraph whose purpose is to explain *cause and effect* or to examine *pros and cons*. Write to convince a reluctant or unconverted reader. Choose a topic like the following:

   - diets
   - protecting nonsmokers
   - cheating on exams
   - a national speed limit
   - graffiti

6. Write a *definition* paragraph that explains and illustrates a current buzzword, such as *lifestyle, quality time, the old boys' network, sexual harassment, prime-time soap,* or *animal rights*.

4

SENTENCE BASICS

Note: The following is a quick rundown of minimum proficiencies in the area covered in this chapter. Remember that there is much more to good writing than meeting minimum standards. However, if you fail to meet the standards summarized here, your message may not reach the reader and you may not get credit for what you do well.

The most basic test of literate English is the ability to write a complete sentence. Periods mark off complete sentences; do not use them to mark off a **sentence fragment.** Do not go to the opposite extreme: merging *several* complete sentences without adequate punctuation.

(1) Correct sentence fragments. Complete English sentences have at least a subject and a complete verb. They bring something into focus and then go on to make a statement about it: Somebody/ does something. Something/happens. Something/exists. In the shortest kind of sentence, the subject and the verb alone make up the complete sentence: Birds/*fly.* Evangelists/*preached.* Usually, however, subject and verb set up the basic structure that other sentence parts fill in:

COMPLETE: Many American **songbirds/fly** south during the winter.
             On Sunday nights, television **evangelists/preached** to the faithful.

- SUBJECT OR VERB MISSING: Fragments happen when a possible subject, or a possible verb, or *part* of the complete verb is missing. (All the following sentence fragments are caused

135

by a **phrase** — a group of words that does not have its own subject and complete verb.)

NO SUBJECT:	The wing hit the ground. **Spun the plane around.** (What spun?)
COMPLETE:	The wing **hit** the ground and **spun** the plane around.
NO VERB:	Chung worked in Washington. **A lobbyist for Taiwan.**
COMPLETE:	Chung, a lobbyist for Taiwan, worked in Washington.
NO COMPLETE VERB:	We spent hours on the road. **Fighting the traffic.**
COMPLETE:	We spent hours on the road fighting the traffic.
NO SUBJECT OR VERB:	We found the host. **In the jacuzzi.**
COMPLETE:	We found the host in the jacuzzi.

■ THE UNUSED LINK: Some fragments do have a subject and complete verb — but they start with a word meant as a *link* to another part of the sentence: *If* they agree to the terms. (If they agree, then what?) The unused links causing fragments are often **subordinators** (subordinating conjunctions). These include *if, when, while, unless, whereas, because, no matter how.* Watch especially for sentence fragments caused by *if* and *whereas*:

FRAGMENT:	We will get a raise. **If the governor signs the budget.**
COMPLETE:	We will get a raise if the governor signs the budget.
FRAGMENT:	The left brain is analytical. **Whereas the right brain is creative.**
COMPLETE:	The left brain is analytical, whereas the right brain is creative.

■ The unused link causing a fragment may be a **relative pronoun**: *who* (*whom, whose*), *which*, or *that*. Correct such fragments by linking the relative pronoun to what it points to: *the man* who, *the law* which, *the plan* that.

FRAGMENT:	He wrote to his friend Jim. **Who served with him in Vietnam.**

COMPLETE: He wrote to his friend Jim, who served with him in Vietnam.

FRAGMENT: It was a California deli. **Which did not serve lox and bagels.**

COMPLETE: It was a California deli, which did not serve lox and bagels.

All the sentence fragments in the last two groups are caused by a **dependent clause** — a group of words that has its own subject and verb but starts with a link to the main part of the sentence.

(2) Correct comma splices. Comma splices are complete sentences too loosely spliced together with only a comma. ("The parking problem is not a problem, it is a disaster.") Use a semicolon to hold such paired sentences together:

COMMA SPLICE: **We scratched** the dog act, **the poodle was** ill.
SEMICOLON: We scratched the dog act; the poodle was ill.

COMMA SPLICE: **The cabin was** empty, **they had gone back** to Maine.
SEMICOLON: The cabin was empty; they had gone back to Maine.

Comma splices also result when only a comma appears between two statements joined by *therefore* or *however*. These and similar conjunctive adverbs require a semicolon:

COMMA SPLICE: The contract expired, **therefore** the nurses went on strike.
SEMICOLON: The contract expired; **therefore,** the nurses went on strike.

(3) Correct fused sentences. A fused sentence runs together two complete statements *without* any grammatical link or any punctuation — not even a comma. Supply a semicolon or a period:

FUSED: She took the exam over **this was her last chance.**
SEMICOLON: She took the exam over; **this was her last chance.**

FUSED: Matthew no longer lives there **he moved to Katmandu.**
PERIOD: Matthew no longer lives there. **He moved to Katmandu.**

OVERVIEW You need to know enough about English grammar to understand how well-written sentences work and why badly written ones break down. Effective writers recognize sentence-building techniques that help them develop, expand, or combine sentences:

BASIC PATTERN:	Americans love sports.
MODIFIERS:	**Many** Americans love the **traditional spectator** sports.
COMPOUNDING:	Many Americans love **football, baseball, and basketball**.
COORDINATION:	Many younger Americans love the traditional spectator sports, **but** they also practice every kind of exercise.
SUBORDINATION:	The older generation drinks beer at football games **while** the younger generation jogs or works out.

8a | BASIC SENTENCE PARTS *gr*

Know the major word classes, or parts of speech.

We assign words to major word classes, or **parts of speech**, according to how they work in a sentence. The basic model of the English sentence has only two basic parts. A complete sentence normally has at least a **subject** and a **predicate**. Somebody acts, or something happens, or something exists:

SUBJECT	PREDICATE
The driver	stopped.
Volcanoes	erupt.
God	exists.

The major word classes are the building blocks we use to make up the two basic parts and to round out the bare-minimum sentences they provide. The four most important word classes are nouns, verbs, adjectives, and adverbs. Look at the way these work in simple sentences:

(1) **The subject of a sentence calls something to our attention.** It brings something into focus, so that the rest of the sentence can make a statement about it. The most important part of the subject is usually a **noun**: *car, student, bulldog, college, education.* We use nouns to name or label things, places, people, animals, ideas. The following clues will help you recognize nouns:

■ Many nouns stand for things we can count. We can usually add the *-s* ending to change a noun from one (**singular**) to several (**plural**): one *car*, several *cars*; one *boy*, several *boys*; one *airplane*, several *airplanes*; one *idea*, several *ideas*. Not all nouns use the *-s* ending for the plural:

REGULAR PLURALS:	books, students, buildings, laws, regulations
IRREGULAR PLURALS:	men, women, mice, children, teeth
UNMARKED PLURALS:	sheep, deer, offspring, people, cattle
SINGULAR ONLY:	chaos, courage, rice

■ Nouns often follow a noun marker like *a, this, my,* or *your*: a *dog*, this *car*, my *friend*, your *neighborhood*. (Often the noun follows the noun marker at a distance: *my* dearest *friend*.) We use three kinds of noun markers over and over:

ARTICLES: *the, a, an*
  the tide, a tree, an apple, a riot, the bill, a surprise

DEMONSTRATIVE ("POINTING") PRONOUNS: *this, these; that, those*
  this street, these tickets; that detour, those requests

POSSESSIVE PRONOUNS: *my, your, his, her, its, our, their*
  my hat, your gloves, his directions, their surprise

■ Nouns often have noun-making endings (**suffixes**) like *-acy, -ance, -dom, -ness,* or *-hood*:

-acy:	literacy, celibacy, delicacy, lunacy
-ance:	importance, attendance, remittance, admittance
-dom:	wisdom, kingdom, Christendom, boredom
-ness:	happiness, darkness, illness, sadness
-hood:	neighborhood, childhood, adulthood, nationhood

PARTS OF SPEECH

NOUNS:	The **jogger** waved a **hand** in my **direction**. **Drivers** shouted **insults** at **pedestrians**.
PRONOUNS:	**I** introduced **them** to **her**. **My** brother left **this** package for **your** friend.
VERBS:	We **greeted** them as they **entered**. They **will screen** those who **have applied**.
ADJECTIVES:	A **young** doctor needs a **big** cemetery. *Proverb* Her **younger** sister wants the **best** grades.
ADVERBS:	We **quickly** closed the window **again**. The train stopped **there unexpectedly**.
CONJUNCTIONS:	She **and** her assistant tried **but** failed. Wake me **if** I am asleep **when** he calls.
PREPOSITIONS:	People **without** umbrellas get wet **in** the rain. We waited **on** the hill **until** sundown.

■ The place of nouns may be taken by noun substitutes, such as the **personal pronouns**: *I, you, he, she, it, we, they.*

He	reads.		*We*	sang.
It	stopped.		*She*	answered.
They	bark.		*You*	win.

> SEE 13 FOR AN OVERVIEW OF PRONOUNS.

(2) The predicate makes a statement about the subject. (Sometimes the predicate asks a question about the subject.) The most important word, or group of words, in the predicate is the **verb**: *reads, stopped, has left, will return, was driving, has arrived.* Verbs report actions, events, or conditions. They often stand for something we can do: *eat* your food; let us *celebrate*; we should *notify* him. The following clues will help you recognize verbs:

■ Verbs can show a *change in time* by a change in the word itself: *steals* (now), *stole* (then); *lies* (now), *lied* (then); *eat* (now), *ate* (then). This change in time is called a change in **tense**. We can change many verbs from present tense to past tense by adding the ending *-d* or *-ed*:

PRESENT:	ask	arrive	request	investigate
PAST:	asked	arrived	requested	investigated

In the present tense, most verbs add *-s* when *he, she,* or *it* could substitute for the subject (**third person singular**). We use this form when speaking about a third party, with "action now":

THIRD PERSON:	My brother **works**.	(He **works**.)
	Jean **travels**.	(She **travels**.)
	The phone **rings**.	(It **rings**.)

■ Complete verbs often consist of several words. The main part of the verb may follow a word like *can, will, have,* or *was: can* work, *was* looking, *will* travel, *have* arrived. Such words are called **auxiliaries**, or helping verbs. More than one auxiliary may come before the same main verb: *will be calling, has been elected, should have known.*

If there are several auxiliaries, an auxiliary like *will (would), shall (should), can (could), may (might)* often comes first. After these there may be a form of *have (has, had).* In the next slot, there may be a form of *be (is, am, are, was, were, be, been): could have been* prevented, *may have been* lost.

■ Verbs often have verb-making suffixes like *-fy, -en,* or *-ize*:

-fy:	notify, magnify, ratify, indemnify, rectify
-en:	darken, weaken, redden, sharpen, lighten
-ize:	organize, synchronize, sympathize, analyze

VERB TENSES

PRESENT (NOW OR USUALLY):
  I **work** at home.

PAST (OVER AND DONE WITH):
  We **sold** the house.

PERFECT (COMPLETED RECENTLY OR TRUE UP TO NOW):
  I **have received** your invitation.
  She **has** always **supported** us.

PAST PERFECT (BEFORE OTHER PAST EVENTS):
  His mother **had worked** in a factory.

FUTURE (STILL TO COME):
  Your friends **will help** you.

FUTURE PERFECT (BEFORE OTHER FUTURE EVENTS):
  They **will have left** by then.

---

(3) Additional words may cluster around a noun. We seldom use the simple noun-and-verb sentence (Birds fly). Usually, we include **modifiers** that develop or narrow the meaning of the basic sentence parts:

Most American songbirds fly **south in the winter**.

Some of these modifiers are single words. **Adjectives** modify nouns, answering questions like "Which one?" or "What kind?" (the *red* convertible, a *tall* order, the *right* answer, *high* hopes). Number adjectives answer questions like "How many?" (*three* blind mice) or "Which in order?" (the *first* date). The following clues will help you recognize adjectives:

■ Adjectives appear in typical adjective positions: "a *reasonable* price," "The price is *reasonable*," "a very *reasonable* price." The most typical position is immediately before a noun (often between a noun marker and the noun):

ADJECTIVE:	the **tall** building	my **foolish** friend
	a **long** lecture	**many** visitors
	expensive cars	the **first** train

■ Most adjectives fit in after words that show differences in **degree**, such as *very, rather,* or *quite*: very *cold*, fairly *tall*, extremely *dangerous*. Unlike nouns or verbs, adjectives have special forms for use in comparisons:

POSITIVE (OR PLAIN FORM)	COMPARATIVE	SUPERLATIVE
tall	taller	tallest
speedy	speedier	speediest
envious	more envious	most envious
bad	worse	worst

■ Suffixes that help us derive adjectives from other words include *-able, -ic, -ish, -ive,* and *-ous*:

-able:	washable, reasonable, usable, dispensable, disposable
-ic:	basic, tragic, allergic, synthetic, generic
-ish:	foolish, Spanish, lavish, squeamish, sheepish
-ive:	expensive, representative, competitive, compulsive
-ous:	famous, enormous, anonymous, ridiculous, marvelous

(4) Additional words may cluster around a verb. The most important of these are **adverbs**. Adverbs answer questions like "How?" "When?" or "Where?" (They also answer questions like "How often?"):

HOW?	carefully, cautiously, silently, quickly, awkwardly
WHEN?	now, then, tomorrow, yesterday, immediately
WHERE?	there, upstairs, downtown, everywhere
HOW OFTEN?	once, twice, frequently, rarely, seldom

The following clues will help you recognize adverbs:

■ Many adverbs, but not all, show the *-ly* ending: *rapidly, individually, basically, dangerously*. (Some exceptional adjectives also have the *-ly* ending: the *friendly* natives, a *leisurely* drive.)

■ Adverbs typically go with a verb: reads *slowly*, spoke *thoughtfully*, asked *twice*. But they have greater freedom of movement than other kinds of words:

> The bell rang **suddenly**.
> The bell **suddenly** rang.
> **Suddenly** the bell rang.

■ Adverbs, like adjectives, often follow words that show degree: very *cheaply*, more *cheaply*, most *cheaply*.

> SEE 14a FOR PROBLEMS WITH ADVERB FORMS.

(5) Two additional parts of speech become important as links between other sentence parts:

■ **Prepositions** are words like *at, of, with, in, on, for, to, with*, or *without*. We use them to tie a prepositional phrase to the rest of the sentence: "Thousands *of* cars were stalled *on* the approaches *to* the bridge." A **phrase** is a group of words that work together, but it does not have its own subject and verb.

■ **Conjunctions** are words like *and, but, if, because, though,* and *whereas*. They help us combine several clauses in a larger, more elaborate sentence. "*Before* we left, we called the agency, *but* a machine answered." A **clause** is a group of words that has its own subject and verb.

> SEE 8d FOR PREPOSITIONS; 8e AND 8f FOR CONJUNCTIONS.

DISCOURSE EXERCISE 1   In each of the following sentences, one word or group of words has been italicized. What kind of word is it? Write the number of the sentence, followed by the right abbreviation:

N	for noun	Adv	for adverb
V	for verb	Pro	for pronoun
Adj	for adjective		

Losing the Space Race

1. The *conquest* of space has long been front-page news.
2. The Russians first sent a *satellite* into orbit.
3. An early Russian space capsule *carried* a dog.
4. Americans *immediately* mobilized their resources.
5. They *gradually* caught up with their competition.
6. *They* poured millions into Project Apollo.
7. American *astronauts* finally landed on the moon.
8. Millions watched the *first* footprints on the lunar surface.
9. *Disastrous* setbacks marred the space race.
10. Three astronauts met a *fiery* death in their capsule.
11. People *had heard* rumors of similar disasters in Russia.
12. Our *government* slowly deemphasized space travel.
13. Meanwhile the Russians *were building* space stations.
14. They invited foreign astronauts to travel in *their* spacecraft.
15. They *may be leading* in the space race for good.

8b | SENTENCE PATTERNS | *gr*

Recognize the basic patterns of the complete English sentence.

Some English sentences need only two basic parts: a subject and a complete verb. But many sentences need one or two additional basic parts to be complete. We call these added essential parts completers, or **complements**.

INCOMPLETE: The carpenter fixed _____ (What?)
COMPLETE: The carpenter fixed **the door**.

INCOMPLETE: Her grandmother had been _____ (What?)
COMPLETE: Her grandmother had been **a photographer**.

THE COMPLETE SENTENCE: BASIC PATTERNS

S–V:	Bees buzz.
S–V–O:	Ranchers dislike coyotes.
S–LV–N:	Her friends were musicians.
S–LV–ADJ:	Silence is golden.
S–V–IO–O:	The delay gave our rivals a chance.
S–V–O–N:	Her lawyer called the driver a menace.
S–V–O–ADJ:	Beer made Milwaukee famous.

---

(1) **Some sentences need only the subject and a complete verb.** In the simplest sentence pattern, the verb alone can make up the predicate; it can tell the whole story. Such a verb "is not going anywhere"; we call it an **intransitive** verb.

SUBJECT	VERB
Planes	fly.
The victims	suffered.
Your letter	has arrived.

(2) **In several sentence patterns, a single complement completes the predicate.** In the first of these patterns, an action verb carries its action across to a target or result (the **direct object**). The object adds a second noun (or equivalent) to the sentence. The kind of verb that "goes on" to an object is called a **transitive** verb.

SUBJECT	ACTION VERB	OBJECT
The student	reads	a book.
Dudley	made	sandals.
A storm	has delayed	the plane.
Our group	will choose	the winner.

In other sentences, the verb is a **linking verb**, which pins a label on the subject. The label may be a noun, called the **predicate noun**.

SUBJECT	LINKING VERB	NOUN
This ape	is	a gorilla.
The supervisor	was	his fiancée.
His story	may have been	a lie.

Note: In the first pattern, someone does something that aims at something else; *A* affects *B*. In the second pattern, the second noun merely puts a label on the first; *A* is the same as *B*. "Susan loved a biker" involves two people; "Susan was a biker" only one.

In addition to the many forms of *be* (*is, are, was, were, has been, will be, may have been*), linking verbs like the following fit this pattern:

SUBJECT	LINKING VERB	NOUN
Jeffrey	**became**	an ornithologist.
Her resignation	**seemed**	a mistake.
Their disappearance	**has remained**	an enigma.

In a third pattern with three basic parts, an adjective instead of a noun follows a linking verb (and is called a **predicate adjective**.)

SUBJECT	LINKING VERB	ADJECTIVE
Our bus	was	late.
The price	seemed	reasonable.
The food	tasted	bland.

(3) In several sentence patterns, the verb is followed by two completers. Sentences that follow these patterns have slots for not just one noun (or equivalent) after the verb; they have slots for two.

INCOMPLETE: Maria sent the agency _____ (What?)
COMPLETE: Maria sent the agency **a letter**.

INCOMPLETE:	The accused called the trial _____ (What?)
COMPLETE:	The accused called the trial **a farce**.

In the first of the four-part patterns, an action verb like *give, lend, send, sell, ask,* or *write* carries the pattern first to the destination (**indirect object**) and then goes on to what was given or sent (**direct object**). The first noun (or equivalent) after the verb tells us *where* something is headed:

SUBJECT	VERB	INDIRECT OBJECT	DIRECT OBJECT
The company	sent	**the victims**	an apology.
Stacey	writes	**her teachers**	notes.
A friend	will lend	**them**	the money.

Many other verbs also work in this pattern:

The manager	**promised**	**me**	a promotion.
The witness	**had told**	**the jury**	the truth.
Brazil	**owes**	**the bank**	billions.

Another pattern also adds a second noun but uses it in a different way. A verb like *call, name, consider, elect,* or *appoint* leads first to a direct object and then pins a label on the direct object. (The second completer is called the **object complement**.) The last two parts of such a sentence point to the same person or thing. In "The editorial called *the official a crook*," the official and the crook are the same person.

SUBJECT	VERB	OBJECT	NOUN
She	called	her ex-husband	**a sponge.**
Marcia	had considered	her manager	**a friend.**
The voters	elected	a Texan	**President.**

A slightly different pattern also pins a label on the object but uses an adjective instead of a noun. (Instead of calling a friend *an idealist*, we call her *idealistic*.)

SUBJECT	VERB	OBJECT	ADJECTIVE
Textiles	had made	the town	**famous.**
The tenants	painted	the walls	**green.**

DISCOURSE EXERCISE 2   In some of the following sentences, added adjectives and adverbs have been used to expand the basic pattern. Do you recognize the basic pattern in each sentence? Write the number of the sentence, followed by the right abbreviations: S–V, S–V–O, S–LV–N, S–LV–Adj, S–V–IO–O, S–V–O–N, or S–V–O–Adj.

Sayings for All Occasions

1. Ben Franklin collected proverbs.
2. Times have changed.
3. His sayings are still good advice.
4. The used key is always bright.
5. You cannot teach an old dog new tricks.
6. A cheerful look makes a dish a feast.
7. Debt makes another person your master.
8. Laziness makes all things difficult.
9. Little strokes fell great oaks.
10. A small leak will sink a great ship.

| **8c** | QUESTIONS, REQUESTS, PASSIVES   *gr* |

Convert simple statement patterns to different uses.

Many sentences ask questions, tell us what to do, or focus on what *was done*. **Transformations** are changes or adaptations that help us convert simple statement patterns to these and other uses. Several simple transformations rearrange (and sometimes delete or expand) familiar sentence parts.

(1) **A simple change in word order can turn statements into questions.** We move all or part of the verb in front of the subject: "You *are* his friend" becomes "*Are* you his friend?"

	SUBJECT	VERB	COMPLETER
Have	our guests	arrived?	
Is	the package		ready?
Will	your friend	pay	the bill?

Sometimes we need to add a form of *do* (*does, did*) and place it in front of the subject:

Do	your friends	agree?	
Does	the guide	speak	English?
Did	the officer	write	a ticket?

(2) **A common transformation helps us turn statements into requests.** It changes the verb to the form used in requests or commands (**imperative**). It omits the subject. "*You* should pay your dues" becomes "Pay your dues!" (Who is supposed to pay is understood.)

VERB	COMPLETER
Shut	the door.
Be	my friend.
Keep	quiet.

(3) **A third transformation changes active to passive sentences.** The **passive** makes the original object the subject of a new sentence. We reverse the order of the original **active** sentence, which goes from the "doer" through the action to the target. The new sentence puts the spotlight on the target:

ACTIVE:	Edison invented **the lightbulb**.
PASSIVE:	**The lightbulb** was invented by Edison.

In the passive sentence, the original subject appears after *by* toward the end of the sentence. (It may also be left out altogether: "*The police* caught the thief" may become "The thief was caught.") The verb appears in its passive form, which uses a form of *be* and the form that usually follows *have*: have *caught*, had *brought*, has *admired* (the **past participle**).

SUBJECT	PASSIVE VERB	
Roses	**should be pruned**	(by the gardener).
The suspect	**has been questioned**	(by the police).
Workers	**are being hired**	(by management).

FOR WEAK OR AWKWARD PASSIVE, SEE **17c** AND **19c**.

REVIEW EXERCISE 3 In each of the following sets, two sentences are very similar in their basic structure. Even though they may have been expanded somewhat, they follow the same sentence pattern, or they have been adapted or transformed the same way. The remaining sentence is different. Write the number of the set, followed by the letter for the *different* sentence.

1. **(a)** The city will host the convention.
   (b) Our computer has made a mistake.
   (c) Has the manager interviewed the applicant?
2. **(a)** Paper is made from wood pulp.
   (b) The documents had been hidden in a suitcase.
   (c) The tenants will pay by the month.
3. **(a)** Reports from the field arrived daily.
   (b) Take your complaints to the manager.
   (c) Report the incident in detail.
4. **(a)** Corruption was common in high places.
   (b) The apartment was searched by the police.
   (c) His sister looked different without her wig.
5. **(a)** Charitable people give generously to charities.
   (b) Please contribute freely to our special fund.
   (c) My father contributed reluctantly to the heart fund.

Recognize the modifiers that flesh out the basic patterns.

In a typical sentence, **modifiers** develop or narrow the meaning of the basic sentence parts. A modifier may be a single word. Or it may be a group of closely related words — a **phrase**.

BARE BONES: The burglar opened the door.
MODIFIED: The burglar **cautiously** opened the **heavy** door.
                The burglar opened the door **to the garden** *by mistake*.

(1) Different kinds of modifiers may cluster around a noun. They tell us more about the noun; they tell us which one or what kind. All of the modifiers boldfaced in the following examples modify the noun *dog*:

A **shaggy** dog barred my way.
A **big, yellow** dog was chewing the rug.
A **police** dog tracked me down.
A dog **with droopy eyes** dozed in the sun.
Let **sleeping** dogs lie.

Of these modifiers, the first three (*shaggy, big, yellow*) are adjectives. Other words or groups of words may modify a noun and serve the same function as an adjective. *Police* in *police dog* is a noun used as an adjective (sometimes called a **modifying noun**). *With droopy eyes* is a prepositional phrase — see (3). *Sleeping* is a **verbal** — a word that is derived from a verb but that can no longer be used as a complete verb by itself (see **8g**).

ADJECTIVE: **yellow** line, **handsome** stranger, **final** offer
MODIFYING NOUN: **police** dog, **track** coach, **home** computer
PREP. PHRASE: house **at the corner**, room **with a view**
VERBAL: **leaking** roof, **scrambled** eggs, **burnt** toast

(2) Different kinds of modifiers may cluster around a verb. They fill in details, answering questions like how, when, where, or how often. All of the modifiers boldfaced in the following examples modify the verb *rang*:

> The bell rang **twice**.
> **Suddenly** the bell rang.
> The bell rang **loudly**.
> The bell rang **at intervals**.

Twice, suddenly, and *loudly* are adverbs. *At intervals* is a prepositional phrase used to modify a verb.

(3) Prepositional phrases may serve the same function as either adjectives or adverbs. Combinations introduced by *with, at, on,* and similar words may modify either nouns or other parts of a sentence:

> The woman **from Chicago** disappeared.   (modifies noun)
> The woman disappeared **from Chicago**.   (modifies verb)

With, at, on, and *from* are **prepositions**. They tie a noun (or equivalent) to the rest of the sentence. Other common prepositions are *about, by, during, in, of, through, to, under, until,* and *without*. A preposition with the noun it introduces is a prepositional phrase. Often several prepositional phrases appear in the same sentence:

> We read **about the accident *in the newspaper***.
> His fear **of earthquakes** kept him **from traveling *to California***.

Such prepositional phrases may in turn include *other* modifiers:

> **In *traditional* textbooks**, our leaders appeared **as *great* men on *white* horses**.

CAUTION: A prepositional phrase alone is not a sentence:

FRAGMENT: The travelers crossed the river. **On a raft**.
COMPLETE: The travelers crossed the river **on a raft**.

A CHECKLIST OF PREPOSITIONS

The following words may all be used as prepositions. Many point out relationships in *time* or in *space*:

about	behind	from	since
above	below	in	through
across	beneath	inside	to
after	beside	into	toward
against	between	like	under
along	beyond	near	until
among	by	of	up
around	despite	off	upon
as	during	on	with
at	except	outside	within
before	for	over	without

The following *combinations* are also used as prepositions:

aside from	in spite of	on behalf of
as to	instead of	out of
as well as	in view of	regardless of
because of	on account of	

PRACTICE EXERCISE 4 Build up the following simple sentences by adding adjectives, adverbs, and prepositional phrases. Use at least one of each kind of modifier in your expanded sentence.

EXAMPLE: The cowboy rode the horse.
ANSWER: The **handsome screen** cowboy **slowly** rode the **magnificent** horse **into the sunset.**

1. The comic strip showed characters.
2. Reporters trailed the candidate.
3. The tourist asked the guide questions.
4. The woman approached the gate.
5. Athletes are tested.
6. Movies feature aliens.

PRACTICE EXERCISE 5 What *prepositions* are needed to fill the blanks in the following sentences? Write down the number of the sentence, followed by the missing prepositions. (Choose those that to you seem to fit best.)

1. The President traveled _____ China _____ a large contingent _____ reporters.
2. _____ the rally, speakers _____ many nations pleaded _____ an end _____ the arms race.
3. Small newspapers _____ many American cities are losing the battle _____ powerful newspaper chains.
4. The restaurant barred customers _____ jackets or _____ bare feet.
5. The road _____ the other side _____ the mountains led _____ tunnels and _____ spectacular bridges.

8e COMPOUNDING

Use compounding to expand simple sentences.

Compound structures are several sentence parts of the same kind, usually tied together by *and* or *or*. Look at the doubling up of different sentence parts in the following examples:

NOUNS: **The walrus and the carpenter** were walking close at hand.

| VERBS: | The hooves **slipped and struggled** on the mountain path. |
| ADJECTIVES: | Korea started to build **cheap and reliable** cars. |

A set of three or more sentence parts of the same kind is called a **series**. Note the commas that separate items in a series.

| VERBS: | In the movie, a robot **is struck** by lightning, **runs** amok, and **achieves** true human consciousness. |

DISCOURSE EXERCISE 6 Find the *compound structure* in each of the following model sentences. Then write a similar sentence of your own. Use or adapt the sentence frame that follows the model.

| EXAMPLE: | Europeans thought of Americans as wealthy, advanced, efficient, and invincible. |
| IMITATION: | Americans thought of Germans as orderly, ruthless, goal-oriented, and emotionless. |

The American Image

1. Europeans have fought insane wars, started disastrous revolutions, and followed fanatical leaders.
   (Americans) (Southerners) (other) have _____
2. To many Europeans, America meant affluence, efficiency, and technological progress.
   To many _____ , _____ meant _____
3. In Western movies, Americans appeared decent, plucky, and generous.
   (In TV shows) (In war movies) (In science fiction movies), _____
4. Refugees discovered people of different races, origins, religions, and values.
   _____ discovered _____ , _____
5. Europeans still imitate American fashions, sports, and gadgets.
   _____ imitate _____

| THE COMBINED SENTENCE *gr*

Join several clauses in a larger combined sentence.

When a short sentence becomes part of a larger whole, we call it a **clause**. A clause has its own subject and verb (unless it is a request, with the subject omitted or understood). The examples in the following pair each combine two **independent** clauses:

INDEPENDENT: The company had sent the bill, **but** the mail was slow.
                The climber slipped; **however**, the rope held.

Independent clauses remain self-sufficient enough to stand by themselves; they could still be punctuated as separate sentences:

SEPARATE: The climber slipped. **However**, the rope held.

In the examples in the following pair, the second clause is a **dependent** clause:

DEPENDENT: Sue will notify us **if** her plans change.
                We need a mechanic **who** knows this kind of car.

In these examples, the second clause cannot stand by itself. It is subordinated to the main clause. A dependent clause alone does not make up a complete sentence.

FRAGMENT: Oil prices will rise. **If consumption goes up**.

Study different links joining two or more clauses:

(1) Clauses remain independent when they are joined by a coordinator. The **coordinating conjunctions** (**coordinators** for short) are *and, but, for, so, yet, or,* and *nor.* Coordinators make two equally important parts of a message "work together." Put a comma between the two clauses, before the *and* or *but* that ties them together:

KINDS OF CONNECTIVES

COORDINATORS:	and, but, for, or, nor, yet, so
CONJUNCTIVE ADVERBS:	however, therefore, moreover, accordingly, furthermore, nevertheless, besides, indeed, consequently, instead, otherwise, hence, thus; in fact, on the other hand
SUBORDINATORS:	when, whenever, while, before, after, since, until, as, if, because, unless, provided, though, although, whereas; so that, no matter how, no matter what, as if, as though
RELATIVE PRONOUNS:	who, whom, whose; which, that
SPECIAL CONNECTIVES:	that, why, whether, how, where, who, what, whoever, whatever

---

Legislators make laws, **and** judges interpret them.

Many are called, **but** few respond to telephone solicitations.

The tombs contained food, **for** the dead needed nourishment on their journey.

Conditions changed, **so** the dinosaurs became extinct.

We are drowning in information, **yet** we are thirsting for knowledge.

Communities must support artists, **or** the arts will wither.

The new law did not lower taxes, **nor** did it simplify them.

(2) Clauses are still considered independent when they are joined by a conjunctive adverb. Conjunctive adverbs (or adverbial conjunctions) include *however, therefore, moreover, nevertheless, consequently, besides, accordingly,* and *indeed,* as well as combinations like *in fact, on the other hand,* and *as a result.*

The assembly passed the law; **however**, the governor vetoed it.

The price of gas went up; **therefore**, we bought a smaller car.

We warned them of the dangers; **nevertheless**, they continued.

Like other adverbs, these words may change their position in the sentence. Use the semicolon, which stays at the juncture between the two clauses even if the adverb shifts its position. Commas set off the adverb from the rest of the second clause in relatively formal prose:

> The assembly passed the law; the governor, **however,** vetoed it.
> We warned them of the dangers; they continued, **nevertheless**.

DISCOURSE EXERCISE 7   In the following *sentence-combining* exercise join each pair of short statements in a larger combined sentence. Of the connecting words given as choices, use the one that seems to fit best.

EXAMPLE: American steel mills used to dominate the market.
          Steel from Korea now floods the country.
ANSWER: American steel mills used to dominate the market, but steel from Korea now floods the country.

It's a Different Campus

(Choose one: *and, but, so, for, yet, or*. Use a comma.)

1. Older students returning to college are in for a surprise.
   The campus scene has changed.
2. Many students tune out political issues.
   Attendance at political rallies is often low.
3. Some of the students may be partying in the pub.
   Others are competing hard for grades.
4. Critics protest against the tyranny of tests.
   Students are taking more tests every year.
5. Today's students have to learn to relax.
   Campuses will turn into deadly serious places.

(Choose one: *therefore, however, moreover, nevertheless, besides, indeed, in fact*. Use a semicolon.)

6. Fraternities still get into trouble for noisy parties.
   Many students today are older and more mature.

7. Student loans have been cut back.
   More students work part-time at scroungy jobs.
8. More students live off campus.
   Many have long commutes every day.
9. For many students with children, day care is a pipedream.
   Some come to campus with their tots in tow.
10. Each campus has a different mix of students.
    The average age of students has gone up nationwide.

---

(3) **A clause becomes a dependent clause when it is joined to the main clause by a subordinator. Subordinating conjunctions,** or **subordinators** for short, are words like *if, when, while, as, unless, where, because, though, although,* and *whereas.* A dependent clause that starts with a subordinator is called an **adverbial clause.** Either no punctuation or a comma separates the two clauses. In each of the following examples, the added clause states an essential **if** or **when**:

NO COMMA: Customers get a discount **if** they buy now. (only then)
            You will be arrested **unless** you pay the fine.
            No flights will depart **until the fog lifts**.

In each of the following examples, the first half of the combined sentence is true *regardless* of what is added:

COMMA: We have a phone, **although** we are not in the phone book.
            Sharks are fish, **whereas** whales are mammals.

When you use a subordinator you can reverse the order of the two clauses, with the dependent clause first. A comma then shows where the main clause starts:

COMMA: **If you act humble**, you may avoid a ticket.
            Where women are honored, the gods are pleased.
            Arab proverb

CAUTION: A dependent clause *alone* is not a complete sentence.

FRAGMENT: The manager will notify you. **If a position opens**.
COMPLETE: The manager will notify you **if a position opens**.

DISCOURSE EXERCISE 8   In the following *sentence-combining* exercise, join each pair of short sentences in a larger combined sentence. Of the connecting words given as choices, use the one that seems to fit best.

EXAMPLES: The rich get richer.
             The poor get poorer.
ANSWER: The rich get richer while the poor get poorer.

The Imbalance of Trade

(Choose one: *when, where, before, after, until, while, as, if, unless, because.* Use no comma.)

1. Unions complain.
    Imported goods take over the market.
2. Domestic industries go out of business.
    They are protected by special tariffs.
3. Hi-tech companies move manufacturing plants to Korea or Taiwan.
    Labor costs are low.
4. Companies prefer to relocate.
    Local taxes are low there.
5. Americans of the future will work for foreign employers.
    Current predictions come true.

(Choose one: *though, although, whereas, no matter how, no matter what.* Use a comma. Put the dependent clause first when it seems appropriate.)

6. The Japanese outperform us in world markets.
    We try hard.
7. They used to be accused of producing cheap imitations.
    They now are known for high-quality goods.
8. Often the merchandise is made in Japan.
    The package carries an American label.

9. The Japanese are leaders in electronics and automotive engineering. Americans still dominate a few other areas.
10. American-built airplanes dominate the sky. Some airlines are flying European-built midsize planes.

---

(4) A clause becomes a dependent clause when it is joined to the main clause by a relative pronoun: *who* (*whom, whose*), *which*, or *that*. The clause that follows a relative pronoun is called a **relative clause**. Relative clauses modify a word in the main clause (*the pause* that refreshes; *people* who care). As a result, they may either follow or interrupt the main clause:

The tickets went to people **who signed up early**.
A Chicago dating service **that helps clients with their image** costs $1,250 a year.

Use *no comma* when you need the added clause to narrow choices — to specify which one or what kind, to single out one among several:

RESTRICTIVE: The candidate **who plagiarized his speeches is** no longer running.

When the added clause does not single out but merely adds details, we use a *comma*, or commas:

NONRESTRICTIVE: President Johnson, **who had been majority leader**, knew the workings of the Senate.

The relative pronouns *whom* and *that* are often left out:

The witnesses [whom] **he had threatened** refused to testify.
Inmates wrote books about the crimes [that] **they had committed**.

CAUTION: A relative clause alone is not a complete sentence.

FRAGMENT: He owned pit bulls. **Which frightened his neighbors**.
COMPLETE: He owned pit bulls, **which frightened his neighbors**.

DISCOURSE EXERCISE 9 In the following *sentence-combining* exercise, join each pair of short statements in a larger combined sentence. Choose one: *who, whom, whose, which,* or *that*. Use a comma, or commas, for the first three examples. Use no comma for the remaining two.

The Natural History of the Sandwich

1. The Reuben sandwich was invented by Reuben Kay.
   He was a wholesale grocer in Omaha.
2. The Earl of Sandwich wanted to snack without using fork and knife.
   His creation was named after him.
3. During a lifetime, the average American eats 2,900 pounds of beef.
   This is equal to six head of cattle.
4. The barbecue sandwich is made up of shredded pork in sauce on a bun.
   People eat it in North Carolina.
5. The hero sandwich was originally eaten by Italian construction workers.
   They had a strong appetite.

---

(5) A special type of dependent clause is not joined to the main clause but replaces one of its nouns. Such a clause-within-a-clause is called a **noun clause**. Noun clauses often start with question words like *who, what, why, where,* and *how*:

NOUN: The reporters asked her **the reason**.
NOUN CLAUSE: The reporters asked her **why she had resigned**.

NOUN: She was excited by **the news**.
NOUN CLAUSE: She was excited by **what she had heard**.

NOUN: **Their fate** remains a mystery.
NOUN CLAUSE: **What happened to the crew** remains a mystery.

That, frequently used as a relative pronoun, also serves to introduce a noun clause, often after words like *say, tell, explain,* or *deny*:

NOUN CLAUSE: The ad campaign told teenagers **that spraypainting the subways with graffiti was not cool**.

Noun clauses blend into the combined sentence without punctuation.

NO COMMA: The article explained **how people without talent become celebrities**.

Note: A sentence that coordinates two or more independent clauses is a **compound** sentence. A sentence that subordinates one or more dependent clauses is a **complex** sentence. A combined sentence using both coordination and subordination is **compound-complex**.

COMPOUND: He hummed, and she sang.
COMPLEX: He hummed when she sang.
COMPOUND-COMPLEX: When they heard the news, he hummed, and she sang.

DISCOURSE EXERCISE 10 How have the two clauses in each of the following sentences been combined? After the number of the sentence, write CO for *coordination*, SUB for *subordination* with a subordinator or relative pronoun, or NC for *noun clause*.

Our Polluted Habitat

1. Government reports show that pollution levels are high.
2. When factories discharge mercury into rivers, fish become toxic.
3. Farm children become sick if adjoining fields are frequently sprayed.
4. Contractors forget where they have dumped toxic wastes.
5. The sites are filled in, and developers build houses.
6. The buyers later wonder why their families suffer from mysterious illnesses.
7. Government agencies reluctantly order cleanups, which cost millions.
8. The injured parties find that law suits drag on forever.

Make good use of appositives and verbals.

We can greatly extend our sentence resources by putting familiar sentence parts to special uses:

(1) Recognize nouns used as appositives. A noun may come *after* another noun to modify that noun and bring added information into the sentence. We call such an added noun an **appositive**: my son, *the doctor*; my friend, *the dean*. The appositive may bring its own noun marker (*a, the, our*) along with it. It may in turn be modified by other material:

APPOSITIVE: Her best friend, **a sophomore**, finished second.
Aunt Minnie, **a vigorous woman of fifty-five**, had come in to help.

CAUTION: An appositive alone is not a complete sentence:

FRAGMENT: She was driving the same car. **An old station wagon**.
COMPLETE: She was driving the same car, **an old station wagon**.

(2) Know the difference between verbs and verbals. Verbals are parts of verbs or special forms of verbs. However, a verbal cannot by itself be the complete verb of a sentence. For instance, "he *writing*" and "the letter *written*" are not complete sentences. We would have to add an auxiliary to turn each verbal into a complete verb: "He *was writing*": The letter *had been written*."

■ Two kinds of verbals can take the place of adjectives and serve as modifiers. The first kind is a form like *burning, falling, hiding, inflating* (**present participles**). The second kind is a form like *burnt, fallen, hidden, inflated* (**past participles**):

VERB: The hall **was burning**.
VERBAL: The spectators fled the **burning** hall.

VERB: The prices **had been inflated**.
VERBAL: The store charged **inflated** prices.

Again, such verbals may carry along other material, making up a **verbal phrase**:

Hiding in the cellar, he heard the officers **searching the house**.
Nobody had found the papers **hidden in the attic**.
Swiss researchers **studying joggers** have found lacerations from bird attacks.

■ When the *-ing* form takes the place of a noun, we call it a **verbal noun** (or **gerund**). In the following examples, verbal nouns serve as subjects or objects, taking the place of nouns:

SUBJECT	VERB	COMPLETER
Speeding	causes	accidents.
Teachers	discourage	**cheating**.

Verbal nouns may have their own objects; together with the object, the verbal then forms a verbal phrase:

The manager	disliked	**paying the help**.

■ Another verbal that can replace a noun is the *to* form, or **infinitive**: *to run, to organize, to have succeeded, to be loved*. In the following examples, infinitives serve as subjects or as completers, taking the place of nouns:

SUBJECT	VERB	COMPLETER
The guests	refused	**to pay**.
To err	is	human.
Herman	hated	**to be ignored**.

Infinitives, like other verbals, keep important features of verbs. For instance, they may have their own objects:

> Joan   refused   to pay **her dues**.

Note: Infinitives have many other uses besides taking the place of nouns. For instance, we use them in combinations like the following:

OBLIGATION: We ought **to go**.
            Aliens had **to register**.

FUTURE: It is going **to rain**.
            I was about **to call you**.

We also use infinitives to modify various parts of a sentence:

We were looking for a place **to stay**.
They would drive five hundred miles **to hear the Grateful Dead**.

CAUTION: Verbals alone cannot be complete sentences.

FRAGMENT: We stopped at a gas station. **To make a phone call**.
COMPLETE: We stopped at a gas station **to make a phone call**.

PRACTICE EXERCISE 11   For each blank in the following sentences, write an *appositive* (a second noun and any additional material) that would provide a brief capsule description.

EXAMPLE: King Kong, _____ , has been the subject of
            several Hollywood movies.
ANSWER: *the big ape with a heart*

1. Penicillin, _____ , was discovered accidentally.
2. Sitting Bull, _____ , defeated General Custer at the battle of Little Bighorn.
3. Iran, _____ , suddenly became the center of media attention.

4. Cities began to convert downtown streets into malls, _____ .
5. Columbus, _____ , landed at San Salvador, _____ .
6. Sigmund Freud, _____ , changed the modern view of the mind.
7. Amelia Earhart, _____ , disappeared over the Pacific during a flight around the world.
8. Tarzan, _____ , travels through the forest with Cheetah, _____ .

DISCOURSE EXERCISE 12 Combine each of the following statements in a single sentence, working the material from the second statement into the first as a *verbal* or *verbal phrase*.

EXAMPLE: Oliver asked for more.
             He was still feeling hungry.
ANSWER: *Still feeling hungry*, Oliver asked for more.

A Sentimental Favorite

1. Many people have laughed and cried over the novels of Charles Dickens.
   They are living in all parts of the world.
2. His books have sold millions of copies.
   They have been translated into many languages.
3. His stories usually have an earnest moral message.
   They were written in Victorian England.
4. Dickens reforms the old miser Scrooge.
   He turns him into a warm-hearted, generous employer.
5. Dickens had a flair for melodrama.
   He often put extreme unselfishness next to grotesque evil.
6. The heroine of *Hard Times* is Rachel.
   She bears misfortune with saintly patience.
7. *A Tale of Two Cities* shows us bloodthirsty revolutionaries.
   They are driven by the spirit of revenge.
8. Dickens found a huge audience around the world.
   He was called sentimental by his critics.

FRAGMENTS AND COMMA SPLICES

OVERVIEW Whatever else you attend to in final editing, check for sentence fragments — incomplete sentences split off from the larger statement of which they should be a part. Check for the opposite problem: fused sentences — two complete sentences blurred without a visible dividing line. Check for comma splices — two complete sentences spliced together loosely without a logical link, connected only by a comma.

SENTENCE FRAGMENTS   *frag*

Use periods to mark off complete sentences.

Except for requests and commands, a sentence needs a subject and a complete verb: *My friends* (S) *vote* (V) for losers. *The team* (S) *was studying* (V) insects. When a period marks off a group of words without a subject and complete verb, the result is a **sentence fragment**.

FRAGMENT: My friends vote for losers. **Most of the time**.
              The team was studying insects. **Roaches, as a matter of fact**.

■Most sentence fragments are **phrases** — groups of words that work together but do not stand up as separate statements. They lack a subject, or they lack all or part of the verb:

ADJECTIVES: The grizzly is a magnificent creature. **Magnificent but deadly**.
PREP. PHRASE: Sarah was studying Hebrew. **In Israel**.
APPOSITIVE: They invited Sandra O'Connor. **The Supreme Court Justice**.
VERBAL: Each day he spent hours on the road. **Fighting the traffic**.
                Kevin had quit the band. **To start a dry-cleaning business**.

■ Many other fragments are **clauses** — dependent clauses that do have their own subject and verb. However, they start with a word meant as a link with an earlier part of the sentence. The unused link causes a fragment. The link may be a subordinating conjunction (subordinator, for short): *if, because, unless, when, before, after, while,* and especially also *whereas* or *although.* Or the unused link may be a relative pronoun: *who, which,* or *that.* Such unused links cause fragments like the following:

SUBORDINATORS: We will refund the money. **If you return the part**.

                          Lawrence is in Kansas. **Whereas Kansas City is in Missouri**.

RELATIVE PRONOUNS: The birds were storks. **Which are common in Egypt**.

                          Our neighbor was an ex-convict. **Who was still on parole**.

Some fragments are a combination of the two kinds: a phrase and a dependent clause. ("My roommate was a foreign student. *An Iranian whose father had served the Shah.*") To revise a sentence fragment, do one of the following:

(1) Reconnect the fragment to the main sentence without a break. Most prepositional phrases and infinitives (*to* forms) should blend into the sentence without punctuation to show the seam:

REVISED: Sarah was studying Hebrew **in Israel**.

                 Kevin had quit the band **to start a dry-cleaning business**.

(2) Reconnect the fragment, using a comma. Use the comma when an appositive or a verbal adds **nonrestrictive** material — nonessential information (or "extras") not used to eliminate possibilities or limit the main point. (See **28b**.)

REVISED: They invited Sandra O'Connor, **the Supreme Court Justice**.

                 Each day he spent hours on the road, **fighting the traffic**.

(3) Use a colon to introduce a list or an explanation. The colon then says "as follows"; note that it comes after a complete statement:

FRAGMENT: Jerry devoted his weekends to his two great loves. **Football and beer**.

REVISED: Jerry devoted his weekends to his two great loves**: football and beer**.

(4) Use a comma when an explanation or example follows a transitional expression. Use a comma before (but not after) *especially* and *such as*:

COMMA: The school attracted foreign students**, especially** Arabs.

Our laws protect religious minorities**, such as** Mormons or Quakers.

Add a second comma after *for example, for instance*, and *namely*. (The second comma is often left out in informal or journalistic writing.)

TWO COMMAS: We learned to like strange food**, for example,** raw fish.

(5) Join a dependent clause to the main clause. Use no punctuation if the added clause is **restrictive** — if it spells out an essential condition or limits our choices:

NO COMMA: We refund the money **if you return the part**.   (only then)

He befriended people **who had money**.   (only those)

Use a comma if the added clause is **nonrestrictive** — if the first statement is true regardless or if what it maps out will not be narrowed down. (See **27d** and **27e**.)

COMMA: Lawrence is in Kansas**, whereas Kansas City is in Missouri**.   (both true)

The birds were storks**, which are common in Egypt**. (true of all storks)

(6) Turn the fragment into a complete separate sentence.
If all else fails, convert the fragment to a complete sentence with its own subject and verb:

FRAGMENT: I appealed to his sense of humor. **Being a futile effort**.
REVISED: I appealed to his sense of humor. **The effort was futile**.

Note: Writers occasionally use **permissible fragments** for a thinking-out-loud effect:

There he is: the brother. **Image of him. Haunting face.**   James Joyce

---

9b | FUSED SENTENCES | *4S*

Separate two sentences that have been run together.

The opposite of the fragment is the complete sentence that has merged with another sentence — without punctuation or a link like *and, but, if,* or *because.* Use a period to separate the two parts of such a **fused sentence** — or a semicolon to show that the two parts are closely related:

FUSED: Matthew no longer lives there **he moved to Katmandu**.
PERIOD: Matthew no longer lives there. **He moved to Katmandu**.

FUSED: She took the exam over **this was her last chance**.
SEMICOLON: She took the exam over**; this was her last chance**.

DISCOURSE EXERCISE 13 Some headlines are *complete sentences* — with a subject and complete verb. Others lack a possible subject or all or part of a verb. The following were selected by the *New York Times* as the ten most important headlines of the twentieth century. Mark each *C* (complete) or *I* (incomplete).

Extra! Extra!

1. Man's First Flight in a Heavier-than-Air Machine
2. The Great Powers Go to War in Europe (1914)
3. The Bolshevik Revolution in Russia
4. Lindbergh Flies the Atlantic Alone
5. Hitler Becomes Chancellor of Germany
6. Roosevelt Is Inaugurated as President
7. Scientists Split the Atom, Releasing Incredible Power
8. The Nightmare Again — War in Europe
9. Surprise Japanese Bombing of Pearl Harbor
10. Men Land on the Moon

PEER EDITOR 14   Revise *sentence fragments* and *fused sentences* in the following examples. Write the italicized part of each example, adding or changing punctuation as necessary. Use a period followed by a capital letter to separate two complete sentences.

1. We were studying pre-Columbian *architecture. Such as Aztec pyramids and Mayan temples.*
2. Outside Mexico City, construction workers found priceless *murals. In buried buildings.*
3. Jobs were plentiful *in the area rents were reasonable.*
4. The lone survivor had hiked *down into the valley. To get help.*
5. One woman was *a jockey the other woman interviewed was a commercial pilot.*
6. Tom Peters co-authored *In Search of Excellence. The best-selling business book in history.*
7. The men of the tribe had *clearly defined roles. Hunting and fishing.*
8. The new management promoted a highly touted *sales technique. With meager results.*
9. Science fiction takes us to the brink *of the impossible. For example, robots with human emotions.*
10. Americans neglect the languages *of the Third World. Especially Arabic and Chinese.*

COMMA SPLICES *CS*

Use the semicolon to correct comma splices.

We often pair two closely related statements. Use a semicolon to show the close tie between the paired sentences if there is no connecting word like *and, but, or, if, unless, although,* or *whereas.* Correct **comma splices,** which use a comma instead of the semicolon and result in a pair of complete statements (independent clauses) too loosely spliced together:

COMMA SPLICE: Paula loved London, it was a wonderful city.
REVISED: Paula loved London; it was a wonderful city.

COMMA SPLICE: Some doctors inform their patients, others keep them in the dark.
REVISED: Some doctors inform their patients; others keep them in the dark.

(1) Use the semicolon also with conjunctive adverbs. A word like *therefore* or *however* may link the two paired sentences. These and similar words are **conjunctive adverbs**: *therefore, however, nevertheless, consequently, moreover, accordingly, besides, indeed,* and *in fact.* Again, a comma used instead of the semicolon would result in a comma splice. Often a comma is used as *additional* punctuation to set the conjunctive adverb off from the second statement. (See **27c.**)

COMMA SPLICE: The weather turned ugly, **therefore** the launch was postponed.
REVISED: The weather turned ugly; **therefore,** the launch was postponed.

(2) Use commas in a set of three parallel clauses. In a set of three or more, commas instead of semicolons are all right. ("I came, I saw, I conquered.")

PEER EDITOR 15   In each of the following pairs, use a semicolon to join two independent clauses. (A comma would cause a *comma* splice.) Write the last word of the first clause and the first word of the second, joined by a semicolon.

EXAMPLE: His hair was very neat every strand was in place.
ANSWER: neat; every

1. I enjoy running it becomes an almost unconscious act.
2. Everyone did calisthenics executives joined the workers and supervisors.
3. The class was inventing imaginary new products one of them was a stringless yo-yo.
4. Cost overruns were horrendous therefore, the project was abandoned.
5. People were shouting commands everyone with a flashlight was directing traffic.
6. The suspect had stepped out of the lobby he was walking down the street.
7. Zoos used to be dismal places however, modern zoos provide more natural habitats.
8. The sloth is genuinely lethargic its metabolism runs at half the normal rate for animals of its size.

5

GRAMMAR FOR WRITERS

Note: The following is a quick rundown of minimum proficiencies in the area covered in this chapter. Remember that there is much more to good writing than meeting minimum standards. However, if you fail to meet the standards summarized here, your message may not reach the reader and you may not get credit for what you do well.

Use the following *editor's checklist* to check your sentences for common grammar problems:

(1) Use standard forms of verbs. Especially, check for verb endings often omitted in nonstandard English or by speakers of English as a second language:

-s ending (verb):   Do not leave off the *-s* ending for one single person or thing (**third person singular**), with action now (**present tense**):

RIGHT: What **does** a motorist do when she **starts** the car? She **puts** the key in the ignition and **turns** it. She **puts** the car in gear and **backs** out of the garage. She **looks** both ways and **avoids** pedestrians.

-ed ending (verb): Many English verbs (**regular** verbs) show a change from present to past by adding the *-ed* (or *-d*) ending: We *travel* now/We travel*ed* in the past. Do not leave off the *-ed* that shows past:

RIGHT: The founders of our country **battled** the British, **secured** our independence, **created** new institutions, **passed** new laws, and **separated** church and state.

(2) Correct faulty agreement. Find the true subject of a sentence and make the verb agree with it. Subject and verb agree when they are both singular or both plural:

SINGULAR:	The **bus/stops** here.	A **siren/was** wailing. (one)
PLURAL:	The **buses/stop** here.	**Sirens/were** wailing. (several)

- Watch for agreement errors when the subject does not come right before the verb:

NO:	The cost of new prisons **are** enormous. (What's enormous?)
YES:	**The cost** of new prisons **is** enormous. (The cost is.)
NO:	Arresting crack dealers **strain** police resources.
YES:	**Arresting** crack dealers **strains** police resources.
NO:	There **was** always people loitering outside. (*Who* was?)
YES:	There **were** always **people** loitering outside. (People *were*.)

- Treat *each, either, neither, everybody,* and *nobody* as singulars — as if you were looking at the items or people involved *one* at a time.

SINGULAR:	**Each** (each one) of these options **has** serious drawbacks.
	Everybody (every single one) in the group **was** tired of the delays.

(3) Use adverb forms to show how something is done. With few exceptions (*fast, much, early*), use one form to tell us what kind (**adjective**) and another to tell us *how* something was done (**adverb**). For many common words, add the *-ly* ending to change the word from a label (a *serious* talk) to the form that tells us how it's done (talked *seriously*):

WHAT KIND:	HOW:
a **considerable** amount	grew **considerably**
slow traffic	turned **slowly**
a **gracious** response	responded **graciously**

(4) Correct dangling or misplaced modifiers. A modifier is left dangling when it points to something that has been left out of the sentence: "*Driving home*, sheep blocked the road." (Who was driving — the sheep?)

DANGLING: **Repossessed for nonpayment**, David claimed that the terms of the contract had not been met. (What was repossessed?)

REVISED: When **his car** was repossessed for nonpayment, David claimed that the terms of the contract had not been met.

A modifier is misplaced when it seems to point to the wrong thing:

MISPLACED: **Blocking the sidewalk, the officer** arrested the street musician.

REVISED: The officer arrested the **street musician blocking the sidewalk**.

(5) Correct vague or confusing pronoun reference. Pronouns like *she* or *they* or *this* need to point clearly to what they stand for.

CONFUSING: **Anne** disliked **Sue**, because **she** was very competitive. (*Who* was — Anne or Sue?)

CLEAR: Because **Anne** was very competitive, **she** disliked Sue.

CONFUSING: They worked in an **asbestos plant**, and **it** got into their lungs. (The *plant* got into their lungs?)

CLEAR: They worked in an asbestos plant, and the **asbestos** got into their lungs.

Especially, avoid shifts in the way you refer to a typical or representative person:

SHIFT: **The typical woman** today does not expect Prince Charming to take care of **their** every need. (We are looking at *one* typical woman.)

REVISED: **The typical woman** today does not expect Prince Charming to take care of **her** every need.

SHIFT: Once **an entertainer** becomes "hot," **you** can write **your**
           own ticket.

REVISED: Once **an entertainer** becomes "hot," **she** can write **her**
           own ticket.

(6) Use the right pronoun forms for different positions in a sentence. Use *I, he, she, we,* or *they* as the subject of a verb. These forms will often point to whoever is active or is doing something in the sentence: *I* arrived; *she* left; *we* procrastinated. Use this **subject form** especially when there is a double subject:

SUBJECT: **He and I** went to the same school. **Her cousin and she**
           both hate country music. **We and they** always disagree.
           (Try each of the two subjects separately: **He** went, and **I**
           went.)

Use *me, him, her, us,* or *them* as the object of a verb. These forms will often point to someone who is a target or recipient: insulted *me*; wrote *him* a letter; warned *them* the last time. Use this **object form** especially when there is a double object:

OBJECT: He put **you and me** on his enemies list. Nobody invited
           him and her to the same party. They had to choose **us or
           them**.
           (Try each of the two objects separately: He put **you** on the
           list, and he put **me** on the list.)

Use the object forms also after a **preposition** — a word like *for, with, between, without, by, on, at, under,* or *near*: for *me*, under *him*, without *her*. Use the object form especially when the preposition has more than one object:

OBJECT: It was a good year **for her and her family**. Your letter has
           meant much **to my collaborators and me**.

(If you can, try each of the two objects separately after the preposition: to my collaborators and **to me**.)

The difference between *I* and *me* or *they* and *them* is called a difference in **case**.

(7) Correct faulty parallelism. Sentences are parallel when several equal or similar sentence parts appear in a row, joined by a word like *and* or *or* or *but*: "People were obsessed with *spies, conspiracies*, and *plots*." (These are all nouns.) "Her friends *partied, took* long vacations, and *bought* their term papers through the mail." (These are all verbs.) But sometimes the second or third element in such a sequence snaps out of the pattern:

FAULTY: A rainy day makes people feel **tired, lazy**, and **in a gloomy mood.** (two adjectives and a prepositional phrase)

PARALLEL: A rainy day makes people feel **tired, lazy**, and **gloomy.** (three adjectives)

OFF BALANCE: *Stoner* is a street word referring to people **who get** stoned, **dress** in jeans, **who have** long hair that looks uncombed, and mainly **Caucasian.**

PARALLEL: *Stoner* is a street word referring to people (usually Caucasian) who **get** stoned, **dress** in jeans, and **have** long hair that looks permanently uncombed. (three verbs)

---

10 **VERB FORMS**

OVERVIEW Verb forms differ in the **standard** English of school and office and the **nonstandard** English that many Americans hear at home, in their neighborhood, or on the job. And verbs are a familiar stumbling block for students speaking English as a second language. Do not let nonstandard forms carry over into your writing.

STANDARD ENGLISH: AN OVERVIEW

Nonstandard	Standard
VERB FORMS:	
he (she) **don't**, I **says**	he (she) **doesn't**, I **say**
we **was**, you **was**, they **was**	we **were**, you **were**, they **were**
knowed, growed, brang	**knew, grew, brought**
I **seen** him, had **went**, has **wrote**	I **saw** him, had **gone**, has **written**
PRONOUN FORMS:	
hisself, theirself	**himself, themselves**
this here book, **that there** car	**this** book, **that** car
them boys, **them** barrels	**those** boys, **those** barrels
CONJUNCTIONS:	
without you pay the rent	**unless** you pay the rent
on account of he was sick	**because** he was sick
being as they missed the plane	**because** they missed the plane
DOUBLE NEGATIVES:	
we **don't** have **no** time	we have **no time**
it **never** hurt **no** one	it **never** hurt **anyone**
wasn't nobody there	**nobody** was there

10a | REGULAR VERBS | *vb*

Use the standard forms of regular verbs.

Verbs can show a change in time by a change in the word itself:
We *meditate* (now); we *meditated* (then). We call the forms that show

TENSES OF ACTIVE AND PASSIVE VERBS

Tenses of Active Verbs

	NORMAL	PROGRESSIVE
Present	I ask, he (she) asks	I am asking
Past	I asked	I was asking
Future	I shall (will) ask	I shall be asking
Perfect	I have asked	I have been asking
Past Perfect	I had asked	I had been asking
Future Perfect	I shall (will) have asked	I shall have been asking

Tenses of Passive Verbs

	NORMAL	PROGRESSIVE
Present	I am asked	I am being asked
Past	I was asked	I was being asked
Future	I shall (will) be asked	____
Perfect	I have been asked	____
Past Perfect	I had been asked	____
Future Perfect	I shall (will) have been asked	____

different relationships of events in time the **tenses** of a verb. Most English verbs, the **regular** verbs, use two basic forms to make up the whole range of forms that show action in the present, the future, or the past: *ask, will ask, asked, had asked.*

(1) Use the -*ed* (or -*d*) ending for the past. Regular verbs draw on two basic forms: *ask/asked, repeat/repeated.* We use the plain form for the **present** tense — something happening now, or done regularly, or about to happen: we *travel* often, I *consent*, they *exercise* regularly, they *depart* tomorrow. We add *-ed* or *-d* for the **past** tense: we *traveled* often, I *consented*, they *exercised*, they *departed* yesterday.

PAST: Many pioneer families **perished** in the desert.
The witness **invoked** the Fifth Amendment.

(2) In the present tense, use *-s* for the third person singular. Use the *-s* ending when talking about one single person or thing, with action now: he *travels*, she *consents*, it *departs*. The **first person** is speaking (*I* or *we*): the **second person** is spoken to (*you*). The **third person** is a third party (or object or idea) that we are talking about: *he, she,* or *it* for singular; *they* for plural. Use the *-s* ending for the third person singular:

THIRD PERSON (PRESENT):   Brian **works** as a shoplifter.   (**He** works.)
Marcia **collects** beer mugs.   (**She** collects.)
Inflation **continues**.   (**It** continues.)

(3) Use the *-ed* (or *-d*) ending for the perfect tenses (and all passive forms). Regular verbs make the *-ed* form do double duty as a verbal (past participle) that follows forms of *have* (*has, had*). Together with *have*, this verbal makes up the perfect tenses: *has called, had called, will have called*. The **present perfect** *has happened* recently, and what has happened usually still matters now. The **past perfect** *had* already *happened* prior to other events in the past. The **future perfect** *will have happened* before some time in the future.

PERFECT: The police department **has consulted** a psychic.
PAST PERFECT: They **had** already **encased** the reactor in cement.
FUTURE PERFECT: The country **will have depleted** its oil reserves.

The verbal ending in *-ed* or *-d* is also used in all forms of the **passive** voice — forms showing that the subject of the sentence is acted upon rather than acting:

PASSIVE: Many elephants **are slaughtered** by poachers.
A protest was **filed** by the Animal Rights Committee.
The passages **had been lifted** verbatim.

(4) Use -*ing* for the progressive construction. The verbal ending in -*ing* (present participle) serves in forms showing an action or event in progress, taking place:

PROGRESSIVE: The agency **is processing** your application.
The architect **was redesigning** the entranceway.

PRACTICE EXERCISE 1   Put each of the following regular verbs through its paces. For each, write a set of sentences following this pattern:

EXAMPLE: We *exercise* now. He (or she) *exercises* now. We *exercised* then. We *have exercised* recently. We *had exercised* before then. We *will have exercised* before then. We *are exercising* regularly.

Use the following five verbs: *work, meditate, relax, improvise, compromise.*

10b | IRREGULAR VERBS | *ub*

Use the standard forms of irregular verbs.

Irregular verbs often have three basic forms, with the past different from perfect: I *write* now. She *wrote* last week. He *has written* regularly. (See chart, "Standard Forms of Irregular Verbs.")

(1) Use the right past tense of irregular verbs. Revise non-standard forms like *knowed, blowed, catched, brung,* and *drug.*

STANDARD: Ancient Greek scientists **knew** that the earth was round.
We cruised all day but **caught** few fish.
Telegrams seldom **brought** encouraging news.

(2) Use the right forms after forms of *have* and *be*. The third of the three listed forms is used after *have (has, had)*. It is the form for the perfect tenses:

STANDARD FORMS OF IRREGULAR VERBS

Group together irregular verbs that follow a similar pattern:

Swim–swam–swum:
begin–began–have begun   drink–drank–have drunk
sing–sang–have sung   sink–sank–have sunk

Blow–blew–blown:
fly–flew–have flown   grow–grew–have grown
know–knew–have known   throw–threw–have thrown

Speak–spoke–spoken:
break–broke–have broken   choose–chose–have chosen
freeze–froze–have frozen

Other -*n* or -*en* words:
draw–drew–have drawn   drive–drove–have driven
eat–ate–have eaten   fall–fell–have fallen
see–saw–have seen   take–took–have taken
tear–tore–have torn   write–wrote–have written

Same form for past and after *have*:
bend–bent–have bent   burst–burst–have burst
deal–dealt–have dealt   dig–dug–have dug
lead–led–have led   send–sent–have sent

One of a kind:
go–went–have gone   come–came–have come
run–ran–have run

STANDARD: Our pious neighbors **had gone** to church.
             The python **has** already **eaten** the rabbit.
             You **should have taken** the blue pills instead.
             Overeager reporter **had** already **written** his obituary.

The same form (past participle) is used in all passive verbs after a form of *be* (*am, are, is, was, were, has been,* and so on):

STANDARD: The fish **is frozen** and shipped by plane.
The bicycle **was stolen** during the night.
The bolt **had been worn** out.

(3) Sometimes we have a choice of two acceptable forms.

Both are right: *lighted* or *lit, dived* or *dove, waked* or *woke, thrived* or *throve, sank* or *sunk.*

PRACTICE EXERCISE 2   What form of the word in parentheses would be right for the blank space in each of the following sentences? Put the right form after the number of the sentence. (Use a single word each time.)

1. (steal)   Radioactive material had been _____ from the plant.

2. (throw)   We spotted the swimmer and _____ her a lifeline.

3. (tear)   Someone had _____ open the envelope.

4. (go)   The witnesses should have _____ to the police.

5. (choose)   Last year, the party _____ a new leader.

6. (know)   Without the ad, she would not have _____ about the job.

7. (break)   Her cabin had been _____ into several times.

8. (grow)   Everything had _____ well in the moist climate.

9. (develop)   In its early years, the company _____ educational software.

10. (write)   He might have _____ a lukewarm letter of recommendation.

11. (know)   When we came home, she already _____ what had happened.

12. (take)   Someone has _____ the papers from the file.

13. (investigate) Last year, a grand jury _____ their dealings.

14. (drown)   Several vacationers have _____ in the lake.

15. (ride)   You never should have _____ in a stranger's car.

10c   *LIE* AND *SIT*   *vb*

Use the standard forms of *lie* and *sit*.

Some verbs have doubles just different enough to be confusing:

(1) Know the difference between *lie* and *lay*. We *lie* in the sun, but we *lay* mines, bricks, tiles, and similar objects of a verb. (We *lie*, and *lie down*, without an object.) For *lie*, the past tense is *lay*, and the third basic form is *lain*:

LIE, LAY, LAIN: Let's **lie** in the shade. We whistled, but he just **lay** there. The statue **had lain** on the ocean floor. You **should lie** down. Coins **were lying** on the ground.

We lay *something*, with *laid* as the past tense (*laid* an egg) and as the form used after *have* (*had laid* the rumors to rest).

LAY, LAID, LAID: Bricklayers **lay** bricks. Our forefathers **laid** the foundation. She **had laid** a wreath at the tomb. He was always **laying** odds.

(2) Know the difference between *sit* and *set*. To *sit* (*sit—sat—sat*) is to be seated. *Sit down* follows the same scheme:

They **sit** in the pew in which their parents **sat** and their grandparents **had sat** before them. (S–V)

Set (*set—set—set*), one of the few verbs with only one basic form, means *place* or *put*. You yourself *sit*, or *sit down*; you *set*, or *set down*, something else:

When you have **set** the timer, **set** the device down behind the screen we **set** up. (S–V–O)

PRACTICE EXERCISE 3   Choose the right forms of *sit* or *set, lie* or *lay.*

1. The folders *sat/set* on the desk while we were *sitting/setting* up a new filing system.

2. Her uncle *set/sat* a record for flagpole *sitting/setting*.
3. This time of year, the tourists *lie/lay* in the sun, while the natives *sit/ set* in the shade.
4. Broken columns were *lying/laying* on the ground; some fragments had been *laid/lain* end to end.
5. Thick dust *lie/lay* on the artifacts that for centuries had *lain/laid* in the tomb undisturbed.

10d | SUBJUNCTIVE | *ub*

Use the subjunctive in special situations.

Many languages have one set of verb forms for straight facts and another set for maybes, wishes, and hypotheses. The factual form is the **indicative** (I know it *was*); the hypothetical form is the **subjunctive** (I wish it *were*).

(1) Choose the hypothetical *were* or the factual *was* after *if, as if, as though*. Use *were* if a possibility is contrary to fact or a remote chance:

SUBJUNCTIVE: For a moment, the statue looked as if it **were** alive.
(It wasn't really.)
If I **were** you, I would resign.   (I'm not really you.)

Use the hypothetical *were* also to show a mere wish:

SUBJUNCTIVE: I wish she **were** more assertive.

Use the factual *is* or *was* when pondering a genuine possibility:

FACTUAL: It looks as if the statue **was** thrown overboard in a storm.   (It probably was.)

(2) Use a subjunctive after verbs asking that something be done. After words like *ask, insist, demand, recommend,* and *suggest,* use a plain or unmarked form (*be, have, go*) instead of the *-s* ending (*is, has, goes*).

SUBJUNCTIVE: Her supervisor insists that she **stay** at her desk.
I move that this question **be** referred to a committee.

PEER EDITOR 4   Choose among *was, were,* or *be,* using the *subjunctive* where appropriate.

1. If *Alice in Wonderland* _____ being written today, Alice would use words like *awesome* and *totally cool*.
2. If neither parent _____ a Catholic, she must be a convert.
3. The measure proposed that utility companies _____ barred from producing nuclear waste within the state.
4. Brian's aunt always acted as if she _____ his mother.
5. Journalists and ministers urged that the sentence _____ commuted.

---

11 AGREEMENT

OVERVIEW   Most nouns and pronouns have different forms for one of a kind (**singular**) and more than one (**plural**): *key/keys, prize/prizes, woman/women, child/children*. Verbs often offer us a similar choice: one *goes*/several *go*; one *is* gone/several *are* gone; one *has* arrived/several *have* arrived. When we match the right forms, the subject and its verb **agree** in number.

SINGULAR: The clock **ticks**. The listener **was** bored. She **writes** often.
PLURAL: The clocks **tick**. The listeners **were** bored. They **write** often.

11a IRREGULAR PLURALS *agr*

Know irregular plurals borrowed from other languages.

Most English nouns use the familiar -*s* plural (car*s*, building*s*, tree*s*, book*s*, petition*s*). But some words borrowed from Greek and Latin have kept irregular plural forms:

SINGULAR	PLURAL	SINGULAR	PLURAL
crisis	crises	criterion	criteria
thesis	theses	phenomenon	phenomena
analysis	analyses	medium	media
hypothesis	hypotheses	stimulus	stimuli
curriculum	curricula	nucleus	nuclei

SINGULAR: The artist's favorite **medium was** acrylic paint.
PLURAL: The **media were** turning the trial into a circus.

SINGULAR: **This phenomenon has** been discovered only recently.
PLURAL: **These phenomena have** been extensively studied.

Note: Acceptable Anglicized plurals are *indexes* for *indices* and *formulas* for *formulae*. Use *data* as a plural to be safe: Data *are* items of information.

EXERCISE 5   In a college dictionary, find the acceptable plural (or plurals) for *alumnus, appendix, beau, cactus, oasis, vertebra,* and *species*.

11b | SINGULAR OR PLURAL *agr*

Know which subjects are singular and which plural.

Sometimes form seems to point one way and meaning another:

(1) Some pronouns seem plural in meaning but are singular in form. Treat as singular *each, either, neither, everybody,* and *everyone*. Though they point to more than one, look at them *one at a time*:

SINGULAR: Each of the students **is** being billed. (each one)
Either of the candidates **seems** weak. (either one)
Everybody (every single one) **approves** of your decision.

(2) Some nouns look plural but are treated as singulars. Words ending in *-ics* — *aeronautics, mathematics, physics, aerobics* — are often singular names for a field or activity: Modern physics *allows* for uncertainty. Some words ending in -*ics* can go either way:

SINGULAR: Politics **bores** me. Statistics **attracts** math majors.
PLURAL: Her politics **have** changed. These statistics **are** suspect.

Collective nouns like *audience, committee, family, police, group, jury,* or *team* are singular when we think of the whole group. They are plural when we think of the *members* of the group:

SINGULAR: The nuclear family **is** the exception, not the rule.
PLURAL: The family **were** gathered around the table.

(3) Expressions showing the whole amount may be singular even when plural in form. They are singular when they point to the sum or total:

SINGULAR: Thirteen dollars **seems** excessive for a small cutlet.
             One third of the world is rich, and two thirds **is** poor.

Number of is singular when it stands for a total: *The number of* joggers *has* declined. It is plural when it stands for "several": *A number of* joggers *were* still on the trail.

Check agreement when there is more than one subject.

When the word *and* joins several subjects, the resulting **compound subject** is normally plural. But the word *or* may merely give us a choice between two singular subjects:

PLURAL: Rafting **and** canoeing **clear** the smog from the lungs.
SINGULAR: Either the surgeon **or** the anesthesiologist **is** to blame.

(1) Two nouns joined by *and* may describe a single thing or person. Corned beef and cabbage *is* good to eat; the President and chief executive *is* one person.

(2) *As well as, together with,* and *in addition to* do not add one subject to another. They merely show that what is said about the subject applies also to other things or persons. (They introduce a prepositional phrase.)

SINGULAR: The mayor's **office**, together with other agencies, **is** sponsoring the event.

The **memo**, as well as the other documents, **has** been shredded.

DISCOURSE EXERCISE 6   In each of the following sentences, solve an *agreement problem* by changing the verb or first auxiliary. Write the changed word after the number of the sentence.

Surviving the Interview

1. Often each of several candidates for a job are reasonably well-qualified.
2. Much feinting, chutzpah, and false humility is required in a successful job interview.
3. Competence or a good track record alone are not enough to assure a good rating.
4. An impressively presented résumé, together with glowing letters of recommendation, put the interviewers in a receptive mood.
5. Statistics about past performance often impresses the listener.
6. A number of topics, like politics and sex, is to be avoided at all costs.

11d | BLIND AGREEMENT *agr*

Make subject and verb agree even when they are separated.

Avoid **blind agreement**: Do not make the verb agree with a word close to it that is *not* its subject.

(1) Check agreement when a plural noun comes between a singular subject and its verb. Disregard any wedge between subject and verb:

SINGULAR: **An ad** [in these small local papers] **produces** results.
            Understanding [the opponent's motives] **is** important.

Beware of blind agreement whenever the subject is one thing singled out among several, one quality shared by several members of a group, or one action aimed at several targets:

SINGULAR: Only **one** of my friends **was** ready in time.
            (not "**were** ready")
SINGULAR: The **usefulness** of these remedies **has** been questioned.
            (not "**have** been questioned")
SINGULAR: **Arresting** the local crack dealers **puts** an impossible strain
            on the courts. (not "**put** a strain")

(2) Check agreement when the subject follows the verb. Do not make the verb agree with a stray noun that stands in front of it:

PLURAL: Inside the yellowed envelope **were** several large bills.
          (What was inside? **Bills** were inside.)

(3) Check for agreement in sentences starting with *there is*, *there are*, and the like. After *there*, the verb agrees with the postponed subject — with whatever is "there":

SINGULAR: There **was** polite **applause** from the better seats.
PLURAL: There **were** scattered **boos** from the balcony.

Use the plural verb even when it comes before a compound subject of which each part is singular:

PLURAL: There **were** a bed and a chair for each patient.

194

(4) Make a linking verb agree with its subject, not the completer. In the following sentence, *problem* is the subject; *parts* is the completer (or complement): "Our chief *problem* is (not *are*) defective parts."

DISCOURSE EXERCISE 7   Rewrite each of the following sentences, changing both subject and verb from singular to plural. Make *no* other changes.

Banning the Dinosaurs

1.   The biology teacher in the local high school teaches evolution.
2.   The scientific theory about the origin of life has become controversial.
3.   A biology textbook is likely to have been revised several times.
4.   In California, a chapter about evolution was first yanked and then put back in.
5.   Meanwhile, the typical American youngster learns all about dinosaurs and fossils from TV.

PEER EDITOR 8   Correct *blind agreement* by changing the verb or first auxiliary. Write the changed word after the number of the sentence.

1.   The description of his appearance and manners hint at turbulent hidden emotions.
2.   As we enter the postmodern period, the style of the office towers subtly change.
3.   For every miracle drug, there is unexpected side effects and tremendous variations in individual response.
4.   The weak chemical bonds among oxygen atoms in ozone allows the molecules to break apart.
5.   Many crime shows make the viewers feel tough by association and boosts their egos.
6.   Computer monitoring of coffee breaks and phone calls are turning offices into electronic sweatshops.

11e   AGREEMENT AFTER *WHO, WHICH,*
AND *THAT*   *agr*

Check for agreement in relative clauses.

Who, which, and *that* often serve as subjects in relative clauses that modify a noun (or pronoun). The verb following the *who, which,* or *that* agrees with the word that is being modified:

SINGULAR: I hate a **person** who **stares** at me.

PLURAL: I hate **people** who **stare** at me.

Watch for agreement in combinations like "one of those who *know*" and "one of those who *believe*." Look at the contrast in the following pair:

PLURAL: Jean is one of **those students who go** to classes after work.
(*Many* students go to classes after work.)

SINGULAR: Jean is **the only one** of those students **who goes** to classes after work.
(Only *one* student goes to classes after work.)

11f   LOGICAL AGREEMENT   *agr*

If necessary, carry agreement beyond subject and verb.

Where the meaning requires it, extend agreement beyond the subject and verb of a sentence.

ILLOGICAL: Average newspaper **readers** go through their whole **life** knowing a little about everything but nothing well.

REVISED: Average newspaper **readers** go through their whole **lives** knowing a little about everything but nothing well.

DISCOURSE EXERCISE 9   Write the correct form after the number of the sentence.

Made (Poorly) in USA

1. Complaints about poor quality *has/have* hurt American efforts to capture overseas markets.
2. The steps that American companies have taken to improve quality control *is/are* producing only limited results.
3. Ford Motor Company as well as other leading manufacturers *has/have* recalled large numbers of cars and trucks.
4. Having to admit that the front seats tend to shake loose *does/do* little for the image of a new car.
5. True, few customers wind up with one of those cars that *spends/spend* more time in the shop than on the road.
6. But a buyer may discover that there *is/are* an electronically controlled door that doesn't open and a windshield wiper motor that has shorted out.
7. According to some foreign customers, computer chips made in America *tends/tend* to be chipped.
8. The ability to turn out high-quality products *is/are* essential if American industry wants to compete around the world.

---

12   PRONOUN REFERENCE

OVERVIEW Pronouns provide a welcome shortcut: *American policy in Central America* can simply become *it* when we mention it the second time. But the *it* has to point clearly to its **antecedent** — to what "went before."

| AMBIGUOUS REFERENCE | *ref*

Make a pronoun point clearly to its antecedent.

Look at the pronoun *she* in the following sentence: "*Linda* disliked *Ann* because *she* was very competitive." Which of the two was competitive? The sentence is **ambiguous**; it confuses the reader because of an unintended double meaning.

CLEAR: Because **Linda** was very competitive, **she** disliked Ann.

Because **Ann** was very competitive, Linda disliked **her**.

If a *they* follows two plural nouns, you might point it at the right one by making the other singular. (Similarly, you might change one of two singular nouns to a plural.)

AMBIGUOUS: **Students** like **science teachers** because **they** are realistic and practical. (realistic teachers? realistic students?)

CLEAR: A **student** usually likes **science teachers** because **they** are realistic and practical.

Note: Make pronouns refer to basic sentence parts rather than to modifiers. The *it* in sentences like the following seems misdirected: "James worked in an *asbestos plant*, and *it* got into his lungs" (the plant?).

CLEAR: James worked in an asbestos plant, and **the asbestos** got into his lungs.

12b | VAGUE *THIS* AND *WHICH* | *ref*

Revise vague idea reference.

Vague idea reference results when a *this* or *which* refers to the overall idea expressed in an earlier statement:

AMBIGUOUS: The police knew the employees were stealing, but management was not aware of **this**. (of the stealing, or of the police knowing?)

CLEAR: The police knew the employees were stealing, but management did not realize **word had got out**.

AMBIGUOUS: Newspapers give prominence to youths who get into trouble, **which** gives a bad name to all young people. (What gives a bad name—the slanted coverage or the trouble-making youths?)

CLEAR: Newspapers give prominence to youths who get into trouble. **This slanted coverage** gives a bad name to all young people.

 12c | VAGUE *THEY* AND *IT*   *ref*

Spell out implied antecedents of *they* and *it.*

Talking informally, we often make a pronoun point to something merely understood: "*They* lost my transcript" (the registrar did). In writing, bring back the lost antecedent:

IMPLIED: In Nebraska, **they** grow mostly wheat.
CLEAR: In Nebraska, **the farmers** grow mostly wheat.

Avoid the orphaned *it* or *they* when you refer to an implied idea in sentences like the following:

AMBIGUOUS: My mother was a musician; therefore, I have also chosen **it** as my profession. (What's **it**?)

REVISED: My mother was a **musician**; therefore, I have also chosen **music** as my profession.

AMBIGUOUS: The prisoner's hands were manacled to a chain around his waist, but **they** were removed at the courtroom door. (What was removed? The prisoner's hands?)

199

REVISED: The prisoner's hands were manacled to a chain around his waist, but the **manacles** were removed at the court-room door.

PEER EDITOR 10 Rewrite the following student sentences to revise ambiguous or unsatisfactory pronoun reference.

1. A five-year-old boy was shot by a police officer mistaking his toy gun for a real weapon.
2. The book's title sounded interesting, but when I read it I found it boring.
3. My father is extremely intelligent, though he does not always express it in a verbal form.
4. Prisons are run by undertrained and underpaid individuals, not to mention that they are hopelessly overcrowded.
5. Many voters know little about Central America, which makes it difficult for the President to gain popular support for his policies.

12d | AGREEMENT OF PRONOUNS | *ref, agr*

Make pronouns agree in number with their antecedents.

To make a pronoun point to what it stands for, make pronoun and antecedent agree in number:

WRONG: **Abortions** should not be outlawed because **it** is often required for medical reasons.

RIGHT: **Abortions** should not be outlawed because **they** are often required for medical reasons.

(1) Make a singular pronoun point to one representative person. Treat as singular *a person, an individual, the typical student,* or *an average American — one* person that represents many:

WRONG:	A person can never be too careful about **their** use of language.
RIGHT:	A person can never be too careful about **his or her** use of language.
WRONG:	**The typical male** is expected to do more parenting, but **they are** often poorly prepared for this task.
RIGHT:	**The typical male** is expected to do more parenting, but **he is** often poorly prepared for this task.

(2) Use a singular pronoun to refer to words like *everybody* and *someone*. These **indefinite pronouns** do not point to one particular person or group: *everybody* (*everyone*), *somebody* (*someone*), *nobody* (*no one*), *anybody* (*anyone*), *one*. Words like *everybody* or *anyone* point to many different people. However, use them as if you were looking at these people *one* at a time:

RIGHT:	**Everybody** on the team did **her** best.
	Nobody should meddle in affairs that are none of **his or her** business.
	It was part of the knight's code that **one** must value **his** (or **one's**) honor more than life.

(3) Deal with the pronoun dilemma. Much spoken English uses the plural pronoun in sentences like "Everybody received *their* copy of the test." Handbooks used to require the singular *he* (*his*, *him*): "Everybody received *his* copy of the test." This **generic** *he*, meant to refer to both men and women, is now widely shunned. Use *he or she* (*his or her*):

NONSEXIST:	Today's executive has a computer by **his or her** desk.

If several uses of *he or she* (and perhaps *himself and herself*) would slow down a sentence, convert the whole sentence to the plural:

SPOKEN:	**Everyone** I knew was increasing **their** insurance to protect **themselves** against lawsuits.
WRITTEN:	**All my friends** were increasing **their** insurance to protect **themselves** against lawsuits.

FOR MORE ON GENDER-BIASED PRONOUNS, SEE 23b.

PEER EDITOR 11   In each of the following student sentences, replace one pronoun in order to solve a problem of *pronoun reference*. Write the changed pronouns after the number of each sentence.

1. Each member had their own private excuse for joining the fraternity.
2. Universities often prove mixed blessings to the towns surrounding it.
3. The bear feeds primarily on roots; to attack livestock, they would have to be desperate.
4. The actress had played roles as a sassy, randy young girl; it had led to her being stereotyped as a hussy.
5. Most medical students are still white males, although admission policies are now less biased in his favor.
6. Nonsmokers are refusing to patronize a restaurant because of the smoke he might inhale.
7. The Founding Fathers intended that someone's religion should be their own responsibility.
8. England consistently had a much lower homicide rate because they enforced strict gun control laws.

---

13   PRONOUN CASE

OVERVIEW   *He* and *she* are **subject forms**. They point to the subject and often tell us *who* is doing something in the sentence. (*He* called. *She* answered.) *Him* and *her* are **object forms**; they point to the object of a verb or a preposition. (The manager interviewed *him*. The customer glared at *her*.) These differences in form are called differences in **case**.

SUBJECT	OBJECT	OBJECT OF PREPOSITION
I congratulated	**him**.	
He recommended	**me**	to **them**.
They prejudiced	**her**	against **me**.

SUBJECT AND OBJECT FORMS   *ca*

Choose the right pronoun forms for subject and object.

Though we might hear "*Me and him* go jogging together," we expect "*He and I* go jogging" in writing. *He* and *I* are both subjects of *go* and should appear in the subject form.

(1) Choose the right form when a pronoun is one of several subjects or objects. To find the right pronoun, try the parts one at a time:

SUBJECT: The supervisor and **I** worked hand in hand.
            (Who worked? **I** worked.)
OBJECT: She asked my brother and **me** to lower the volume.
            (Whom did she ask? She asked **me**.)

(2) Be careful with pronoun-noun combinations. Choose between *we girls — us girls* or *we Americans — us Americans*. Use the subject form when the combination serves as the subject of the sentence:

SUBJECT: **We Americans** pride ourselves on our good intentions.
            (Who does? **We** do.)
OBJECT: The border guard questioned **us Americans** at length.
            (Questioned whom? Questioned **us**.)

(3) Use object forms after prepositions: *with* her; *because of* him; *for* me. Use the object form for a pronoun that is the second or third object in a prepositional phrase:

OBJECT: This kind of thing can happen to you and **me** [not "to you
            and **I**"].
OBJECT: I knew there was something between you and **her** [not
            "between you and **she**"].

AN OVERVIEW OF PRONOUNS

	SUBJECT FORM	OBJECT FORM
Personal pronouns	I	me
	you	you
	he, she, it	him, her, it
	we	us
	you	you
	they	them

	FIRST SET	SECOND SET
Possessive pronouns	my	mine
	your	yours
	his, her, its	his, hers, its
	our	ours
	your	yours
	their	theirs

	SINGULAR	PLURAL
Reflexive pronouns (also "intensive")	myself	ourselves
	yourself	yourselves
	himself, herself, itself	themselves
Demonstrative pronouns ("pointing" pronouns)	this	these
	that	those
Indefinite pronouns	everybody (everyone), everything somebody (someone), something nobody (no one), nothing anybody (anyone), anything one, each, either, neither	
Relative pronouns	who (whom, whose), which, that	
Interrogative pronouns ("question" pronouns)	who (whom, whose), which, what	

(4) Use the right pronoun after *as* and *than*. Often the part of the sentence they start has been shortened. Fill in enough to see whether the pronoun would be subject or object:

SUBJECT: He felt as unloved as **I** (did).

His sister earned more than **he** (did).

OBJECT: I owe you as much as (I owe) **them**.

They liked my rival better than (they liked) **me**.

(5) Use subject forms after linking verbs. These introduce not an object of an action but a description of the subject:

FORMAL: The only ones absent were **she** and a girl with measles.

(**She** and the other girl were absent.)

FORMAL: It was **he** who had initiated the proposal.

(6) Avoid the *self-* pronouns (reflexive pronouns) as informal substitutes for the plain subject or object form. Use forms like *myself* or *himself* to point *back*: "*I* questioned *myself*." "*The owner herself* showed me the door." Use forms like *I, me, him,* or *her* (personal pronouns) to point:

SPOKEN: My friend and **myself** made a low-cholesterol pact.

WRITTEN: My friend and **I** made a low-cholesterol pact.

SPOKEN: The jury listened spellbound to his lawyer and **himself**.

WRITTEN: The jury listened spellbound to his lawyer and **him**.

CAUTION: *Hisself, theirself, theirselves,* and *themself* are nonstandard.

PEER EDITOR 12 In each of the following sentences, change *one pronoun* to the form that is right for written English. Write the changed form after the number of the sentence.

1. Jane's lawyer brought bad news for she and her mother.
2. I recognized the man's face; it was him who had thrown the pie.
3. This information should remain strictly between you and I.
4. Visitors from space might snigger at the technology that us Earthlings possess.

5. The report cited she and her fellow officer for bravery.
6. Teachers do not necessarily always know more than us students.
7. My brother and myself were always bickering, but now we tolerate each other.
8. The losing candidate seemed as well qualified as her.

| **13b** | *WHO AND WHOM* | *ca* |

Know when to replace *who* with *whom*.

Use *who* as the subject form, *whom* as the object of a verb and also of a preposition.

(1) Choose *who* or *whom* at the beginning of a question. *Who* asks a question about the subject. *Whom* asks a question about an object. Apply the *he-or-him* or *she-or-her* test:

SUBJECT:	**Who** put the ice cream back in the freezer? (**He** did.)
OBJECT:	**Whom** did the jurors believe? (They believed **her**.)
OBJECT:	To **whom** did she leave her fortune? (To **him**.)

The *he-or-him* test will also work in more complicated questions:

| SUBJECT: | **Who** do you think will win? (I think **she** will win.) |
| OBJECT: | **Whom** did you expect to come? (I expected **her** to come.) |

(2) Choose *who* or *whom* at the beginning of a dependent clause. To apply the *he-or-him* test to a dependent clause, separate it from the rest of the sentence. In the following examples, *who* (or *whoever*) is the subject of a verb:

SUBJECT:	We asked/**who** discovered the body. (**He** did.)
	Rita was the auditor/**who** had discovered the forgeries. (**She** had.)
	He offered a gold doubloon to/**whoever** first saw the whale. (**He** did.)

In the following examples, *whom* is the object of a verb or of a preposition:

OBJECT: She adored her brother, **whom** most people detest.
(People detest **him**.)
We all need coworkers/on **whom** we can rely.
(We can rely on **them**.)

PEER EDITOR 13   Choose *who* or *whom* and write it after the number of the sentence.

1. People *who/whom* we knew only slightly called and offered to board the cat.
2. Some people never discover *who/whom* their real friends are.
3. The visitors had little respect for the people with *who/whom* they worked.
4. People *who/whom* are asked to play themselves are often less convincing than actors.
5. For *who/whom* the message was intended never became clear.

---

14   ADVERBS AND MISPLACED MODIFIERS

OVERVIEW Modifiers, which help us build up bare-bones sentences, range from single words to long prepositional or verbal phrases:

ADJECTIVE: **Angry** buyers called the **escape** clause a **cheap** trick.
ADVERB: The star will **probably** stalk off the set **again soon**.
PREP. PHRASE: A woman **in grimy overalls** was standing **on the ladder**.
VERBAL PHRASE: The pot **waiting at the end of the rainbow** is not always gold.

Check your sentences to see if the right form of a modifier is in the right place.

| **14a** | ADJECTIVES AND ADVERBS | *adv* |

When you have a choice, use the distinctive adverb form.

Often the only difference between an adjective and an adverb is the *-ly* ending: *sad/sadly, probable/probably, careful/carefully*. We use the **adjective** to modify nouns, telling the reader which one or what kind: the *sad* song, *probable* cause, a *careful* driver, an *immediate* reply. We use the **adverb** to modify verbs, telling the reader how, when, or where something is done: talk *sadly*, *probably* left, drove *carefully*, should reply *immediately*.

(1) Use the adverb form to modify a verb. Choose the distinctive adverb form to tell the reader *how*:

ADVERB: The inspectors examined every part **carefully**.
               We have changed the original design **considerably**.
               No one took the new policy **seriously**.

Note: Some words ending in *-ly* are not adverbs but adjectives: a *friendly* talk, a *lonely* life, a *leisurely* drive. And for words like *fast, much,* and *early*, the adjective and the adverb are the same: *Fast* trains move *fast*; *early* risers get up *early*.

(2) Avoid the informal adverbs of casual talk. Use *well* and *badly* as adverbs instead of *good* and *bad*. Change "I don't hear *good*" to "I don't hear *well*"; "I write pretty *bad*" to "I write *badly*." Replace informal adverbs like *slow, quick,* and *loud*: drive *slowly*, react *quickly*, speak *loudly*.

(3) Use adverbs to modify other modifiers. Use the adverb form to modify either an adjective or another adverb:

ADVERB + ADJECTIVE: It was a **surprisingly beautiful** bird.
ADVERB + ADVERB: You sang **admirably well**.

Edit out informal expressions like *real popular, awful expensive,* and *pretty good.* Use *very* in such combinations or a distinctive adverb form like *really, fairly,* or *extremely*: Punk rock was *extremely popular.* The crowd was *fairly well-behaved.*

Note: Adjectives instead of adverbs follow linking verbs. After a **linking verb**, an adjective points back to the subject; it pins a label on the subject:

ADJECTIVE: These bottles are **empty**. (**empty** bottles)
              The speaker seemed **nervous**. (a **nervous** speaker)
              The rains have been **heavy**. (**heavy** rains)

- *Feel* is a linking verb in "We *felt bad* when we heard the news."
- *Well* used as an adjective means healthy: "He is not *well*."

PEER EDITOR 14 In each of the following sentences, change one word to the distinctive *adverb form*. Write the changed word after the number of the sentence.

1. When the witness testified, she spoke nervously and very defensive.
2. He was tired and unable to think logical.
3. I read the questions as careful as panic allowed.
4. Toward the end of the story, the events unfold very sudden, as they sometimes do in real life.
5. My father regarded life more philosophical than most plumbers do.
6. Macbeth interpreted the prophecies of the weird sisters very literal.
7. During the time Judy spent in France, her horizon widened considerable.
8. Computers solve math problems faster and more efficient than the fastest human mathematician.
9. An experienced cryptographer can decipher a simple code very easy.
10. Sebastian went in for arm wrestling because he didn't do good in other sports.

14b   MISPLACED AND DANGLING
MODIFIERS   *DM, MM*

Make modifiers point clearly to what they modify.

Moving a modifier will often change the meaning of a sentence:

Riots **almost** broke out at every game.   (but never did)
Riots broke out at **almost** every game.   (they often did)

(1) Shift a misplaced modifier to the right position. If necessary, rewrite the whole sentence:

MISPLACED: The manager looked at the room we had painted **with ill-concealed disgust**. (painted with disgust?)

REVISED: **With ill-concealed disgust**, the manager looked at the room we had painted.

MISPLACED: **Made of defective material**, the builder had to redo the sagging ceiling.

REVISED: **Since it was made of defective material**, the builder had to redo the sagging ceiling.

(2) Link a dangling modifier to what was left out of the sentence. Dangling modifiers usually start with verbals like *to fall, falling, fallen,* or *having fallen.*

DANGLING: **To become a computer specialist**, an early start is essential. (Who wants to become a computer specialist?)

REVISED: To become a computer specialist, a **student** needs an early start.

DANGLING: **Having watched *Dallas* and *Dynasty***, real people will seem dull.

REVISED: Having watched *Dallas* and *Dynasty*, **viewers** will find real people dull.

(3) Keep a squinting modifier from pointing two ways at once:

SQUINTING: I feel **subconsciously** Hamlet wanted to die.
            (**Your** subconscious feelings — or Hamlet's?)
REVISED: I feel that Hamlet **subconsciously** wanted to die.

Note: Some verbal phrases are not meant to modify any one part of the main sentence. These are called **absolute constructions**. The most common ones clarify the attitude or intention of the speaker:

RIGHT: **Generally speaking**, traffic is getting worse.
            They had numerous children — seven, **to be exact**.

Some of these constructions carry their own subjects along with them:

RIGHT: **The air being warm**, we left our coats in the car.
            Escape being impossible, we prepared for the worst.

PEER EDITOR 15   Rewrite each of the following student sentences to eliminate unsatisfactory *position of modifiers*.

1. Having run for an hour, the carrot juice tasted great.
2. The car was towed away by John, having exploded on Interstate 59.
3. Unsure of my future, the navy was waiting for me.
4. After ringing for fifteen minutes, the bellhop answered the phone.
5. He was hit by a rotten egg walking back to the dorm.
6. After graduating from high school, my stepfather asked me to vacate the premises.
7. When traveling during the night without sufficient lighting, other motorists will have difficulty seeing the vehicle.
8. These magazines appeal to immature readers with torrid love affairs.

| 15 | **CONFUSING SENTENCES** |

OVERVIEW Final editing is your last chance to catch sentences that are awkwardly put together, with badly matching parts. Often such a sentence seems to set up one pattern but then switches to another:

MIXED: The typical background of women who get abortions are two-thirds white and more than half childless. (The background . . . are . . . **white**?)

CONSISTENT: Of the women who get abortions, **two thirds are white**, and more than half are childless.

| 15a | OMISSION AND DUPLICATION | *st* |

Check for omitted or duplicated elements.

Revise omission or duplication that results from hasty writing, inaccurate copying, or careless typing.

(1) Supply sentence parts that you have left out. Fill in the missing *a, the, has, be, we,* or *they*:

INCOMPLETE: Our astronauts walked on the moon but have faltered since.   (**Who** faltered?)

COMPLETE: Our astronauts walked on the moon, but **we** have faltered since.

(2) Delete duplicated words. Check especially for doubling up of words like *of* and *that*:

DUPLICATED: They had built a replica of the Eiffel Tower **of** which they were very proud **of**.

REVISED: They had built a replica of the Eiffel Tower **of** which they were very proud.

DUPLICATED:	Economists claim **that** because of political pressures in an election year **that** the deficit will grow.
REVISED:	Economists claim **that** because of political pressures in an election year the deficit will grow.

DISCOURSE EXERCISE 16   Catch *omission and duplication* in careful proofreading. Rewrite the following passage with all necessary corrections.

All the Trivia Fit to Print

Some readers look in newspaper for trivia, of which they never tire of. They love read that because of an ancient law that a citizen of Lower Liguria not allowed to wash clothes on a Saturday. They ponder the information that stamp machines in hotel lobbies take two quarters but only one 25-cent and two 5-cent stamp. They love ads for toy sumo wrestlers fight in ring that can made out package in which they came in. My favorite example of trivia article described muskrat dinners served at restaurant in Delaware. Ingenious traps drown the muskrats and call them "marsh rabbits" when this local delicacy appears on menu.

15b   MIXED CONSTRUCTION   *mx*

Do not mix two ways of expressing the same idea.

We sometimes start a sentence one way and finish it another. To revise such a sentence, retrace your steps. Disentangle the two ways of saying what you had in mind:

MIXED:	**In case of** serious flaws in design **should have been reported** to the regulatory agency.
REVISED:	Serious flaws in design **should have been reported** to the regulatory agency.

213

> In case of serious flaws in design, **the regulatory agency** should have been notified.

MIXED: The course was canceled **because of** not enough students registered.

CONSISTENT: The course was canceled **because not enough students registered**.

The course was canceled **because of insufficient enrollment**.

Note: Avoid the "Because . . . does not mean" sentence, where the adverbial clause starting with *because* appears as if it were the subject of a verb. Use a noun clause starting with *that*:

MIXED: **Because** we listened to his proposal **does not mean** we approve.

REVISED: **That** we listened to his proposal **does not mean** that we approve.

Make sure what the predicate says fits the subject.

The predicate of a sentence makes a statement about the subject: "The choice (subject) *was difficult* (predicate)." Make sure the statement made by the predicate can apply logically to the subject:

ILLOGICAL: **The choice** of the new site **was selected** by the mayor.

(What was selected? The site, not the choice.)

LOGICAL: **The new site was selected** by the mayor.

(1) Revise equations when they link two labels that do not stand for the same thing. In "*Dinosaurs* were *giant reptiles*," the dinosaurs are reptiles, and the reptiles are dinosaurs. But in "*Her job* was *a mail carrier*," the mail carrier is not really a job but a person:

"She *worked* as a mail carrier." (Or "Her job was *that* of a mail carrier.")

ILLOGICAL: **A student** with a part-time job **is a common cause of** poor grades. (A student is not a cause.)

LOGICAL: A student's **part-time job** is a common cause of poor grades.

(2) Revise faulty equation caused by *is-when* or *was-when* sentences. Avoid sentences like "Conservation is *when* we try to save energy." Conservation is not a time when something happens but a practice or a goal.

ILLOGICAL: Parole **is when** a prisoner is set free on condition of good behavior.

LOGICAL: Parole **is the practice of** setting prisoners free on condition of good behavior.

(3) Revise faulty equation caused by prepositional phrases. Such phrases typically tell us not what something is but how, when, or where it is done. Use an infinitive (or a similar noun equivalent) instead:

WRONG: Their only hope is **by appealing** to the governor.
RIGHT: Their only hope is **to appeal** to the governor.

| **15d** | FAULTY APPOSITIVES | *at* |

Make sure appositives fit the nouns they follow.

An **appositive** is a noun that tells us more about another noun: "Ferraro, *the vice-presidential candidate*, had served in Congress." Here, Ferraro and the candidate are the same person. Revise sentences when the second label does not logically fit:

ILLOGICAL:	They had only one **vacancy, the assistant manager**.
	(The manager is not vacant; the position is.)
LOGICAL:	They had only one **vacancy, the position of** assistant manager.

PEER EDITOR 17   Revise each of the following confusing sentences. Look for examples of mixed construction, mismatched subjects and predicates, and faulty labels.

1. Usually it takes a minimum of brain power to watch *Dallas* than it does to read a book.
2. While attending college and working at the same time makes it hard to shine as a scholar.
3. Typical playground equipment fails to keep in mind the needs of the tot.
4. The players up for the team were about even in ability and was a hard decision to make.
5. A person who fails in various things might give him an inferior feeling.
6. Assimilation is when we make every Spock a clone of Captain Kirk.
7. Because little of the pledged money actually came in does not mean we have to abandon the project.
8. Scientists know how to distill drinking water from salt water, but the cost of such a project is too unprofitable.
9. By cutting the number of jurors in half greatly reduces the time used in selecting a jury.
10. The legislators were flooded with angry letters, mostly members of the NRA.

---

16   INCOMPLETE CONSTRUCTIONS

OVERVIEW Look for comparisons that do not spell out clearly what is being compared. Look for combined statements that have telescoped elements that need to be different in form.

Complete incomplete comparisons.

Revise unsatisfactory comparisons:

(1) Spell out what is being compared. Revise incomplete comparisons using *more* and *the most*:

INCOMPLETE:	The company employed **more tax lawyers**. (than what?)
COMPLETE:	The company employed **more tax lawyers than engineers**.
INCOMPLETE:	The author turned the life of Mozart into **the most exciting play**.
COMPLETE:	The author turned the life of Mozart into **the most exciting play of the season**.

(2) Compare things that are really comparable. Revise sentences like the following: "The *fur* was as soft as a *kitten*." The fur was as soft as a *kitten's* (fur), or as soft as *that* of a kitten.

ILLOGICAL:	**Her personality** was unlike **most other people** I have known.
LOGICAL:	**Her personality** was unlike **that of** most other people I have known.

(3) Clarify three-cornered comparisons. When you mention three comparable items, which two are being compared?

CONFUSING:	**We** distrusted the **oil companies** more than the **local governments**.
CLEAR:	**We** distrusted the oil companies more than **we did** the local governments.
	We distrusted the oil companies more than the local governments **did**.

(4) Correct overlapping comparisons. Comparisons like the following are blurred: "The forward was faster than *any player on her* *team.*" The forward is part of the team and cannot be faster than *any player* on the team, including herself.

RIGHT: The forward was faster than **any other player** on the team.

DISCOURSE EXERCISE 18 Rewrite the following passage to complete or clarify unsatisfactory comparisons.

The New Yellow Journalism

Readers of today's newspapers find as much blood and gore as the yellow journalism of old. Journalists looking for lurid scandals track politicians as eagerly as evangelists. Nevertheless, tabloids serve up a fare more sensational than any national publications. In the world of tabloids, the death of a husband who swallowed seven fish hooks as part of his fish dinner is more important than John Kennedy. A headline like "Fisherman Hooked on Wife's Soup" attracts more readers than the Polish economy. There seem to be more stories about aging widows piling an unbelievable twenty tons of garbage three feet high in a neglected rat-infested home. The balance sheet of a firm marketing a bad-breath detector rates more attention than the Bank of America.

<table>
<tr><td>**16b**</td><td>INCOMPLETE COORDINATION *inc*</td></tr>
</table>

Check coordinate elements for excessive shortcuts.

When items of the same kind are coordinated by *and, or,* or *but,* leave out only those forms that would cause unnecessary duplication.

(1) Check for completeness when shortening one of several similar verbs. Leave out only words that would be exactly identical: "It can [*be done*] and will *be done.*"

INCOMPLETE:	The bear **was given** an injection and the instruments **made** ready.
COMPLETE:	The bear **was given** an injection, and the instruments **were made** ready.

(2) Revise shortcuts of the "as-good-if-not-better" type: "Korean cars are *as good if not better than* ours." The complete forms would be *as good as* and *not better than*:

REVISED:	Korean cars are **as good as, if not better than**, ours.
BETTER:	Korean cars are **as good as ours**, if not better.

(3) Check several linked prepositional phrases. Keep prepositions that are not identical but merely express a similar relationship.

WRONG:	I have great **respect and faith in** our leadership.
RIGHT:	I have great **respect for** and **faith in** our leadership.
	I have great **admiration and respect for** our leadership.

PEER EDITOR 19   Make each of the following *incomplete sentences* more complete by rewriting the italicized part. Write the rewritten part after the number of the sentence.

1. People today live longer and eat up more resources *than the previous century*.
2. *Juries have always and will always be swayed* by the grandstanding of a lawyer.
3. Taxpayers are already *familiar and hostile to the usual explanations*.
4. The population of China is already *bigger than any country*.
5. *The club had in the past and was still barring* "undesirables" from membership.
6. The Sears Building in Chicago is *as tall or taller than any building in New York City*.
7. The statistics for rape are much less complete *than robbed banks or stolen bicycles*.

8. Few of my friends were *preoccupied or even interested in the love lives of celebrities*.
9. Children understand other children *better than adults*.
10. The liberal arts are excellent preparation *for such practical professions as engineers and lawyers*.

---

17   SHIFTS AND PARALLELISM

OVERVIEW Sentences should stay within a consistent time frame or maintain a consistent perspective. When they do not, they are like a road full of unexpected twists and turns. They slow down and confuse the reader.

17a   SHIFTS IN TENSE

Revise confusing shifts in time.

Verbs have a built-in reference to time: We *agree* (now). We *agreed* (then). When describing a situation or telling a story, be aware of the **tense** forms you are using to show time.

(1) Avoid shifting from past to present. Do not switch to the present when something becomes so real that it seems to be happening in front of you:

SHIFT: We **were waiting** for the elevator when suddenly all lights **go** out.

REVISED: We **were waiting** for the elevator when suddenly all lights **went** out.

(2) Show differences in time to avoid confusion. For instance, signal the difference between what *happened* in the past and what *had happened* before then in the more distant past (**past perfect**).

SHIFT:	Linda **was** only a messenger, but she **was** now the supervisor of the whole floor.
CONSISTENT:	Linda **had been** only a messenger, but she **was** now the supervisor of the whole floor.
	(Working as a messenger came before promotion.)
SHIFT:	My uncle always **talked** about how farming **has changed**.
CONSISTENT:	My uncle always **talked** about how farming **had changed**.

(3) Be consistent when dealing with possibilities. Note the difference between factual reference to a possibility and the **conditional**, which makes the possibility seem less probable, more remote:

SHIFT:	If they **come** here, the government **would** refuse them asylum.
FACTUAL:	If they **come** here, the government **will** refuse them asylum. (*Both* are real possibilities.)
CONDITIONAL:	If they **came** here, the government **would** refuse them asylum. (Both are more remote possibilities.)
FACTUAL:	If terrorists **threaten** to use a nuclear weapon, what **will** we do?
CONDITIONAL:	If terrorists **threatened** to use an atomic weapon, what **would** we do?

(4) Adjust tense forms in indirect quotation. In **direct quotation**, a speaker may talk about events in the past, but they were then the present time: She *said*, "I *feel* elated. I *am* proud to be here." In **indirect quotation**, we are no longer using the speaker's exact words. When *we* talk about her feelings, they are in the past: She *said* that she *felt* elated and *was* proud to be there.

DIRECT:	Roosevelt said, "We **have** nothing to fear but fear itself."
INDIRECT:	Roosevelt said that the nation **had** nothing to fear but fear itself.

Failure to adjust the tenses in indirect quotations can lead to sentences like the following:

SHIFT: Chamberlain **said** that there **will** be peace in our time.
CONSISTENT: Chamberlain **said** that there **would** be peace in our time.

17b | SHIFTS IN REFERENCE *ref*

Revise confusing shifts in reference.

Edit out shifts that result when your system of referring to people is not clearly worked out:

(1) Edit out the informal generalized *you*. In your writing, use *you* only to mean "you, the reader."

SPOKEN: Sailing to the colonies, **you** had to worry about pirates. (Your reader wasn't there.)
WRITTEN: Sailing to the colonies, **travelers** had to worry about pirates.

Avoid shifting to *you* after the person involved has already been identified:

SHIFT: I would not want to be a celebrity, with people always knowing what **you** are doing.
CONSISTENT: I would not want to be a celebrity, with people always knowing what **I** am doing.

(2) Avoid shifts to the request form. Giving directions or instructions, we naturally use the form for requests or commands (**imperative**): *Dice* the carrots. *Remove* the hubcaps. But avoid shifting to the request form when giving more general advice:

SHIFT: Managers **should stop** tallying every move of the employee and every trip to the restroom. **Build** employee morale and **stimulate** group loyalty, as the Japanese do.

CONSISTENT: Managers **should stop** tallying every move of the employee and every trip to the restroom. **They should build** employee morale and **stimulate** group loyalty, as the Japanese do.

17c SHIFTS TO THE PASSIVE   *sf*

Do not shift to the passive when the same person is still active.

Active sentences put the spotlight on who does what: *Poachers are decimating* the herds (**active voice**). Passive sentences put the spotlight on the target or the victim: *The elephants are being slaughtered* (**passive voice**). Avoid a shift in perspective when the same person is still active and important.

SHIFT: He **retyped** his résumé, and it **was mailed** the same day. (by whom?)
REVISED: He **retyped** his résumé and **mailed** it the same day.

Avoid awkward shifts to the passive in instructions or advice:

SHIFT: After **you complete** the form, **it should be returned** to the agency.
REVISED: After **you complete** the form, **you should return** it to the agency.

PEER EDITOR 20   Rewrite the following sentences to revise shifts in *time, pronoun reference, or grammatical perspective*. More than one such shift may occur in a sentence.

1. A sure-fire prescription for disaster is for a cocaine addict to come off a binge and try to drown your depression in alcohol.
2. As I was getting ready to leave the elevator, I notice two men who are watching me out of the corner of their eyes.

3. Office workers discovered that computers monitored the time you took to staple memos or open envelopes.
4. The police were warning us that if the crowd did not calm down, arrests will be made.
5. Only when one faces the decision of whether to have an abortion can you really feel what a tough issue it is.
6. Parents must take an active interest in what their children are doing. Coach a ball team or be a counselor to a scout troup.
7. My favorite television program was already in progress, but right in the middle of a dramatic scene, the station goes off the air.
8. Teenagers armed with rags and towels swarmed around the still dripping car, and quickly the outside is wiped dry and the chrome polished.

17d | FAULTY PARALLELISM *¶,//*

Use parallel structure for repeated sentence parts.

Sentence parts joined by *and, or,* and *but* should be **parallel,** fitting into the same grammatical category. The words in a set like "red, white, and blue" are parallel (three adjectives); the words in a set like "handsome, personable, and in a red convertible" are not (two adjectives and a prepositional phrase).

(1) Revise mismatched sentence parts joined by *and, or,* or *but.* For instance, "*ignorant* and a *miser*" is off balance because it joins an adjective and a noun. You could change *ignorant* to a noun ("He was an *ignoramus* and a miser") or *miser* to an adjective ("He was ignorant and *miserly*").

FAULTY: They loved **the wilderness** and **to backpack** to solitary lakes.

PARALLEL: They loved **to explore** the wilderness and **to backpack** to solitary lakes.

Look especially for an *and who* or *and which* that changes a pattern in midstream:

FAULTY:	We met a painter **living** in Paris and **who had known** Picasso.
PARALLEL:	We met a painter **who lived** in Paris and **who had known** Picasso.

(2) Avoid mixing a noun and an adjective as modifiers.

LUMPY:	Schools serve **personal and society** needs as they evolve.
PARALLEL:	Schools serve **personal and social** needs as they evolve.

(3) Check for parallelism when using paired connectives.
Such pairs (**correlative conjunctions**) are *either . . . or, neither . . . nor, not only . . . but also,* and *whether . . . or*:

FAULTY:	I used to find him either **in the spa** or **chatting with his friends**.
PARALLEL:	I used to find him either **soaking in the spa** or **chatting with his friends**.
MISPLACED:	Judge Hardball **not only** threatened the lawyer with expulsion **but also** jail. (We expect to hear that the judge not only **threatened** but also **did** something else.)
REVISED:	Judge Hardball threatened the lawyer with **not only** expulsion **but also** jail.

(4) Avoid faulty parallelism in a series of three or more elements.
Sometimes we read what looks like a series, only to have the last element snap out of the expected pattern:

FAULTY:	He loved to **talk, drink wine,** and **good food**.
PARALLEL:	He loved **conversation**, good **wine**, and good **food**.
	He loved to **talk, drink** good wine, and **eat** good food.

If the elements in a series are not really parallel in meaning, your revision might break up the series altogether:

FAULTY:	The new manager was **ambitious, hard-driving,** and **an MBA from Harvard**.
REVISED:	The new manager, **an MBA from Harvard**, was ambitious and hard-driving.

DISCOURSE EXERCISE 21   Rewrite the following passage to revise all examples of faulty parallelism.

Updating the Vampire

Fans of vampire movies should neither be committed vegetarians nor made easily sick by the sight of blood. In the classic vampire story, the vampire lives in a gloomy castle, tricks unwary tourists, and sucking their blood during the night. Today's vampires are more up-to-date and definitely catering to a modern audience. Coming to our modern world, they neither totally abandon their blood-sucking ways nor their costumes. They can read minds but perhaps unable to use a touch-tone phone. At a rock concert, they can blend in without a special costume or needing special makeup. The modern vampire zaps roaches in a microwave, lifts jets into orbit around a different planet, and similar high-tech exploits. Audiences are not always sure whether to thrill with horror or should they laugh at a biting satire of the modern world.

18	AWKWARD SENTENCES

OVERVIEW   Learn to diagnose and improve sentences that turned out stiff, awkward, or roundabout.

18a	DEADWOOD	*w, awk*

Prune your sentences of deadwood.

Revise sentences where too many words are unnecessary props or mere filling. Cross out **redundant** words, which merely duplicate a meaning: Write *October* instead of *the month of October, consensus* instead of *consensus of opinion.*

(1) Take out wordy, roundabout tags. Edit out **circumlocutions** — talky constructions that "take the long way around."

INFLATED	BRIEF
because of the fact that	because
during the time that	while
a large number of	many
at an early date	soon
in the event that	if

(2) Remove unneeded props. Instead of "*those of* adolescent *age*," write *adolescents*. Trim superfluous *there are's* and *who were's*, especially if several pad the same sentence.

AWKWARD: **There are** many farmers in the area **who are** planning to attend the protest meeting **which is** scheduled for Memorial Day.

REVISED: Many farmers in the area plan to attend the protest meeting scheduled for Memorial Day.

18b   AWKWARD REPETITION   *rep*

Avoid unintentional repetition of sounds, words, or phrases.

Revise for awkward repetition like the following:

AWKWARD: Commercials seldom make for entertain**ing** and relax**ing** listen**ing**.

BETTER: Commercials seldom entertain and relax the listener.

AWKWARD: Close examin**ation** of the results of the investig**ation** led to a reorganiz**ation** of the organiz**ation**.

BETTER: Close study of the results of the inquiry led to a reorganization of the company.

AWKWARD: We listened to an account **of** the customs **of** the inhabitants **of** the village.

BETTER: We listened to an account of the villagers' customs.

Revise for unintentional repetition especially when the similarity
in sound covers up a *shift in meaning or relationship*.

The investors lost their money because they **banked on** [better: "re-
lied on"] the well-established reputation of our hometown **bank**.

DISCOURSE EXERCISE 22 Rewrite the following sentences to eliminate *deadwood and awkward repetition*.

The Bionic Athlete

1. As an athlete, it is essential to attain the best physical shape as far as
   body conditioning is concerned.
2. It is an unfortunate fact, however, that many of today's athletes in this
   modern day and age excel because of the fact that chemicals build
   up their muscles and speed up their performance.
3. Doctors warn of the risks of pumping the body full of drugs of different kinds.
4. This year has been a discouraging one for those who are committed
   to keeping steroids from skewing athletic competitions in the sports
   arena.
5. Increasingly, runners and swimmers more and more find themselves
   stripped of their medals and well-paying lucrative advertising contracts in the event that banned chemicals are found in their bodies.

| **18c** | AWKWARD PASSIVE | *pass, awk* |

Avoid unnecessary roundabout passives.

An active sentence goes from the "doer" through the action to
the target or result. A passive sentence turns this perspective around
and puts the target first:

ACTIVE: NASA aborted the mission.

PASSIVE: *The mission* was aborted by NASA.

The passive works well when the target or product seems more important than the performer. The passive is also appropriate when the doer or performer is beside the point or hard to identify.

LEGITIMATE: The **dusky**, a subspecies of the seaside sparrow, **has never been found** anywhere except on Merritt Island and along the St. John's River.

LEGITIMATE: **Marcia's parents were killed** in a car accident when she was very young.

Avoid *unneeded* passives that make sentences roundabout and impersonal. Many verbs work best in an active sentence; they work best when a sentence tells us who does what.

AWKWARD: Monumental traffic jams **are endured by** many motorists on the way to work.

ACTIVE: Many motorists **endure** monumental traffic jams on the way to work.

AWKWARD: After each simplification of the tax laws, longer instructions **must be puzzled out** by the taxpayer.

ACTIVE: After each simplification of the tax laws, the taxpayer **must puzzle out** longer instructions.

> ON SHIFTS TO THE PASSIVE, SEE 17c.

PEER EDITOR 23   Rewrite the following sentences to convert *awkward or unnecessary passives* back to active statements.

1.   When an application for a badly needed loan is turned down by a bank because of the customer's gender, a feeling of impotent rage may be experienced.

2.   All instructions should be read carefully and all blank spaces filled in before this form is signed by the applicant.

3.   If any experimenting endangering human lives is to be done by the government, the voters should be consulted first.

4. When information about summer school is received, the necessary deadlines may have already passed.
5. Various ways of living are being tested today and experimented with by youth whose dominant characteristic is the desire for flexibility.

18d   IMPERSONAL CONSTRUCTIONS   *awk*

Make impersonal sentences more direct.

The introductory *there is/there are* and the impersonal *one* (meaning anybody, a person) can make a sentence roundabout. Often, a *there is* merely postpones the main point and causes an awkward reshuffling later in the sentence:

AWKWARD: In 1986, **there was** a protest march to the state capitol participated in by 15,000 people.

REVISED: In 1986, 15,000 protesters marched to the state capitol.

Avoid the impersonal **one** when it serves as a mere prop:

ROUNDABOUT: **If one is a citizen of a democracy, she** should exercise her voting rights.

DIRECT: **A citizen of a democracy** should vote.

18e   SENTENCE OVERLOADS   *awk*

Lighten the load in overburdened sentences.

Look for the following:

(1) Revise interlocking dependent clauses. Several dependent clauses may create a logjam of confusing provisos and specifications. For instance, interlocking *that-if, if-because, which-when* constructions are often awkward:

AWKWARD: I think **that if** there were less emphasis on conformity in high school, college students would be better prepared for independent thinking.

IMPROVED: In my opinion, college students would be better prepared for independent thinking **if** there were less emphasis on conformity in high school.

(2) Revise "house-that-Jack-built" sentences. Several dependent clauses of the same kind may cause a sentence to trail off into a confusing succession of explanations:

AWKWARD: Nitric oxides have an overfertilizing effect on deciduous trees, **which** are trees **that** lose their leaves during the winter, **that** has the effect of encouraging them to keep their leaves far into the winter, **which** makes them sensitive to frost.

REVISED: Nitric oxides have an overfertilizing effect on deciduous trees — trees **that** lose their leaves during the winter. The excess fertilizer encourages them to keep their leaves too far into the winter and thus makes them vulnerable to frost.

(3) Revise an awkward string of introductory clauses. Sometimes too many similar dependent clauses delay the main point:

AWKWARD: **When** children are constantly watched **when** they are born and **while** they are babies, the reason is that parents want to see whether their children are developing as the books say they should.

IMPROVED: Some parents constantly watch their young children to see whether they are developing as the books say they should.

(4) Revise seesaw sentences. Seesaw sentences start with an important reason or condition but end with a reason or condition that seems to ignore or overrule the first:

AWKWARD: **Because** many students change their majors, they take more than four years to graduate, **because** most majors are loaded with requirements.

REVISED: Most majors are loaded with requirements. As a result, students who change their majors often take more than four years to graduate.

(5) Keep lengthy modifiers from breaking up the pattern of a sentence. Lengthy appositives, verbal phrases, or dependent clauses sometimes separate elements that belong together:

AWKWARD: The pilot told his friends that he had flown Clinton Morris, **a resident of New York City sought by the government for income tax evasion**, out of the United States.

REVISED: The pilot told his friends about a passenger he had flown out of the United States: Clinton Morris, **a resident of New York City sought by the government for income tax evasion**.

PEER EDITOR 24 Rewrite the following *awkward, overburdened, or confusing sentences*.

1. We watched the officer who questioned the suspects who had been apprehended.
2. There was an antinuclear demonstration participated in by over 20,000 people.
3. There will be an investigation by the mayor's office of the unauthorized distribution of this information.
4. When people are constantly under supervision when at work and asked immediately where they are going when they leave their station, a feeling of harassment is experienced.
5. Motorists are quickly informed of the whereabouts of restaurants, motels, and, of course, speed traps set by the police, by other CB operators.
6. The dreary weather, mainly rain, that never seemed to stop, and my problems with my parents, which were serious, upset me.
7. A child's first impressions of people and places shape the course of her future life, frequently.
8. Financial independence between partners was rarely practiced in a traditional marriage.

OVERVIEW Well-written sentences have the right **emphasis**: They help us take in the main points and keep lesser points in perspective. They have a satisfying **rhythm**: They line up related ideas and balance off opposing points.

19a EFFECTIVE PREDICATION *st, emp*

Rewrite weak sentences on the "Who does what?" model.

Try the following to strengthen weak sentences:

(1) Make the subject and verb answer the question: "Who does what?" Make the subject name the key agent or doer — put the spotlight on whoever took action or whatever was the cause. Then let the verb and the rest of the predicate make the point:

UNFOCUSED: **It was not the usual procedure** of the nuns to pamper their students.

FOCUSED: **The nuns** did not usually pamper their students.

(2) Shift the action from a noun to a verb. When a noun ending in *-ion, -ment, -ism,* or *-ing* serves as the subject of a sentence, it may blur our view of who does what. When such nouns label actions, events, or activities, try specifying the agent or doer while shifting the action to a verb.

STATIC: Violent **arguments took place** in front of the children.

ACTIVE: **Our parents** often **argued** violently in front of us.

STATIC: **Confusion marked** the opening speech.

ACTIVE: **The opening speaker confused and lost** the audience.

(3) Convert a weak use of *to be* to a more active verb. Many electronic editing programs flag uses of *to be* (*is, was, has been, will be*, and so on) to make you check whether you should use a stronger, more active verb.

TO BE: The parents' income **was** the criterion of eligibility.

NOT *TO BE*: The parents' income **determined** eligibility.

PEER EDITOR 25 Rewrite the following sentences for more *effective predication*. If possible, make the subject and the predicate tell the reader who does what.

1. The result of restrictive new laws will be to force women back to illegal abortion mills.
2. Vigorous discussion of current political events often took place among the patrons.
3. It is very probable that intimidation of witnesses will result from such threatening remarks by the defendant.
4. A recent development is the encouragement of new technology for extracting oil by the Canadian government.
5. As the result of unruly demonstrations, repeated interruptions of the committee's deliberations took place.
6. A plan for safe driving is of no use if the cooperation of the individual driver is not present.

Use coordination when two ideas are equally important.

When we coordinate two things, we make them work together. If you doubt the appropriateness of a coordinator like *and* or *but*, test the sentence by inserting "equally important":

EFFECTIVE: Radioactivity is a threat to workers at nuclear plants, **and** [equally important] radioactive wastes are a threat to the environment.

To correct **excessive coordination**, remember that *and* merely says "more of same." Use modifiers and compounding to tighten the relationship between ideas:

LOOSE: Salmon return to the same spot upstream where they were hatched, **and** they have to go against the stream to get there, **and** that takes much strength and determination.

TIGHTER: Salmon return to the same spot upstream where they were hatched, **struggling against the current to get there, showing tremendous strength and determination**.

PEER EDITOR 26   Rewrite the following passages to correct *excessive coordination*. Tighten relationships by replacing coordinators with subordinators (such as *if, when, because, although*) or relative pronouns (*who, which, that*).

1. Gun owners were fighting back against the new restrictions, and the city council passed a new ordinance, and it omitted the requirement for a 14-day records search.
2. My father came from a wealthy family, and my mother came from a very poor home, and it was strange that she held the purse strings in the family.
3. Many high school teachers follow a textbook word for word, and they go over each page until everyone understands it. In college, many teachers just tell the student to read the textbook, and then they start giving lectures on the material covered in the text, but they don't follow it word for word.

19c   EFFECTIVE SUBORDINATION   *sub, emp*

Use subordination to tighten relationships in a sentence.

Often subordination helps us integrate sentences that are loosely strung together. Subordinators (*when, while, since, because, if, though*) and relative pronouns (*who, which,* and *that*) add a **dependent** clause to the main clause. When sentences are too loosely strung together, use effective subordination to show the relationships between ideas:

(1) Use subordination to help the main idea stand out in a larger combined sentence. Use the main clause for the idea that deserves special **emphasis**:

SIMPLE: The term *democracy* originated in ancient Greece. Different people have used it to describe quite different political systems. Often the person who uses the word thinks it has only one meaning.

COMBINED: **Democracy**, a term that originated in ancient Greece, **has been used to describe quite different political systems**, though the person who uses it usually thinks it has only one meaning.

(2) Use subordination to clarify relationships in a sentence. Merely placed next to each other, the following statements may seem disjointed: "Mertens was kidnapped and held hostage for eleven months. He had been a bureau chief for the CIA." They make more obvious sense when one is subordinated to the other:

EFFECTIVE: Mertens, **who had been a bureau chief for the CIA**, was kidnapped and held hostage for eleven months.

(3) Avoid upside-down subordination. "*I was four* when men landed on the moon" focuses our attention on your age. "When I was four, *men landed on the moon*" focuses our attention on the moon. **Upside-down subordination** results when the wrong item seems to stand out:

IRONIC: The wage was considered average by local standards, **though it was not enough to live on**.

STRAIGHT: **Although it was considered average by local standards**, the wage was not enough to live on.

DISCOURSE EXERCISE 27   Combine the separate sentences in each of the following sets, making use of *effective subordination*. In each new combined sentence, use at least one dependent clause, starting with a subordinator (*if, when, because, where, although, whereas,* or the like) or with a relative pronoun (*who, which,* or *that*).

Our Cousins the Apes

1. Human beings are constantly encroaching on animal habitats. Many species are already extinct.
2. The great apes are endangered. We are fascinated with them. They include gorillas and orangutans.
3. Monkeys are of low intelligence. They are imitative. They can be trained to perform simple tasks.
4. Primates are our close cousins biologically. They are ideally suited for experiments. These cannot be performed on human beings.
5. Animal rights advocates appeal to our sympathy for these animals. They suffer atrociously. They are used for medical experiments.

19d ·   EFFECTIVE MODIFIERS   *ɪt*

Use modifiers to help a sentence carry added freight.

Observe the tightening of relationships when separate statements are combined in a compact sentence:

SEPARATE: Dolphins can send distress signals to other members of their group. They communicate by beeps and clicks.

COMBINED: Dolphins, **communicating by beeps and clicks**, can send distress signals to other members of their group.

SEPARATE: I lay on the couch in the kitchen. I was reading *The Last Days of Pompeii*. How I wished I could have been there.

COMBINED: I lay on the couch in the kitchen, **reading** *The Last Days of Pompeii* and **wishing** I were there.   Alice Munro

---

SENTENCE PRACTICE 28   Use *modifiers* to build up the following simple sentences with additional details. Use different kinds of modifiers in various positions. Example:

SIMPLE: A girl plays "Silent Night."

MODIFIED: A small, skinny girl plays "Silent Night" with two fingers on an untuned piano in a garage.

237

1. A woman runs.
2. A dog crossed the road.
3. The rider mounted the horse.
4. Energy is in short supply.
5. Her cousin bought a new car.

Vary your sentences to bring a plodding passage to life.

An effective writer uses sentences of different length and structure for variety and emphasis. Try the following:

(1) Avoid excessive use of short, choppy sentences. They can easily make your writing sound immature:

CHOPPY: We listened to AM radio most of the day. The format never seemed to change. There was one advertising jingle after the other. The fast-talking DJ would give a number to call. You name the song and you win a prize. You could call an agency for tickets to this concert or that. The DJ would play oldies but goodies and then the current number-one song, the big hit.

REVISED: We spent most of the day listening to AM radio, whose format never seemed to change. Punctuating the advertising jingles, the DJ would give a number to call so listeners could name the song to win a prize or order tickets to this concert or that. The DJ would play oldies but goodies and then the current number-one song, the big hit.

(2) Pull a modifier to the front of the sentence. The introductory modifier can give a sprightly or energetic quality to a passage:

VARIED: The Trans World Terminal stems from the work of contemporary architects like Corbusier of France and Nervi of Italy, masters of the curve in concrete. **Like a true eagle**, this building is all curves and muscle, no right angles.

> **Built of reinforced concrete**, the whole structure swoops
> and turns and rises.   Ken Macrorie

(3) Shift a completer to the beginning of the sentence. A writer may move an object or other completer from its usual position after the verb and pull it out in front for a change in emphasis. ("*His horses* he loved more than his family" highlights the person's love of horses.) The introductory complement often links two sentences by taking up something mentioned earlier:

LINKED: Ma's Café catered to locals and tourists. **The tourists** she
             charged extra.

(4) Save the predicate of the main clause till the end. Work modifiers or other supporting material into the sentence earlier before you go on to the main verb. Try shifting the main point toward the end, especially if a **belated modifier** sounds like a lame afterthought:

LAME: Richard Wagner became one of the most successful com-
             posers of all time **in spite of the jeers of his contempo-
             raries**. (We may remember the jeers rather than the com-
             poser's success.)
IMPROVED: Richard Wagner, **though jeered at by his contemporaries**,
             became one of the most successful composers of all time.

SENTENCE PRACTICE 29   Each of the following sentences varies the usual subject-verb or noun-verb-noun order. Choose five of these as model sentences. For each, write a similar sentence of your own.

1.   Stronger than the mighty sea is almighty God.
     SAMPLE IMITATION: Bleaker than a misspent youth is life without experience.
2.   The rhinoceros, an animal built like a tank, faces extinction.
3.   Goaded beyond endurance, Igor turned on his pursuers, shaking his fists.
4.   Her face drawn, her lips tight, the mayor announced her decision.
5.   Heads up, swinging with the music, the right arm swinging free, they stepped out.   Ernest Hemingway

---

6

THE RIGHT WORD

Note: The following is a quick rundown of minimum proficiencies in the area covered in this chapter. Remember that there is much more to good writing than meeting minimum standards. However, if you fail to meet the standards summarized here, your message may not reach the reader and you may not get credit for what you do well.

Effective writers use the right word — right for the purpose, right for the occasion. From the full range of our English vocabulary, they choose the word that carries exact information or conveys the right attitude.

(1) Use accurate words. Effective writers choose the word with the right shade of meaning: *eloquent* (using words with special power), *articulate* (especially good at putting ideas into words), *terse* (preferring few words), or *taciturn* (hardly saying anything at all). They use specific words that call to mind actual movements, shapes, or textures: *stride, shuffle,* or *slink* instead of just *walk*; *sparrow, quail,* or *robin* instead of just *bird*. They use technical words correctly (*entitlements, entropy, empathy*) and, if necessary, provide brief, pointed explanations.

(2) Correct excessively informal English and slang. Language that is too brash or slangy suggests that you are not taking your subject or your reader seriously. Edit out informal words like *flunk, kids, folks, cop, bust* (arrest), *bitch* (complain), *ticked off, pot, prof, bushed,* and *broke*. Avoid expressions like "knock it off," "give me a break," and "only kidding."

(3) Avoid sexist language and racial or ethnic slurs. Instead of words like *stewardess* (always women's work?) or *policeman* (always men's work?), use unisex terms like *flight attendant, police officer, mail carrier, chair* or *chairperson, firefighter,* and *member of Congress.* When referring to a typical doctor, nurse, executive, secretary, or politician, use the double pronoun *he or she* to show that you are not limiting occupations to either sex. Use the more inclusive *humanity* and *human beings* instead of so-called generic terms like *mankind* or *the history of man.*

(4) Edit for clichés and jargon. Clichés are familiar overused expressions that sound as if we had written them with our minds shut off: *in the final analysis, last but not least, easier said than done, burn the midnight oil, Mother Nature.* Jargon is pretentious pseudo-scientific language that writers use to make themselves or their subject sound important. Write "during the planning" instead of "during the pre-planning phase" and "thinking about goals" instead of "conceptualizing desired outcomes."

(5) Edit for mixed and distracting metaphors. Metaphors are compressed imaginative comparisons that bring vivid images into our prose: "When someone yells racial insults at me from a passing car, I don't like to think that someday these *solo artists* might make up a *chorus,* especially on my own campus." Avoid metaphors that make readers say: "What's wrong with this picture?" ("*Waves* of new immigrants *stepped* boldly into the *melting pot* of America" — waves don't step, and people don't step into pots.)

20 USING YOUR DICTIONARY

OVERVIEW Some users turn to the dictionary only to check a spelling (*develop* or *develope?*) or an unusual word (*phlegmatic, serendipity*). But many writers turn to the dictionary regularly for information and advice.

Familiarize yourself with the information in your dictionary.

College dictionaries are becoming more alike. They compete in including new words: *sitcom, unisex, upscale, hot tub, pro-life, interface, preppie.* They vie with each other in covering the language of science and technology, from *entropy* and *laser* to *microfiche* and *quark.* Nevertheless, widely recommended dictionaries differ in how they present information and in how they envision their intended audience.

■ *Webster's Ninth New Collegiate Dictionary* is published by Merriam-Webster, Inc., whose collection of citation slips has been called the "national archives of the language." The *Collegiate* is based on *Webster's Third New International Dictionary,* the most authoritative unabridged dictionary of American English. Historical information about a word comes first, followed by meanings in the order they developed. The current *Ninth New Collegiate* includes the year of the first recorded appearance of a word. The editors do not use the label *informal* (too arbitrary or subjective); they rarely use the label *slang.* Sample entry:

> **fem·i·nism** \'fem-ə-,niz-əm\ *n* (1895) **1** : the theory of the political, economic, and social equality of the sexes **2** : organized activity on behalf of women's rights and interests — **fem·i·nist** \-nəst\ *n or adj* — **fem·i·nis·tic** \,fem-ə-'nis-tik\ *adj*

■ *Webster's New World Dictionary* stands out because of its clear and helpful definitions. Historical information comes first; lists of idioms provide an excellent guide to the manifold uses of a word. The editors have a good ear for informal English and slang; they pay special attention to Americanisms — expressions first found in the United States. Sample entry:

> **Goth·am** (gäth'əm, gō'thəm; *for 1, Brit.* gät'-) **1.** a village near Nottingham, England, whose inhabitants, the "wise men of Gotham," were, according to legend, very foolish **2.** *nickname for* NEW YORK CITY —**Goth'am·ite'** (-īt') *n.*

vocabulary entry ——

pronunciation

syllabication dots

beau·ty (byoo′tē), *n.*, *pl.* **-ties** for 2–6. **1.** a quality that is present in a thing or person giving intense aesthetic pleasure or deep satisfaction to the senses or the mind. **2.** an attractive, well-formed girl or woman. **3.** a beautiful thing, as a work of art, building, etc. **4.** Often, **beauties.** that which is beautiful in nature or in some natural or artificial environment. **5.** a particular advantage: *One of the beauties of this medicine is the absence of aftereffects.* **6.** a person or thing that excels or is remarkable of its kind: *His black eye was a beauty.* [ME *be(a)ute* < OF *beaute;* r. ME *beaute* < OF, var. of *beltet* < VL **bellitāt-* (s. of **bellitās*) = L *bell(us)* fine + *-itāt-* *-ITY*] **—Syn. 1.** loveliness, pulchritude.

synonym lists ——

part of speech and ——
inflected forms

be·gin (bi gin′), *v.*, **be·gan**, **be·gun**, **be·gin·ning.** —*v.i.* **1.** to proceed to perform the first or earliest part of some action; commence or start. **2.** to come into existence; originate: *The custom began during the Civil War.* —*v.t.* **3.** to proceed to perform the first or earliest part of (some action): *Begin the job tomorrow.* **4.** to originate; be the originator of: *Civic leaders began the reform movement.* [ME *begin(en),* OE *beginnan* = *be-* BE- + *-ginnan* to begin, perh. orig. to open, akin to YAWN] **—be·gin′ner,** *n.*

etymology ——

synonym study ——

—Syn. 3. BEGIN, COMMENCE, INITIATE, START (when followed by noun or gerund) refer to setting into motion or progress something that continues for some time. BEGIN is the common term: *to begin knitting a sweater.* COMMENCE is a more formal word, often suggesting a more prolonged or elaborate beginning: *to commence proceedings in court.* INITIATE implies an active and often ingenious first act in a new field: *to initiate a new procedure.* START means to make a first move or to set out on a course of action: *to start paving a street.* **4.** inaugurate, initiate. **—Ant. 1.** end.

antonym ——

be·la·bor (bi lā′bər), *v.t.* **1.** to discuss, work at, or worry about for an unreasonable amount of time: *He kept belaboring the point long after we had agreed.* **2.** to scorn or ridicule persistently. **3.** *Literary.* to beat vigorously. Also, *Brit.,* **be·la·bour.**

variant spelling ——

hyphenated entry ——

belles-let·tres (Fr. bel le′tRª), *n.pl.* literature regarded as a fine art, esp. as having a purely aesthetic function. [< F: lit., fine letters] **—bel·let·rist** (bel le′trist), *n.* **—bel·let·ris·tic** (bel′li tris′tik), *adj.* **—Syn.** see literature.

word element ——

bene-, an element occurring in loan words from Latin where it meant ''well'': *benediction.* [comb. form of *bene* (adv.) well]

consecutive
definition numbers

be·neath (bi nēth′, -nēth′), *adv.* **1.** below; in or to a lower place, position, state, or the like. **2.** underneath: *heaven above and the earth beneath.* —*prep.* **3.** below; under: *beneath the same roof.* **4.** further down than; underneath; lower in place than: *The first drawer beneath the top one.* **5.** inferior in position, rank, power, etc.: *A captain is beneath a major.* **6.** unworthy of; below the level or dignity of: *beneath contempt.*

usage note ——

bent[1] (bent), *adj.* **1.** curved or crooked: *a bent bow; a bent stick.* **2.** determined, set, or resolved (usually fol. by *on*): *to be bent on buying a new car.* —*n.* **3.** a direction taken by

example contexts ——

bet·ter[1] (bet′ər), *adj.*, compar. of **good** with **best** as superl. **1.** of superior quality or excellence: *a better coat.* **2.** morally superior; more virtuous: *He's no better than a thief!* **3.** of superior value, use, fitness, desirability, acceptableness, etc.: *a better time for action.* **4.** larger; greater: *the better part of a lifetime.* **5.** improved in health; healthier: *Is your mother better?* —*adv.*, compar. of **well** with **best** as superl. **6.** in a more excellent way or manner: *to behave better.* **7.** to a greater degree; more completely or thoroughly: *I probably know him better than anyone else.* **8.** more: *I walked better than a mile to town.* **9. better off, a.** in better circumstances. **b.** more fortunate; happier. **10. go (someone) one better,** to exceed another's effort; be superior to. **11. had better,** would be wiser or more reasonable to; ought to: *We had better stay indoors today.* **12. think better of,** to reconsider and decide more favorably or wisely: *She was tempted to make a sarcastic retort, but thought better of it.* —*v.t.* **13.** to make better; improve; increase the good qualities of. **14.** to improve upon; surpass; exceed: *We have bettered last year's production record.* **15. better oneself,** to improve one's social standing, financial position, or education. —*n.* **16.** that which has greater excellence: *the better of two choices.* **17.** Usually, **betters.** those superior to one in wisdom, social position, etc. **18. for the better,** in a way that is an improvement: *His health changed for the better.* **19. get the better of, a.** to get an advantage over. **b.** to prevail against. [ME *bettre,* OE *betera;* c. OHG *bezziro* (G *besser*), Goth *batiza* = *bat-* (akin to BOOT[2]) + *-iza* comp. suffix] **—Syn. 13.** amend; advance, promote. See **improve.**

idiomatic phrase ——

- *The Random House College Dictionary*, Revised Edition, is based, like *Webster's Ninth New Collegiate*, on a larger unabridged dictionary. The most frequently used meanings come first; historical information is last. Both informal English and slang are marked; usage notes recognize many traditional restrictions. Sample entry:

> **cal·i·ber** (kal′ə bər), *n.* **1.** the diameter of something of circular section, esp. that of the inside of a tube. **2.** *Ordn.* the diameter of the bore of a gun taken as a unit of measurement. **3.** degree of competence, merit, or importance: *a mathematician of high caliber; the high moral caliber of the era.* Also, *esp. Brit.,* **cal′i·bre.** [var. of *calibre* < MF < early It *calibro,* ? alter. of Ar *qālib* mold, last < Gk *kalópous* shoemaker's last = *kálo(n)* wood + *poús* foot] —**cal′i·bered;** *esp. Brit.,* **cal′i·bred,** *adj.*

- *The American Heritage Dictionary*, Second College Edition, is intended as a sensible (moderately conservative) guide, less forbidding than traditional dictionaries. Definitions branch out from a central meaning that may not be historically the earliest sense of the word. Sample entry:

> **Im·promp·tu** (ĭm-prŏmp′tōō, -tyōō) *adj.* Performed or conceived without rehearsal or preparation: *an impromptu speech.* —*adv.* Spontaneously. —*n.* **1.** Something made or done impromptu, as a speech. **2.** *Mus.* A short lyrical composition esp. for the piano. [Fr. < Lat. *in promptu,* at hand : *in,* in + *promptus,* ready. —see PROMPT.]

DISCOURSE EXERCISE 1   What does your dictionary tell you about the meaning or uses of each bold-faced word?

The Sleeping Giant

1. China is a **homogeneous** nation with a traditional respect for its **mandarins** and the wisdom of its **sages**.

2. Mao's revolution destroyed the ancient **caste** system and the power of **feudal** warlords.

3. He maintained revolutionary **fervor** by mass rallies, propaganda **tirades**, and media **fanfare**.

4. After his death, the new leaders stretched the **procrustean** bed of Maoism to fit new needs.

5. China's students have repeatedly been in the **vanguard** of **cataclysmic** change.

Explore the full range of meaning of a word.

Dictionaries furnish other useful information before they explain the meaning of a word: spelling and division into syllables (in•aus•pi•cious), pronunciation, and grammatical label. However, the bulk of a dictionary consists of definitions that tell us what a word means and how it is used.

(1) Take in exact technical information. For scientific and historical terms, for instance, dictionaries try to provide exact and helpful information in a short space.

TECHNICAL: A *laser* is a device that amplifies light rays (including rays with the frequencies of ultraviolet and infrared) and concentrates them in extremely narrow, intense, powerful beams that are used, for instance, in surgery, communications, and various industrial processes.

(2) Take in shades of meaning. Look beyond the general idea covered by a word to its special implications. For instance, *terse* means more than "brief":

terse: intentionally brief and pointed; deliberately avoiding the superfluous, devoid of idle chatter

(3) Choose the right meaning from the full range of meanings of a word. Often you will have to work your way down a numbered list of meanings, like the meanings listed for the word *cell* in the *Webster's Collegiate*:

1   a small cabinlike house for a religious person

2a   a hermit's cell

2b   a monk's or nun's cell in a monastery or nunnery

3a   a cell in a beehive

3b   a cell in an insect's wing structure

4   a biological cell

5   an electric cell

6   a statistical cell

7   a (Communist) party cell

8   a meteorologist's term

(4) Let your dictionary guide you to the right meaning for the context. The **context** of a word may be another word (*square* meal), a whole sentence or paragraph ("*Square* your theories with your practice"), a whole publication (a treatment of *square* roots in an algebra text), or a situation (a tourist asking for directions to a *square*). Dictionaries show how context determines meaning by showing a word in a phrase or sentence and by specifying an area like economics or geometry:

pro·duce (prə do͞os′, -dyo͞os′; *for n.,* präd′o͞os, -yo͞os; prō′do͞os, -dyo͞os) *vt.* **-duced′, -duc′ing** [L. *producere* < *pro-*, forward + *ducere*, to lead, draw: see PRO-[2] & DUCT] **1.** to bring to view; offer for inspection [to *produce* identification] **2.** to bring forth; bear; yield [a well that *produces* oil] **3.** *a*) to make or manufacture [to *produce* steel] *b*) to bring into being; create [to *produce* a work of art] **4.** to cause; give rise to [war *produces* devastation] **5.** to get (a play, motion picture, etc.) ready for presentation to the public **6.** *Econ.* to create (anything having exchange value) **7.** *Geom.* to extend (a line or plane)

From *Webster's New World Dictionary*

DICTIONARY WORK 2 How does your dictionary help you with the different meanings of each of the following words? Show how the *context* guides you to the right meaning of each phrase.

1. straight to the point, straight party line, straight alcohol, thinking straight
2. a head of government, a head of steam, heads or tails, head off complaints
3. committed to the cause, committed to an institution, committed no crime
4. a sense of duty, an off-duty police officer, duty-free shop, the duties of a nurse
5. an undertakers' convention, the conventions of punctuation, revolt against convention, the Geneva Convention

---

| **20c** | SYNONYMS AND ANTONYMS | *d* |

Let the dictionary help you distinguish between closely related terms.

The quickest way to show the meaning of a word is to give a double, or **synonym** (*systematic* for *methodical*). We often get further help from its opposite, or **antonym** (*legitimate* for *illicit*). Synonyms usually mean *nearly* the same; they are not simply interchangeable. *Burn, char, scorch, sear,* and *singe* all refer to the results of exposure to extreme heat, but whether a piece of meat is charred or merely seared makes a difference to the person who has it for dinner. "Synonymies" like the following help the writer make accurate distinctions:

> *SYN.*—**alien** is applied to a resident who bears political allegiance to another country; **foreigner,** to a visitor or resident from another country, esp. one with a different language, cultural pattern, etc.; **stranger,** to a person from another region who is unacquainted with local people, customs, etc.; **immigrant,** to a person who comes to another country to settle; **émigré,** to one who has left his country to take political refuge elsewhere

From *Webster's New World Dictionary*

DISCOURSE EXERCISE 3 What meaning do the synonyms in each set have in common? How do they differ, or what sets them apart?

The Theory of Revolution

1. Revolutions may start with a localized protest against **inequities** and develop into a full-blown attack on **injustice**.

2. In Russia, a sailors' **mutiny** led to widespread **revolt** and finally full-scale **revolution**.

3. Often **idealistic** leaders develop a **visionary** or **utopian** blueprint for a new society.

4. The more **zealous** or **doctrinaire** elements may steer the revolution in a more **fanatical** direction.

5. Or a more **pragmatic** leadership may adopt **expedient** or even **opportunistic** policies.

6. A revolution may in turn produce a **paternalistic, authoritarian,** or **totalitarian** government.

| **20d** | CONNOTATION | *d* |

Use the dictionary as a guide to the associations of words.

Words carry attitudes and emotions as well as information. *Demagogue, politician, mercenary, crony,* or *bureaucrat* do not simply point to people. They point the finger; they reveal the likes and dislikes of the speaker. We call the added freight of attitudes, feelings, or value judgments the **connotations** of a word.

Connotative words most commonly mirror our likes and dislikes. When we like the bright colors of a shirt, we call it *colorful*; when we dislike it, we call it *loud*. Often synonymies alert us to attitudes and feelings. To make a scheme sound impressive, we call it a *project*; to belittle a project, we call it a *scheme*:

SYN.—**plan** refers to any detailed method, formulated beforehand, for doing or making something [vacation *plans*]; **design** stresses the final outcome of a plan and implies the use of skill or craft, sometimes in an unfavorable sense, in executing or arranging this [it was his *design* to separate us]; **project** implies the use of enterprise or imagination in formulating an ambitious or extensive plan [a housing *project*]; **scheme,** a less definite term than the preceding, often connotes either an impractical, visionary plan or an underhanded intrigue [a *scheme* to embezzle the funds]

From *Webster's New World Dictionary*

CAUTION: Remember that words carrying an emotional charge may set off the *wrong* reaction on the part of the reader:

JARRING: She sings music that pleases listeners of all races and **emits** a feeling of love and warmth. (The word *emit* is too cold; we expect something to "emit" radiation or shrill sounds of warning.)

REVISED: She sings music that pleases listeners of all races and **creates** a feeling of love and warmth.

DISCOURSE EXERCISE 4　How do the words bold-faced in each sentence differ in *connotation*?

The Media as Mirror

1. The media have the power to **shape, slant,** or **manipulate** our perceptions of reality.
2. Action taken by an official may be labeled **rash, timely,** or **precipitate**.
3. People who are dissatisfied may be said to **protest, complain, squawk,** or **whine**.
4. A new law may be described as **tough, severe,** or **punitive**.
5. A governor may take the advice of **associates, insiders,** or **cronies**.
6. Resistance to change may be labeled **caution, delay,** or **obstruction**.
7. A program to help the poor may be called **compassionate, sentimental,** or (a favorite) **misguided**.
8. A response to insults by a foreign government official may be called **temperate, timid, gutless,** or **abject**.

Check clues to how a word functions in a sentence.

Here is the kind of grammatical information that dictionaries provide:

- The word *human* is usually labeled both as an **adjective** (adj.) and as a **noun** (n.), with some indication that the latter use ("a human" rather than "a human being") is not generally accepted.
- The word *annoy* is labeled a **transitive verb** (v.t.); it is incomplete without an object. In other words, we usually annoy somebody or something; we don't just annoy. *Set* also is usually transitive ("*set* the bowl on the table"), but it is labeled **intransitive** (v.i.) when applied to one of the celestial bodies. The sun doesn't set anybody or anything; it just sets.

DICTIONARY WORK 5   Answer the following questions about *grammatical functions* of words after consulting your dictionary.

1.   Is *incompetent* used as a noun?
2.   Which of the following words are used as verbs: *admonition, loan, lord, magistrate, minister, sacrilege, spirit, war*?
3.   Are the following used as adjectives: *animate, predominate, very*?
4.   Are the following used as intransitive verbs: *entertain, censure, promote*?

Use the dictionary as a guide to idiomatic phrases.

Set expressions are called **idioms**. To write idiomatic English, you have to develop an ear for individual ways of saying things. For

IDIOMATIC PREPOSITIONS — AN OVERVIEW

abide **by** (a decision)
abstain **from** (voting)
accuse **of** (a crime)
acquiesce **in** (an injustice)
agree **with** (a person), **to** (a proposal), **on** (a course of action)
apologize **for** (a mistake)
assent **to** (a proposal)
avail oneself **of** (an opportunity)

capable **of** (an action)
charge **with** (an offense)
compatible **with** (recognized standards)
comply **with** (a request)
concur **with** (someone), **in** (an opinion)
confide **in** or **to** (someone)
conform **to** (specifications)

deficient **in** (strength)
delight **in** (mischief)
deprive **of** (a privilege)
derived **from** (a source)
die **of** or **from** (a disease)
disappointed **in** (a friend)
dissent **from** (a majority opinion)
dissuade **from** (an action)

identical **with** (something looked for)
ignorant **of** (a fact)

inconsistent **with** (sound procedure)
independent **of** (outside help)
indifferent **to** (praise)
infer **from** (evidence)
inferior **to** (a rival product)
insist **on** (accuracy)
interfere **with** (a performance), **in** (someone else's affairs)

jealous **of** (others)

object **to** (a proposal)
oblivious **of** (warnings)

part **with** (possessions)
partial **to** (flattery)
participate **in** (activities)
persevere **in** (a task)
pertain **to** (a subject)
prevail **on** (someone to act)
prevent someone **from** (acting)

refrain **from** (wrongdoing)
rejoice **at** (good news)
required **of** (all members)
resolve **on** (a course)

secede **from** (the Union)
succeed **in** (an attempt)
superior **to** (an alternative)

instance, we *do* a certain type of work, *hold* a job or position, *follow* a trade, *pursue* an occupation, and *engage in* a line of business.

(1) Revise garbled or upside-down idioms. Look out for expressions that mix or reverse familiar expressions:

WRONG IDIOM: Older people are worried about the ardent **devotion** that young people **pay** to new religious cults.
(We **show** devotion; we **pay** attention.)
RIGHT: Older people are worried about the ardent **devotion** that young people **show** to new religious cults.

(2) Use idiomatic prepositions. (See chart.) In particular, avoid the informal prepositions in *borrow off* and *wait on*:

INFORMAL: He constantly **borrowed** money **off** his friends.
FORMAL: He constantly **borrowed** money **from** his friends.

INFORMAL: The audience was **waiting on** the next performer.
FORMAL: The audience was **waiting for** the next performer.

PEER EDITOR 6   Write a more idiomatic preposition after the number of each unsatisfactory sentence.

1. To seek a good grade at someone else's expense would be a violation to our standards of conduct.
2. Several families volunteered to take care for the children of flood victims.
3. Only the prompt help of the neighbors prevented the fire of becoming a major disaster.
4. During the first years of marriage, we had to deprive ourselves from many things that other people take for granted.
5. The arrival of the ship to its destination caused general rejoicing.

6. As an instrument of the popular will, the Senate suffers from defects inherent to its constitution.

OVERVIEW College dictionaries often give a quick rundown of a word's **etymology**, or history, using abbreviations like OE and ME (for Old and Middle English), ON (for Old Norse or early Scandinavian), or IE (for Indo-European, the hypothetical common parent language of most European languages). Here is a capsule history of a word that came into English from Latin by way of Italian and French:

> **pop·u·lace** \'päp-yə-ləs\ *n* [MF, fr. It *popolaccio* rabble, pejorative of *popolo* the people, fr. L *populus*] (1572) **1** : the common people : MASSES **2** : POPULATION

From *Webster's Ninth New Collegiate Dictionary*

The basic vocabulary of English goes back to the language the Anglo-Saxon tribes brought to England after A.D. 450 from what is now Denmark and Germany. Many everyday words come from these **Anglo-Saxon** or **Old English** roots: *father, mother, hand, house, bread, water, sun, moon.* Throughout its history, English has borrowed heavily from Latin, (which Christian missionaries first brought to England as the language of the Roman Catholic church) and Greek (the language of ancient Greek literature, science, and philosophy). When the French-speaking Normans conquered England after A.D. 1066, French became for a time the language of law, administration, and literature. Over the next two centuries, thousands of French words were absorbed into **Middle English**.

Since the beginning of **Modern English** (about 1500), English has borrowed words from languages like Italian, Spanish, and Portuguese. This process of borrowing and assimilation continues today, as we are getting used to seeing words from Arabic, Russian, and Japanese.

Know the most common Latin and Greek roots.

Modern English uses thousands of words that came originally from Greek or Latin. Modern scientific and technological terms draw heavily on Latin and Greek roots.

(1) Know the most common Latin and Greek roots. Knowing the Latin root *mal-* for "bad" helps us understand *malpractice, malfunction, malnutrition, malformation,* and *malfeasance.* Knowing that the Greek root *bio-* means "life" helps us with *biopsy, biochemistry, biomass, biofeedback,* and *bionics.*

ROOT	MEANING	EXAMPLES
arch-	*rule*	monarchy, anarchy, matriarch
auto-	*self*	autocratic, autonomy, automation
chron-	*time*	chronological, synchronize, anachronism
doc-	*teach*	docile, doctrine, indoctrinate
graph-	*write*	autograph, graphic, seismograph
hydr-	*water*	dehydrate, hydraulic, hydrogen
phon-	*sound*	euphony, phonograph, symphony
port-	*carry*	portable, exports, deportation
terr-	*land*	inter, terrestrial, subterranean
urb-	*city*	suburb, urban, urbane
vit-	*life*	vitality, vitamin, revitalize
vol-	*will*	volition, involuntary, volunteer

(2) Know common prefixes and suffixes. Prefixes and **suffixes** are exchangeable attachments at the beginning or end of a word: *pre*war, *post*war, *anti*war; organ*ize*, organ*ic*, organ*ism*. Knowing that the Latin prefix *sub-* means "under" helps explain *subconscious, submarine, subterranean,* and *subzero.* The Latin suffix *-cide* means "killing"—helping us understand not only *homicide* and *suicide* but also *fratricide* (killing of a brother) and *parricide* (killing of a parent).

PREFIX	MEANING	EXAMPLES
bene-	*good*	benefactor, benefit, benevolent
bi-	*two*	bicycle, bilateral, bisect
contra-	*against*	contraband, contradict, contravene
dis-	*away, apart*	disperse, disorganize, discourage
ex-	*out*	exclude, exhale, expel
extra-	*outside*	extraordinary, extravagant, extrovert
mono-	*one*	monarch, monopoly, monolithic
multi-	*many*	multilateral, multinational, multiethnic
omni-	*all*	omnipotent, omnipresent, omniscient
per-	*through*	percolate, perforate, permeate
poly-	*many*	polygamy, polysyllabic, polytheistic
post-	*after*	postpone, postwar, postscript
pre-	*before*	preamble, precedent, prefix
re-	*back*	recall, recede, revoke, retract
tele-	*distant*	telegraph, telepathy, telephone
trans-	*across, beyond*	transatlantic, transmit, transcend

DICTIONARY WORK 7   What does your dictionary tell you about the *history* of the following words? Select five and report briefly on the history of each. What language did it come from? How did it acquire its current meaning?

algebra	hogan	police	Sabbath
crusade	laissez faire	propaganda	virtuoso
ecology	millennium	pundit	xenophobia

DICTIONARY WORK 8   How does the *shared root or suffix* help explain each word in the set?

1. anesthetic — anemic — amoral
2. antibiotic — biography — biology
3. audiovisual — audition — inaudible
4. cosmic — cosmopolitan — microcosm
5. disunity — discord — dissent
6. heterogeneous — heterosexual — heterodox
7. magnify — magnificent — magnitude
8. monarchy — oligarchy — anarchy

| **21b** | BORROWINGS FROM OTHER SOURCES | *d* |

Recognize major sources of our English vocabulary.

Here are kinds of historical information found in a good dictionary:

(1) Thousands of words came into English from French. England was conquered by the French-speaking Normans in the years following 1066. For a time the language of law, administration, and literature was French. When English gradually reestablished itself, thousands of French words were retained. Many of these mirror the political and military role of the Normans: *castle, court, glory, mansion, noble, prison, privilege, servant, treason, war.*

(2) Foreign languages have influenced the vocabularies of special fields of interest. Since the beginning of **Modern English** (about 1500), many words have come into English from French, Italian, Spanish, and other sources.

FRENCH:	apartment, ballet, battalion, façade, negligee, patrol
ITALIAN:	concert, falsetto, solo, sonata, soprano, violin
SPANISH:	alligator, cocoa, mosquito, potato, tobacco, tomato

(3) Foreign words are still coming into English from other languages. We use *apartheid*, from Dutch as spoken in South Africa, for the system of racial segregation there. We are getting used to encountering words from Russian or Japanese:

RUSSIAN:	troika, sputnik, gulag, nomenklatura, glasnost
JAPANESE:	samurai, shogun, kamikaze, hibachi, karate, haiku

When such words are not yet fully naturalized, your dictionary may put a special symbol in front of them or label them French, Chinese, or whatever is appropriate.

DICTIONARY WORK 9   What does each of the following expressions mean? What language did it come from? Which of them does your dictionary still consider foreign rather than English?

ad hoc	El Dorado	paparazzo
aficionado	fait accompli	quod erat demonstrandum
blitz	habeas corpus	reich
de jure	karma	samurai

21c | NEOLOGISMS | *d*

Make discriminating use of recent coinages.

Dictionaries compete in their coverage of **neologisms**, or newly coined expressions. Technology, space exploration, genetics, medicine, and computers create a constant demand for new words. Many fill an obvious need and are rapidly accepted: *astronaut, fallout, data base, flextime, space shuttle, aerobics, fax, high tech*. Other new words at first sound clever but soon become convenient shorthand for what they stand for: *palimony, no-show, baby boomer, floppy disk, boat people, laugh track*. Some coinages, however, sound cute, awkward, or farfetched. Avoid coinages that smack of media hype, advertising prose, or bureaucratic jargon:

MEDIA HYPE:	megabuck, docudrama, infomercial, sexploitation
ADVERTISING WORDS:	jumboize, paperamics, moisturize, usership
BUREAUCRATIC:	escapee, definitize, prioritize, socioeconomic

DICTIONARY WORK 10   What's *new* in dictionaries? How up to date, or how far behind, is your dictionary in its coverage of the following words? Report on its treatment of *five* of the words. For several of those that are missing, write a short but informative definition that would help an editor bring the dictionary up to date.

acid rain	body stocking	fast breeder	survivalist
aerobics	brain dead	hospice	tokenism
aerospace	buzzword	interface	unisex
airbag	CAT scan	no-show	upscale
bleep	Chicano	payload	voiceover

22   APPROPRIATE WORDS

OVERVIEW Not all words are right for all occasions. Traditionally, dictionaries have identified three varieties of *spoken* English likely to seem out of place in serious writing: **Nonstandard** English is for many Americans the workaday speech of street, neighborhood, or construction site; it differs from the **standard** English of the media, of school and office. **Informal** language is the variety of English we use in casual conversation; it is the chatty kind of language we use when at ease or with our friends. **Slang** is extremely informal language, usually too freewheeling and disrespectful for use in serious discussion.

In addition, dictionary makers use usage labels to show that a word is used only in part of the English-speaking world or that it is no longer in common use.

22a   NONSTANDARD WORDS   *NS*

Recognize words that suggest nonstandard speech.

Standard English is the language of education, business, journalism, and government. It is the language of teachers, lawyers, office workers, and others whose work keeps them in daily contact with books, records, forms, memos, notes, and other uses of the written word.

Nonstandard English is for many people the natural speech of home, neighborhood, or job. Historically, nonstandard speech has often been associated with a way of life that required little formal schooling or with jobs that required little reading of instructions and writing of reports. Many of the features of nonstandard speech stand out and are clearly out of place in writing. Here are some examples of nonstandard usage:

NONSTANDARD:	ain't	being that	nohow	off of
STANDARD:	isn't, hasn't	because	not at all	off, from
NONSTANDARD:	irregardless	hisself	theirself	nowheres
STANDARD:	regardless	himself	themselves	nowhere

> SEE THE GLOSSARY OF USAGE FOR *A/AN*, DOUBLE NEGATIVE, DOUBLE COMPARATIVE.

PEER EDITOR 11 Rewrite each sentence, editing out all *nonstandard* expressions.

1. Being that their parents died young, my cousins early learned to take care of theirself.
2. He was determined to have hisself promoted irregardless of the cost.
3. If she ain't eligible, we'll have to take her name off of the list.
4. We couldn't find the records anywheres.
5. He bought hisself a new car at hundreds of dollars off of the listed price.

22b INFORMAL WORDS *inf*

Recognize words that are too informal for serious writing.

The right kind of English for most of your college writing will be **edited written English**—more formal than casual everyday talk, serious enough for the discussion of issues and ideas. In most of your writing, the right tone will be near the midpoint between extremely formal and extremely informal language.

(1) Sift out the catchall words that punctuate everyday talk. Avoid the routine use of words like *nice, neat, cute, terrific, great, wonderful.*

(2) Limit words with a distinctly folksy or casual touch to informal personal writing. Words like the following suggest casual talk:

INFORMAL	FORMAL	INFORMAL	FORMAL
boss	superior	kid	child
bug	germ	sloppy	untidy
faze	disconcert	snoop	pry
flunk	fail	stump	baffle

Other familiar words are generally acceptable in one sense but informal in another. Informal are *alibi* in the sense of "excuse," *aggravate* in the sense of "annoy," *funny* in the sense of "strange," and *mad* in the sense of "angry."

Replace informal combined verbs like the following:

INFORMAL	FORMAL	INFORMAL	FORMAL
chip in	contribute	come up with	find
get across	communicate	cut out	stop
check up on	investigate	get on with	make progress

(3) Edit out informal tags and abbreviations. Avoid informal tags like *kind of, sort of, a lot, lots.* Revise clipped forms that have a "too-much-in-a-hurry" effect: *bike, prof, doc, fan mag, exec, econ.* (But shortened forms like *phone, ad,* and *exam* are now commonly used in serious writing.)

(4) Improve on tired informal expressions. Avoid the familiar overused figurative expressions of informal speech. (See **25b** for more on trite language, or **clichés**.)

TRITE: have a ball   polish the apple   jump the gun
        butter up   shoot the breeze   play ball

A Note on Slang: Dictionaries may disagree, but for most readers, words like *zilch, crock, the fuzz, far out, yo-yo, ballsy,* and *mooning* have the true slung-about quality of slang. New slang is often colorful or pointed (*spaced out, ripoff*), but much of it wears out from repetition. At any rate, much slang is too crude or disrespectful for most writing: *pig out, chew the fat, blow one's top, lay an egg.*

DISCOURSE EXERCISE 12   Rewrite the sentences, replacing each informal word or expression with one more appropriate in serious writing.

The Rise of the Yuppie

1. The student hero of the seventies had been John Belushi, **pigging out** and **yukking it up** with his **frat brothers**.
2. By the early eighties, **grinds** were **in**, and slobs were no longer considered **cool**.
3. Yuppies were becoming role models for everyone who did not **hate their guts**.
4. MBAs were becoming a **hot item, mediawise**.
5. Business schools **packed in** students whose goal was to **cash in**.

DISCOURSE EXERCISE 13   Point out words and expressions that make for a breezy or jazzy informal style.

Advertising is relatively a Johnny-come-lately. It did not exist in the mass-market form that we know much before World War I, and did not exist in any form at all before the late nineteenth century. But before advertising, there were newspapers and magazines. They were very much as we know them today, except of course that the pages were filled with news instead of paid hustle. Since they had almost no other source of revenue, the publications of that time lived or died by the reader's penny spent, and charged an honest price; if a publication cost five cents to produce, you can bet a publisher charged at least five cents for it and hoped like hell that what the paper had to say was interesting enough to get enough people to pony up their nickels. It is no coincidence that the great muckraking magazines of American legend flourished under these game conditions; who pays the piper calls the tune, and the only paymaster was their readers, who apparently liked what the muckrakers were playing.   Warren Hinckle, "The Adman Who Hated Advertising," *Atlantic*

22c | REGIONAL LABELS | *d*

Notice labels for words in use mainly in one region.

During the centuries before travel, books, and finally radio and television exercised their standardizing influence, languages developed regional varieties.

(1) Vocabulary differs somewhat from one English-speaking country to another. American travelers in England notice the British uses of *tram, lorry, lift, fortnight*.

BRITISH: lift (elevator), torch (flashlight), wireless, bonnet (hood of a car), chemist (druggist)

Dictionaries increasingly discuss special terms or special uses of words in Canadian, Australian, or South African English:

CANADIAN: province, governor general, Grey Cup, permanent force, Calgary Stampede
SOUTH AFRICAN: apartheid, veldt, trek

(2) Regional varieties within a country are called dialects. A poet to whom a church is a "kirk" and a landowner a "laird" is using one of the **dialects** of Scotland and Northern England. American speech shows some regional differences. However, the intermingling of settlers from many areas and the growth of mass media have kept American dialects from drifting very far apart.

DIALECTAL: dogie, poke (bag), reckon (suppose), tote (carry), you all

| **22d** | OBSOLETE AND ARCHAIC | *d* |

Notice labels for words no longer in common use.

Some words, or meanings of words, have gone out of use altogether; they are **obsolete**. Examples of obsolete meanings are *coy* (quiet), *curious* (careful), and *nice* (foolish). Some words or meanings are no longer in common use but still occur in special contexts; they are **archaic**. The King James version of the Bible preserves archaisms that were in common use in seventeenth-century England: *thou* and *thee*, *brethren*, *kine* (cattle). In the following entry, five meanings of *brave* are labeled obsolete:

> **brave** (brāv) *adj.* **brav·er, brav·est** **1.** Having or showing courage; intrepid; courageous. **2.** Making a fine display; elegant; showy. **3.** *Obs.* Excellent. — *v.* **braved, brav·ing** *v.t.* **1.** To meet or face with courage and fortitude: to *brave* danger. **2.** To defy; challenge: to *brave* the heavens. **3.** *Obs.* To make splendid. — *v.i.* **4.** *Obs.* To boast. — *n.* **1.** A man of courage. **2.** A North American Indian warrior. **3.** *Obs.* A bully; bravo. **4.** *Obs.* A boast or defiance.

From *Standard College Dictionary*

DICTIONARY WORK 14   Which of the following words carry usage labels in your dictionary? Which are labeled informal or slang? Which have regional or dialect uses? Which are archaic or obsolete?

bonkers	cove	habitant	Sooner
boodle	gig	hangup	sweetie
bower	goober	one shot	tube
complected	goodman	petrol	wonted

23 SEXIST LANGUAGE

OVERVIEW Fair-minded readers have no use for language that mirrors prejudice. They object to expressions that slight people because of race, sex, age, national origin, sexual orientation, or disability. Many government agencies and many publications require authors to observe guidelines on how to avoid offensive or prejudiced language.

In particular, readers increasingly object to language that belittles women. Doing without sexist language is not just a matter of avoiding terms like *chick, doll,* or *gal.* Many readers increasingly object to terms once considered neutral and used freely by both men and women writers. For instance, *man* as a **generic** term for the human species (*early man, the history of mankind*) was said to include both men and women. It made people picture primarily the male of the species nevertheless. Current textbooks therefore use terms like *humanity, humankind, human beings*, or just plain *people* instead.

| 23a | REVISING SEXIST LANGUAGE | *sx* |

Revise gender-biased language.

Steer clear of sexist language:

(1) Replace biased labels for occupations. Replace labels that seem to reserve some occupations for men while shunting women off into others:

STEREOTYPED	UNBIASED
fireman	firefighter
policeman	police officer
mailman	mail carrier
weatherman	meteorologist
salesman	sales representative
Congressman	Representative
stewardess	flight attendant

Some terms recommended in official guidelines still sound artificial to many writers, causing them to try alternatives:

STEREOTYPED	UNBIASED	ALTERNATIVES
chairman	chairperson	chair, head
spokesman	spokesperson	voice, representative, speaker
businessmen	businesspersons	business people, executives, the business community

(2) Revise expressions that imply there is something odd about men or women in a given situation or line of work. Avoid the condescending *lady doctor* or *lady lawyer*. Do not make a big point about a *female* pilot or a *male* secretary. You can often fill the reader in simply by using the right pronoun: "The new secretary handled *his* workload well."

(3) Mention sex, marital status, or family evenhandedly. Provide such information equally for people of either sex, or omit it when it is irrelevant. Use courtesy titles impartially, and use first names or nicknames evenhandedly for either sex. (*Ms.*, like *Mr.*, allows people to keep their marital status their own business, although women who prefer *Mrs.* or *Miss* may so indicate by using them in signing their correspondence.)

NO: Mr. John Greuber, local builder, and Mrs. Vitell, mother of three, were elected to the board.

YES: John Greuber and Ann Vitell, both long active in community affairs, were elected to the board.

NO: Mr. Pfitzer and Jane will show you the plant.

YES: Mr. Pfitzer and Ms. Garner will show you the plant.

23b | THE PRONOUN DILEMMA | *sx*

Avoid using pronouns with sexist implications.

English does not have a personal pronoun that refers impartially to persons of either sex. There is no single pronoun that would help us avoid choices like the following: "A police officer needs strict guidelines for the use of (*his? her? his or her?*) gun."

(1) Replace gender-biased pronouns. Beware of stereotyping occupations by using *he* or *she* selectively when talking about typical representatives. Avoid loaded pairs like "the doctor — *he*, the nurse — *she*." Use the **double pronoun** *he or she* (or *his or her*) to refer to a typical doctor, nurse, teacher, secretary, or executive. Or sidestep the pronoun problem by talking about typical doctors, teachers, or secretaries *in the plural*:

STEREOTYPED: A successful manager keeps a certain distance from **his** employees.

DOUBLE PRONOUN: A successful manager keeps a certain distance from **his or her** employees.

PLURAL: Successful **managers** keep a certain distance from **their** employees.

The plural usually works best when several *he-or-she, his-or-her,* and *himself-or-herself* combinations in a row would make a sentence awkward.

(2) Replace the generic *he*. Use the double pronoun *he or she* also to replace the **generic** *he* in reference to the generalized expressions like *everyone, somebody, anybody, anyone, nobody,* or *one* (**indefinite pronouns**). Everyday speech uses the plural *they* or *their* after these: "*No one* should be required to inform on *their* own family." Grammarians used to require the singular *he* or *him* (or *himself*): "*Everyone* has the right to make *his* own mistakes." In your own writing, use the unbiased *he or she*, or change the generalized pronouns to a plural:

UNBIASED: **Everyone** has the right to make **his or her** own mistakes.
PLURAL: We **all** have the right to make **our** own mistakes.

PEER EDITOR 15   Rewrite the sentences to eliminate *sexist language*.

1. Risking his life for unconcerned or unappreciative citizens is part of a policeman's or a fireman's job.
2. Evolutionists are rewriting the history of mankind to show that early man branched off the evolutionary tree before the chimpanzee.

3. A doctor can walk away from his patients after a brief consultation; the nurse spends most of her day dealing with their pain and fear.

4. Everybody takes American history at least three or four times in his career as a student.

5. On Secretaries' Day, the boss is expected to show his appreciation for the ladies in the office.

6. A business traveler may take out his anger on the stewardess if he misses his connecting flight.

7. The ambition of every Congressman is to become the chairman of an important House committee.

8. While the convention-goer attends his meetings, his spouse can do her shopping or use the legendary recreational facilities.

---

24   EFFECTIVE LANGUAGE

OVERVIEW Effective writers know how to choose the right word — the word that brings an idea clearly into focus or brings a vivid image to the reader's mind. They use language that does justice to important distinctions and shades of meaning; they use language that makes us see, hear, and feel.

24a   ACCURATE WORDS

Aim at accurate words and exact shades of meaning.

Speaking or writing in a hurry, we often settle for words that merely come close — words that express the intended meaning almost but not quite. In revising a quick first draft, look for the following:

(1) Use the exact word, not a roundabout description. Avoid **circumlocutions** ("taking the long way around").

ROUNDABOUT: The skipper and **the people working for him on the boat** were lost.

EXACT: The skipper and **the crew** were lost.

(2) Use the exact word, not one that is only half right. Replace an approximate word with the word that is exactly right:

BLURRED: Many parents today do not have time to **adhere** to the needs of their children.
(We **adhere to** — or stick to — an agreement. We **attend to**, or **satisfy**, someone's needs.)

ACCURATE: Many parents today do not have time to **attend to** the needs of their children.

(3) Watch out for the right word used the wrong way. Some words carry the right idea but are used the wrong way in a sentence:

WRONG: **The news** about corruption was first **exposed** in the local press.

RIGHT: **The news** about corruption first **broke** in the local press.
(Evildoers are **exposed**; the news about their doings **breaks** or is **reported**; the truth about them is **revealed**.)

GARBLED: Most American teenagers do what they want without **consenting** their parents.

REVISED: Most American teenagers do what they want without **consulting** their parents (or without **obtaining** their consent).

(4) Watch out for words easily confused. Do not confuse words close in sound or meaning:

CONFUSED: Similar choices **affront** every student (should be **confront**).
Self-control is an **envious** asset (should be **enviable**).

PEER EDITOR 16 Write down a *more accurate* word or expression for each word or phrase italicized in the following sentences.

1. My parents have always *placed a high standard* on a good education.
2. Having high-spirited parents has given me a *jest* for life.
3. Diane soon discovered some of the problems *coherent* in managing a large department.
4. Her parents were idealists and tried to raise healthy, *opinionated* children.
5. In my *analogy* of this essay, I hope to show its strengths and weaknesses.
6. The woman *braved* her life to save her fellow passengers.

24b | SPECIFIC WORDS | *d*

Use specific, informative words.

Do the following to make your writing more vivid and informative:

(1) Call things by their names. Instead of lumping something in a general category, use names that call up shapes, textures, and colors. "Small animal" is colorless; *gopher, chipmunk, squirrel,* and *raccoon* call up contours, movements, habits. Instead of a colorless, general word like *building*, use a more expressive word like *barn, mansion, warehouse, bungalow, tenement, shack, workshop,* or *cabin. Tenement* carries more information than *building*, making it possible for the reader to visualize an actual structure.

(2) Use concrete words—words that appeal to our five senses. **Concrete** words bring us close to what we can see, hear, and feel; they seem to conjure up sights, sounds, smells, textures, and motions.

GENERAL	CONCRETE
look	gaze, stare, peer, squint, ogle
walk	stride, march, slink, trot, shuffle, drag
sit	slump, squat, lounge, hunch, crouch
take	seize, grab, pounce on, grip
throw	hurl, pitch, toss, dump, flip

DISCOURSE EXERCISE 17   Ernest Hemingway was known as a stickler for the right word. Look at the general, colorless word at the beginning of each of the following sentences. Then compare it with the more *concrete word* that Hemingway used in one of his short stories. What does the concrete word add to the more general meaning?

Camping in the Michigan Woods

1. (throw) The handler had *pitched* Nick's bundle out of the door of the railroad car.
2. (move) The river *swirled* against the logs of the bridge.
3. (rock) There were big *boulders* at the bottom of the stream.
4. (flow) A mist of sand gravel was raised in *spurts* by the current.
5. (reflection) Looking for the river, Nick caught *glints* of the water in the sun.
6. (turn) There were big grasshoppers with wings *whirring out* from their sheathing.
7. (eat) He saw the grasshopper *nibble* at the wool of his sock.
8. (stand) By a *grove* of trees was a bare space for his tent.

24c   TECHNICAL TERMS   *d*

Explain technical terms to the outsider.

Explain and illustrate new or difficult terms. In a paper on a mountain-climbing trip, you may need to define terms like the following:

bivouac: a temporary encampment in the open, with only tents as
an improvised shelter

traverse: to move sideways across a mountain slope, making a slant-
ing path

In a passage like the following, a writer uses necessary technical
terms while making their meaning clear to the newcomer or outsider:

> The **disk drive** works like a very fast tape recorder, recording
> information on a magnetic medium, the **floppy disk**. When the user
> needs that stored information, she tells the computer to load the
> information into its own **short-term** memory (RAM—for "random
> access memory"), where the data can be examined and revised.

SENTENCE PRACTICE 18 What specialized fields do the following
technical terms represent? Which of these terms would you expect a
college student to know? For five of these, write a one-sentence definition
for the newcomer or outsider.

EXAMPLE: *Type-A* personalities are those uptight, compulsive, competitive, aggressive overachievers likely to suffer early
heart attacks unless they modify their behavior.

a priori	camshaft	meltdown	syncopation
black box	hard disk	solstice	thyroid
black hole	lien	symbiosis	venire

Use figurative language to bring your writing to life.

Figurative language employs imaginative comparisons, or **figures of speech**, to translate ideas into striking images. A brief comparison signaled by *as* or *like* is called a **simile**: "In much modern

fiction, happiness is found only briefly and in unexpected places, *like a flower growing in the crack of a sidewalk.*" An implied comparison that presents one thing as if it actually were the other is called a **metaphor**: "For many beginning poets, the traditional rhymed four-line stanza is *a jug into which the syrup of verse is poured.*"

(1) Figurative expressions should be apt. The implied analogy has to fit:

APT: In many of the author's stories, language is **like signals from vessels in distress, telling us of desperate needs**. (Distress signals are particularly urgent language.)

INEPT: **Lacking the ignition** of advertising, our economic engine would run at a slower pace. (An engine without ignition would just be dead.)

(2) Figurative expressions should be consistent. Avoid the **mixed metaphor**, which at first sails smoothly along and then suddenly jumps the tracks (hard to do on the trackless sea).

CONSISTENT: If the new industrial robots have become the **arms and eyes** of our factories, computers have become their **brains**.

MIXED: Enriched programs give the good student a chance to **dig** deeper into the large **sea** of knowledge. (We dig on solid ground rather than at sea.)

(3) Figurative language should not be strained. Reaching for a striking image, we can easily strain our metaphor:

DISTRACTING: Helplessly, Fred watched from his desk while his stomach tied itself into knots.

REVISED: As Fred watched the event helplessly from his desk, he experienced a sick, tense feeling in the pit of his stomach.

(4) Figurative language should not be stale. Some figurative expressions have been used over and over and over. Avoid **clichés**, including *the bottom line, the cutting edge,* and *the melting pot,* not to mention *smart as a whip* and *blind as a bat.*

DISCOURSE EXERCISE 19   Find and discuss *figurative expressions* in the following passage. What images or associations do they bring to mind? Which of these figurative expressions are familiar? Which are fresh or provocative?

Loaded Words

A great many words bring along not only their meanings but some extra freight—a load of judgment or bias that plays upon the emotions instead of lighting up the understanding. These words deserve careful handling—and minding. They are loaded. Such words babble up in all corners of society, wherever anybody is ax-grinding, arm-twisting, back-scratching, sweet-talking. Political blather leans sharply to words (*peace, prosperity*) whose moving powers outweigh exact meanings. Merchandising depends on adjectives (*new, improved*) that must be continually recharged with notions that entice people to buy. In casual conversation, emotional stuffing is lent to words by inflection and gesture: The innocent phrase, "Thanks a lot," is frequently a vehicle for heaping servings of irritation. Traffic in opinion-heavy language is universal simply because most people, as C. S. Lewis puts it, are "more anxious to express their approval and disapproval of things than to describe them."   Frank Tippett, "Watching Out for Loaded Words," *Time*

PEER EDITOR 20   Rewrite the following sentences. Use *more apt or fresh* figurative language to replace expressions that are mixed, stale, or overdone.

1.   The original educator is the family, which plants the seeds that teachers later build upon.
2.   Immigrants bring new blood into our country to help us recharge our batteries.
3.   The grocery store is alive with the stuffed carts that will fill the growling stomachs of the customers.
4.   This cat was in our driveway when the kiss of death took him by surprise.
5.   It is common for people to be unaware of the more difficult gut issues that are propelling them forward.

6. The jagged teeth of the powerful saw bit into the flesh of the tree like a hungry shark crushing its prey.

---

25   PLAIN ENGLISH

OVERVIEW   Ideally, we would all write vigorous plain English that carries our message without static. In practice, however, words may get in the way, slowing down, confusing, or misleading the reader.

25a   WORDINESS   *w*

Avoid wordiness.

Redundancy is the use of more words than are necessary. The phrase *basic fundamentals* is redundant because fundamentals are already basic by definition. *Newly renovated* and *free gift* tell us nothing that *renovated* and *gift* wouldn't tell us on their own.

(1) Avoid direct duplication. In the following sentences, one or the other way of expressing the same idea should be omitted:

REDUNDANT: **As a rule**, summers there are **usually** unbearably hot.
Prisoners were awakened **in the morning** at six **a.m.**
The President knew more than **seemed apparent**.

(2) Watch for redundant pairs. Prune the adjectives in *future plans* (plans are always for the future) or *true facts*.

REDUNDANT	ECONOMICAL
consensus of opinion	consensus
past memories	memories
anticipate in advance	anticipate

(3) Avoid familiar wordy tags. Much inflated language is caused by tags like the following:

WORDY	BRIEF
at the present time	now
due to the fact that	because
under the prevailing circumstances	as things are
in this time and age	today
at a period of time when	when

(4) Use simple, direct transitional expressions. Often a simple *for example, however,* or *therefore* can replace a mouthful like *Taking these factors into consideration, we must conclude that.*

WORDY: **In considering the situation, we must also take into account the fact that** the current residents often do not share our enthusiasm for redevelopment.

BRIEF: The current residents, **however**, often do not share our enthusiasm for redevelopment.

(5) Avoid vague all-purpose words. Words like *element, factor, aspect, situation,* or *angle* are often mere padding.

PADDED: Another **aspect** that needs to be considered is the consumer relations **angle**.

REVISED: We should also consider consumer relations.

PEER EDITOR 21   Rewrite each sentence to eliminate wordiness.

1. We are planning to move because in terms of employment there are few jobs in this area at the present time.
2. Mormons fleeing persecution founded the beginning of our community.
3. In due time, a new fad will eventually replace this current craze.
4. Many plants are closing due to the fact that a flood of cheap products is inundating the market.
5. In my opinion, I have always felt that a popular entertainer should be a happy, smiling type of person.

6.   The central nucleus of the tribe was based around the institution of the family.
7.   At a period of time when schools face skyrocketing insurance costs, the aspect of insurance pools deserves consideration.
8.   In the modern world of this day and age, computer projections are among the basic fundamentals of business planning.

Phrase ideas freshly in your own words.

Clichés are ready-made phrases, worn out from overuse. Like phrases stored in the memory of an electronic typewriter, they practically type themselves: "*few* and . . . *far between*," "easier said . . . *than done*," "last but . . . *not least*." Many folksy clichés have outlived a rural past (*put the shoulder to the wheel, put the cart before the horse*). Other trite phrases survive from old-fashioned, flowery oratory (*intestinal fortitude, dire necessity, the bitter end*). Still others sound like part of a sales talk that has been replayed too many times (*let's look at the facts, look at the big picture, look at the bottom line*). To *say the least,* for *all intents and purposes*, the *bloom is off* such expressions, and *in the final analysis*, they *do more harm than good.*

Avoid clichés like the following:

believe it or not	burn the midnight oil
better late than never	crying shame
beyond the shadow of a doubt	Mother Nature
bolt out of the blue	off the beaten track
easier said than done	pride and joy
few and far between	rear its ugly head
first and foremost	rude awakening
in one fell swoop	a shot in the arm
it goes without saying	sink or swim
last but not least	sneaking suspicion
the last straw	straight and narrow
let's face it	to all intents and purposes

PEER EDITOR 22   Rewrite each sentence to get rid of trite language.

1. We try to give foreign competition a run for their money, but in many areas, cheap foreign labor has forced American management to throw in the towel.

2. In a very real sense, politicians dealing with tax legislation often cannot see the forest for the trees.

3. Catching the street-corner pusher has become small potatoes. The major effort now is international, and it is a pathway strewn with political pitfalls.

4. In the final analysis, party platforms never get down to brass tacks.

5. The meetings scheduled with the candidate will give people from every walk of life a chance to stand up and be counted.

6. When we try to give our neighborhoods a shot in the arm, appealing to self-interest is our best bet.

25c	JARGON	*d*

Avoid pretentious pseudoscientific language.

Jargon is pretentious, pseudoscientific language that tries to make the trivial sound important: "Mandatory verification of your attendance record is required of all personnel exiting the work area." (Punch your time card when you leave.)

(1) Deflate inflated substitutes for straightforward words. In each of the following pairs avoid the big word if the simple word will do:

BIG WORD	SIMPLE WORD	BIG WORD	SIMPLE WORD
interrelationship	relation	maximize	develop fully
methodology	methods	insightful	intelligent
prioritize	rank	preadolescence	childhood

(2) Lower the abstraction count. Watch for such symptoms as the piling up of too many words ending in *-ion: verification, utilization, implementation, modification, conceptualization.* Be wary of *factors, aspects, elements, facets, phenomena, strata.*

JARGON: **An element of society that is most prevalent** in advertising is the desire for a carefree existence.

PLAIN ENGLISH: Advertising mirrors the yearning for a carefree life that is strong in our society.

(3) Avoid impersonal tags. Even in formal research reports, overuse of phrases like the following produces a stilted effect:

STILTED	PLAIN
reference was made	I mentioned
the hypothesis suggests itself	we can tentatively conclude
a realization of desired outcomes	producing the desired results

PEER EDITOR 23   Translate the following examples of *jargon* into plain English.

1. In camp, cooking is done over open fires, with the main dietary intake consisting of black beans and rice.
2. To be frank about it, today an inadequacy can bring about the ruination of a person in later life when it happens in education.
3. The English language and its use have become very important factors in correlation with communication to large audiences.
4. In these two books, there are basic differences in character representation that are accountable only in terms of the individual authors involved.
5. Further insight into the article discovered that the writing insinuated a connection between the conviction of the accused and his working-class background.

6. Advertisements similar to those of Certs and Ultra-Brite are creating a fallacy in the real cause of a person's sex appeal.

7. The fact that we are products of our environmental frame of reference ensures that each of us has deeply ingrained within the fiber of our being preconceived ideas that influence our thoughts, actions, and reactions.

8. We say we believe in democracy while denying the partaking of its first fruits, justice and equality, to diverse members of our society. This is true in many aspects of our lives, but especially so in the context of racial prejudice.

25d | EUPHEMISMS | *d*

Prefer plain English to euphemisms.

Euphemisms are "beautiful words" — words more beautiful than what they stand for: *memorial park* for *cemetery, correctional facility* for *jail.* Some euphemisms are merely polite: *intoxicated* for *drunk, stout* for *fat.* But many try to upgrade ordinary realities: *human performance* (physical education), *sanitary engineer* (plumber), *research consultant* (file clerk). In much public-relations prose and other kinds of doublespeak, euphemisms cover up facts that the reader is entitled to know: *straitened financial circumstances* for "bankruptcy"; *negative economic growth* for "recession."

An effective writer knows when to be diplomatic but also when to be blunt and direct:

EUPHEMISM	BLUNT
immoderate use of intoxicants	heavy drinking
lack of proper health habits	dirt
below the poverty line	poor

| FLOWERY DICTION *d* |

Avoid language that is flowery or overdone.

Resist the temptation to weave a flowery garland of fancy words around simple everyday events:

FLOWERY: The **respite** from study was devoted to a **sojourn** at the **ancestral mansion**.

PLAIN ENGLISH: I spent my vacation at the house of my grandparents.

Here is a brief list of words that can make your writing seem affected:

FLOWERY	PLAIN	FLOWERY	PLAIN
astound	amaze	nuptials	wedding
betrothal	engagement	obsequies	funeral
demise	death	pulchritude	beauty

PEER EDITOR 24 Cut through the *euphemisms* and *flowery language* in the following examples and rewrite them in plain English.

1. Ready to leave the parental nest, I decided to pursue my education at an institution of higher learning.
2. After a most rewarding bout with a social research paper, something stirred my intellect and I possessed a burning desire to stay in school for another three-week session.
3. Offenders who have paid their debt to society at a correctional institution should be given a chance to become productive participants in community life.
4. All personnel assisting in preparation of food should observe proper hygiene after using the sanitary facilities.

281

7

PUNCTUATION: WHEN AND WHY

PUNCTUATION MARKS: REFERENCE CHART

COMMA

before coordinators (*and, but, or*)	**27b**
with nonrestrictive adverbial clauses	**27d**
after introductory adverbial clauses	**27d**
with nonrestrictive relative clauses	**27e**
with nonrestrictive modifiers	**28b**
after introductory modifiers	**28c**
with conjunctive adverbs (*therefore, however*)	**27c**
with *especially, namely, for example*	**29e**
with *after all, of course*	**28c**
between items in a series	**29a**
in a series of parallel clauses	**27a**
between coordinate adjectives	**29b**
with dates, addresses, and measurements	**29c**
with parenthetic elements	**30c**
between repeated or contrasted elements	**29d**
with direct quotations	**31a**

SEMICOLON

between paired sentences	**27a**
before conjunctive adverbs	**27c**
before coordinators if clauses have commas	**27b**
in a series with items containing commas	**29a**

PERIOD

at end of sentence	**9a, 26a**
for ellipsis	**31c**
with abbreviations	**39a**

COLON

to introduce a list or an explanation	**29e**
to introduce a formal quotation	**31a**

DASH

to show a break in thought	**30a**
to set off modifier with commas	**30a**

QUOTATION MARKS

with direct quotations	**31a**
with end marks	**31b**
with technical terms	**31e**
to set off titles	**31f**

PUNCTUATION ESSENTIALS: *Minimum Proficiencies*

Note: The following is a quick rundown of minimum proficiencies in the area covered in this chapter. Remember that there is much more to good writing than meeting minimum standards. However, if you fail to meet the standards summarized here, your message may not reach the reader and you may not get credit for what you do well.

Among punctuation essentials, revising the periods that split off sentence fragments and the commas that splice comma splices has the highest priority. Next in importance are the items covered by the following *eight basic rules.*

(1) COMMA WITH *AND* AND *BUT*. When we link two statements in a larger combined sentence, we call them clauses. Use a comma if the link between the two clauses is *and, but, for, so, or, nor,* or *yet.* These are coordinating conjunctions (**coordinators**, for short); they make two statements "work together." In the following combined sentences, each statement (or clause) has its own subject and verb.

COMMA: The thin look was in, **and** yogurt sales soared.

Jogging is fine, **but** walking is healthier.

Auditors are unpopular, **for** they trace misspent funds.

(2) SEMICOLON WITH *HOWEVER* AND *THEREFORE*. Use a semicolon if the link between two statements is a word like *however* or *therefore* (**conjunctive adverbs**). Other words in this group include *nevertheless, consequently, accordingly, besides, moreover, indeed,* and *in fact.* Use an additional comma (or commas) to set the *however* or *therefore* off from the second statement.

SEMICOLON: I had friends; **however,** they disappeared on weekends.

Many Soviet citizens are not Russian; **in fact,** they learn Russian in school.

Like other adverbs, conjunctive adverbs can move in a sentence. Keep the semicolon at the juncture between the two statements:

SEMICOLON: We hear much of miracle drugs; most, **however,** have severe side effects.

The hall was nearly empty; the show went on, **nevertheless**.

(3) NO COMMA WITH *IF* AND *WHEN*. Words like *if, unless, when, while,* or *where* bring essential conditions into a sentence (a rebate only *if you act now*). Do *not* use a comma. Words like *if* and *when* are subordinating conjunctions (**subordinators,** for short). Words like *before, after, since,* and *until* are subordinators when they start a statement with its own subject and verb (*before* I knew her; *since* he joined the band).

NO COMMA: Hundreds will perish **if** the dam breaks.

The phone will be disconnected **unless** you pay.

The added *if* or *unless* narrows or restricts the original statement; it adds a **restrictive** clause. When we use a subordinator, we can put the condition first. Use a comma to show where the main statement starts:

COMMA: **When** the killer bees arrived, the villagers panicked.

If the bond issue fails, the project is dead.

(4) COMMA WITH *ALTHOUGH* AND *WHEREAS*. Subordinators like *though, although, whereas,* and *no matter how* show that two statements are each true regardless of what the rest of the sentence says: "He kept charging to his card (regardless), *although* his account was overdrawn."

COMMA: Reactors produce nuclear wastes, **whereas** coal leaves inert ash.

The figures were wrong, **no matter what** the computer said.

(5) COMMA/NO COMMA WITH *WHO, WHICH,* AND *THAT*. *Who, which,* and *that* are **relative pronouns** when they join two clauses in a larger combined sentence: "The manager hates tenants *who complain.*" "Tenants *who wanted to complain* could never find the manager." Use *no* comma when the added clause (**relative clause**) is needed to tell us which one or what kind (drugs *that kill pain*).

NO COMMA: The odds favor candidates **who** raise tons of money.
                The evil **that** men do lives after them.

Use a comma (or commas) when the *who*-clause or *which*-clause merely adds information. We then already *know* who or what (dinosaurs, *which became extinct*). The nonessential *who* or *which* often follows a name (which already tells us who or what).

COMMAS: Amelia Earhart, **who** had flown around the world, disappeared over the Pacific.

Remember: The essential *who* or *that* restricts — it identifies, singles out, or narrows down. (The clause is **restrictive** — no comma.) The nonessential *who* or *which* merely tells us more about something already singled out. (The clause is **nonrestrictive** — use a comma or commas.)

(6) COMMAS WITH A SERIES. Commas mark off the elements in a **series**. A series is a set of three or more sentence parts of the same kind, usually tied together by *and* or sometimes *or: red, white,* and *blue; single, married,* or *divorced; milk, coffee,* or *tea.* Include the last comma (before the *and*):

COMMAS: Yuppies jog, bicycle, **and** work out in health clubs.
                The stand sold nuts, raisins, apples, **and** every other kind of organic lunch.

(7) COMMA BETWEEN CITY AND STATE. Mark off city from state with a comma:

COMMA: Tulsa, Oklahoma; Austin, Texas; Mobile, Alabama; New York, New York

(8) COMMA AFTER INTRODUCTORY ELEMENT. When we *frontload* a sentence with introductory material before the subject, a comma shows where the main part of the sentence starts: Use the comma if you start with a **prepositional phrase** of *three* words or more: *on the average, in the meantime, by a lucky accident, for best results*. Prepositional phrases are modifiers using words like *at, by, in, or, for, like, with, without, under, over, before, after*. These and other **prepositions** become part of a **phrase** — a group of words that does not have its own subject and verb.

COMMA: **At** Valerie's school, boys and girls wore uniforms to class.
With players earning a million dollars a year, the price of tickets keeps creeping up.

Use the comma after an introductory **verbal** — a form like *writing, written,* or *to write*. Use the comma regardless of whether the verbal starts the sentence alone or brings other material with it.

COMMA: **Smiling,** he tore up the check.
Scribbled on an envelope, the message was barely legible.
To get a refund, customers had to fill in a form in triplicate.

---

26 **END PUNCTUATION**

OVERVIEW Punctuation regulates the flow of material on the page. The most important kind is end punctuation, which brings what we are saying to a complete stop. We use it to set off complete sentences — units that can stand by themselves and that we can take in one at a time.

26a | SENTENCES AND FRAGMENTS *frag*

Use the period at the end of a complete statement.

A complete statement normally needs at least a subject and a complete verb. Look at the complete verbs that help turn each of the following into a separate sentence:

COMPLETE: Malpractice insurance **pays** for your doctor's mistakes.
              Marcia **was selling** billboard space.
              Drunk drivers **will be sent** to traffic school.

Revise two familiar kinds of incomplete statements that cause **sentence fragments**.

(1) Do not use a period to mark off fragments without both a subject and complete verb. *In the backyard* is a fragment because it does not tell us who does what in the backyard. *Orbiting around Jupiter* is a fragment because (a) it does not tell us *what* is in orbit around Jupiter and (b) it lacks the *is* or *was* that would turn *orbiting* into a complete verb.

NO SUBJECT: The wing hit the ground. **Spun the plane around.**
                     (What spun?)
COMPLETE: The wing **hit** the ground and **spun** the plane around.

NO VERB: Chung worked in Washington. **A lobbyist for Taiwan.**
COMPLETE: Chung, a lobbyist for Taiwan, worked in Washington.

NO COMPLETE VERB: We spent hours on the road. **Fighting the traffic.**
COMPLETE: We spent hours on the road fighting the traffic.

NO SUBJECT OR VERB: We found the host. **In the jacuzzi.**
COMPLETE: We found the host in the jacuzzi.

All the sentence fragments in this group are caused by a **phrase** — a group of words that does not have its own subject and verb.

(2) Do not use a period to mark off fragments starting with an unused link like *if* and *whereas* (subordinators) or *who* and *which* (relative pronouns). Words like *if* and *whereas* are meant to link a dependent clause (*if you need me*) to the main clause (*I'll be here if you need me*). When you mark off the *if*-clause by a period, it will be a fragment — even though it has a subject and a complete verb:

FRAGMENT: The clinic will be closed. **If the governor's veto is upheld**.
COMPLETE: The clinic will be closed **if the governor's veto is upheld**.

FRAGMENT: Charles Schulz created *Peanuts*. **Which became a national institution**.
COMPLETE: Charles Schulz created *Peanuts*, **which became a national institution**.

(3) Use a period to separate two complete sentences that have been run together. If there is no punctuation to separate two complete sentences, the result is a **fused sentence**. Supply the missing period (or a semicolon to show an exceptionally close relationship):

FUSED: *Star Trek* became an American myth **it will run forever**.
REVISED: *Star Trek* became an American myth**. It will run forever**.
           Star Trek became an American myth**; it will run forever**.

SEE **9a** AND **9b** ON REVISING FRAGMENTS AND FUSED SENTENCES.

26b | QUESTIONS AND EXCLAMATIONS   *?/!*

Signal questions and exclamations.

Not all of our sentences are simple statements, marked off by periods.

(1) Use the question mark to mark direct questions. These appear exactly as you would ask them of another person. ("Who shredded the documents?") Remember to use question marks at the end of questions that are long or involved.

QUESTION: Are our needs shaped by advertisers, or do advertisers cater to our needs?

CAUTION: Do not keep the question mark when you convert a direct question to an indirect question. In an indirect question, you no longer use the exact words of the original speaker or writer. You change time and pronouns to show that you are looking at what is said from your own perspective:

DIRECT: She asked the guide: "Why **do you call** the *Mona Lisa* La Gioconda?"

INDIRECT: She asked the guide why **he called** the *Mona Lisa* La Gioconda.

WRONG: She asked the guide why he called the *Mona Lisa* La Gioconda?

(2) Use the exclamation mark for emphasis. Use it to mark an order or a shout, to signal indignation or surprise. Note that the exclamation mark appears rarely in ordinary prose.

EMPHASIS: Win a trip to Tahiti!
             The jury found him not guilty!

DISCOURSE EXERCISE 1   Rewrite the italicized part of each example, using the right punctuation. (Use a period to separate the two parts of a fused sentence. Join any sentence fragments you find here to the main sentence *without* punctuation.)

EXAMPLE: Voting is a *responsibility. In democratic countries*.
ANSWER: responsibility in democratic countries.

The Voter's Dilemma

1.   Many voters have become *disillusioned they stay home.*
2.   What is the use of choosing between two *candidates who both dance around the issues.*

3. Presidential campaigns have become a media *circus. Why should voters bother.*

4. Candidates heed the *polls. And not their own judgment.*

5. Old political warhorses go foraging among the *grassroots. Before they support a candidate.*

6. A whistlestop used to be a chance to sway local *voters it's now little more than a photo opportunity.*

7. Why does a campaign have to be a demolition *derby won by the last battered survivor.*

8. Voters who really care still *exist. In other parts of the world.*

LINKING PUNCTUATION

OVERVIEW When several statements become part of a larger whole, we call each subsentence in the combined sentence a **clause**. Independent clauses are self-contained; they could be separated again by a period.

INDEPENDENT: We hear much about miracle drugs; however, they often have severe side effects. (one combined sentence)

ALSO RIGHT: We hear much about miracle drugs. However, they often have severe side effects. (two separate sentences)

Dependent clauses have been welded together more permanently, so that they cannot be simply pulled apart.

DEPENDENT: Addiction sounds less grim **when we call it substance abuse**.

WRONG: Addiction sounds less grim. **When we call it substance abuse**.

   (The dependent clause has become a sentence fragment.)

Much punctuation signals the connection between two or more clauses that work together in a larger combined sentence.

LINKING PUNCTUATION — AN OVERVIEW

SEMICOLON ONLY:

_____ ; _____ .

COORDINATORS:

_____ , and _____ .
_____ , but _____ .
_____ , so _____ .

CONJUNCTIVE ADVERBS:

_____ ; therefore, _____ .
_____ ; however, _____ .
_____ ; _____ , however, _____ .
_____ ; _____ , nevertheless.

SUBORDINATORS:

Restrictive   _____ if _____ .
                     _____ when _____ .
Nonrestrictive   _____ , although _____ .
                     _____ , whereas _____ .
Introductory   If _____ , _____ .
                     When _____ , _____ .

RELATIVE PRONOUNS:

Restrictive   _____ who _____ .
                     _____ that _____ .
Nonrestrictive   _____ , who _____ .
_____ , which _____ , _____ .

SPECIAL CONNECTIVES (WITH NOUN CLAUSES):

_____ what _____ .
_____ how _____ .
_____ that _____ .

SEMICOLON ONLY   *CS or /;*

Use a semicolon between two paired statements.

Often two statements go together as related information; they are part of the same story. When a semicolon replaces the period, the first word of the second statement is *not* capitalized:

SEMICOLON: The thin look is in; yogurt sales soared.
We constantly coin new words: Governments spread *dis-information*; executives are protected by *golden parachutes.*

CAUTION: Do not use a comma alone to join two independent clauses. A **comma splice** runs on from one independent clause to the next with only a comma between them. (See **9c**.)

COMMA SPLICE: I loved London, it is a wonderful city.
REVISED: I loved London; it is a wonderful city.

Note: If you wish, use *commas* instead of semicolons to link three or more clauses that are exceptionally close in meaning and parallel in form:

COMMA: Be brief, be blunt, be gone.

PEER EDITOR 2   In each of the following combined sentences, two independent clauses would cause a comma splice if joined only by a comma. Write down the last word of the first clause and the first word of the second clause; put a semicolon between the two words.

EXAMPLE: Carl's appearance had changed he had spiked hair.
ANSWER: changed; he

1.   A boutique is on the ground floor above it is a cheap tourist hotel.
2.   A flaming car wreck cannot daunt our superhero he emerges from the inferno intact.
3.   Automobile plants in Japan maintain a minimal inventory things are used right away.

4. The sloth is genuinely lethargic its metabolism runs at half the normal rate for animals of its size.

5. A modern zoo is less crowded the animals live in more natural habitats.

6. Poverty is a major problem in our world it is found in every city in the United States.

7. I enjoy running it becomes an almost unconscious act.

8. People were shouting commands everyone with a flashlight began directing traffic.

27b COORDINATORS *p or ⌃*

Use a comma when a coordinator links two clauses.

Use a comma before a **coordinating conjunction** (coordinator, for short): *and, but, for, so, or, nor,* and *yet.* Put a comma before — but not after — the *and, but,* or *so:*

COMMA:
The lights dimmed, **and** a roar went up from the crowd.
She remembered the face, **but** she forgot the name.
The picnic fizzled, **for** it started to rain.
The star was late, **so** the warmup band played forever.
We had better apologize, **or** we won't be invited again.
Her parents did not approve of divorce, **nor** did her spouse.
Reporters knew the truth, **yet** no one dared to print it.

(1) Do not use a comma with a coordinator that joins two words or two phrases. In a sentence like the following, the *and* merely adds a second verb to the same clause: "The earthquake *rattled* windows *and toppled* shelves."

(2) For clarity, use a semicolon between clauses with internal commas. The semicolon then marks the major break:

SEMICOLON: Now in the Big Bend the river encounters mountains in a new and extraordinary way; **for** they lie, chain after chain of them, directly across its way.   Paul Horgan

27c CONJUNCTIVE ADVERBS   *p or /;*

Use a semicolon with conjunctive adverbs.

Conjunctive adverbs are adverbs used as connectives: *therefore, however, nevertheless, furthermore, consequently, moreover, accordingly, besides,* as well as *hence, thus, indeed,* and *in fact.* The two statements they join are often linked by a **semicolon** rather than by a period. A period, nevertheless, would still be acceptable:

RIGHT: Business improved; **therefore**, we changed our plans.
ALSO RIGHT: Business improved. **Therefore**, we changed our plans.

RIGHT: The hall was empty; **nevertheless**, the curtain rose.
ALSO RIGHT: The hall was empty. **Nevertheless**, the curtain rose.

(1) Do not use just a comma with a conjunctive adverb. If a comma replaces the semicolon, the sentence turns into a **comma splice**:

COMMA SPLICE: The weather turned ugly, **therefore** the launch was postponed.
RIGHT: The weather turned ugly; **therefore,** the launch was postponed.

(2) If the conjunctive adverb moves, keep the semicolon at the juncture between the two clauses. Put the semicolon where the two clauses join, even if the connective follows later.

Demand had dropped off; **nevertheless,** prices remained high.
Demand had dropped off; prices, **nevertheless,** remained high.
Demand had dropped off; prices remained high, **nevertheless**.

RECOGNIZING CONJUNCTIVE ADVERBS

ADDITION:	furthermore, moreover, similarly, besides, likewise, also
LOGICAL RESULT:	therefore, consequently, accordingly, hence, thus, then
OBJECTION:	however, still, nevertheless, nonetheless, on the other hand
OPTION:	otherwise, instead
EMPHASIS:	indeed, in fact
TIME:	meanwhile, subsequently

---

(3) In relatively formal writing, use additional commas. Note the *two* additional commas when the conjunctive adverb interrupts the second clause.

FORMAL: We liked the area; rents**, however,** were impossible.
INFORMAL: We liked the area; rents **however** were impossible.

DISCOURSE EXERCISE 3 Write the italicized part of each combined sentence, adding punctuation as necessary. (Include the added commas that set off conjunctive adverbs from the second clause.) Do not add punctuation if a coordinator merely joins parts of a single clause.

EXAMPLE: Gershwin developed a brain *tumor and the studio* fired him.
ANSWER: tumor, and the studio

Hollywood and Small-Town America

1. Most early movie moguls came from immigrant *backgrounds but their pictures* showed a sanitized WASP America.

2. The cities were crowded with poor *immigrants therefore the movies showed idealized rural towns.*

3. These idyllic towns had white clapboard houses with *broad verandas and tidy streets* with quaint little shops.

4. The boys living in these houses looked like *Mickey Rooney so the studio* dyed Danny Kaye's hair blond.

5. Selfish people might cause *trouble the people of good will however always* win out in the end.

6. The banker might *be a skinflint a kindly Jimmy-Stewart type would best him nevertheless.*

7. Small-town values are *alive and well or our politicians* wouldn't cater to them so eagerly.

8. We dream of a more *innocent America for we want* a world without conflict, drugs, and crime.

27d | SUBORDINATORS | *p or ⌃*

Use a comma or no punctuation with subordinators.

Subordinating conjunctions (subordinators, for short) start **adverbial clauses** — clauses that tell us when, where, why, or how. Subordinators include words like *if, when, unless, because, although,* and *whereas.* An *if* or a *because* changes a self-sufficient, independent clause into a **dependent clause**, which normally cannot stand by itself. "If I were in charge" does not become a complete sentence until you answer the question "If you were in charge, *then what?*"

FRAGMENT: He failed the test. **Because he ran out of time.**
REVISED: He failed the test **because he ran out of time.**

(1) Use no comma when a restrictive clause comes last. A **restrictive** clause limits the scope of the main clause, imposing essential conditions. "I will raise wages" sounds like an unqualified promise. "I will raise wages *after we strike oil*" puts a restriction on

---

RECOGNIZING SUBORDINATORS

TIME AND PLACE:	when, whenever, while, before, after, since, until, as soon as, as long as, where, wherever
REASON OR CONDITION:	because, if, unless, provided
COMPARISON:	as, as though, as if
CONTRAST:	though, although, whereas, no matter how, even though
RESULT:	so that, in order that

---

the offer. Such restrictive clauses are essential to the meaning of the whole sentence.

RESTRICTIVE:	Hundreds will perish **if the dam breaks**.
	Gold prices rise **when the dollar falls**.
	They would not treat the patient **unless we signed a release**.

(2) Set off a nonrestrictive clause. Use a comma before *though, although,* and *whereas.* These introduce **nonrestrictive** material, which does not impose essential restrictions or conditions. Rather, they set up a contrast; both statements are separately true. Similarly, *whether or not* and *no matter how* show that the main statement is true regardless:

NONRESTRICTIVE:	Many applied for the job, **although the salary was low**.
	Reactors produce nuclear wastes, **whereas coal pollutes the air**.
	The figures were wrong, **no matter what the computer said**. (They were wrong *regardless*.)

(3) Set off any adverbial clause that comes first. When a subordinator joins two clauses, you can reverse their order. When the dependent clause comes first (restrictive or not), use a comma to show where the main clause starts:

COMMA: **If the dam breaks,** hundreds will perish.
After we noticed the police car, we drove more slowly.

Note special uses of some connectives: *though* used as a conjunctive adverb (with a semicolon); *however* used as a subordinator (with a comma):

Henry Ford II went to Yale**; he didn't graduate, though.**
(used like *however*)
His underlings could not please him**, however hard they tried.**
(used like *no matter how*)

27e | RELATIVE CLAUSES *p or ⌃*

Use commas or no punctuation with relative clauses.

Relative clauses are clauses that start with a **relative pronoun:** *who (whose, whom), which,* or *that.* Such clauses add information about one of the nouns (or pronouns) in the main part of the sentence. They may, therefore, appear at different points in the sentence, *interrupting* rather than following the main clause:

AT THE END: The odds favor candidates **who raise tons of money**.
They dug in Kenya**, which is rich in fossil remains**.
WEDGED IN: The address **that they gave us** does not exist.
Those **who know how to talk** can buy on credit. Creole proverb

(1) Do not set off restrictive relative clauses. They are **restrictive** when we need them to know "Which one?" or "What kind?"

Such relative clauses narrow the possibilities. They help us identify; they single out one person or group: the runner *who tripped*. Restrictive clauses are *essential* to the author's message.

NO COMMA:
People **who live in glass houses** should not throw stones.   (only those)
Call the woman **whose name appears on this card**. (only her)

Note: The pronoun *that* almost always introduces a restrictive clause. Shortened relative clauses with a pronoun like *that* or *whom* left out are always restrictive:

NO COMMA:
The forms **[that] we sent** were lost in the mail.
The lawyer **[whom] she recommended** charged large fees.

(2) Set off nonrestrictive relative clauses. A **nonrestrictive** clause does not single out one from a group or one group among many. We know which one or what kind; we merely learn more about something already identified: Beethoven, *who was deaf*; aspirin, *which kills pain*. Nonrestrictive clauses are *nonessential*; the essential point would come through without them.

COMMA:
Sharks differ from **whales, which surface to breathe**. (all do)
We drove down **Pennsylvania Avenue, which leads past the White House**.

Use *two* commas when the nonrestrictive clause interrupts the main clause:

TWO COMMAS:
Computers, **which perform amazing feats,** do break down.

Note: Punctuate other clauses that modify nouns as you would relative clauses. Sometimes a clause starting with *when, where,* or *why* modifies a noun:

RESTRICTIVE: The place **where I work** has no heat.   (which place?)
NONRESTRICTIVE: Minnesota, **where I was born**, has cold winters.

DISCOURSE EXERCISE 4   Write the italicized part of each sentence, adding a comma if and where needed.

EXAMPLE: Geological maps stay *the same whereas political* maps become obsolete.

ANSWER: the same, whereas political

The Politics of Maps

1.   Nations often change *place names that carry* an unwanted legacy from the past.
2.   *St. Petersburg which was the capital of Czarist Russia is* now Leningrad.
3.   English and French names were widely used *in Africa until the new nations* became independent.
4.   After the Belgians *left the Congo names like* Leopoldville disappeared.
5.   Maps no longer *show Rhodesia which was named* after a British explorer.
6.   Older names *usually survive only if they are not linked* with the colonial past.
7.   A Malaysian city had been named *after Jesselton who was a British empire builder*.
8.   The *city that bore his name is now* called Kinabalu.

| 27f | NOUN CLAUSES | *p* |

Do not set off noun clauses.

Use no punctuation when the place of a noun is taken by a clause within a clause. Clauses that take the place of a noun are called **noun clauses**:

NOUN: The mayor announced **her plans**.
NOUN CLAUSE: The mayor announced **that she would retire**.

NOUN: The *Post* first revealed **his identity**.
NOUN CLAUSE: The *Post* first revealed **who had leaked the news**.

Noun clauses start with words like *that, why, how, where, who,* and *which*: explain *why you came back*; ask her *where she lives*. Other words that might start a noun clause are *whoever, whatever, whichever*:

NOUN CLAUSE: They voted for **whomever the party picked**.

PEER EDITOR 5   Choose the right answer for the blank space left in each sentence. After the number of the sentence, write *C* for comma, *SC* for semicolon, or *No* for no punctuation.

1. She wasn't a big-time photographer _____ but she had enough work to keep up her studio.
2. Students who needed financial aid _____ were grilled like suspects in a bank robbery.
3. Space exploration is astronomically expensive _____ therefore, only the richest nations take part.
4. The new law aimed at drug dealers _____ who carry guns.
5. Lawmakers must stop computer crime _____ before it reaches epidemic proportions.
6. When meteors hit the surface _____ they form craters like those made by volcanoes.
7. Her parents tolerated her friends _____ though one was a body builder with a shaved head.
8. The plaintiff was never told _____ why the application was denied.
9. The sun, which is the final source of most of our energy _____ is a gigantic nuclear furnace.
10. Human beings could not survive on other planets _____ unless they created an artificial earthlike environment.

OVERVIEW   Modifiers help us build up the basic "Birds fly" sentence. Much of the added information that we feed into a short sentence blends in without a break:

NO COMMAS: Scientists have ridiculed newcomers.
STILL NO COMMAS: **Established** scientists have **often** ridiculed newcomers **with revolutionary new ideas**.

To use internal commas, you need to ask how essential a modifier is to the meaning of a sentence. **Restrictive** modifiers are essential to the sentence and are not set off. We use them to narrow the field: cars *built in Japan* (only those); students *eligible for aid* (only those).

Nonrestrictive modifiers merely add information about something already identified. They are set off by a comma, or *two* commas if they interrupt the sentence. They leave the term they follow unrestricted or generally applicable: the sparrow, *a pesky bird* (applies to all of them); soap operas, *watched by millions* (applies to the whole type).

28a | UNNECESSARY COMMAS   *p* |

Do not use commas between basic sentence elements.

Do not use a comma between the subject and its verb, or between the verb and one or more objects. In the following sentence, there should be no comma between the **compound** (or double) **subject** and the verb:

SUPERFLUOUS COMMA: Unfortunately, **information and common sense, do** not always **prevent** the irresponsible use of dangerous substances.

In addition, do *not* set off the many modifiers that blend into a simple sentence without a break. These include many single-word modifiers: adjectives and adverbs. They also include most prepositional phrases. (See the chart on p. 304.)

WRONG: Forms **with unanswered questions**, will be returned.
RIGHT: Forms **with unanswered questions** will be returned.

WRONG: The next Olympic Games were to be held, **in 1992**.
RIGHT: The next Olympic Games were to be held **in 1992**.

UNNECESSARY COMMAS — A SUMMARY

CAUTION: Avoid commas in the following situations. Omit the circled commas.

■ between subject and verb:

The needle on the dial⊘ **swung** erratically.

■ before an ordinary prepositional phrase:

She had first flown a plane⊘ **in Ohio** in 1972.

■ with restrictive modifiers and clauses:

The hunt was on for migrants⊘ **entering illegally**.
American diplomats⊘ **who speak Chinese**⊘ are rare.

■ with coordinators joining words or phrases:

The Vikings reached Greenland⊘ **and North America**.

■ after coordinators:

WRONG: He promised to call **but**⊘ he never did.
RIGHT: He promised to call, **but he never did**.

■ before coordinators joining two dependent clauses:

He told the court **that** the building had been only partially
insured⊘ **and that** the policy had lapsed.

■ before noun clauses:

We already know⊘ **what the future holds** for the poor.

■ after *such as:*

The new plan called for more teaching of basics, **such
as**⊘ English and algebra.

■ between adjective and noun:

Clint Eastwood movies are known for their crude, **brutal**⊘ **violence**.

■ after last items in a series:

Natives, tourists, **and pickpockets**⊘ mingled in the square.

28b	RESTRICTIVE AND NONRESTRICTIVE *p or ⌃*

Know when to use commas with modifiers.

Punctuation may be required when a modifier follows a noun (or a pronoun). **Restrictive** modifiers help us narrow the possibilities or single out one among several. They are an essential part of the sentence and are *not* set off:

RESTRICTIVE: Gamblers **willing to place $1,000 bets** were invited to the tournament. (only those)

Nonrestrictive modifiers merely give added information about something already identified. They are set off by a comma, or *two* commas if they interrupt the sentence. They leave the term they follow unrestricted or generally applicable:

NONRESTRICTIVE: My friends**, willing to risk a few quarters,** joined me in the casino. (They all joined in.)

(1) Set off most appositives. An **appositive** is a second noun that modifies the first. Most appositives are nonrestrictive. They do not winnow one possibility from among several; they answer questions like "*What else* about the person?" or "*What else* about the place?" ("Her aunt, *a lawyer*, lived in Boston, *my favorite city*.") A proper name is usually adequate identification, and the appositive that follows it is set off:

COMMA: She joined the Actors' Theater**, a repertory company**.
COMMAS: H. J. Heinz**, the Pittsburgh pickle packer,** keeps moving up in the food-processing industry.

Occasionally, however, a restrictive appositive helps us tell apart two people of the same name:

NO COMMAS: I find it hard to distinguish between Holmes **the author** and Holmes **the Supreme Court Justice**.

305

(2) Set off nonrestrictive verbals and verbal phrases. A **verbal phrase** modifying a noun usually starts with a form like *running, explaining, starting* or like *dressed, sold, taken*. Such phrases are restrictive when used to narrow a general term or single out one among several:

NO COMMAS: The person **running the place** talked like a drill sergeant.
The restaurant excluded guests **dressed in togas**.

Verbal phrases are *non*restrictive when they merely *tell us more* about something we have already identified:

COMMAS: We saw the bride, **dressed in white**.

(3) Set off nonrestrictive adjective phrases. An **adjective phrase** is made up of several adjectives, or of an adjective and other material:

RESTRICTIVE: We collected containers **suitable for recycling**.
(We discarded the others.)

NONRESTRICTIVE: The climbers, **weary but happy**, started down.
(applies to all the climbers)
We approached the lake, **smooth as a mirror**.
(We have already focused on one lake.)

(4) Use dashes to set off a modifier that already contains one or more commas. The **dashes** then signal the major breaks:

DASHES: Her sister — **a stubborn, hard-driving competitor** — won many prizes.

<table>
<tr><td>**28c**</td><td>SENTENCE MODIFIERS</td><td>*p or* ∧</td></tr>
</table>

Set sentence modifiers off by commas.

Modifiers may modify sentence elements other than nouns. They may also modify the sentence as a whole rather than any part of it.

(1) Verbals and verbal phrases modifying a verb may be either restrictive or nonrestrictive. Notice the **comma** showing the difference:

RESTRICTIVE: He always rushed into the office **reading from fan letters just received**.   (contains main point)

NONRESTRICTIVE: Deadline newspaper writing is rapid because it cheats, **depending heavily on clichés**.   (elaborates main point)

(2) Set off long introductory modifiers. Use a **comma** to show where the main sentence starts. Use this comma after prepositional phrases of three words or more:

COMMA: **Like many good reporters,** they deplored the low status of the journalistic rank and file.

Set off *introductory verbals and verbal phrases* even when they are short:

COMMA: **Smiling,** the officer tore up the ticket.
To start the motor, turn the ignition key.

(3) Always set off verbal phrases modifying the sentence as a whole. Such phrases are often called **absolute constructions**:

COMMA: **To tell you the truth,** I don't even recall his name.
Our new manager has done well, **considering her lack of experience**.

(4) If you wish, use the optional commas with transitional expressions. Expressions like *after all, of course, unfortunately, on the whole, as a rule,* and *certainly* often help us go on from one sentence to another. If you pause for such a modifier when reading, set it off by a comma:

COMMA: **After all,** we are in business for profit.
On the other hand, the records may never be found.
You will submit the usual reports, **of course**.

Sentence modifiers that are set off require *two* commas if they do not come first or last in the sentence:

COMMAS: A great many things, **to be sure,** could be said for him.

PEER EDITOR 6   Punctuate the following sentences. For each blank, write *C* for comma, *NC* for no comma, or *D* for dash.

1. In spite of repeated promises _____ the shipment never arrived.
2. Whipped by the wind _____ five-foot swells splash over the deck.
3. The book told the story of Amelia Earhart _____ a true pioneer.
4. An engraved receipt was promised to listeners _____ sending in large donations.
5. The owner, a large woman with mean eyes _____ watched us the whole time.
6. The city, on the other hand _____ has shown no interest in the proposed arena.
7. The mechanics working on a competitor's car _____ are racing against the clock.
8. The wooden benches, bolted to the planks _____ were torn loose by the waves.
9. My uncle—a jovial, fast-talking man _____ sold earthquake insurance.
10. Their performance has been unsatisfactory _____ to say the least.

---

29   **COORDINATION**

OVERVIEW   When we coordinate parts of a sentence, we make related sentence parts work together. We pull together information that might have appeared in separate statements: "The Russians took *first place*. They also took *second place*. And they took *third place*." Coordination enables us to line up the three related sentences in a single sentence: "The Russians finished *first, second, and third.*" The commas together with the coordinator *and* help us tie the three related sentence parts together.

| SERIES | *p or ⁁*

Use commas between items in a series.

A **series** is a set of three or more parts of the same kind: *red, white,* and *blue* (adjectives); *eat, drink,* and *be* merry (verbs); *life, liberty,* and the *pursuit* of happiness (nouns). Link the elements in a set of three by commas, with the last comma followed by an *and* or *or* that ties the whole group together. Not every series follows the simple one,-two,-and-three pattern:

(1) The basic *A, B, and C* pattern can be stretched to four elements or more:

COMMAS: The stand sold **nuts, raisins, apples,** and **every other kind** of organic lunch.

(2) Groups of words in a series may already contain commas. To prevent misreading, use **semicolons** to show the major breaks:

SEMICOLONS: Three people were left out of her will: **John, her greedy brother; Martin, her no-account nephew;** and **Helen, her one-time friend**.

PEER EDITOR 7 Rewrite the following sentences, adding *series punctuation* and other needed marks.

1. In the tabloids homelessness the national debt and economic disaster do not exist.

COORDINATION — AN OVERVIEW

SERIES:	Russian gymnasts finished **first, second, and third.**
INTERCHANGEABLE ADJECTIVES:	**slanted, sensational** reporting
DATES:	It was **Monday, December 5, 1983.**
ADDRESSES:	They lived at **48 Broadway, Phoenix, Arizona.**
MEASURES:	It stood **three feet, five inches** high.
CONTRAST:	**People, not things,** should come first.
ENUMERATION:	Different sports become popular: **soccer, jogging, lacrosse.**

---

2. The room is fitted with three turntables a huge electric clock and a cantilevered microphone over a console of switches buttons and dials.
3. For their new friends yoga was a way of life a cause and a religion.
4. Advertising sells good services candidates and ideas.
5. After a while the messenger arrives with the cholesterol special a triple order of bacon two fried eggs over easy and bagels split and buttered.

29b | COORDINATE ADJECTIVES   *p or* ∧

Use a comma between coordinate adjectives.

Coordinate adjectives work together to modify the same noun: a *tall, handsome* stranger. They are interchangeable adjectives; use a comma between them when you can reverse their order: *slanted, sensational* reporting or *sensational, slanted* reporting. Use the comma only when an *and* could take the place of the comma:

RIGHT: a **disappointed, angry** customer   (both disappointed and angry)

CAUTION: Often an adjective combines with a noun to indicate a type of person or object: a *public servant*, a *short story*, a *black market*. An adjective that comes before such a combination modifies the combination as a whole.

NO COMMA: a **long** *short story* (not "long *and* short")
              a **dedicated** *public servant* (not "dedicated *and* public")

29c | DATES AND ADDRESSES   *p or ⌐*

Use commas with information in several parts.

Dates, addresses, page references, and the like often come in several parts, kept separate from each other by a comma. The last item is followed by a comma if the sentence continues:

DATE: On **March 28, 1979,** several water pumps stopped working at Three Mile Island, a nuclear power plant near Harrisburg, Pennsylvania.

ADDRESS: Please send my mail to **113 Robin Street, Birdsville, Alabama,** starting the first of the month.

REFERENCE: The quotation is from **Chapter 5, page 43, line 7,** of the second volume.

Remember the comma that separates city and state: *Chicago, Illinois; New York, New York*. Commas also separate the parts of *measurements* employing more than one unit of measurement. Here the last item is usually *not* separated from the rest of the sentence:

MEASURE: The boy is now **five feet, seven inches** tall.
                Nine pounds, three ounces is an unusual weight for this
                fish.

Note: The comma is left out if the day of the month precedes
rather than follows the month: "12 November 1991."

29d | REPETITION AND CONTRAST   *p or* ∧

Use commas to signal repetition or contrast.

Use commas between expressions that repeat the same idea:

REPETITION: **Produce, produce!** This is the law among artists.
RESTATEMENT: We were there in the nine days before Christmas, **the
                Navidad**.

Use commas also to separate words or phrases that establish a
contrast:

CONTRAST: The prices were **stunning,** the food **average**.
                We should **welcome, not discourage,** dissent.

29e | ENUMERATION   *:/or* ∧

Use a colon or comma to introduce details.

We often need punctuation when we continue a sentence to
illustrate (give examples) or to enumerate (list several items).

**(1) Use the colon to introduce an explanation or a more
detailed list for something already mentioned. The colon then
means "as follows":**

EXPLANATION: Marcia had a single wish: **a home computer.**

LIST: Military life abounds with examples of regimentation: **fixed hours, a rigid meal schedule, the dress code.**

Avoid a colon after a verb:

WRONG: His two mistakes were: obeying orders and offending Congress.

RIGHT: His two mistakes were obeying orders and offending Congress.

(2) Use a comma when explanation or illustration follows transitional expressions. Use the comma before *such as* or *especially*:

COMMA: They studied computer languages**, such as** Fortran.

TWO COMMAS: Recent immigrants**, especially** Vietnamese, now live downtown.

Use a comma before and after *namely, for example, for instance,* and *that is*:

TWO COMMAS: American colleges neglect major world languages**, for example, Chinese and Russian.**

DISCOURSE EXERCISE 8 Rewrite the following sentences, adding all necessary punctuation.

The Buck Starts Here

1. The Bureau of Engraving and Printing in Washington D.C. and the mints in Philadelphia Pennsylvania and Denver Colorado are the nation's money factories.

2. For Americans today money is the ticket to the good life not the source of all evil.

3. Part of the Bureau's job is to replace currency that has been torn burned soaked and chewed.

4. Banks weed out bills too limp too faded or too creased to be of further use.

5. Citizens from Columbia South Carolina and Corpus Christi Texas send in evidence of lost currency incinerated mattresses scorched filing cabinets and a cow's stomach with the remains of several hundred dollars.

6. The Philadelphia mint produces 35 million sparkling gleaming coins a day.

7. Inspectors weed out mistakes such as one-dollar bills with the five-dollar imprint on the back.

8. Collectors pay good money for botched coins for example off-center pennies.

OVERVIEW Use dashes, parentheses, or commas to set off parenthetic elements — elements that interrupt the normal flow of thought. They suspend the normal traffic of sentence elements for a while the way an officer might briefly halt motor traffic to let a pedestrian cross.

30a   DASHES   *p or —/*

Use the dash — sparingly — to signal a sharp break.

A speaker may pause for dramatic effect. Or a speaker may stop in the middle of a sentence to supply some missing detail or additional clarification. In writing, set such material off from the rest of a sentence by **dashes** (made up of two hyphens in typed manuscript). Note: Overuse of the dash creates a disjointed, thinking-out-loud effect.

(1) Make a word or phrase stand out for emphasis. Use the dash (or dashes) to produce a dramatic or climactic effect:

PARENTHETIC ELEMENTS — AN OVERVIEW

SHARP BREAK: He opened the door — **a serious mistake**.

ASIDE: The trophy **(her first)** stood on the mantelpiece.

DIRECT ADDRESS: Your friends, **John,** are worried about you.

COMMENT: The loan was denied, **it seems**.

TAG OPENING: **No,** she is not here.

TAG QUESTION: She is your friend, **isn't she**?

UNUSUAL ORDER: Work, **for her father's generation,** was a religion.

DRAMATIC BREAK: Every time we look at one of the marvels of modern technology, we find a by-product — **unintended, unpredictable, and often lethal**.

It seems possible that two billion people — **half of the human beings on earth** — would be destroyed in a thermonuclear war.

(2) Set off a complete sentence that interrupts another sentence. (Note that the first word of the interrupting sentence is *not* capitalized.)

INSERTED POINT: The cranes — **these birds were last sighted three years ago** — settled down on the marsh.

(3) Set off modifiers that already contain internal commas. Dashes then signal the stronger breaks:

COMMAS IN MODIFIER: The old-style family — **large, closely knit, firmly ruled by the parents** — is becoming rare.

(4) Set off a list that interrupts rather than follows a clause.

INSERTED LIST: The group sponsored performers—**dancers, poets, musicians**—from around the world.

(5) After an introductory list, show where the sentence starts over with a summarizing *all,* *these,* **or** *those:*

LIST FIRST: **Arabs, Japanese, Vietnamese, South Americans**—all these are a familiar part of the campus scene.

| PARENTHESES | *p or* /( ) |

Use parentheses for less important material (or asides).

Parentheses are useful in the following situations:

(1) Use parentheses for a quick interspersed explanation or clarification:

QUICK HELP: The lowest forms of life, such as the amoebae, normally **(that is, barring accidents)** do not die.   Susanne K. Langer

(2) Use parentheses for optional backup information. Use parentheses around dates, addresses, page references, chemical formulas, and similar information if it might interest some readers but is not an essential part of the text: (*p. 34*) (*first published in 1910*) (*now called Market Street*).

CAUTION: When the inserted aside is a complete sentence (*this is an example*), do not capitalize the first word. When a sentence in parentheses begins *after* end punctuation, end punctuation is required inside the final parenthesis:

INSIDE: Local British soccer teams were banned from the continent. **(The national team was allowed to play.)**

30c | COMMAS FOR PARENTHETIC
ELEMENTS   *p or ⌄*

Use a comma, or commas, to signal slight interruptions.

Use commas with parenthetic elements that blend into a sentence with only a slight break.

(1) Use commas when you address the reader or comment on what you are saying:

DIRECT ADDRESS: Few remember**, dear reader,** the crash of 1929.
COMMENT: Romance**, it seems,** is not the same as a relationship.

(2) Use commas to set off introductory tags. These include greetings and exclamations, as well as an introductory *yes* or *no*. Such introductory tags frequently precede a statement in conversation and in informal writing:

TAG OPENING: **Why,** 'tis a loving and a fair reply. *Hamlet*

(3) Use commas to set off echo questions. Such **tag questions** are often added to a statement to ask for agreement or confirmation:

TAG QUESTION: They signed the agreement**, didn't they?**

(4) Use commas for slight breaks caused by unusual word order.

UNUSUAL ORDER: Laws**, to be cheerfully obeyed,** must be both just and practicable.

DISCOURSE EXERCISE 9 Rewrite the italicized part of each sentence, adding all necessary punctuation.

EXAMPLE: *Fusion (the philosopher's stone of modern alchemists promises* unlimited cheap and safe energy.

ANSWER: Fusion (the philosopher's stone of modern alchemists) promises

Running Out of Energy

1. Most of the energy we use — whether *from coal oil or water ultimately comes* from the sun.

2. We use up our fossil *fuels (as ecologists have told us for years at an alarming rate*

3. Politicians (and investors) talk less now about alternative *sources (wind power solar energy*

4. Geothermal power in one's backyard, unless there is *a geyser on the property is just not feasible.*

5. *Nuclear power though first heralded* as a boon to humanity, has become a huge headache for utility companies.

6. Nuclear fuel would create an enormous waste problem (as indeed *there is already with our existing uranium plants*

7. *Americans Russians Germans the French these and other nations are* having second thoughts about the atom.

8. New parties like the Greens clamor for nuclear-free zones. *(The Greens are German environmentalists*

PEER EDITOR 10 Copy the following sentences, adding all punctuation needed for *parenthetic elements*.

1. Why this town my friends has weathered far worse storms.

2. Well Your Honor that is only one version of the incident. Other witnesses you realize have told a different story.

3. To change the rules all the time we revised them twice last year does not make sense does it?

4. Well this theory it seems to me was rejected long ago.

QUOTATION

OVERVIEW We use **direct quotation** when we quote someone verbatim, word for word. Direct quotation ranges from complete sentences or longer passages to quoted words or phrases:

FULL QUOTATION: Mark Twain said, "One man's comma is another man's colon."

PARTIAL QUOTATION: One engineer called the company's drug-testing program "a paranoid overreaction."

We use **indirect quotation** when we put someone else's ideas in our own words. In indirect quotation, we do *not* use quotation marks. We rely on an introductory source statement or credit tag to inform the reader who is likely to ask: "Who said?"

INDIRECT QUOTATION: The National Academy of Sciences reports that the cholesterol we were supposed to give up may not be bad for us after all.

31a | DIRECT QUOTATION   *p or "/*

Use quotation marks when you repeat someone's exact words.

Use a comma to separate the quotation from the **credit tag**—the statement that identifies the source. Use a colon for a more formal or emphatic introduction:

COMMA: The Irish essayist Robert Lynd once said, "The last person in the world whose opinion I would take on what to eat would be a doctor."
           "News stories deal with food as if it were a foreign agent," the article said.

COLON: The rule says: "No tools will be taken from this building."

PUNCTUATING QUOTATIONS — AN OVERVIEW

STANDARD:	Keats said, "Truth is beauty."
FORMAL:	The rules were explicit: "No guns allowed."
QUOTED PHRASE:	The cry of "Yanks go home" was heard again.
SPLIT QUOTATION:	"Today," she said, "we start anew."
	"We accept," she said. "We cannot wait."
QUOTE-WITHIN-QUOTE:	He said, "Stop calling me 'Honey.'"
QUOTED QUESTION:	She always asked, "Where were you?"
QUESTIONED QUOTE:	Did she really say, "I don't care"?
OMISSION:	The law says: "All businesses . . . require a license."
ADDITION:	The entry read: "My birthday [April 4] was a disaster."
INDIRECT:	He always asked where I had been.

---

(1) Check punctuation if the credit tag interrupts a quotation. Use commas before and after if the credit tag splits one complete sentence:

COMMAS: "Both marijuana and alcohol," **Dr. Jones reports,** "slow reaction times on a whole spectrum of tasks."

Use a comma before and a period (or semicolon) after if the credit tag splits two complete sentences. Avoid a **comma splice**:

COMMA SPLICE: "Language habits are changing," the article said, "a lover is now a significant other."

PERIOD: "Language habits are changing," the article said. "Love is now a relationship."

SEMICOLON: "Language habits are changing," the article said; "forming close ties is now called bonding."

No comma is required when the credit tag follows a question or exclamation:

NO COMMA: "To rest is to rust!" the poster said.

(2) Use no comma with partial quotations. Use no comma when you quote only part of a sentence, or when a very short quoted sentence becomes part of a larger statement:

NO COMMA: Goodman said that food should not be considered a po-
              tential poison; it "should be eaten and enjoyed."
              "The small family lives better" was the official slogan of
              the campaign to curb population growth.

(3) Use single quotation marks when you shift to a quotation within a quotation:

SINGLE MARKS: As Goodman says, "The urge to take charge of our lives
               has led us headlong into the arms of the 'experts.'"

(4) Type long quotations as block quotations. Set off quotations of more than four typed lines — *no* quotation marks, indented *ten* spaces. Do not indent the first line of such **block quotations**:

```
The sense of outrage felt by the relatives of vic-
tims was expressed by David H. Berg, a criminal law-
yer, in an article in Newsweek:
←———————→A deputy sheriff held my brother's skull
(10 spaces)  for a photograph that appeared in the cen-
             ter of the front page. . . .  The suffer-
             ing of my family is not unique.  Someone
             is murdered by a gunshot every 48 minutes
             in America, about 10,000 people a year, a
             figure that has quadrupled since my broth-
             er's death.
```

Note: Set off lines of poetry as block quotations, but center them on the page (indent fewer than ten spaces if necessary). You may run in one or two lines of poetry with your continuous text. A **slash** (with a space on either side) then shows where a new line begins:

RUN-IN: With her usual gift for upsetting conventional expectations, Plath makes the rat seem amusing and harmless: "Droll, vegetarian, the water rat **/** Saws down a reed. . . ."

| END MARKS IN QUOTATIONS *p or "/* |

End quotations correctly.

Remember to use quotation marks to *end* your quotation, and know where to place them in relation to other marks.

(1) Keep commas inside, semicolons outside a quotation:

COMMA: As he said, "Don't worry about me," the boat pulled away.

SEMICOLON: You said, "I don't need sympathy"; therefore, I didn't offer any.

(2) Keep end punctuation inside the quotation except in special situations. Make sure a period comes before a final quotation mark:

PERIOD: The letter said: "You have been selected to receive a valuable gift."

Usually, a question mark or exclamation mark will also come before the final quotation mark. However, keep it *outside* the quotation if you are asking a question or exclaiming about the quotation:

QUOTED QUESTION:	He asked, "Where are they now?"
QUESTIONED QUOTE:	Who said, "To err is human"?
QUOTED SHOUT:	She shouted: "The dam broke!"
SHOUTED QUOTE:	He actually said, "You don't count"!

(3) Do not normally duplicate a terminal mark at the end of a quotation. Use only one question mark when you ask a question about a question:

Did you ever ask, "What can I do to help?"

DISCOURSE EXERCISE 11 Rewrite the italicized part of each sentence to add marks needed for satisfactory punctuation of *quoted material*.

EXAMPLE: Tabloids love headlines like "Fergie Pregnant *with Sextuplets?*

ANSWER: with Sextuplets?"

Alien Space Mummy Found in Glass Coffin

1. A recent article in *Smithsonian* magazine was titled: "With Tabloids, 'Zip! You're *in Another World!*
2. The world of tabloids is what science fiction writers call a "parallel *universe*
3. In the words of the *Smithsonian* author, "It's like ours, but *with more gusto!*
4. "Cave Explorers Find *Alien Mummy! proclaimed one* screaming headline.
5. The article claimed that a Turkish scientist had found a humanlike creature with green skin and wings "in a glass coffin that dates back to the *Ice Age*

6. "With a creature such *as this the scientist said I'm not* at all certain it really is dead."
7. "300-lb. Mom Swaps Twins *for Cookies said another* recent headline.
8. Who could pass up another recent classic, "Woman *Eaten by Pigs*

31c   INSERTIONS AND OMISSIONS   *p or "/*

Show changes you have made in the original text.

Signal insertions and omissions:

(1) Identify comments of your own. Put them in **square brackets**:

ADDITION: The note read: "Left Camp B Wednesday, April 3 [actually April 4]. Are trying to reach Camp C before we run out of supplies."

If your keyboard does not have square brackets, compose them by using a slash and two horizontal lines:

```
In the words of the judge, "the members of the tribe   /‾the
Paiutes̲/  were denied their treaty rights."
```

(2) Show that you have left out unnecessary or irrelevant material. Indicate the omission by three spaced periods (called an **ellipsis**):

OMISSION: The report concluded on an optimistic note: "All three patients . . . are making remarkable progress toward recovery."

If the omission occurs after a complete statement in the original text, use a sentence period and then add the ellipsis. (Use four spaced periods if you leave out a whole sentence.)

| **31d** | INDIRECT QUOTATION | *p or "/* |

Use no quotation marks when quoting in your own words.

In an **indirect quotation,** you look at the time frame and the people from your (and not the original author's) perspective. "She said, 'I adore you'" becomes "She said *she adored me.*"

(1) Use no comma when an indirect quotation becomes a noun clause. Indirectly quoted statements are often noun clauses introduced by *that.* Indirectly quoted questions are often noun clauses introduced by words like *whether, why, how,* and *which.* Remember: *No* introductory comma or colon, *no* quotation marks.

DIRECT: The mayor replied, "I doubt the wisdom of such a move."
INDIRECT: The mayor replied **that she doubted the wisdom of such a move**.

(2) Use a comma (or commas) when an indirect quotation is introduced or interrupted by a parenthetical credit tag.

COMMA: **According to the mayor,** the initiative was a foolish move.
COMMAS: Which of the drawings, **he wondered**, did I like best?

DISCOURSE EXERCISE 12   The following quotations are from Richard Rodriguez' *Hunger of Memory.* Convert all sentences to *indirect quotation* (but keep special quoted phrases in quotation marks).

325

A Bilingual Childhood

1. Richard Rodriguez remembers: "I was a bilingual child, but of a certain kind: 'socially disadvantaged.'"
2. He tells us: "I had been preceded by my older brother and sister to a neighborhood Roman Catholic school."
3. He was surprised: "I was fated to be the 'problem student.'"
4. Rodriguez says about his family: "We were the foreigners on the block."
5. Speaking Spanish at home, he and his family felt: "We are speaking now the way we never speak out in public — we are together."

Use quotation marks or italics for special words.

Set off the following:

(1) Use quotation marks for an expression that is not your own:

IRONIC: At a New York restaurant, lone diners share companionship over pasta at a special **"friendship table."**

Avoid apologetic quotation marks for slang or offensive language:

APOLOGETIC: Many skilled positions have been "infiltrated" by women.
BETTER: Many skilled positions have been filled by women.

(2) Use quotation marks or italics for technical words and words discussed as words. Italics are shown by underlining in a typed paper:

TECHNICAL: She described the "Skinner box," a device used by be-
haviorist psychologists.

WORD AS WORD: The word *comet* comes from the Greek *aster kometes,*
meaning long-haired star.

(3) Use italics to identify foreign words. Italicize words borrowed from foreign languages but not yet fully assimilated:

FOREIGN: For a Bolivian *campesino,* the pay for a bird for the illegal
parrot trade is not bad.

Many legal and scientific terms from Latin or Greek are in this
category:

LEGAL: A writ of *certiorari* is used by a superior court to obtain
judicial records from an inferior court.

BOTANICAL: The California live oak — *Quercus agrifolia* — began to
evolve more than ten million years ago.

31f | TITLES OR NAMES SET OFF *"/ or ital*

Use quotation marks or italics to set off titles or names.

Know the kinds of titles and names that need to be set off:

**(1) Distinguish between whole publications and their
parts.** Put quotation marks around the titles of poems, articles, songs,
and other pieces that would normally be *part* of a larger publication
("The Tiger"). Italicize (underline in typing) the title of a *complete*
publication — a magazine, newspaper, or book (*The Poems of William
Blake*).

PUBLICATION: Joan Didion's "Notes of a Native Daughter" was reprinted in *Slouching Towards Bethlehem*.

Do *not* use italics when naming the Bible or its parts (or other sacred writings: Talmud, Koran).

SCRIPTURE: She opened the Bible and read from the Book of Job.

(2) Italicize the titles of works of art or entertainment. Italicize (underline) the titles of plays, major musical works including operas and ballets, movies, television and radio programs, and such works of art as paintings and sculptures:

ENTERTAINMENT: My aunt wanted us to watch *Romeo and Juliet* or *Swan Lake* rather than *I Love Lucy* or *The Price Is Right*.
ART: Every summer, an army of tourists troops past the *Mona Lisa*.

(3) Italicize the names of ships and aircraft. Italicize (underline) the names of ships and other craft, including space vehicles, planes, or trains: the *Queen Mary, Apollo IX,* the *Hindenburg*.

FOR MORE ON ITALICS, SEE 38d.

PEER EDITOR 13   Rewrite the following sentences, *setting off words and phrases* as needed.

1.   In the chapter titled Pestilence in her History of Medieval Europe, Grumberg blames the black rat for the spread of the plague.
2.   Our word assassin, from the Arabic hashshashin, originally meant hashish smoker.
3.   The loss of the Titanic, the Hindenburg, or the Challenger seems pale when compared with disaster movies like The Poseidon Adventure or The Towering Inferno.

4. Adrienne Rich reexamined the novel Jane Eyre in an essay titled Jane
    Eyre: The Temptations of a Motherless Woman, included in her col-
    lection On Lies, Secrets, and Silence.
5. The Los Angeles Times, in an editorial titled A Face from the Past,
    called the appointment a setback for glasnost and perestroika.

8

SPELLING HELP

Note: The following is a quick rundown of minimum proficiencies in the area covered in this chapter. Remember that there is much more to good writing than meeting minimum standards. However, if you fail to meet the standards summarized here, your message may not reach the reader and you may not get credit for what you do well.

Work on the several dozen most predictable spelling problems. Go over them again and again — till you can type the correct spelling in your sleep.

(1) Never misspell the dozen unforgivables. Learn to cope with them by using memory devices (or learner's crutches) like the following:

definitely	It's **it** in definite. (We definitely need a definitive definition.)
receive	*E* first after *c*. (The receptionist received the receipts for the day's receipts.)
separate	She played below **par** on separate days. (The separation led to separate rooms.)
believe	Look for the **Eve** in believe. (The beliefs were believable to the true believer.)
similar	Similar is similar to popular. (Similar — dissimilar — similarities)
athlete	Do not spell with *e* before *l*. (The athletic athlete loved athletics.)

perform	Not **pre** but **per** in **per**form. (The **per**former **per**formed in a **per**fect **per**formance.)
basically	**Basic** plus **-ally**. (Basic/basic**ally**, accident/accident**ally**, incident/incident**ally**)
writing	**Writing** rhymes with **biting**; **written** rhymes with **bitten**.
used to	Get use**d** to the **-d** in use**d** to. (They use**d** to sell use**d** cars.)
a lot	Not to be used a whole **lot** — and then always *two* words. (The builder paid **a lot** for **a lot**.)
could have	Never use *could of/might of/should of*. RIGHT: could **have** written, might **have** tried, should **have** called.

(2) Know the troublesome doubles. Several pairs of sound-alikes trip the unwary:

accept/except	You **ex**cept something when you make an **ex**ception — you take something *out*. You **ac**cept something when you receive something willingly — you take something *in*.
affect/effect	Late papers may **af**fect a grade. (They change it *in part*.) We put a new law into **ef**fect (in its *entirety*).
conscious/ conscience	When we are con**scious**, we are *aware* (and when we are uncon**scious**, we are not). Our con**science** makes us feel *guilty* when we do something wrong.
to/too	**To** often means *toward*: **to** town, **to** school, **to** bed. Double the *o* when you are talking about *degree*: **too** much, **too** soon, **too** hot.
then/than	**Then** tells us wh**en** (th**en** and now). Th**an** helps us compare (larger th**an** life, sweeter th**an** wine).
there/their	**There** tells us wh**ere** (here and th**ere**; th**ere**'s no th**ere** there). Th**eir** tells us *whose* (they and th**eir** friends, players and th**eir** coaches). They're is short for *they are* (they're friends).

(3) After a single stressed vowel, double a final consonant when adding endings like - *er*, - *ed*, - *ing*, or - *ance*. Write occur but occurred, stop but stopped, plan but planning, occur but occurrence.

■ Double only at the end of a *stressed* syllable: perMIT and permiTTED, but EDit and Edited. Watch especially: reFER and reFERRED but REFerence.

■ Do not double after a double vowel (b*oa*t/b*oa*ting, sw*oo*n/sw*oo*ned, l*ea*d/l*ea*der) or after a long vowel signaled by a silent -*e* (hop*e*/hoping). Watch especially: write and writing but written.

(4) Work on the top sixty. Have someone dictate the following sentences to you, and make a list of all the words you misspell. Work on them till they no longer give you trouble.

The *independent candidate* cared for the *environment*.
Huge *debts* were owed by *foreign governments*.
They *preferred studying* in the *library*.
She will *probably* need the same *quantity* in *February*.
I *doubted* that she considered *criticism indispensable*.
Amateurs benefited more than other *athletes*.
The *committee* heard every *conceivable opinion*.
Manufacturers developed a new *device*.
We kept all *business decisions confidential*.
Her *appearance was definitely* a *surprise*.
She *accused* her *opponent* of *hypocrisy*.
The *absence* of *controls* proved *disastrous*.
We met a *prominent professor* of *psychology*.
Their *marriage succeeded exceptionally* well.
These *privileges* are *undoubtedly unnecessary*.
The *sponsor* was *dissatisfied* with the *performance*.
Their *approach* was *strictly practical*.
Companies can seldom just *eliminate* the *competition*.
A *repetition* of the *tragedy* is *inevitable*.
This *subtle difference* is *irrelevant*.

32 **SPELLING PROBLEMS**

OVERVIEW Poor spelling, like static, comes between you and the audience. Advice like the following should help you develop good spelling habits:

(1) Check for the true unforgivables. A handful of common words again and again trip up the poor speller. Copy them, read them over, spell them out — until the correct spelling becomes second nature:

accept	definite	occurred	probably
all right	environment	occurrence	receive
a lot	believe	perform	similar
athlete	conscience	preferred	studying

(2) Start a record of your own personal spelling problems. Whenever a piece of writing is returned to you, write down all the words that you misspelled.

(3) Fix each word firmly in your mind. At each sitting, take up a group of ten or twenty spelling words. Try putting them on a set of small note cards that you can carry around with you. Run your eyes over each word until you can see both the individual letters and the whole word at the same time. If you learn mainly by ear, read each word aloud. Then spell each letter individually: *Receive* — R-E-C-E-I-V-E. If you learn best when you can bring your nerves and muscles into play, try writing each word in large letters. Trace it over several times.

(4) Make use of memory devices. Remember the following, or make up your own:

all right:	ALL RIGHT means ALL is RIGHT.
beginning:	There's an INNING in begINNING.
business:	The drive-IN stayed IN busINess.
criticism:	There's a CRITIC in CRITICism.
environment:	There's IRON in the envIRONment.

government:	People who GOVERN are a GOVERNment.
library:	The LiBRarians BRought BRicks for the LIBRARY.
surprise:	The SURfer had a SURprise.
villain:	There's a VILLA in VILLAin.

32a | SPELLING AND PRONUNCIATION   *sp*

Watch for differences between speech and writing.

Some words become spelling problems because the gap between spelling and pronunciation is unusually wide.

(1) Watch for sounds not clearly heard in informal speech.

accident**a**lly	can**d**idate	library
basic**a**lly	government	proba**b**ly
Feb**r**uary	incident**a**lly	quan**t**ity

(2) Watch for silent consonants. Know how to spell the following:

SILENT LETTERS: | condem**n** | de**b**t | mortgage |
| forei**g**n | dou**b**t | soverei**g**n |

(3) Watch for vowels in unstressed positions. The vowels *a*, *e*, and *i* blur in endings like *-ate* and *-ite*, *-ant* and *-ent*. As a memory aid, link the word with a close cousin: *definite* (defin*i*tion); *indispensable* (dispens*a*ry).

a: accept**able**, accept**ance**, advis**able**, attend**ance**, attend**ant**, brilli**ant**, perform**ance**

e: consist**ent**, excell**ence**, excell**ent**, exist**ence**, experi**ence**, independ**ent**, persist**ent**, tend**ency**

i: irresist**ible**, plaus**ible**, poss**ible**, suscept**ible**

(4) Never write *of* for *have* in combinations like *could have been* and *might have been*.

WRONG:	could of been	should of known	might of failed
RIGHT:	could **have** been	should **have** known	might **have** failed

---

32b	VARIANT FORMS	*vp*

Watch for different forms of the same word.

Some words are confusing because they appear in different forms.

(1) Watch out for different spellings of the same root. The root *-cede* is spelled with a single *e* in *secede* (from the union), *precede* (causing a *precedent*), and *intercede* (stepping in). However, *exceed* and *proceed* have a double *e*, as do the *proceeds* of a sale. (Then, the double *e* disappears again in *procedure*.) Watch out for similar pairs:

till/until:	**till** dark	but	**until** dark
four/forty:	**four** and **fourteen**	but	**forty** thieves
nine/ninth:	**nine** and **ninety**	but	the **Ninth** Symphony

(2) Know how to spell pairs representing different parts of speech. For instance, when we *absorb* something well (verb), the result is complete *absorption* (noun). Study similar pairs:

advise/advice: We **advise** somebody (verb), but we give **advice** (noun).

conscience/conscientious: If we are not **conscientious** (adjective), we may suffer from a bad **conscience** (noun).

genius/ingenious: A clever person is not a **genius** (noun) but merely **ingenious** (adjective).

pronounce/pronunciation: When I **pronounce** a word wrong (verb), you may correct my **pronunciation** (noun).

Also: *courteous/courtesy, curious/curiosity, generous/generosity.*

(3) Change a spelling to show a change in grammatical form. For instance, we "ch*oo*se" and "l*ea*d" in the present, but we "ch*o*se" and "l*e*d" in the past. Some plurals trip up the unwary: one *man* but several *men*, one *woman* but several *women*. Similarly, we write one *freshman* but several *freshmen*, one *Irishman* but several *Irishmen*.

■ Most words like *piano* simply add *-s* for the plural (*pianos, radios, studios, rodeos, sopranos*). Some words ending in *-o* add *-es* instead:

SINGULAR:	hero	potato	tomato	veto
PLURAL:	hero**es**	potato**es**	tomato**es**	veto**es**

■ Most words like *roof* simply add *-s* for the plural (*roofs, chiefs, chefs, reefs, beliefs*). Some words change the final *-f* to *-ves*:

SINGULAR:	life	wife	calf	wolf	knife	loaf
PLURAL:	li**ves**	wi**ves**	cal**ves**	wol**ves**	kni**ves**	loa**ves**

Be sure to add the *-ed* (or *-d*) for *past tense* or *past participle* in words like the following:

used to:	He use**d** to sell used cars.
supposed to:	She was suppose**d** to be opposed.
prejudiced:	They were prejudice**d** (biase**d**) against me.

Note: For some nouns, two different spellings are acceptable for the plural: zero/zero**s** or zero**es**, buffalo/buffalo**s** or buffalo**es**, cargo/cargo**s** or cargo**es**, tornado/tornado**s** or tornado**es**; scarf/scarf**s** or scar**ves**, hoof/hoof**s** or hoo**ves**, elf/elf**s** or el**ves**, wharf/wharf**s** or whar**ves**.

SPELLING PRACTICE 1 What form of the missing word would fit the context? Write the missing form after the number of the sentence.

1. use   China _____ to experience large-scale famines.

2. woman   We recognized the voices of several of the _____ .

3. freshman   A _____ was expected to live in the dorms.
4. prejudice   The townspeople were _____ against the new immigrants.
5. pronounce   The French teacher kept correcting my _____ .
6. advise   Her counselors had given Donna bad _____ .
7. hero   The new movies presented vigilantes as _____ .
8. woman   The convention chose a _____ for its vice-presidential candidate.

CONFUSING PAIRS

Watch for words that sound similar or alike.

accept/except	**accept** responsibility (take it on); make an **except**ion (take it out)
Capitol/capital	the **Capitol** (buildings) is in the **capital**
cite/site/sight	**cited** for careless driving (give a **citation**), the **site** of the new school (where it is **situated**), the miracle of **sight**
conscious/conscience	we are **conscious** (aware); we have a **conscience** (moral sense)
council/counsel	**councilors** are part of the city **council**; camp **counselors counsel** young people
desert/dessert	**deserts** appear on maps, **desserts** on menus (and when a friend **deserts** us, we hope he will get his just **deserts**)
effect/affect	it has **effects** (results); it **affects** (alters) my grade

lose/loose	win or **lose**; fast and **loose**
personal/personnel	a **personal** (private) matter; a **personnel** (staff) matter
presents/presence	bring **presents** (gifts); **presence** or absence
principal/principle	the **principal's** office, the **principal** (main) reason; against my **principles** (convictions)
quite/quiet	**quite** (entirely) true; peace and **quiet**
than/then	bigger **than** life (comparison); now and **then** (time)
there/their	here and **there**; they and **their** friends
to/too	back **to** Georgia (direction); **too** much **too** soon (degree); you **too** (also)
whether/weather	**whether** or not (choice); foul **weather** (climate)

SPELLING PRACTICE 2   Write the choice that fits the context.

1. The governor *accepted/excepted* the resignation of two top aides.
2. The decision *affected/effected* thousands of commuters.
3. Macbeth was tormented by a guilty *conscious/conscience*.
4. Marcel was *to/too* tall to play Napoleon.
5. Brokers know dozens of ways to *lose/loose* money.
6. Basques invoked the *principal/principle* of self-determination.
7. Several people had parked *their/there* motorcycles in the driveway.
8. No one knew *whether/weather* we could meet the deadline.
9. Anything was better *then/than* going back down the mountain.
10. Most farms were *then/than* family-owned.
11. He always lectured us about sound business *principles/principals*.
12. She cherished the *quiet/quite* moments between visits.

OVERVIEW Spelling rules help you memorize words that follow a common pattern. Let a few simple rules help you with some familiar spelling problems.

33a | *I* BEFORE *E* *sp*

Put *i* before *e* except after *c*.

The combinations *ie* and *ei* often stand for the same sound. (*Relieved* rhymes with *received*.) Sort out the words in question:

ie: achieve, believe, chief, grief, niece, piece (of pie), relieve
cei: ceiling, conceited, conceive, perceive, receive, receipt

In the second group of words, the *ei* follows the letter *c*. It is *i* before *e* except after *c*. Exceptions: (*ei*) either, leisure, neither, seize, weird; (*cie*) financier, species.

SPELLING PRACTICE 3   Insert *ei* or *ie*: ach ___ vement, bel ___ ver, dec ___ tful, f ___ ld, inconc ___ vable, misch ___ f, perc ___ ve, rec ___ ving, rel ___ f, s ___ ze, w ___ rd, y ___ ld.

33b | DOUBLED CONSONANT *sp*

Double a final consonant after a stressed single vowel.

Often, we double a single final consonant before an ending (or **suffix**) that begins with a vowel: *-ed, -er, -est, -ing*. The word *plan* has a single final *n*; we double the *n* in *planned, planning,* and *planner*. Two conditions apply:

(1) Double the final consonant only after a short or single vowel. There is no doubling after a long or double vowel: *ai, oo, oa, ea, ee,* or *ou* (boat/boating, read/reading). Some long vowels are shown by a silent final *e* (bite/biting, hope/hoping, bare/baring).

(2) Double the final consonant only at the end of a stressed syllable. There is no doubling when the stress shifts *away* from the final syllable.

DOUBLING	NO DOUBLING
ad**mit**, admitted, admittance for**get**, forgetting, forgettable be**gin**, beginning, beginner re**gret**, regretted, regrettable over**lap**, overlapping	**ed**it, edited, editing **ben**efit, benefited **hard**en, hardened pro**hib**it, prohibited, prohibitive de**vel**op, developing
pre**fer**, preferred, preferring re**fer**, referred, referring	**pref**erence, **pref**erable **ref**erence

Remember especially:

DOUBLING: (occur) occu**rr**ed, occu**rr**ence, occu**rr**ing
NO DOUBLING: (write) wri**t**ing, wri**t**er (but wri**tt**en)

SPELLING PRACTICE 4   Which choice fits the context? Write it after the number of the sentence.

1. bared/barred   Commoners were _____ from the club.
2. bating/batting   He knew the _____ average of every player.
3. hoping/hopping   The prisoners were _____ for a reprieve.
4. planed/planned   The raid had been meticulously _____ .
5. robed/robbed   The choristers were _____ in white.
6. pined/pinned   The rejected lover _____ away.
7. biding/bidding   The agents were _____ their time.
8. caned/canned   The expedition lived on _____ meat.

33c   Y AS A VOWEL   *sp*

Change *y* to *ie* before *s*.

As a single final vowel, *y* changes to *ie* before *s* (one city — several cit*ies*; the sixt*ies*, the eight*ies*). It changes to *i* before all other endings except -*ing* (*dried* but *drying*, *burial* but *burying*).

ie: family — famil**ies**, fly — fl**ies**, study — stud**ies**, try — tr**ies**, quantity — quantit**ies**

i: beauty — beaut**i**ful, bury — bur**i**al, busy — bus**i**ness, copy — cop**i**ed, dry — dr**i**er, lively — livel**i**hood, noisy — nois**i**ly

y: bur**y**ing, cop**y**ing, stud**y**ing, tr**y**ing, worr**y**ing

When it follows another vowel, *y* is usually preserved: *delays, joys, played, valleys*. Exceptions: *day — daily, gay — gaily, lay — laid, pay — paid, say — said*.

33d   FINAL *E*   *sp*

Drop the final silent e before an added vowel.

Drop a silent *e* before an ending that starts with a vowel. Keep it before an ending that starts with a consonant:

	DROPPED *e*	KEPT *e*
bore	boring	bore**d**om
hate	hating	hate**f**ul
like	liking, likable	like**l**y
love	loving, lovable	love**l**y

Remember the following exceptions:

DROPPED *e*:   (argue) argument, (due) duly, (true) truly, (whole) wholly, (judge) judgment, (acknowledge) acknowledgment

KEPT *e*:   (mile) mil**e**age, (dye) dy**e**ing (tinting or coloring as against *die — dying*)

Note: A final *e* may signal the difference in the final sound of *rag* and *rage*, or *plastic* and *notice*. Keep such a final *e* not only before a consonant but also before *a* or *o*:

ge: advantage—advanta**ge**ous, change—chan**ge**able, courage—coura**ge**ous, outrage—outra**ge**ous

ce: notice—noti**ce**able, peace—pea**ce**able

SPELLING PRACTICE 5 Combine the following words with the suggested endings: accompany ___ ed, advantage ___ ous, argue ___ ing, benefit ___ ed, carry ___ s, come ___ ing, confide ___ ing, differ ___ ing, excite ___ able, friendly ___ ness, lively ___ hood, occur ___ ing, prefer ___ ed, remit ___ ance, sad ___ er, satisfy ___ ed, shine ___ ing, sole ___ ly, study ___ ing, tragedy ___ s, try ___ s, use ___ ing, valley ___ s, whole ___ ly, write ___ ing.

SPELLING PRACTICE 6 For each blank space, what would be the right form of the word in parentheses? Put the right form after the number of the sentence.

1. (family) Several _____ were reunited.
2. (study) My friends were _____ in the library.
3. (regret) I have always _____ this oversight.
4. (city) We visited three _____ in one week.
5. (pay) They had already _____ the bill.
6. (love) They never stopped hating and _____ each other.
7. (quantity) Great _____ of food had been consumed.
8. (occur) The thought had _____ to us.
9. (begin) My patience was _____ to wear thin.
10. (copy) He had _____ whole paragraphs.
11. (refer) Your doctor should have _____ you to a specialist.
12. (lay) We had _____ the tile ourselves.
13. (admit) Marcia had _____ her mistake.
14. (refer) She was _____ to a famous incident.
15. (forget) She kept _____ my name.

34 **WORDS OFTEN MISSPELLED**

Watch for words frequently misspelled.

The following are among the words most frequently misspelled in student writing. Take up one group of twenty or twenty-five at a time. Find the ones that would cause you trouble.

absence	allowed	article
abundance	all right	artistically
accessible	already	ascend
accidentally	altar	assent
acclaim	altogether	athlete
accommodate	always	athletic
accompanied	amateur	attendance
accomplish	among	audience
accumulate	amount	authority
accurately	analysis	
accuses	analyze	balance
accustom	annual	basically
achievement	anticipate	basis
acknowledgment	anxiety	beauty
acquaintance	apologize	becoming
acquire	apology	before
acquitted	apparatus	beginning
across	apparent	belief
actuality	appearance	believe
address	applies	beneficial
adequate	applying	benefited
admit	appreciate	boundaries
adolescence	approach	breath
advantageous	appropriate	brilliant
advertisement	approximately	Britain
afraid	area	buses
against	argue	business
aggravate	arguing	
aggressive	argument	calendar
alleviate	arising	candidate
allotted	arrangement	career

careless
carrying
category
ceiling
cemetery
challenge
changeable
character
characteristic
chief
choose
chose
clothes
coarse
column
comfortable
comfortably
coming
commission
committed
committee
companies
competition
competitive
completely
comprehension
conceivable
conceive
concentrate
condemn
confident
confidential
conscience
conscientious
conscious
considerably
consistent
continually
continuous

control
controlled
convenience
convenient
coolly
courageous
course
courteous
criticism
criticize
cruelty
curiosity
curriculum

dealt
deceit
deceive
decision
definite
definitely
definition
dependent
describe
description
desirability
desirable
despair
desperate
destruction
devastate
develop
development
device
difference
different
difficult
dilemma
dining
disappear

disappearance
disappoint
disastrous
discipline
disease
disgusted
dissatisfaction
dissatisfied
doesn't
dominant
due
during

ecstasy
efficiency
efficient
eighth
eliminate
embarrass
embarrassment
eminent
emphasize
endeavor
enforce
enough
entertain
environment
equipped
especially
etc.
exaggerate
excellent
exceptionally
exercise
exhaust
exhilarate
existence
experience
explanation

extraordinary
extremely

familiar
families
fascinate
finally
financial
financier
foreign
forward
friend
fulfill
fundamentally
further

gaiety
generally
genius
government
governor
grammar
guaranteed
guidance

happily
happiness
height
heroes
heroine
hindrance
hopeful
huge
humorous
hundred
hurriedly
hypocrisy
hypocrite

ignorant
imaginary
imagination
immediately
immensely
incidentally
indefinite
independent
indispensable
inevitable
influence
ingenious
insight
intellectual
intelligence
interest
interpret
interrupt
involve
irrelevant
irresistible
itself

jealous

knowledge

laboratory
laid
leisure
likelihood
literature
livelihood
loneliness
losing

magnificence
maintain

maintenance
manageable
manufacturer
marriage
mathematics
meant
medieval
merely
mileage
miniature
minute
mischievous
muscle
mysterious

naive
necessarily
necessary
ninety
noticeable

obstacle
occasion
occasionally
occurred
occurrence
omit
operate
opinion
opponent
opportunity
optimism
original

paid
parallel
paralysis
paralyze

particularly
passed
past
peace
peculiar
perceive
perform
performance
permanent
persistent
persuade
pertain
phenomenon
philosophy
phrase
physical
piece
pleasant
possess
possession
possible
practical
precede
prejudice
prepare
prevalent
privilege
probably
procedure
proceed
professor
prominent
propaganda

prophecy
psychology
pursue

quantity

really
recommend
regard
relief
relieve
religion
repetition
representative
resource
response
rhythm
ridiculous
roommate

safety
satisfactorily
schedule
seize
sense
separate
sergeant
shining
significance
similar
sincerely
sophomore
speech

sponsor
strength
stretch
strictly
studying
subtle
succeed
successful
summarize
surprise

temperament
tendency
therefore
thorough
together
tragedy
transferred
tries

undoubtedly
unnecessary
useful
using

various
vengeance
villain

weird
writing

9

SPECIAL MARKS AND MECHANICS

Note: The following is a quick rundown of minimum proficiencies in the area covered in this chapter. Remember that there is much more to good writing than meeting minimum standards. However, if you fail to meet the standards summarized here, your message may not reach the reader and you may not get credit for what you do well.

Use correctly the special marks that are not heard but show only on the written page. Capital letters and apostrophes are easy to miss when we write, but they are conspicuous by their absence when we read.

(1) Capitalize proper names and major words in titles. Capitalize the names of days, months (but not seasons), places, states, ships, schools: Monday, August (but summer), the South, Wyoming, the Titanic, Yale. Be sure especially to capitalize the names of *countries, nationalities,* and *languages*: English, American, Australian, Polish, Mexican, Spanish, Chinese, Arabic, Russian, British (the country is spelled Britain), Japanese. Also capitalize the names of parties and religions: Democrats, Catholics, Muslims.

Capitalize the first and last words in a title. Also capitalize all major words *within* a title — no capitals for articles (*the, a, an*), conjunctions (*and, but, when*), and prepositions of four letters or less (*in, with, at, for* — but *About, Within*).

The Graying of America	Much Ado About Nothing
The Man with the Golden Arm	The Agony and the Ecstasy

(2) Use the apostrophe in shortened forms or contractions: *don't, doesn't, isn't, won't, can't; we're* ready, *she's* fine, *you're* late, *they're* wrong.

(3) Use the apostrophe with possessives. The apostrophe marks forms that tell us whose: my *brother's* grades, the *coach's* salary, *Russia's* neighbors. Remember four basic rules:

■ Apostrophe first and then *s* if you are talking about *one*: a *cowboy's* horse, the *President's* speech, my *friend's* divorce.

■ The *s* first and then the apostrophe if you are talking about *several*: my *parents'* divorce, other *countries'* problems.

■ Apostrophe first and then *s* for unusual plurals without the plural *s* (such as several *men*, all the *people*): *women's* rights, the *men's* locker room, the *children's* hour, the *people's* right to bear arms.

■ Singular or plural possessive for expressions dealing with time or value: *today's* world, *yesterday's* newspaper, *tomorrow's* election; a *week's* wage (singular), two *months'* salary (plural).

(4) Use *it's* only if it is short for *it is*. The major exceptions to the use of the apostrophe for possessives are **possessive pronouns**: The money is **yours**. The car must be **hers**. The bank paid off **its** creditors. *It's* is *not* a possessive but short for *it is*.

WRONG: The band played *it's* favorite songs at *it's* last concert.
RIGHT: The band played *its* favorite songs at *its* last concert.

(5) Use the hyphen for words temporarily joined together: *Polish-American, cost-effective, mother-in-law, in-laws.* Use the hyphen when several words combine to take the place of an adjective telling us what kind: a *state-of-the-art* design, another *cost-cutting* measure.

OVERVIEW　The apostrophe, causes trouble two ways: People who spell by ear leave it out where it clearly belongs ("a *mothers* love" should be "a *mother's* love"). People with a shaky grasp of the rules put it in where it's wrong ("the *player's* were leaving the field").

35a　　CONTRACTIONS　　　　　　　　*ap*

Use the apostrophe in informal shortened forms.

Use the apostrophe to show that part of a word has been left out: *o'clock, ma'am, class of '85.* Avoid common misspellings.

(1) Use the apostrophe in common contractions or short-ened forms. Remember that *they're* is short for *they are*; *let's* is short for *let us*.

(we *are* ready)	**we're** ready
(she *is* a friend)	**she's** a friend
(he *will* be back)	**he'll** be back

(2) Use the apostrophe in combined forms that include a shortened form of *not*. Remember that *can't* is short for *cannot; won't* is short for *will not*.

(he *could not* stay)	he **couldn't** stay
(they *have not* paid)	they **haven't** paid
(you *are not* safe)	you **aren't** safe
(it *is not* true)	it **isn't** true

CAUTION:　Make sure not to misspell *don't* and *doesn't*. These are shortened forms of *do not* and *does not*.

(3) Know familiar confusing pairs. Use *it's* (= it is) only when it's really an abbreviation. Otherwise use *its* — the possessive pronoun that shows where something belongs: a nation and *its* leaders (tells us *whose* leaders); the bird beat *its* wings (tells us *whose* wings).

it's (it *is*, it *has*):	**it's** true, **it's** raining, **it's** a shame; **it's** been cold
its (of it):	took **its** course, lost **its** value, heavy for **its** size
who's (who *is* or *has*):	**Who's** to blame? **Who's** seen him? the one **who's** guilty
whose (of whom):	**Whose** turn is it? friends **whose** help counts
they're (they are):	**they're** late, **they're** glad, if **they're** here
their (of them):	**their** belongings, **their** friends, they and **their** parents

Note: Contractions are common in informal speech and writing. Avoid them in formal reports, research papers, and letters of application. Use them sparingly in ordinary prose.

Use the apostrophe for the possessive of nouns.

The **possessive** form of nouns shows who owns something (*Macy's*) or to whom something belongs (*the driver's seat*). We usually add an apostrophe plus *s* to the plain form:

WHOSE?	my **sister's** car	Mr. **Smith's** garage
	the **family's** debts	one **person's** opinion
	our **mayor's** office	the **mind's** eye

Besides ownership, the possessive signals other relationships that tell us whose: the *senator's* enemies, the *defendant's* innocence, the *committee's* activities. Usually the possessive comes before another noun, but sometimes it's been cut loose from it:

WHOSE?   It's either the owner's car or her **son's.**   (her **son's car**)

(1) Distinguish between singular and plural possessives. If a plural noun already ends in -*s*, we add only the apostrophe — not a second *s*: a *lovers'* quarrel, the *slaves'* revolt.

SINGULAR: the **twin's** bicycle, a **parent's** duties, one **family's** home
PLURAL: the **twins'** birthdays, both **parents'** duties, both **families'** homes

However, use the regular possessive when a plural noun does not end with the plural -*s* (*children, women, men,* and *people*).

PLURAL: **children's** toys | **women's** rights
            men's wear | **people's** prejudices

CAUTION: Do not use the apostrophe with nouns that are *not* possessives.

WRONG: The **player's** went on strike.
RIGHT: The **players** went on strike. (Who?)
RIGHT: The **player's** jersey had ripped. (Whose?)

(2) Use the apostrophe in expressions dealing with time or value. Distinguish between singular and plural:

SINGULAR	PLURAL
a **week's** pay	two **weeks'** pay
an **hour's** drive	three **hours'** drive
a **dollar's** worth	two **dollars'** worth

The following are possessive forms and need the apostrophe:

a **moment's** notice   **today's** paper   a **day's** work

(3) Know when to use the apostrophe with pronouns. Use the apostrophe with the possessive forms of **indefinite pronouns**: *everyone (everybody), someone (somebody), anyone (anybody), no one (nobody),* and *one*:

to **everybody's** surprise	**anyone's** guess
at **someone's** suggestion	**nobody's** fault
(also: at someone **else's** house)	**one's** best friends

CAUTION: Do *not* use the apostrophe with **possessive pronouns**: *its, hers, ours, yours, theirs.* Remember *its* has no apostrophe when used as a possessive (the movie and *its* sequel, the college and *its* faculty). Use *it's* only to mean *it is*: "*It's* too late."

NO APOSTROPHE: both **its** ears | it was **hers** | this is **yours**

(4) Know how to use the apostrophe with combinations or groups of words. Treat compound words or combinations that stand for a single entity the way you would single words. Put the apostrophe plus -*s* or the apostrophe alone at the end of the last word in the group:

SINGULAR:	the **commander-in-chief's** orders
	a **father-in-law's** hopes
PLURAL:	her **brothers-in-law's** store
	my **in-laws'** support

Note: When the singular form of a noun already has a final -*s*, you may or may not add another *s*, depending on whether you would expect an extra syllable in pronunciation. With words like the following, the additional syllable seems clearly required: the *boss's* office, the *waitress's* tip. We usually do *not* add the extra syllable to the word *Jesus* or to Greek names: for *Jesus'* sake, in *Sophocles'* plays. With many other names, either form would be right:

| BOTH RIGHT: | **Dolores'** trip | **Dolores's** trip |
| | **Dickens'** novel | **Dickens's** novel |

SPELLING PRACTICE 1   Choose the right spelling in each pair.

1. The *judge's/judges* ruling changed both *lawyer's/lawyers'* strategies.
2. Since the *mayor's/mayors* resignation, many *voter's/voters* have been worrying about *whose/who's* going to succeed her.
3. *Mens/Men's* and *womens/women's* cycling found enthusiastic *spectators'/spectators* when introduced as new Olympic sports.
4. In *today's/todays* competitive world of sports, a *gymnast's/gymnasts* training takes up many hours every day.
5. *It's/Its* not easy for *parent's/parents* to let a child find *it's/its* own answers.
6. *Lets/Let's* borrow *someones/someone's* car and go for an *hour's/hours'* drive.

35c   PLURALS OF LETTERS AND SYMBOLS *ap*

Use the apostrophe for plurals of letters and symbols.

Traditionally, the apostrophe has been used before the plural *-s* added to the name of a letter, a number, an abbreviation, or a word named as a word: the early 1900's, average I.Q.'s.

LETTERS:	Teachers were giving more **C's** and **D's**, fewer **A's**.
NUMBERS:	The phone number started with **3's** and ended with **7's**.
ABBREVIATIONS:	People with **Ph.D.'s** were driving cabs.

Remember that letters of the alphabet and words discussed as vocabulary items should be italicized (or underlined in typing). Do not italicize the plural -*s*:

ALPHABET: She spelled her name with two **e's** and two **s's**.

WORDS: His talk was full of **Honey's** and **Darling's**.

Note: Writers more and more tend to leave out the apostrophe for the plural except with letters of the alphabet and abbreviations using a period.

BOTH RIGHT: the **1830's** or the **1830s**

several **6's** in a row or several **6s** in a row

---

36 | **CAPITALS**

OVERVIEW We capitalize the first word of a sentence and the pronoun *I*. In addition we use capital letters for names and for words in titles.

36a | PROPER NAMES | *cap*

Capitalize proper names.

Capitalize names — of people, places, languages, periods, ships and other craft, days of the week, months, organizations, institutions, and religions: *Daniel Boone, Kalamazoo,* the *Everglades, Zimbabwe, Arabic,* the *Middle Ages,* the *Challenger, Saturday, July,* the *Salvation Army, Harvard, Islam.* Do not capitalize the names of the seasons: *spring, summer.*

(1) Capitalize words derived from proper names. Capitalize words that use the name of a country, place, or religion. In particular, capitalize the names of languages and nationalities:

CAPITALS: Imports from **Japan** replaced **German** cameras, **Swiss** cuckoo clocks, **British** motorcycles, and **American** cars. **Marxist** intellectuals criticized the role of **Christian** missionaries and **Buddhist** monks.
Few **Americans** study **Arabic, Chinese,** or **Japanese**.

In some words, the proper name involved has been lost sight of, and a lowercase letter is used:

LOWERCASE: **pasteurized** milk, **guinea** pig, **india** rubber

(2) Capitalize words that become part of a name. When it combines with a proper name, capitalize the general label for a title, family relationship, institution, or geographic feature: *Sergeant Bilko, Nuclear Energy Commission, Silicon Valley.* Some titles point to one person only and are capitalized like a proper name: the *Pope*, the *Queen* (of England).

(3) Capitalize a general word put to special use as a proper name. A general label may double as a proper name:

GENERAL WORD	PROPER NAME
democratic (many institutions)	**D**emocratic (name of the party)
orthodox (many attitudes)	**O**rthodox (name of the church)
history (general subject)	**H**istory 31 (specific course)
west (general direction)	Middle **W**est (the specific area)
my **m**other (common relationship)	**M**other (name you call one person)

Note: Practice varies for the *P*resident or *p*resident (of the United States), the *F*ederal or *f*ederal government, the (U.S.) *C*onstitution or *c*onstitution. Believers capitalize pronouns used in reference to the deity: "She believed that *G*od would not abandon *H*is people."

357

A CHECKLIST OF CAPITALIZED NAMES

PEOPLE:	Eleanor Roosevelt, Martin Luther King, Albert Einstein, Edna St. Vincent Millay
TITLES:	Dr. Brothers, Senator Kennedy, Queen Elizabeth, Pope John Paul
CONTINENTS:	Asia, America, Europe, Australia, the Antarctic
COUNTRIES:	United States of America, Canada, Great Britain, Mexico, Denmark, Japan, Zimbabwe
LANGUAGES:	English, Spanish, Chinese, Russian, French
REGIONS:	the South, the East, the Middle East, the Midwest
STATES:	Kansas, North Dakota, Louisiana, Rhode Island
CITIES:	Oklahoma City, Dallas, Baltimore, Los Angeles, Washington, D.C.
SIGHTS:	Lake Erie, Mount Hood, Death Valley, the Grand Canyon
ADDRESSES:	Park Lane, Fleet Avenue, Oak Street
MONTHS:	January, March, July, October
WEEKDAYS:	Monday, Wednesday, Saturday, Sunday
HOLIDAYS:	Labor Day, Thanksgiving, Easter, the Fourth of July
INSTITUTIONS:	the Supreme Court, the Department of Agriculture, the U.S. Senate, the FBI
BUSINESSES:	Ford Motor Company, General Electric, Sears
SCHOOLS:	Oakdale High School, Las Vistas Junior College, University of Maine
GROUPS:	the Democratic Party, the American Legion
FAITHS:	Christian, Muslim, Jewish, Buddhist
DENOMINATIONS:	Methodist, Mormon, Unitarian, Roman Catholic

Capitalize major words in titles.

A capital letter marks the first and last word and all major words in the title of a publication or work of art. Words not counting as major are articles (*a, an,* and *the*) and also prepositions (*at, in, on, from, with*) or conjunctions (*and, but, if, when*). Even these are capitalized when they have five or more letters (*Through, Because*). Observe these rules in the titles of your papers:

Raising the Mirth Rate
Travels with a Camel Through Arid Country
How I Quit Drugs and Learned to Love the Police

The same rules apply to titles of publications cited in a sentence:

TITLES: *New York Times Magazine's* "About Men" column is the weekly counterpart of the older "Hers" column; *Esquire* has published numerous articles on subjects like "Men, Babies, and the Male Clock" or "The Pain of the Divorced Father."

PEER EDITOR 2 Which words should be *capitalized*? After the number of each sentence, write down and capitalize all such words.

1. Players from brazil and argentina have played for france and italy in the world cup.
2. The authenticity of some of rembrandt's most popular paintings — *the man with the golden helmet* and *polish rider* — has been challenged.
3. Delegates met in manhattan to celebrate the centennial of the union of american hebrew congregations, founded in cincinnati by rabbi isaac wise.
4. At columbia and barnard, at atlanta's morehouse college and the university of virginia, economics was the subject to take.

5. Seven novels by mickey spillane are among the thirty best-selling novels of all time, along with *gone with the wind, peyton place, lady chatterley's lover,* and *in his steps*, by charles monroe sheldon, 1897.

6. Like other newspapers, the *new york journal-american* had learned the art of catering to irish catholics.

THE HYPHEN

OVERVIEW Watch out for high-frequency uses of the hyphen:

in-law words	daughter-in-law, father-in-law, in-laws
self-words	self-conscious, self-confidence, self-correcting
double numbers	twenty-four, sixty-seven
ethnic labels	Irish-American, Asian-American, Polish-American
new blends	trade-off, cancer-causing, cost-effective

37a COMPOUND WORDS *hy*

Know which compound words require a hyphen.

Some **compound words** differ from ordinary combinations in both speech and writing: "a wild LIFE" but "our WILDlife"; "a dark ROOM" but "a DARKroom." Such unmistakable compounds are *headache, highway,* and *stepmother.* In many similar pairs, however, the parts are kept separate: *high school, labor union.* Still other compound words require the hyphen: *cave-in, great-grandfather, mother-in-law.*

(1) Know how to spell common compound words.

ONE WORD: bridesmaid, stepfather, checklist, highlight, headquarters, blackout, bittersweet

---

COMMON TYPES OF HYPHENATED WORDS

in-laws, off-season, drive-in, sit-in, off-duty, take-off, trade-off

---

ten-speed, six-pack, one-sided, three-cornered, second-rate, one-way, two-dimensional

---

Polish-American, Asian-American, Anglo-Saxon, Greco-Roman

---

law-abiding, Spanish-speaking, cancer-causing, award-winning, money-losing

---

dark-haired, Washington-based, air-conditioned, computer-aided, career-oriented, middle-aged, foreign-born, college-bound, single-handed

---

fuel-efficient, cost-effective, oil-rich, water-repellent, image-conscious, toll-free

---

self-conscious, ex-husband, all-purpose, great-grandfather, co-star, pro-Arab, non-Catholic

---

south-southeast, north-northwest

---

two-by-four, cash-and-carry, fly-by-night, father-in-law

| TWO WORDS (OR MORE): | commander in chief, goose flesh, vice versa, off year, high command |
| HYPHEN: | able-bodied, bull's-eye, drive-in, court-martial, six-pack, in-laws, vice-president, Spanish-American, one-sided, off-season, in-group, President-elect |

(2) Hyphenate compound numbers from *twenty-one* to *ninety-nine*. Also hyphenate fractions used as modifiers:

NUMBERS:	There were **twenty-six** passengers.
	The plan was **one-third** empty.
	The tank was **three-quarters** full.

Practice varies for other uses of fractions:

FRACTIONS: **Two thirds** (or **two-thirds**) remained poor.

CAUTION: Be sure to spell correctly combinations that are often misspelled:

ONE WORD: today, tomorrow, nevertheless, nowadays
TWO WORDS: all right, a lot (of time), be able, no one, even though

---

37b | PREFIXES | *hy*

Know which prefixes require a hyphen.

Many hyphenated compounds combine a word and its prefix. A **prefix** can be attached at the beginning of many different words.

(1) Use a hyphen with *all-*, *ex-* ("former"), *quasi-*, *self-*, and sometimes *co-*. Hyphenate words like *all-knowing, ex-husband, quasi-judicial, self-contained, co-worker.*

> *all-:*   all-powerful, all-American, all-male, all-star
> *ex-:*   ex-champion, ex-convict, ex-wife, ex-governor
> *self-:* self-confident, self-conscious, self-image, self-destruct

(2) Use a hyphen with all prefixes before a capital letter. Hyphenate *anti-American, pro-British, un-American, non-Catholic, Pan-Arabic.*

(3) Use a hyphen to separate two identical vowels or a third identical consonant. Hyphenate *anti-intellectual, semi-independent,* (also *fall-like*).

Use the hyphen with group modifiers.

Hyphenate words that work together as a modifier before a noun:

HYPHENS: a **middle-of-the-road** policy | **off-the-cuff** remarks
a **low-income** neighborhood | **wall-to-wall** carpeting
an **in-depth** interview | a **step-by-step** account

Use no hyphens when the same combinations serve other functions: tend toward the **middle of the road**; explain a process **step by step**.

Use no hyphen when a modifier before a noun is in turn modified by an adverb ending in *-ly*: a *fast-rising* executive but a *rapidly growing* city; a *well-balanced* account but a *carefully documented* study.

PEER EDITOR 3 After the number of each sentence, pull out and change all combinations that should be *hyphenated or written as one word*.

1. New style managers developed cost effective procedures for labor intensive industries.
2. Italian Americans protested against the poor self image and low self esteem created by negative stereotypes.
3. The room was about one fourth full, with forty five people scattered in two hundred seats.
4. This is the story of a flabby middle aged two pack a day smoker who transformed himself into a 160 pound marathon runner.
5. Though at times her son in law seemed self conscious, he never the less had a well balanced personality.
6. The self righteous law and order candidate promised to crack down on ex convicts.

OVERVIEW Make the outward appearance of your manuscript show that you care about your readers' convenience and respect their standards.

38a | PENMANSHIP AND TYPING *ms*

Prepare a legible and attractive manuscript.

Write legibly, pruning your handwriting of excessive loops and curlicues. (Do *not* print or leave every other line blank unless instructed to do so.) Type on unlined paper of standard size and weight, double-spacing all material. When in doubt about the quality of the printout delivered by a word processor, show a sample to your instructor.

(1) Observe conventional spacing. Leave one space after most punctuation marks (comma, semicolon) but *two* spaces after end punctuation.

TWO SPACES: `They invested in a restaurant.  It failed.`

After a colon, leave one space if the colon appears before the end of the sentence. Leave two spaces if it appears at the end.

ONE SPACE: `We saw new construction: offices and hotels.`
TWO SPACES: `The news was out:  The test had been`
               `postponed.`

Use two hyphens — with no space on either side — to make a **dash**:

DASH: `Use two hyphens--with no space on either`
             `side.`

Note: Leave no space after a period that occurs *within* an abbreviation — but leave one space each if several initials are part of a person's name:

ABBREVIATIONS: `The U.S. Supreme Court    T. S. Eliot`

(2) Leave adequate margins. Leave about an inch and a half on the left and at the top, an inch on the right and at the bottom. *Indent* the first line of a paragraph — about an inch in longhand, or five spaces in typed copy.

(3) Make necessary final corrections. Always make time for final proofreading. If necessary, make handwritten last-minute corrections. Draw a line through a word to delete it or to write the corrected word above. (Use a snaking line to revise the order of two transposed letters.)

```
                  deep
Critics found profound meaning in in Laurel and
Hardy.
```

To separate two words, draw a vertical line; to close up a space, use two curved lines. Insert a **caret** (^) to show where a missing word is to go:

```
                                    the
Film|critics have in vestigated symbolism of King
Kong.
```

To start a new paragraph, insert the symbol ¶; to take out a paragraph break, insert "no ¶" in the margin.

| TITLES OF PAPERS | *ms*

Use standard form for the titles of your papers.

Capitalize words in the titles of your papers as you would in titles of publications (see **36b**). Capitalize the first and last word. Capitalize all other words except articles (*the, a, and*) and prepositions (*in, at, with*) or conjunctions (*and, when, if*). Capitalize even prepositions or conjunctions when they have five or more letters (*around, because*).

TITLES: My Teacher the Computer
            Was Granddad a Monkey?
            Drugs on the Job
            All About Graft

CAUTION: Do not italicize (underline) your own title. Do not put it in quotation marks unless you want to identify it as a quotation. Use a question mark or exclamation mark as appropriate, but do not use a period even if your title is a complete sentence.

QUOTATION:	"A Kinder, Gentler America"
QUESTION:	Marriage: Bond or Bondage?
SENTENCE:	Chivalry Is Dead

38c | DIVIDING WORDS | *div*

Observe conventional syllabication.

Use a hyphen to divide words at the end of a line. Dictionaries generally use centered dots to indicate where a word may be divided:

ad·dress   af·fec·ta·tion   en·vi·ron·ment   mal·ice

(1) Recognize recurrent patterns. For instance, divide words before the *-ing* ending, but keep the added consonant with the ending when you have doubled a final consonant:

play·ing	sell·ing	edit·ing
plan·ning	hum·ming	submit·ting

Divide between two consonants when they go with two separate syllables in slow pronunciation:

op·tics *but* neu·tral | fac·tor *but* su·preme

(2) Do not divide names and combinations that form a single unit. Avoid dividing names (*Kiplinger, Washington*). Do not divide contractions (*doesn't, wouldn't*) and abbreviations (*NATO, UNESCO, UCLA*). Do not split sums (*$1,175,000*) or expressions using abbreviations like *a.m.* and *B.C.*

(3) Do not set off single letters. Do not divide words like *about, alone,* and *enough* or like *many* and *via.* Similarly, do not set off the ending *-ed* in words like *complained* or *renewed*. (Do not divide one-syllable words: *strength, through*.)

(4) Divide hyphenated words at the original hyphen. Do not break up the *American* in "Un-American" or the *sister* in "sister-in-law."

(5) Do not divide the last word on a page.

38d | ITALICS | *ital*

Use italics to set off special words and phrases.

Italics (or slanted type) are signaled in handwritten and most typed manuscript by underlining.

(1) Italicize for emphasis. Use italics (underlining) to call attention to important words or to words that will prevent misunderstanding.

EMPHASIS: The group was a professional ***association***, not a union.

(2) Italicize words discussed as words or words still considered foreign.

WORD AS WORD: Dictionaries lag behind, only slowly beginning to include
                hot tub, prime time, gulag, preppie, and ***putdown***.
FOREIGN: He developed a taste for ***tostadas*** and the music of the
                mariachis.

(3) Italicize titles of whole publications. Italicize or underline titles of books (*Veil: The Secret Wars of the CIA*), magazines (*Popular Mechanics*), newspapers (*Chicago Tribune*), and other complete publications. Put in quotation marks the titles of articles, poems, short stories, songs, and other items that are *part* of a larger publication: "The Love Song of J. Alfred Prufrock"; "The Lottery"; "I Got You, Babe."

Note: The name of the Bible and the names of its parts (Genesis, Book of Job) are usually *not* italicized.

(4) Italicize the names of works of art, music, and entertainment. Use italics (underlining) for the names of paintings, ballets, operas, major orchestral works, plays, movies, radio and television shows.

ART: He dreamed of seeing Michelangelo's **David** in Florence or listening to **Lohengrin** in Bayreuth.

(5) Italicize the names of trains, aircraft, ships, and other vessels.

VESSELS: Legendary ships from the **Mayflower** and the **Titanic** to the **Hindenburg** and **Apollo IX** have been symbols of human hopes and fears.

---

39   ABBREVIATIONS AND NUMBERS

OVERVIEW Abbreviations like *Mr.* and *a.m.* are all right anywhere, but we expect to see *NY, lb.*, and *in.* only in addresses, invoices, charts, and other very businesslike kinds of communication. We expect numerals for exact sums, but we prefer to have the figures spelled out in "2 out of 3 voted for the 3rd party candidate."

39a   ABBREVIATIONS   *ab*

Spell out inappropriate abbreviations.

Some abbreviations (*Mr., CIA, a.m.*) are generally acceptable, others (*lb., Ave., NY*) only in invoices, addresses, and other special contexts.

(1) Use the acceptable abbreviations for titles and degrees. Before and after names, use the titles *Mr., Mrs., Ms., Dr.,* and *St.* (Saint), and the abbreviations *Jr.* (Junior) and *Sr.* (Senior). Use standard abbreviations for degrees: *M.D., Ph.D.* Use *Prof.* only before the full name.

TITLES: **Mr.** John J. Smith, Jr.

Dr. Alice Joyce *or* Alice Joyce, **M.D.**

Prof. Shelby F. Jones *but* Professor Jones

(2) Use familiar initials for organizations. Use familiar initials (*KGB*) or **acronyms** (UNICEF) for agencies, organizations, firms, technical processes, chemical compounds, and the like.

INITIALS: IBM, AFL-CIO, FBI, CIA, UNESCO, PTA, FM radio, CBS

Note: Use the **ampersand** (&) and abbreviations like *Inc.* and *Bros.* only when organizations use them in their official titles: *Smith & Company, Inc.*

(3) Use familiar abbreviations related to time and number. Before or after numerals, use *A.D.* and *B.C., a.m.* and *p.m.* (also *A.M.* and *P.M.*), *no.* (also *No.*):

YEARS: Augustus reigned from 27 **B.C.** to **A.D.** 14.

HOURS: Planes leave at 11 **a.m.** and 2:30 **p.m.**

NUMBER: This issue was Volume 7, **no.** 2.

(4) Spell out addresses and geographic names. Use abbreviations like *NY* or *CA* only when writing an address for a letter or the like. (Exceptions: *USSR; Washington, D.C.;* and *U.S.* in combinations like *U.S. Navy.*)

WRONG: When in the **U.S.**, she lived on Grant **Ave.** in San Francisco, **Calif.**

RIGHT: When in the **United States**, she lived on **Grant Avenue** in **San Francisco, California**.

(5) Spell out most measurements. In ordinary prose, *lb.* (pound), *oz.* (ounce), *ft.* (foot), and *in.* (inch) are usually spelled out.

Some units of measurement are more unwieldy and are abbreviated, provided they are used with figures: *45 mph, 1500 rpm*. Spell out % (percent) and ¢ (cent), but use $ for exact figures: $287.55.

MEASUREMENTS: He used to weigh 305 **pounds**, which made him a bit
sluggish in competition.

PEER EDITOR 4   Rewrite the following sentences, using only *abbreviations appropriate in ordinary prose*.

1. Cab drivers in NYC are as likely to be from the USSR as from Boston Mass. or Athens GA.
2. Doctor Brenner was a lit. prof. teaching Gen. Ed. at Baylor U.
3. The Internal Rev. Service office is on N. Front St. and is open in the a.m.
4. She spent eighty % of her time lobbying for the U.S. Navy in Washington, D.C.
5. A local cheese co. made a cheese that was two ft. long and weighed twenty lb.

39b	NUMBERS	*num*

Use figures in accordance with standard practice.

Figures are generally appropriate in references to the day of the month (*May 13*), the year (*1917*), street numbers (*1014 Union Avenue*), and page numbers (*Chapter 7, page 18*). For other uses of numbers, observe the following conventions:

(1) Spell out round numbers. Numbers from one to ten, and round numbers requiring no more than two words, are usually spelled out: *three dollars a seat, ten thousand copies, about seventy-five reservations*.

WORDS: My aunt came from Ireland a **hundred** years ago, when she was **seven** years old.

FIGURES: The church was **350** years old and had withstood a major earthquake **125** years ago.

Note: In ordinary prose, the words *million* and *billion* are usually preferable to figures using large numbers of zeros: *4.8 million* (instead of *4,800,000*).

(2) Use numerals for exact figures. Use numerals for exact counts, exact sums, technical measurements, decimals, numbers with fractions and percentages:

FIGURES: 500,867 inhabitants $3.86   65 mph
            4.3 miles   3½ hours   92% (or 92 percent)

Use numerals also for references to time using *a.m.* or *p.m.*

TIME: 2:30 p.m. (*but* three o'clock, half past twelve)

(3) Avoid numerals at the beginning of a sentence. Write "Fifteen out of 28 replied" or "When questioned, 15 out of 28 replied." Except in special situations like this one, avoid changes from figures to words (and vice versa) in a series of numbers.

(4) Hyphenate compound numbers. When spelled out, compound numbers from 21 to 99 are hyphenated: *twenty-five, one hundred and forty-six*.

PEER EDITOR 5   Rewrite the following sentences, using *abbreviations and numerals* in accordance with standard practice:

1. She had lived at Eighteen N. Washington St. since nineteen-hundred and forty-four.
2. Though he weighed only one hundred and twenty-six lb. and measured little more than 5 ft., he was an ardent devotee of the rugged life.
3. He found 2$ and 36 cts. left in his account.

10

GLOSSARY OF USAGE

Note: The following is a quick rundown of minimum proficiencies in the area covered in this chapter. Remember that there is much more to good writing than meeting minimum standards. However, if you fail to meet the standards summarized here, your message may not reach the reader and you may not get credit for what you do well.

Make sure not to let nonstandard forms carry over into your writing. Correct any of the following:

a/an   Use the *an* before a vowel: *an* eye for *an* eye, *an* earful, *an* A, *an* accident, *an* informed reader, *an* unimportant point. Vowels are *a, e, i, o,* and *u.* (Use *an* before *u* if it sounds like the *u* in *up*, not like "you": *an* upturn, but *a* U-turn.) Use *a* before a consonant: *a* desk, *a* launch, *a* hotel, *a* beehive. Go by what you hear, not by what you see spelled. It's *an* F (pronounced *eff*) and *an* honest man (pronounced *onnest*).

WRONG: **a** ear, **a** accident, **a** athlete, **a** automobile
RIGHT: **an** ear, **an** accident, **an** athlete, **an** automobile

double negative   Double negatives say no twice: (In standard English, a double negative is a no-no.)

WRONG: I didn't do **nothing**. **Nobody** calls here **no more**.
RIGHT: I didn't do **anything**. **Nobody** calls here **anymore**.

he don't, she don't   *Don't* instead of *doesn't* is nonstandard for one single person or thing (**third person singular**), with action now (**present tense**). Use *doesn't* after *he, she,* or *it* or any single subject:

WRONG: She **don't** live here. He **don't** like it. It **don't** matter. The insurance **don't** cover it.

RIGHT: She **doesn't** live here. He **doesn't** like it. It **doesn't** matter. The insurance **doesn't** cover it.

hisself, theirself, themself   Use *himself* and *themselves*.

knowed, blowed, had went   Irregular verbs signal the past by a change in the word itself: *know* it now/*knew* it then. They usually change again when they appear after *have* (*has, had*): I *had* always *known*. This third form also appears after forms of *be* (*am, is, was, were, has been*) when the subject is the target or product of the action: The truth *will be known* (**passive voice**). Know the standard forms for sets of three like the following:

RIGHT: It **grows** now/it **grew** in the past/it **had grown**
We **go** now/we **went** then/we **had gone** before
It **takes** time/it **took** longer/nothing **was taken**

these kind   *These kind* and *those kind* are grammatical hybrids, half plural and half singular. Use "*This kind* of car *is* . . ." (all singular) or "*These kinds* of nuts *are* . . ." (all plural). Similarly, use *that kind of house* or *those kinds of houses*.

40   GLOSSARY OF USAGE

Avoid expressions that many readers find objectionable.

The advice given in this glossary will help you write the kind of *serious edited English* that is acceptable to a large cross section of educated readers.

Note: Check **32c** for confusing pairs like *advise/advice, affect/ effect, lose/loose,* or *than/then.*

a, an   Use *a* only before words that begin with a consonant when pronounced: *a desk, a chair, a house, a year, a* C, *a university*. Use *an* before words that begin with a vowel when pronounced (though in writing the first letter may be a consonant): *an eye, an answer, an honest mistake, an* A, *an* M, *an uninformed reader.* The *a* before a vowel is nonstandard.

aggravate   In writing, use to mean "make worse or more grave." Avoid its informal use in the sense of "annoy" or "irritate":   U2

FORMAL: When you **irritate** him, you **aggravate** his condition.

ain't   Nonstandard for *am not, isn't, aren't,* or *hasn't* (She *ain't* been seen since).   U3

all right   Spell as *two* words. (Although *alright* appears in some dictionaries, most readers will consider it a misspelling.)   U4

allusion, illusion   An *allusion* is a brief mention that reminds us of a story or an event (the speaker's *allusion* to Watergate). An *illusion* is a deceptive appearance or false hope (The Vietnam war destroyed many *illusions*).   U5

a lot   Always spell as *two* words. "*A lot* of money" is informal; "*lots* of money" is slang: U6

FORMAL: She owed us **a large amount** of money.

already, all ready   "They *already* (ahead of time) had our equipment *all* (completely) *ready*."   U7

altogether, all together   "It is *altogether* (completely) too late to bring these people *all* (every one of them) *together*."   U8

amount, number   Use *amount* only when thinking about bulk or a sum (the total *amount* of the debt). Use *number* when thinking about countable items (the *number* of whooping cranes).   U9

RIGHT: A large **number** (not **amount**) of people were waiting.
            The **number** (not **amount**) of unsold cars on dealers' lots was growing steadily.

and and but at the beginning of a sentence   A traditional rule banned *and* and *but* at the beginning of a sentence. But many modern writers start sentences with *and* or *but* merely to avoid more formal words like *moreover, furthermore, however,* and *nevertheless*. Don't overdo or overuse the initial *and* or *but*.   U10

and/or   *And/or* is sometimes necessary in commercial or official documents. Avoid it in ordinary writing.   U11

angle, approach, slant   *Angle, approach,* and *slant* are overused as synonyms for "attitude," "point of view," "position," or "procedure."   U12

U13 **anyone, anybody** *Anyone* and *anybody* stand for "any person at all." *Any one* singles out: "Take any *one* of those three." *Any body* refers to the physical body.

U14 **anyways, anywheres, anyplace** In writing, use *anyway* or *anywhere*.

U15 **apt, liable** In formal usage, *apt* suggests that something is likely because of someone's aptitude ("She is *apt* to become a successful artist"). *Liable* suggests that what is likely is burdensome or undesirable ("He is *liable* to break his leg").

U16 **as** *As* is nonstandard as a substitute for *that* or *whether* ("I don't know *as* I can come"). It is also nonstandard as a substitute for *who* ("Those *as* knew her avoided her").

U17 **at** Omit the redundant *at* in *where at*. Use "*Where* does he live?" instead of "*Where* does he live *at*?"

U18 **attribute, contribute** *Attribute* means "to trace to a cause" or "to credit to a source." *Contribute* means "to give one's share" or "to have a share" in something.

RIGHT: She **attributed** her success to perseverance.

U19 **awful, awfully** In writing, use *awful* only for something truly horrible (The plane went down with *awful* loss of life). Do not use *awful* or *awfully* as an informal substitute for *very* or *extremely* (That was *awful* close).

INFORMAL: Their parents had been **awfully** mean to them.
FORMAL: Their parents had been **extremely** mean to them.

U20 **bad, badly** Use the adjective *bad* after the linking verb *feel*, which shows a condition: "His resignation made everyone feel *bad*." Use the adverb *badly* to show how something is done: "She handled the assignment *badly*."

U21 **being as, being that** Nonstandard as substitutes for *because* or *since* ("being *that* I was ill").

U22 **between, among** Use *between* in references to two of a kind (distinguish *between* right and wrong). Use *among* in references to more than two (distinguish *among* different shades of color). *Between* is also right when more than two things can be considered in pairs of two:

RIGHT: Bilateral trade agreements exist **between** many countries.

broke Very informal for being out of money. Do not use *broke* in- U23
stead of *broken*: "Someone *had broken* (not *had broke*) the glass."

burst, bursted, bust, busted *Bursted* is a nonstandard form of U24
burst: "The tank *burst* (not *bursted*) and killed two of the workers."
Bust as a verb meaning "*break*" or "*arrest*" is slang.

but what Use *that* instead of *but what* after words like *doubt*: "We U25
never doubted *that* (not *but what*) they would return."

but yet, but however Expressions like *but yet* or *but however* are U26
redundant; they say *but* twice. Use only one of the logical links at a
time: "The full amount had been paid, *but* (not *but yet*) the computer kept sending us bills."

calculate, reckon, expect, guess In written English, *calculate* and U27
reckon imply computing or systematic reasoning. *Expect* implies
expectation or anticipation; *guess* implies conjecture. In the sense
of "think," "suppose," or "consider," these verbs are informal or
dialectal.

can and may Formal English uses *can* in the sense of "be able to." U28
It uses *may* to show permission. The use of *can* to indicate permission, common in speech and writing, is often considered informal:

INFORMAL: **Can** I speak to you for a minute?
FORMAL: Visitors **may** (are permitted to) enter the country only if
         they **can** (are able to) prove their identity.

cannot help but *Cannot help but* is often criticized as illogical or U29
confused. Use either *cannot help* or *cannot but*:

RIGHT: I **cannot help** wishing that I had never met you.
RIGHT: I **cannot but** wish that I had never met you.

can't hardly, can't scarcely These expressions, like double nega- U30
tives, duplicate the negative idea. Use *can hardly, can scarcely*.

WRONG: The country **can't hardly** pay the interest on its debt.
RIGHT: The country **can hardly** pay the interest on its debt.

censor, censure To *censor* means to meddle with speech or writing U31
to make it conform to the censor's standards (or to ban it outright).
Censorship is the result. To *censure* is to express disapproval in a
very serious official manner (a vote of *censure*).

center around Logical readers expect a discussion to *center on* an U32
issue, not to *center around* it.

U33 **compare with, compare to** We compare two cities *with* each other to see what they have in common. We compare a city *to* an anthill to show what a city is like.

U34 **complement, compliment** The first word means "complete" or "supplement." The second word means "say nice things, flatter." *Complementary* findings round out or complete a picture. *Complimentary* remarks flatter. (*Complimentary* tickets are given away free.)

U35 **conscience, conscious** We are usually *conscious* and sometimes un*conscious*, and some of our feelings are buried in the sub*conscious*. Our *conscience* makes us feel guilty when we do something wrong.

U36 **couple of** In formal writing, *couple* refers to two of a kind, a pair. Used in the sense of "several" or "a few," it is informal. Used before a plural noun without a connecting *of*, it is nonstandard:

INFORMAL: We had to wait **a couple of** minutes.

NONSTANDARD: We had only **a couple** dollars left.

U37 **data** Though now often used as a singular, the word is originally a Latin plural (meaning "facts"):

SAFE: **These** data **are** part of a growing body of evidence.

U38 **different than** *Different from* used to be expected in formal English. *Different than*, widely used in speech, is becoming acceptable in writing.

ECONOMICAL: We tried a different method **than** we had used last year.

LESS ECONOMICAL: We tried a different method **from the one** we had used last year.

U39 **disinterested, uninterested** In formal English, *disinterested* means "not swayed by personal, selfish interest" or "impartial." Avoid using *disinterested* in the sense of "uninterested" or "indifferent."

RIGHT: We were sure she would be a **disinterested** judge.

U40 **don't, doesn't** Put the apostrophe where the *o* would have been in *do not* and *does not*. Standard English doesn't use *don't* after *he, she,* or *it* (third person singular): She *doesn't* smoke. He *doesn't* work. It *doesn't* matter.

U41 **double comparative, double superlative** Short adjectives usually form the comparative by adding the suffix *-er (cheaper)*, the superlative by adding the suffix -*est (cheapest)*. Long adjectives, and adverbs ending in -*ly*, usually employ the intensifiers *more* and *most* instead (*more expensive, most expensive; more carefully, most carefully*). Forms using both the suffix and the intensifier are nonstandard (*more cheaper, most cheapest*).

double negative   Double negatives say no twice. The use of addi- **U42** tional negative words to reinforce a negation already expressed is nonstandard: "I *didn't* do *nothing*"; "*Nobody* comes to see me *no more*."

RIGHT: I **didn't** do **anything**.
           Nobody comes to see me **anymore**.

Similar to double negatives are expressions like *couldn't hardly* or *couldn't scarcely:*

RIGHT: I **could hardly** keep my eyes open during the talk.

due to as a preposition   Use *due to* as an adjective: "His absence **U43** was *due to* ill health." "His absence, *due to* ill health, upset our schedule." (In these examples, you could substitute another adjective: "His absence was *traceable* to ill health.") Avoid *due to* as a preposition meaning "because of ":

WRONG: Computer chips fail **due to** poor quality control.
RIGHT: Computer chips fail **because of** poor quality control.

each other, one another   Conservative writers distinguish be- **U44** tween *each other* (referring to two persons or things) and *one another* (referring to more than two):

The bride and groom had known **each other** since childhood.
The members of his family supported **one another**.

enthuse, enthused   Avoid these very informal shortcuts for "turn **U45** enthusiastic" and "enthusiastic."

etc.   *Etc.*, the Latin abbreviation for "and so on," often serves as a **U46** vague substitute for additional examples or illustrations. Furthermore, *ect.* is a common misspelling. "And etc." and "such as ... etc." are redundant. To avoid trouble, steer clear of *etc.* altogether.

except, accept   Use *except* when you make an *exc*eption — you take **U47** something *out*. Use *accept* when you receive something willingly — you take something *in*.

U48 farther, further; all the farther   A traditional rule requires *farther* in references to space and distance ("We traveled *farther* than we had expected"). It requires *further* in references to degree and quantity ("We discussed it *further* at our next meeting") and in the sense of "additional" ("without *further* delay"). *Further*, however, is now widely accepted as appropriate in all three senses.

　　All the farther in the sense of "as far as" ("This is *all the farther* we go") is nonstandard or dialectal.

U49 flaunt, flout   We *flaunt* (show off) wealth or possessions ("If you have it, *flaunt* it"). We *flout* (defy or ignore) laws.

U50 get   Several uses of the verb *get* are informal: "We finally *got* to see him" (succeeded); "He never *got* it" (understood); "What *gets* me is that he is always late" (irritates). For many readers, *get* used instead of *be* (*am, are, was, were*) for the passive has an informal ring: "Her Mustang *got hit* by a truck."

U51 get, got, gotten   In American English, *have gotten* is an acceptable alternative to *have got* in the sense of "have obtained" or "have become." For example: "Her grandparents had *got* (or *gotten*) wealthy after the Civil War."

U52 hadn't ought to   In formal English, *ought*, has no form for the past tense. *Hadn't ought* is informal; *had ought* is nonstandard:

INFORMAL:　You **hadn't ought** to ask him.

FORMAL:　You **ought not to have** asked him.

U53 hopefully   When used instead of "I hope," *hopefully* is widely considered illogical.

RIGHT:　She looked at the bulletin board **hopefully** (with hope).

POOR:　**Hopefully**, she will look at the bulletin board.

BETTER:　**We hope** she will look at the bulletin board.

U54 if, whether   *If* is sometimes criticized when used to express uncertainty after such verbs as *ask, don't know, wonder, doubt*. The more formal subordinator is *whether:* "I doubt *whether* his support would help."

U55 immigrate, emigrate   People *immigrate* to a new country, where they arrive as *immigrants*. People *emigrate* from the old country, where they leave as *emigrants*.

U56 impact   *Impact* is fashionable jargon when used to mean "affect," "change," or "alter." Try a more exact word like *improve, strengthen,* or *reduce*: "These cuts greatly *worsened* (not *impacted*) the housing situation in the city."

in, into   Formal writing often requires *into* rather than *in* to indicate   *U57* direction: "He came *into* (not *in*) the room."

infer, imply   Use *imply* to mean "hint or suggest a conclusion." Use   *U58* *infer* to mean "draw a conclusion on the basis of what has been hinted or suggested." A speaker *implies* something; the audience *infers* what is meant from the speaker's hints.

in terms of   A vague all-purpose connective frequent in jargon: *U59* "What have you seen lately *in terms of* new plays?"

JARGON:	What did she expect **in terms of** salary?
BETTER:	What salary did she expect?

irregardless   Use *regardless*.   *U60*

it's, its   Use *it's* only when it's short for *it is*. Use *its* (no apostrophe)   *U61* to show possession: the band and *its* admirers, the orchestra and *its* conductor.

it's me, it is I   Grammarians require *it is I* on the grounds that the   *U62* linking verb *is* equates the pronoun *I* with the subject *it* and thus makes necessary the use of the subject form. *It's me* is now freely used in informal speech. Avoid it and parallel uses of other pronouns (*us, him, her*) in your writing:

INFORMAL:	I thought it was **him**. It could have been **us**.
FORMAL:	It was **she** who paid the bills.

judicial, judicious   A judicial decision is reached by a judge or by   *U63* a court. A judicious decision shows sound judgment.

kind of, sort of   Avoid as informal substitutes for *rather* or *some-*   *U64* *what*: "We were all *sort of* (should be *rather*) tired at the end of the lecture."

later, latter   *Later* is the opposite of *earlier*. The *latter* is the opposite   *U65* of the *former*. "Although both Alfred and Francis were supposed to arrive at eight, the *latter* came *later*."

learn, teach   In standard English, the teacher *teaches* (rather than   *U66* *learns*) the learner.

leave, let   In formal usage, *leave* does not mean "allow" or "permit."   *U67* You do not "leave" somebody do something. Nor does *leave* take the place of *let* in suggestions like "Let us call a meeting."

𝒰68 lend, loan We *lend* money (using the verb), thus giving someone *a loan* (using the noun).

𝒰69 less, fewer Use *less* in references to extent, amount, degree (*less* friction, *less* money, *less* heat). Do not use it in references to things you can count: *fewer* people, *fewer* homes, *fewer* requirements.

𝒰70 like as a conjunction In informal speech, *like* is widely used as a subordinator replacing *as* or *as if* at the beginning of a clause. Avoid this informal *like* in your writing:

INFORMAL: Do **like** I tell you.
FORMAL: Do **as** I tell you.

INFORMAL: The patient felt **like** he had slept for days.
FORMAL: The patient felt **as if** (or **as though**) he had slept for days.

In formal usage, *like* is acceptable as a preposition, followed by an object: *like* a bird, *like* a cloud. It is not acceptable as a conjunction that starts a clause, with its own subject and verb: *like* a bird flies, *like* a cloud had passed.

𝒰71 literally *Literally* literally means "in plain fact." Do not use it figuratively to mean "figuratively."

RIGHT: They **literally** leveled the village.
WRONG: They **literally** (should be **completely**) blanketed the city with leaflets. (They did not use an actual blanket.)

𝒰72 media *Media* is originally the plural of *medium*, and many of your readers will expect to see it used as a plural: "The *media are* not just reporting but shaping and sometimes creating political events."

𝒰73 moral, morale We talk about the "moral" of a story but about the "morale" of workers. People with good morale are not necessarily moral, and vice versa.

𝒰74 most, almost *Most* is informal when used in the sense of "almost" or "nearly": "*Most* everybody was there." "Jones considers herself an authority on *most* any subject." Use "*almost* everybody," "*almost* any subject."

𝒰75 myself, yourself, himself, herself The *-self* pronouns are reflexive pronouns; they usually "point back" to someone already mentioned:

The **woman** introduced **herself**.
He **himself** gave me the key.

Conservative readers object to these pronouns when they do not point back but are used as simple substitutes for *I* or *me, he* or *him*:

FORMAL: My brother and **I** (not **myself**) met him at the station.

FORMAL: We have reserved seats for Jean and **you** (not **yourself**).

nohow, nowheres, nowhere near *Nohow* and *nowheres* are non- *U76* standard for *in no way* and *nowhere*. *Nowhere near* is informal for *not nearly*: "They were not nearly as clever as they thought."

off of Nonstandard for *off* or *from*: *U77*

STANDARD: Take it **off** (not **off of**) the table.

STANDARD: She deducted two dollars **from** (not **off of**) the price.

OK, O.K., okay All three spellings are acceptable, but the expres- *U78* sion itself is informal:

FORMAL: The mayor gave us her formal **approval** (not "her formal **OK**").

on account of Nonstandard as a substitute for *because*: *U79*

NONSTANDARD: When promoted, people may stop trying **on account of** (should be "because") they have reached their goal.

parameter *Parameter* is a useful technical word for exact margins *U80* or outside limits. For ordinary limits, try *limits* or *boundaries*.

plan on In your writing, plan to substitute *plan to*. *U81*

INFORMAL: My parents had **planned on** us taking over the farm.

FORMAL: My parents had **planned to** have us take over the farm.

plus *Plus* is acceptable in writing when used about figures, sums, *U82* and the like. Avoid using it as an informal substitute for *and* or *also*: "He dresses shabbily, *and* (not *plus*) he smells."

possessives with verbal nouns A traditional rule requires that a *U83* verbal noun (**gerund**) be preceded by a possessive in sentences like the following:

FORMAL: He mentioned **John's winning** a scholarship.

I am looking forward to **your mother's** staying with us.

In informal English, the plain form is common:

INFORMAL: Imagine **John winning** a scholarship!

A combination of a pronoun and a verbal with the *-ing* ending may express two different relationships. In the sentence "I saw *him* *returning* from the library," you actually saw *him*. In the sentence "I object to *his using* my toothbrush," you are not objecting to *him* but merely to one of *his* actions. Use the possessive pronoun (*my, our, his, their*) when the object of a verb or of a preposition is not the person but one of his or her actions, traits, or experiences:

RIGHT: We investigated the chances of **his** being elected.

There is no excuse for **their** not writing sooner.

U84 predominate   *Predominate* is a verb: "Shirt sleeves and overalls *predominated* in the crowd." *Predominant* is the adjective: "Antiwar feeling was *predominant*." "Democrats were the *predominant* party."

U85 preposition at the end of a sentence   The preposition that ends a sentence is idiomatic, natural English, though more frequent in informal than in formal use:

INFORMAL: She found her in-laws hard to live **with**.

FORMAL: Let us not betray the ideals **for which** these men died.

U86 prepositions often criticized   *Inside of* (for *inside*), *outside of* (for *outside*), and *at about* (for *about*) are redundant.

Back of for *behind* (*back of* the house), *inside of* for *within* (*inside of* three hours), *outside of* for *besides* or *except* (no one *outside of* my friends), and *over with* for *over* (it's *over with*) are informal.

As to, as regards, and *in regard to* often seem heavy-handed and bureaucratic:

AWKWARD: I questioned him **as to** the nature of his injury.

PREFERABLE: I questioned him **about** his injury.

As to whether, in terms of, and *on the basis of* flourish in all varieties of jargon.

Per (a dollar *per* day), *as per* (*as per* your request), and *plus* (quality *plus* service) are common in business and newspaper English but inappropriate in a noncommercial context.

U87 prior to, previous to   These sound like old-fashioned business jargon or bureaucratese. Try *before*.

JARGON: He always had an elaborate strategy session **previous to** (should be **before**) an important exam.

U88 provided, provided that, providing   *Provided, provided that,* and *providing* are interchangeable in a sentence like "He will withdraw his complaint, *provided* you apologize." However, only *provided* has escaped criticism and is therefore the safest form to use.

reason is because   *The reason . . . is because* is redundant, since   *U89*
because repeats the idea of cause already expressed in the word
reason.

INFORMAL: **The reason** that the majority rules **is because** it is strongest.

FORMAL: **The reason** that the majority rules **is that** it is strongest.

respective, respectful   When we are respectful, we show respect.   *U90*
The use of *respective* in expressions like "They went to their *respec-*
tive rooms" sounds jargony to many readers. Try "They *each* went
to their rooms."

shall, will   In current American usage, *will* usually indicates simply   *U91*
that something is going to happen. (I will ask him tomorrow.) The
more emphatic *shall* often shows determination, obligation, or
command:

We **shall** do our best.
Wages of common laborers **shall** not exceed twenty dollars a day.

   Handbooks no longer require *shall* for simple future in the
first person: "I *shall* see him tomorrow."

so and such   Informal English often uses *so* or *such* without going   *U92*
on to the *so . . . what?* "They were *so* frightened" (that what?).
"There was *such* an uproar" (that what?). Substitute "They were
extremely frightened" or add the *so . . . what?*

RIGHT: They were so frightened **that they were unable to speak**.
   There was such an uproar **that the judge banged the gavel
in vain**.

split infinitives   Occasionally, a modifier breaks up an infinitive,   *U93*
that is, a verbal formed with *to* (*to come, to promise, to have written*).
A split infinitive can be awkward if the modifier that splits the
infinitive is more than one word:

AWKWARD: He ordered us **to** with all possible speed **return** to our
stations.

BETTER: He ordered us **to return** to our stations with all possible
speed.

U94   **superlative in reference to two**   In informal speech and writing, the superlative rather than the comparative frequently occurs in comparisons between only two things. This use of the superlative is often considered illogical:

INFORMAL: Which of the two candidates is the **best** speaker?
FORMAL: Which of the two candidates is the **better** speaker?

U95   *sure*   In writing, use *surely* or *certainly* as the adverb:

INFORMAL: The guide **sure** knew all the answers.
FORMAL: The guide **certainly** knew all the answers.

U96   *take and, try and, up and*   *Take and* (in "I'd *take and* prune those roses") and *up and* (in "He *up and* died") are dialectal. *Try and* for *try to* ("I'd *try and* change his mind") is informal.

U97   *these kind*   Avoid "*these kind* of cars" and "*those kind* of fish." Agreement requires "*this kind* of car" (both singular) or "*these kinds* of fish" (both plural).

U98   *this here, that there*   Use only the *this* or *that*.

U99   **titles:** *Dr., Prof., Reverend*   In references to holders of academic degrees or titles, *Dr. Smith* and *Professor Brown* are courteous and correct. *Professor* is sometimes abbreviated in addresses, but only when it precedes the full name: *Prof. Martha F. Brown*. In references to clergy, *Reverend* is usually preceded by *the* and followed by the first name, by initials, or by *Mr.* (*the Reverend William Carper; the Reverend W. F. Carper; the Reverend Mr. Carper*).

U100   *type, type of, -type*   Omitting the *of* in expressions like "this *type* of plane" is informal. Avoid -*type* used as a suffix to turn nouns into adjectives: "an *escape-type* novel," "a *drama-type* program." Use "an *escape* novel," "a *dramatic* program."

U101   *unique*   It is often argued that one thing cannot be *more unique* than another. Either it is unique (one of a kind) or it isn't. Formal English therefore often substitutes *more nearly unique*.

U102   *used to, didn't use to, used to could*   *Used to* in questions or negative statements with *did* is informal. Avoid it in writing:

INFORMAL: She **didn't use to** smoke.
FORMAL: She **used not to** smoke.

Used to could is nonstandard for *used to be able*.

wait for, wait on   Informal English uses *wait on* both when we wait *U103* *for* others and when we wait *on* (or serve) them. In writing, use *wait for* when someone is keeping you waiting.

INFORMAL: They had been **waiting on** him in the parking lot.
FORMAL: They had been **waiting for** him in the parking lot.

where, where at, where to   In formal English, *where* takes the *U104* place of *where to* ("*Where* was it sent?") and *where at* ("*Where* is he?"). *Where* used instead of *that* ("I read in the paper *where* a boy was killed") is informal.

who, which, and that   *Who* and *whom* refer to persons ("the man *U105* *whom* I asked"). *Which* refers to ideas and things ("my son's car, *which* I bought"). A *which* introducing a restrictive clause should be replaced by *that*.

FORMAL: The people **whom** I asked liked the car **that** I bought.

-wise   People often change a noun into an adverb by tacking on *U106* *-wise*; this practice is common in business or advertising jargon:

JARGON: The delay was advantageous **tax-wise**.
BETTER: The delay was advantageous **for tax purposes**.

without   *Without* is nonstandard when used as a conjunction *U107* (subordinator) introducing a clause:

NONSTANDARD: The owner won't let me stay **without** I pay the rent.
STANDARD: The owner won't let me stay **unless** I pay the rent.

you with indefinite reference   Formal writing limits *you* to the *U108* meaning of "you, the reader." Much informal writing uses *you* with indefinite reference to refer to people in general.

INFORMAL: In Rome, **you** had to be a patrician to be able to vote.
BETTER: In Rome, **only patricians** were able to vote.

11

THE RESEARCH PAPER

STARTING YOUR SEARCH

OVERVIEW In a research paper, you investigate a limited subject by bringing together information and comment from several sources. A successful research paper provides reliable information on a subject about which many readers have only vague general impressions. The research paper will take you two steps beyond ordinary writing projects: First, you will be *synthesizing* material from a wider range of sources. You will draw on the best available information or the best current thinking on your subject. Second, you will *document* your sources, identifying them fully, enabling your reader to trace them and check the use you have made of them.

GUIDELINES FOR RESEARCH

Think of your research paper as a writing task.

Remember the following guidelines when choosing a promising topic and charting your course:

(1) Work on a subject that is worth the time and energy you invest. A topic may be right for you because it satisfies a latent curiosity: You might want to investigate space stations, solar energy, or nineteenth-century railroads. Or a topic may be right for you because it relates to a personal commitment, like Amnesty International or computers for the blind.

(2) Close in on a limited part of a general subject. The threat to animal life on our planet is a vast general subject. To arrive at a workable topic, you may want to focus on changing attitudes toward predators like the wolf or the coyote or on the vanishing habitats for the big birds: the condor or the bald eagle.

(3) Make full use of your library. Discover the full range of library resources and of more informal sources available to you. A good researcher perseveres in hunting down promising leads and manages not to be discouraged by those that don't work out.

(4) Synthesize material from a range of sources. Avoid subjects that would make you lean heavily on one main source, such as an encyclopedia entry or a survey article in a magazine. Your task is to sift the best current information and the most authoritative opinion. Be prepared to bring together scattered data and to weigh conflicting points of view.

(5) Stay close to the evidence you present. A research paper tests your ability to be **objective**, to follow the evidence where it leads. Your stance toward the audience should be: "This is the evidence. This is where I found it. You are welcome to check these sources and to verify these facts."

(6) Document your sources. Identify and describe the sources of all material you have used or adapted in your paper. The running text of your paper will identify your sources briefly, usually including an exact page reference in parentheses. A final alphabetical listing of "Works Cited" will give full publishing data, enabling the reader, for instance, to find the right article in a magazine, or the right edition of a book. This final list may include both print and nonprint sources and is therefore often more than strictly a **bibliography** (literally, a listing of *books*).

AVOIDING PLAGIARISM

Protect yourself against charges of plagiarism.

Careful documentation helps a writer avoid **plagiarism**. Writers who plagiarize lift material from their sources without acknowledgment. Whenever you draw on a source, anticipate questions like the following: Who said this? Who found this out? Who drew these conclusions?

Granted, many facts and ideas are common knowledge. Major historical dates and events or key ideas of scientific or philosophical movements are easily found in reference books. However, identify your source whenever you use information recently discovered or collected, whenever you adopt someone's personal point of view.

NO SOURCE: George Washington was elected to the Virginia assembly in 1758. (This is common knowledge, the kind of fact recorded in public documents and found in many history books.)

SOURCE SHOWN: Samuel Eliot Morison describes Washington as "an eager and bold experimenter" in new agricultural methods (62). (This is a judgment the historian made on the basis of firsthand investigation.)

(1) Never copy whole phrases or sentences without quotation marks. It is true that you will often condense or summarize. You will often **paraphrase** — pulling out and restating important ideas in your own words. Even so, use quotation marks — both in your notes and in your actual paper — whenever you transcribe word for word characteristic phrases, parts of sentences, or whole sentences. Much unintentional plagiarism results when students include in their notes — *without* quotation marks — material that is an only slightly shortened or superficially adapted version of the original text.

ORIGINAL: The Green parties of Western Europe point to the Industrial Revolution and nuclear power as unmitigated evils, as sins against nature.

BADLY ADAPTED: The environmentalists of Western Europe treat modern technology and nuclear power as unmitigated evils, as sins against nature.

SAFE: The environmentalists of Western Europe think of modern technology and nuclear power "as unmitigated evils, as sins against nature."

(2) Never take notes without including a source tag. As a practical precaution, make sure that a brief **source tag** — showing author, publication, and page number — always accompanies borrowed material in your notes and in successive drafts.

(3) Don't simply appropriate other people's thinking. Never simply take over someone else's plan, procedure, or strategy without acknowledgment.

41c	CHOOSING A SUBJECT

Focus on a manageable subject.

Carve out a topic from a general area like the following:

1. *Saving the animals:* the history of a major endangered species; the story of the disappearance of the buffalo or other nearly vanished animal; current conservationist efforts to protect endangered species of birds or other animals; the struggle to protect fur-bearing animals; in defense of the wolf or the coyote.

2. *The limits of technology:* Is manned space travel necessary? Are animal experiments necessary for medical research? Do heart transplants have a future? Was the green revolution a success?

3. *Running out of energy:* the future of solar energy; the story of coal; wind power through the ages; fission and fusion; damming the last wild rivers.

4. *The price of progress:* the story of the supersonic passenger plane; natural versus synthetic foods; more about additives; the automobile and the environment; acid rain; toxic waste.

5. *Fighting words in American history:* the abolitionist movement; the American suffragette; the tradition of populism; the story of segregation; the roots of unionism; robber barons or captains of industry.

6. *Future shock:* talking computers; the future of space stations; life on other planets; robots.

7. *The story of censorship:* controversial authors and the schools (Kurt Vonnegut, J. D. Salinger, Joyce Carol Oates); creationism and evolution; the definition of obscenity; unwelcome books (*1984, Grapes of Wrath, Brave New World*).

8. *The American Indian:* the story of a forgotten tribe; the Cherokee nation; the pueblos of the Southwest; the last wars; assimilating the native Americans.

Note: By and large, you will want to stay away from highly technical subjects, which may require more knowledge of mathematics, physics, biochemistry, or the law than you can muster or than you can explain to the nonspecialist reader.

WRITING WORKSHOP 1   Your instructor may ask you to prepare a *planning report* for a paper on a tentative research topic. Include the why, what, and how. What previous interest or exposure can you build on? What do you hope to accomplish? What are possible sources or promising leads? What might be your overall plan or strategy? Are you aiming at a special audience or the general reader? Present your report for discussion by the class or a small group.

OVERVIEW The experienced investigator knows where to look. To conduct a successful search, you have to know how to tap the resources of your college library. Although your search strategy will vary from subject to subject, you will normally explore three major kinds of materials:

- *reference works* (encyclopedias, specialized dictionaries, guides) that provide an overview or summary of your subject
- *magazine or newspaper articles* that deal with limited areas of your subject or with current developments
- *books* (or sections of books) that deal with your subject in some depth

Remember that your library is not the *only* source of information. Your phone book has a special section listing government agencies where you might write for advice or enlightenment. Your college as well as local businesses and organizations will employ experts who might consent to be interviewed.

42a EVALUATING SOURCES

Draw on reliable information from authoritative sources.

When evaluating possible sources, keep in mind test questions like the following:

(1) Is the writer an authority on the subject? Experts are not infallible, but it's good to know that an author has written and lectured widely on the subject and is frequently quoted or consulted. It's comforting to find that an author writing about agribusiness has been in the fields to talk with workers and supervisors, has studied government and corporate reports, and has read recent studies of relevant trends.

(2) Is the work a thorough study of the subject? Does it show a grasp of the historical background; does it seriously explore causes and effects? Does it take the opinions of others seriously, carefully weighing the pro and con on debated issues?

(3) Does the author draw on primary sources? Reliable authorities do not simply accept secondhand accounts; they settle important questions by turning to **primary sources** — legal documents, diaries, letters, eyewitness reports, transcripts of speeches and interviews, reports on experiments, statistical surveys.

(4) Is the author biased? The bailout of a large automobile manufacturer through government loans will be viewed one way in the autobiography of the company's chief executive. The story will be told differently by an aggressive critic of corporate politics. Whenever possible, try to look at both sides.

(5) Is the work up to date? Has it profited from recent research or newly discovered facts? If it was first published ten or twenty years ago, is there a revised, more recent edition? Keep in mind that a writer may have been left behind by new findings and new thinking in a burgeoning field.

42b | USING REFERENCE WORKS

Learn to use the reference tools available to every investigator.

Commonly available reference works range from weighty multi-volume sets to handy manuals and guides. You will find specialized reference works in a guide like Eugene P. Sheehy's *Guide to Reference Books*, published by the American Library Association. Here is a sampling of reference works that are often consulted:

ENCYCLOPEDIAS An encyclopedia is sometimes a good place to start — but not to finish — an investigation.

- The *Encyclopaedia Britannica* (an American publication) is the most authoritative of the general encyclopedias. It is brought up to date each year by the *Britannica Book of the Year*. A complete revision, called *The New Encyclopaedia Britannica*, was published in 1974 and has been updated since. It has two major sections: a ten-volume quick-reference index (the *Micropaedia*) and a nineteen-volume guide to more detailed information on many subjects (the *Macropaedia*).
- The *Encyclopedia Americana* is sometimes recommended for science and biography. General subjects are broken up into short articles, arranged alphabetically. The annual supplement is the *Americana Annual*.
- The one-volume *Columbia Encyclopedia* serves well for a quick check of people and places.

BIOGRAPHY In addition to biographical entries in encyclopedias, libraries usually have ample materials for a paper reassessing the role or reputation of a famous person.

- *Who's Who in America*, a biographical dictionary of outstanding living men and women, provides capsule biographies of important contemporaries. (The original *Who's Who* is a British publication. Specialized offshoots of the same publication include *Who's Who of American Women*.)
- The *Dictionary of American Biography (DAB)* gives a more detailed account of the lives of significant persons. (The British counterpart is the *Dictionary of National Biography*.)
- The *Biography Index* is a guide to biographical material in books and magazines.

LITERATURE A library project may deal with an author's schooling or early reading, recurrent themes in the books of a well-known novelist, or the contemporary reputation of a nineteenth-century poet.

- The fifteen-volume *Cambridge History of English Literature* and the *Cambridge Bibliography of English Literature* take stock of English authors and literary movements.

- The Spiller-Thorp-Johnson-Canby *Literary History of the United States*, with its supplementary bibliographies, lists as its contributors an impressive roster of American literary scholars.
- *Harper's Dictionary of Classical Literature and Antiquities* is a comprehensive scholarly guide to Greek and Roman history and civilization.

OTHER FIELDS OF INTEREST   Every major field of interest has its own specialized reference guides: specialized encyclopedias, dictionaries of names or technical terms, or yearbooks reporting on current developments. Here is a sampling of specialized reference works frequently consulted:

- *American Universities and Colleges* and *American Junior Colleges* provide basic facts about educational institutions.
- The *McGraw-Hill Encyclopedia of Science and Technology* is kept up to date by the *McGraw-Hill Yearbook of Science and Technology*.
- The *Encyclopedia of Computer Science and Technology* is a multivolume guide to a rapidly growing field.
- The *Dictionary of American History* by J. T. Adams is a six-volume guide.
- Langer's *Encyclopedia of World History* is a long-established reference guide in one volume.
- The *International Encyclopedia of the Social Sciences* is a multivolume reference work.
- *Grove's Dictionary of Music and Musicians*, a multivolume reference guide for music lovers, covers biography, history, and technical terms.
- The *McGraw-Hill Encyclopedia of World Art* has fifteen volumes.
- The Funk and Wagnalls *Standard Dictionary of Folklore, Mythology, and Legend* is one of several well-known guides to basic themes in folk culture and folk tradition.
- *Vital Speeches of the Day* can help you find recent speeches by government officials or business executives on topics like Third World debt or the impact of new technologies on employment.

BIBLIOGRAPHIES   For many subjects of general interest, you will be able to find a printed **bibliography** — an inventory of important books and other sources of information. Shorter bibliographical listings often appear at the end of an entry in an encyclopedia or a chapter in a textbook. Especially helpful are **annotated bibliographies** that provide a capsule description of each source. The following might be a sample entry:

> *Edsels, Luckies, & Frigidaires* by Robert Atwan, Donald McQuade, and John W. Wright (New York: Dell, 1972) is a large-format paperback which resembles nothing so much as a 100-year scrapbook of American advertising. Over 250 full-page ads are organized under three main headings, "Advertising and Social Roles," "Advertising and Material Civilization," and "Advertising and the Strategies of Persuasion." Chronological arrangement of the ads reflects changes in the "good life" over the last century.

BOOK REVIEWS   The *Book Review Digest* excerpts book reviews written shortly after publication of a book. Book review sections are a regular feature of many professional publications. The following is an example of a short book review from the *Library Journal*:

> **De Santis, Marie. Neptune's Apprentice: adventures of a commercial fisherwoman.** Presidio Pr. Jun. 1984. c.256p. illus. by Patricia Walker. ISBN 0-89141-200-X. $15.95.
>
> SOC SCI. PER NAR
>
> There are innumerable books about the lure of the sea but very few are by women. De Santis was a doctoral student in the late 1960s when she heard the siren call and, after brief apprenticeships on California commercial fishing boats, she determined to be her own captain. To describe the way the sea "shaped the spirit of its people" she tells of the people in the fleet for the eight years she fished: toil, fear, acceptance by the fishing fraternity, greed, fish and game bumbling—and always the search for the elusive fish. She left just before much of the fishing collapsed, but the sea remained with her. This is a fine testament to an individual's maturing and to the environment. Recommended, not just for libraries near the sea.—*Roland Person: Southern Illinois Univ. Lib., Carbondale*

LIBRARY WORK 2 Study *one* of the following often-mentioned *reference tools*. Prepare a brief report on its scope, usefulness, and format. Try to provide useful advice to prospective users; include some interesting sidelights.

1. *Books in Print*
2. *National Union Catalog (NUC)*
3. *Library of Congress Subject Headings*
4. *Sociological Abstracts*
5. *Contemporary Authors*
6. *Who's Who of American Women*
7. *Wall Street Journal Index*
8. *Historical Abstracts*
9. *Dictionary of Scientific Biography*
10. *Comprehensive Dictionary of Psychological and Psychoanalytic Terms*
11. *McGraw-Hill Dictionary of Art*
12. *Concise Encyclopedia of Living Faiths*

42c FINDING ARTICLES IN PERIODICALS

Know how to find articles in magazines and newspapers.

Much information or comment is published in **periodicals** — publications that appear at regular intervals, ranging from the daily newspaper to monthly and quarterly magazines. Most libraries have a compact catalog for all periodicals to which the library subscribes. This catalog, separate from the general catalog of the library, will show the location of recent issues and back issues, as well as availability on microfilm or microfiche.

COMPUTERIZED INDEXES Many libraries now have a central computerized index that will call up for you a battery of current magazine articles on a given subject. Trying to find material on changing patterns of modern marriage, you might punch in the key word MARRIAGE. The following might be a partial printout of what would appear on the screen:

```
                                   InfoTrac Database
                                   1/20/91 at 12:28
MARRIAGE
 —ADDRESSES, ESSAYS, LECTURES
      Changing relationships between men and
   women; scope of the problem.  (transcript)
   Vital Speeches—Oct 1 '84 p757(8)
MARRIAGE
 —ANALYSIS
      What is this state called marriage? by
   Elaine Brown Whitley il Essence Magazine—Feb
   '85 p54(5)
   #32D2299
MARRIAGE
 —CASE STUDIES
      First marriage after 40, by Lynn Normont il
   Ebony—Jan '83 p28(7)
   #15A2292
MARRIAGE
 —ECONOMIC ASPECTS
      The money side of marriage. il Changing
   Times—June '85 p32(6)
   #27K5219
      Equal pay for different work saved our
   marriage.  (physician pays wife for domestic
   duties) by Daniel L. Brick, Medical Econom-
   ics—Feb 4 '85 p95(3)
```

PRINTED PERIODICAL INDEXES To find magazine articles on your subject, you will often search the printed periodical indexes in your library. Published in monthly or semimonthly installments, these are later combined in huge volumes, each listing articles for a period of one or more years.

- The *Readers' Guide to Periodical Literature* indexes magazines for the general reader, from *Time*, and *Newsweek* to *Working Woman, Science Digest,* and *Technology Review*.

In the *Readers' Guide*, articles are listed twice — once under the author's name and once under a subject heading. Compare two entries for the same article:

AUTHOR ENTRY: **HARRIS, Michael**
Junk in outer space. il Progressive 42:16-19 N '78

SUBJECT ENTRY: **SPACE pollution**
Junk in outer space. M. Harris. il Progressive 42:16-19 N '78

The author entry begins with the full name of the author; the subject entry begins with the general subject: space pollution. The title of the article is "Junk in Outer Space." (The *il* shows that the article is illustrated.) The name of the magazine comes next: *Progressive*. Note:

- The *volume number* for the magazine is 42. *Page numbers* for the article follow after the colon: 16 through 19. (Sometimes the symbol + appears after the last page number; it shows that the article is concluded later in the magazine.)
- The *date of publication* was November 1978. (For magazines published more than once a month, the exact date is given. For example "N 10 '78" means "November 10, 1978.")

Other guides to periodicals intended for a general audience:

- *Essay and General Literature Index* may help you when you are not satisfied with what you find in the *Readers' Guide.*
- *Poole's Index to Periodical Literature,* covering the years from 1802–1907, is a guide to British and American magazines of the past.
- *Popular Periodicals Index,* published since 1973, will prove helpful to students of popular culture.

The following are guides to periodical literature in specialized areas:

- *Applied Science and Technology Index* (see the *Industrial Arts Index* for years before 1958)
- *Art Index*
- *Biological and Agricultural Index* (*Agricultural Index* before 1964)
- *Business Periodicals Index*
- *Education Index*
- *Engineering Index*
- *General Science Index*
- *Humanities Index* (now a separate publication, combined with the *Social Sciences Index* during the years 1965–1973)
- *Social Sciences Index* (formerly *International Index*)

CURRENT EVENTS   A number of special reference guides are useful for papers on a political subject or on current events:

- *Facts on File* is a weekly digest of world news, with an annual index. It gives a summary of news reports and comments, with excerpts from important documents and speeches.

- The *New York Times Index* (published since 1913) is a guide to news stories published in the *New York Times*.

- The annual index to the *Monthly Catalog of the United States Government Publications* lists reports and documents published by all branches of the federal government.

ABSTRACTS You can often identify useful articles by looking at **abstracts** — short summaries of articles, usually collected and published several times a year. The following is from Volume 30 of *Sociological Abstracts*:

82M2679

Fly, Jerry W., Reinhart, George R. & Hamby, Russell (Georgia Coll, Milledgeville 31061), **Leisure Activity and Adjustment in Retirement,** *Sociological Spectrum,* 1981, 1, 2, Apr-June, 135–144.
¶ A sample of retired persons (N = 134) in a southern metropolitan area responded to a questionnaire designed to investigate the interrelationship between level of leisure activity & adjustment in retirement. Adjustment was measured by two indices, life satisfaction & alienation. Results show that persons who have more leisure activities are more satisfied with their lives & are less alienated than those who have few leisure activities. 2 Tables. HA

COMPUTERIZED RESEARCH Computerized information services and research tools simplify and speed up a writer's search for sources.

- A system like INFOTRAC provides an instant listing of relevant current newspaper and magazine articles from hundreds of publications. By typing in key words or retrieval codes, you call up (and print out) a wide range of sources on subjects like marriage, acid rain, recessions, or men's fashions. You can call up book reviews, articles by or about a person, or information about a company or business.

■ The WILSEARCH system provides access to periodical indexes including the *Readers' Guide to Periodical Literature, Biography Index, General Science Index, Social Sciences Index, Art Index,* and *Book Review Digest.*

■ The DIALOG information service provides access to many different **databases** — collections of information stored in large computers. The service allows you to tap into sources of information covering areas like government statistics, science, medicine, law, business, finance, or current news events. A printed index (or a librarian) can help you find the right **descriptors** — subject labels or key words that will help the computer search for material on your topic. If your home computer has a **modem**, or telephone hookup, you may be able to have a complete reprint of an article produced on your own printer.

If you use the DIALOG service in your search for articles on your research topic, it will provide a printout describing possible sources in the following format. For inclusion in your records, note the item number (EJ 281390) and the file number (IR 511297):

```
EJ281390  IR511297
   Censorship Today and Probably Tomorrow.
   204elson, Ken
   Canadian Library Journal, v40 n2 p83-89 Apr 1983
   Language: English
   Document Type: JOURNAL ARTICLE (080); POSITION
   PAPER (120)
   Journal Announcement: CIJSEP83
   Examines preconceptions of censorship, citing
problems posed to librarians and teachers.
Highlights include censored books; individual
censors (including the Gablers); organized groups
including Save Our Schools (SOS), Phyllis
Schlafly's Eagle Forum, and the Moral Majority;
teacher and librarian censors (moral, literary,
sociological); and those who aid and abet
censors. (EJS)
```

LIBRARY WORK 3 In the *Readers' Guide, Social Sciences Index,* or *Humanities Index,* find an article on *one* of the subjects that follow. Write a brief report. Include the facts of publication, the purpose of the article, intended audience, main point or points, overall plan or strategy. Comment on level of difficulty, handling of technical terms or difficult material, and the like. Include one or two key quotations.

- talking computers
- the artificial heart
- sign language for apes
- schizophrenia
- reevaluations of the CIA or FBI
- competency tests for teachers
- women executives
- dissent in the Soviet Union
- drug testing for athletes
- basketball recruiting

 42d

FINDING BOOKS IN THE LIBRARY CATALOG

Learn to use the general catalog of your library.

Many libraries today are in transition from the card catalogs of the print age to the online catalogs of the computer age. The traditional catalog has been a card catalog with rows of drawers holding printed index cards in alphabetical order. Today, users increasingly view computerized catalog information on screens. However, the kind and arrangement of the information will be similar under the different systems. An important difference is that the computer catalog is likely to be set up for searches by key word. For instance, if you use the key words SPORTS MEDICINE, the computer will provide a listing of all the books in your library that have the words SPORTS and MEDICINE in their titles.

New-style computer entries may look like this:

```
Call#:        JX 1944.H68 1978b

Author:       Howard, Michael Eliot, 1922—

Title:        War and the liberal conscience /
              by Michael Howard. New Brunswick,
              N.J.: Rutgers University Press,
              1978. 143 p. ; 23 cm.

Series:       The Trevelyan lectures ; 1977.

Notes:        Includes bibliographical
              references and index.

Subjects:     Peace—History
              World politics—To 1900
              World politics—20th century
              War—History
              Liberalism
              Europe—Politics and government.
Also listed
under:        Trevelyan lectures ; 1977.
```

In the typical library catalog, the same book is listed several times: by *author* (under the author's last name), by *title* (under the first word of the title, not counting *The, A,* or *An*), and by *subject.*

AUTHOR ENTRIES Author entries give you complete publishing information about each separate book by an author, with titles arranged in alphabetical order. Entries for books *about* the author may follow at the end. Know how to read the information on the typical Library of Congress card:

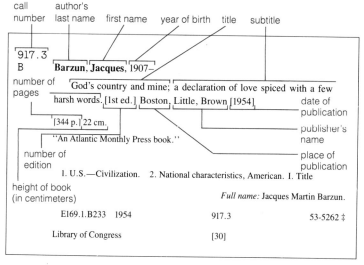

SAMPLE AUTHOR CARD

Look for clues to the nature of the book:

■ *The number or description of the edition.* If the catalog lists both the original edition and another marked "2nd ed." or "Rev. ed.," generally choose the one that is more up to date.

■ *The name and location of the publisher.* For instance, a book published by a university press is likely to be a scholarly or specialized study. The *date of publication* is especially important for books on scientific, technological, or medical subjects, where information dates rapidly.

■ *The number of pages* (with the number of introductory pages given as a lowercase Roman numeral). If the book contains *illustrations* or a *bibliography*, the card will carry a notation to that effect.

■ *The subject headings* (which show under what headings the book will be listed in the catalog). The listing for the Barzun book shows that the book will be of interest to students of the American national character.

TITLE ENTRIES Title entries carry the same information as author entries — except that the title is repeated at the top for alphabetical listing. The following might be a locally generated title card:

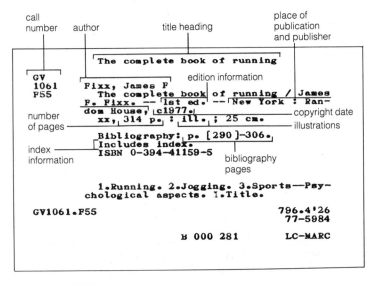

call number · author · title heading · place of publication and publisher

```
                  The complete book of running
                                   edition information
 GV
 1061        Fixx, James F
 F55             The complete book of running / James
            F. Fixx. -- 1st ed. -- New York : Ran-
            dom House, c1977.
                 xx, 314 p. : ill. ; 25 cm.

                 Bibliography: p. [290]-306.
                 Includes index.
                 ISBN 0-394-41159-5

                 1.Running. 2.Jogging. 3.Sports--Psy-
            chological aspects. I.Title.

 GV1061.F55                                796.4'26
                                           77-5984

                  B 000 281              LC-MARC
```

number of pages · copyright date · illustrations · index information · bibliography pages

SAMPLE TITLE CARD

SUBJECT ENTRIES Subject entries will often be your best hope for finding usable books. For instance, books on the American Civil War might appear under *U.S. — History — Civil War*, under *U.S. — History — Military*, under *Slavery in the United States*, or under *Abolitionists*. Try to think of other key terms that might appear in the catalog: *Confederacy* or *Emancipation*. Here is an example of a typed subject card from the card catalog of a special division of a college library:

```
978        MORMONS AND MORMONISM - HISTORY
S

           Stegner, Wallace Earle, 1909-

           The gathering of Zion; the story of the
      Mormons, by Wallace Stegner. 1st ed. New York,
      McGraw-Hill, 1964

      331 p. illus. maps 23 cm (American Trails
      series)

      Bibliography: pp. 315-319
```

SAMPLE SUBJECT CARD

CALL NUMBERS   Once you decide that you should consult a book, copy its call number. The **call number** directs you, or the librarian, to the shelf where the book is located. Your library may use either the Library of Congress system or the Dewey decimal system.

■ The **Library of Congress system** divides books into categories identified by letters of the alphabet. It then uses additional letters and numerals to subdivide each main category. For instance, the call number of a book on religion starts with a capital *B*. The call number of a book on education starts with a capital *L*.

■ The **Dewey decimal system** uses numerals to identify the main categories. For instance, 400–499 covers books on language; 800–899 covers books on literature. The 800 range is then further subdivided into American literature (810–819), English literature (820–829), and so on. Additional numerals and letters close in on individual authors and individual works by the same author.

LIBRARY WORK 4 Through the central catalog of the library, find *one* of the following books. Study its preface or introduction, table of contents, and a key chapter or sample entries. Then prepare a brief *book review* that tells your reader about the purpose of the book, its intended audience, the scope of the book, and its overall plan. Include one or two characteristic or revealing quotations.

- Bruno Bettelheim, *The Uses of Enchantment*
- Leo Rosten, *The Joys of Yiddish*
- G. M. Trevelyan, *History of England*
- Barbara W. Tuchman, *A Distant Mirror*
- Norma Lorre Goodrich, *Ancient Myths*
- Margaret Mead, *Male and Female*
- Alden T. Vaughan, *New England Frontier: Puritans and Indians*
- Robert Coles, *Children of Crisis*
- Desmond Morris, *The Naked Ape*
- Joseph Campbell, *The Hero with a Thousand Faces*
- Alice Walker, *In Search of Our Mothers' Gardens*
- Adrienne Rich, *On Lies, Secrets, and Silence*
- Maxine Hong Kingston, *China Men*

42e YOUR WORKING LIST OF SOURCES

Keep a complete record of promising sources.

Prepare a separate **source card** or source entry for each book, pamphlet, article, or nonprint source. Some of the information in your preliminary list of sources is mainly for your own use in locating the book or article: the complete call number or a location in the library. But most of the information will be essential when you identify your sources in your finished paper.

SOURCE CARDS FOR BOOKS When preparing your source cards for books, use the format that you will need to observe when later typing your final list of works used (or cited) in your finished paper: Start with the last name of the author. Underline (italicize) title and any subtitle. Indent the second line five spaces. A typical entry might look like this:

```
HV
947        Mitford, Jessica.  Kind and Usual
M58             Punishment:  The Prison Business.
1073            New York:  Random, 1973
```

SOURCE CARD — BOOK

For accurate identification of a book, give the *full name of the author* — last name first to facilitate alphabetizing. Second, give the *full title* of the book, including any subtitle (separate it from the main title by a colon). Underline or italicize title and subtitle of a book, pamphlet, or other work that appeared as a separate publication. (Underlining in a handwritten or typed manuscript converts to italics in print.)

The publishing data, or *facts of publication*, for a book may include the following:

- *editor's or translator's name* if the book has been put together or translated by someone other than the author(s): "Shakespeare, William. *The Complete Works*, ed. G. B. Harrison" or "Chekhov, Anton. *The Cherry Orchard*, trans. Tyrone Guthrie and Leonid Kipnis."

- *number or description of the edition* if the book has been revised or brought up to date: "3rd ed." or "Rev. ed."
- *number of volumes* if a work consists of several and all relate to your investigation: "2 vols."
- *place of publication* (usually the location of the main office of the publishing house, or of the first office listed if several are given).
- *name of the publisher*, leaving out such tags as "Inc." or "and Company": "Random"; "McGraw-Hill."
- *date of publication* (if no date is listed on the title page, use the latest copyright date listed on the reverse side of the title page).
- *number of the volume used* (if only one volume of a larger work seems relevant to your investigation): "Vol. 3."

SOURCE CARDS FOR ARTICLES For accurate identification of an article, record both the *title of the article* (in quotation marks) and the *title of the periodical* (underlined or italicized). The quotation marks show that an article, story, or poem was *part* of a larger publication. An annotated card, including brief reminders about the article, may look like this:

Periodical Room   Schorer, Mark. "D. H. Lawrence: Then, During, Now," *Atlantic* March 1974 : 84-88.

The author, one of Lawrence's biographers, traces Lawrence's reputation as a writer from its low point at the time of his death to its present "position of primacy among great twentieth-century prose writers in English" (84).

Normally, your entry for a journal or newspaper article will not include the publisher's name or the place of publication, though the latter is sometimes needed to identify a small-town newspaper: *Daily Herald* [Ely, NV]. Record the *date* of the issue and complete *page numbers: Surfer's Companion* Sept. 1989: 13–18. *The Honolulu Enquirer* 10 Jan. 1990, 24–26. In case you decide later to make or request a photocopy, you might want at this point to include complete page numbers when an article is interrupted and then concluded later in the magazine (12–17, 45–46). However, a plus sign will signal the continuation in your final listing of sources (12–17 +).

You may need additional data like the following:

■ In many professional or technical journals, page numbers are consecutive through the issues of the same *volume* — usually all the issues published in one year. Record the number of the volume (in Arabic numerals), the year (in parentheses), and the page numbers of the article: *Modern Ornithology* 7 (1987): 234–38. When page numbers of different issues are *not* consecutive for the same volume, you may have to include the number of the issue: *Birdwatcher's Quarterly* 17.3 (1988): 17–20 (for volume 17, no. 3).

■ The full-service modern newspaper often publishes more than one daily edition, with several sections whose pages are not numbered consecutively throughout the issue. Include the specifics needed to guide your reader: *Bogtown Gazette* 25 Oct. 1988, late ed.: C18. (Include *p.* or *pp.* for page or pages only if omitting them might cause confusion.)

LIBRARY WORK 5   Prepare *annotated source cards or entries* for three possible sources for a research report on changing public attitudes on a current issue. Choose *one* of the following:

■ nuclear safety
■ prison reform
■ age and aging
■ safe sex
■ damage awards
■ capital punishment

- mercy killings
- space flights

For your sources, choose one book indexed in the central catalog, one article indexed in the *Readers' Guide*, and one current magazine article. Provide full information; include call numbers when appropriate.

OVERVIEW   Good writers are often good note takers; they have an eye for material that will serve them well later. When deciding whether to note or not to note, ask yourself:

- Am I *learning* something here about my topic?
- Does this help answer a *question* that has come up earlier?
- Does this *raise* a question to which I should try to find the answer?
- Does this furnish *evidence* or support for a working hypothesis or tentative conclusion?
- Does this represent an objection or *contrary evidence* that I will have to address?
- Does this help clarify a *key term* related to my topic?

CAUTION: Make sure that at a later stage your notes will tell you clearly *who* said *what* and *where*.

Take accurate notes as raw material for your first draft.

Whether you write your notes by hand, type them, or feed them directly into your word processor, accurate and usable notes provide the essential supply line for your paper. For handwritten or typed notes, 3″ × 5″ or 4″ × 6″ note cards enable you to shuffle your information as the pattern of your paper takes shape. The following procedures will save you time and grief:

■ Include a *heading* — first only a specific identifier, but later also the tentative subdivision of your paper — with each card or entry. If you feed notes into your word processor, use a clear **retrieval code** (like WS for women in sports), followed by a specific identifier (like "track coach interview" or "women's Olympic marathon"). Refine your retrieval code later as subdivisions of your paper take shape (for instance WS — hst for "Women in Sports — history").

■ Include the *author and title* of your source (in shortened form) at the end, along with exact page numbers.

■ Use each card or entry for *closely related information* or for quotations centered clearly on one limited point. (This way you will not have to disentangle material later for use at different points in your grand design.)

■ Use *quotation marks* to identify all quoted phrases, parts of sentences, or whole sentences.

In taking notes, do not simply copy big chunks of material. Adapt the material to suit your purposes as you go along. Learn to use several major techniques:

(1) Summarize background information; condense lengthy arguments. Here is a note card that condenses several pages of introductory information in John G. Neihardt's book *Black Elk Speaks*:

```
Last Battles

    In the fall of 1930, a field agent helped
Neihardt meet Black Elk, a holy man of the
Oglala Sioux who was a second cousin to Chief
Crazy Horse.  Black Elk was nearly blind and
knew no English.  Neihardt, speaking to him
through an interpreter, gained his confidence
partly by respecting the holy man's long si-
lences.  In the spring of 1931, Black Elk took
many days to tell his life story, including the
story of his share in the defeat of General
Custer, which Black Elk witnessed as a young
warrior.

Neihardt, Black Elk vii-xi
```

SAMPLE NOTE CARD

(2) Make strategic use of brief, well-chosen direct quotations. When we quote **verbatim**, we quote directly word for word. Quote characteristic or striking phrases. Quote sentences that sum up well a step in an argument. Look for sentences that show well the point of view or intentions of the quoted author.

```
Indian Education

    Indian children were put in crowded boarding
schools and fed at the cost of 11 cents a day
(with their diet supplemented by food that could
be grown on school farms).  From the fifth grade
up, children put in half a day's labor on the
school farm.  They were taught "vanishing trades
of little or no economic importance."

Johnson, "Breaking Faith"  240
```

(3) Use extended direct quotation for key passages. Quote at some length to let the original author sum up a major argument.

Let authors speak in their own words on difficult or controversial points. Quote verbatim an author's striking summing up of a key issue or a current trend:

Vegetarianism

"Welcome to Vegetarian Chic, the latest
consuming consequence of healthier attitudes
among Americans. While few people have totally
forsworn meat, they're loading their plates high
with veggies and fruits--11 percent more of the
former and 7 percent more of the latter than
five years ago. According to a 1985 Gallup
poll, some 6.2 million Americans now call themselves vegetarians (although many eat the odd
morsel of fish or chicken or even beef)."

Givens, "Going for the Greens" 79

---

(4) Paraphrase less important material. In a **paraphrase**, we put information and ideas into our own words. This way we can emphasize what is most directly useful. We can cut down on what is less important. At the same time, we show that we have *made sense* of what we have read. The following sample note card paraphrases an author's statement and support of one key point:

Rehabilitation

    Trades or vocational skills taught in
today's prisons are often outdated or unrealis-
tic. In one case, a New York medium-security
prison provided detainees with a course in
operating diesel trucks. The course was very
popular and was supported by local charitable
organizations. Ironically, after their release
the prisoners found that the law prohibited them
from obtaining a Class One driver's license for
more than five years in most cases. In the
interim, many returned to the professions that
had put them behind bars in the first place. As
a result, over half returned to prison.

Menninger, "Doing True Justice" 6

LIBRARY WORK 6 Select a magazine article or a chapter in a book on one of the topics listed below. Assume that you are extracting information or opinions for use in a larger research project. Prepare five note cards illustrating various techniques of *note taking:* Include examples of summary, paraphrase, mixed indirect and direct quotation, and extended direct quotation. Choose one:

- deregulation
- the history of advertising
- the history of photography
- Hollywood's early stars
- the Cherokee nation
- the suffragette (suffragist) movement
- space stations
- the war on drugs

<table>
<tr><td>**43b**</td><td>USING QUOTED MATERIAL</td></tr>
</table>

Use quoted material to advantage in your own text.

As you start your first draft, you work material from your notes into your own text. Study effective ways of integrating material from your notes in your paper. In your final draft, quotations of *more than four typed lines* should be set off as **block quotations** — double-spaced, indented *ten* spaces, with *no* quotation marks.

(1) Long quotation — to be used sparingly:

```
In her biography of President Johnson, Doris Kearns
summed up the factors that weakened the role of the
traditional political party:
          The organization of unions, the development
          of the Civil Service, and the rise of the
```

PUNCTUATING QUOTATIONS — AN OVERVIEW

DIRECT QUOTATION: quotation marks, introduced by comma or (more formally) by colon:

According to the report, "Engineering, medicine, and law are no longer male bastions."
The author emphasized her conclusion: "Engineering, medicine, and law are no longer male bastions."

QUOTED WORDS OR PHRASES: *no* introductory comma or colon:

Like Horace Mann, Americans have long considered education the "great equalizer" in society.

QUOTE-WITHIN-QUOTE: single quotation marks when someone you quote is in turn quoting someone else:

The article concluded: "She is a hard worker and, in the words of a fellow judge, 'very much in charge of herself.'"

EXCERPTED QUOTATION: Use an **ellipsis** — three spaced periods — to show that you have omitted material in order to shorten a quotation. (Use four periods, with *no* extra space before the first period, if the omission occurs after a complete sentence.)

The reviewer called the book a "searing indictment of the extent to which Americans . . . failed to respond to the plight of European Jews."

ADDITIONS: Use **square brackets** to show interpolations:

According to the report, "Powerful tribal antagonisms are a basic political fact of life in countries like Nigeria and Rhodesia [now Zimbabwe]."

> welfare state deprived the party of its ca-
> pacity to provide jobs, foods, and services
> to loyal constituents, thus severing its
> connection with the daily lives and needs
> of the people. . . . Technology provided
> access to new forms of amusement and recre-
> ation, such as movies and television, which
> were more diverting than party-sponsored
> dances and made it unlikely that people
> would attend political meetings and
> speeches for their entertainment value.
> During the 1960's, more and more people de-
> clined to affiliate themselves with a party
> and identified themselves as independents.
> (162)

COMMENT: The introductory sentence sums up the point of the quotation. The excerpt is set off as a **block quotation** — *indented ten spaces, no quotation marks*. The introductory sentence gives credit to the original author; the full title of her book will appear after her name in the final listing of "Works Cited." The number in parentheses at the end of the quotation directs the reader to the exact page.

Note: Use no additional paragraph indentation with block quotations unless the quotation runs to more than one paragraph. An additional *three* spaces then shows the beginning of each actual paragraph in the original source.

(2) Plagiarized version — illegitimate, unacknowledged paraphrase:

> The political party no longer plays its traditional
> role. The growth of the unions and the welfare state
> deprived the party of its capacity to provide jobs,
> food, and services to people. New forms of amuse-
> ment and recreation, such as movies and television,

```
were more diverting than party-sponsored dances and
made it unlikely that people would attend political
meetings for their entertainment value.  More and
more people declined to affiliate themselves with a
party and became independents instead.
```

COMMENT: The passage takes over someone else's words in a slightly shortened, less accurate form — *and without acknowledgment.* Even if the source were identified, this method of adapting the material would be unsatisfactory. Far too much of the original author's way of putting things has been copied — without the use of direct quotation: "deprived the party of its capacity," "more diverting than party-sponsored dances."

(3) Legitimate paraphrase — attributed to the original author:

```
As Doris Kearns reminds us, major changes in our so-
ciety weakened the traditional political party.  The
old-style party had provided jobs, favors, and even
free food to the party faithful, but the unions, the
Civil Service, or the welfare state took over many
of these functions.  People no longer depended on
social events sponsored by the party or on rousing
political speeches for entertainment; they had mov-
ies and television instead.  During the 1960's,
fewer and fewer people declared a party affiliation;
many listed themselves as independents (162).
```

COMMENT: This paraphrase (followed by the page reference) keeps the essential meaning of the original. But the information is given to us in the adapter's own words, sometimes with added touches that help make the point clear or vivid: "the party faithful," "rousing political speeches."

(4) Part paraphrase, part direct quotation — worked closely into the text:

> In her biography of President Johnson, Doris Kearns
> traces the changes that weakened the role of our po-
> litical parties. The growing labor unions, the ex-
> panding Civil Service, and the welfare state began
> to provide the jobs, the favors, and the free food
> that the old-style party had provided for the party
> faithful. These changes cut off the party's close
> "connection with the daily lives and needs of the
> people." Movies and television made the old-style
> party-sponsored dances and rousing political
> speeches obsolete as entertainment. During the
> 1960's, voters more and more "declined to affiliate
> themselves with a party and identified themselves as
> independents" (162).

COMMENT: The adapter explains the main points but at the same time keeps some of the authentic flavor of the original. Direct quotation is limited to characteristic phrases and key points.

(5) Legitimate summary — for preview or overview:

> Doris Kearns shows how the unions, the Civil Ser-
> vice, the welfare state, and the mass media all
> helped weaken party affiliation. They provided the
> jobs, the favors, and the entertainment for which
> voters once turned to the traditional party organi-
> zations (162).

COMMENT: This summary, getting at the gist of the passage, could serve as an overview of major points.

WRITING WORKSHOP 7   Alice Walker wrote the following excerpt in her first published essay, "The Civil Rights Movement: What Good Was It?" (*The American Scholar*, Autumn 1967). Prepare several different versions of a passage that would use material from this excerpt:

- a passage introducing an excerpted *block quotation*
- a passage using an extended *paraphrase* of much of the material
- a passage combining paraphrase and *direct quotation*
- a passage using only a brief *summary*

In each version, identify author and source. Introduce the material; make the reader see its point or significance.

> The life of Dr. King, seeming bigger and more miraculous than the man himself, because of all he had done and suffered, offered a pattern of strength and sincerity I felt I could trust. He had suffered much because of his simple belief in nonviolence, love, and brotherhood. Perhaps the majority of men could not be reached through these beliefs, but because Dr. King kept trying to reach them in spite of danger to himself and his family, I saw in him the hero for whom I had waited so long.
>
> What Dr. King promised was not a ranch-style house and an acre of manicured lawn for every black man, but jail and finally freedom. He did not promise two cars for every family, but the courage one day for all families everywhere to walk without shame and unafraid on their own feet. He did not say that one day it will be us chasing prospective buyers out of our prosperous well-kept neighborhoods, or in other ways exhibiting our snobbery and ignorance as all other ethnic groups before us have done; what he said was that we had a right to live anywhere in this country we chose, and a right to a meaningful well-paying job to provide us with the upkeep of our homes. He did not say we had to become carbon copies of the white American middle class; but he did say we had the right to become whatever we wanted to become.

43c   COMBINING DIFFERENT SOURCES

Combine material from different sources in a paragraph.

A paragraph in your finished paper will often combine material from different note cards. The paragraph will often begin with the general conclusion that the evidence on several related cards suggests. Study the three sample cards on the following page. Then study the way the material has been integrated in the following finished paragraph:

> For years, nature lovers have been keeping an anxious count of such endangered species as the bald eagle and the whooping crane. When the bald eagle became the national symbol soon after Independence, there were nesting pairs everywhere in what is now the continental United States. Two hundred years later, Frank Graham, Jr., writing in Audubon magazine, reported a current estimate of 5,000 bald eagles left in the lower forty-eight states. According to his figures, only 627 nests remained active, and they produced approximately 500 young (99). In 1981, Steven C. Wilson and Karen C. Hayden, writing in the National Geographic, reported a count of 76 for wild whooping cranes left in the United States, up from a dismal count of 21 thirty years earlier (37–38). Another estimate puts the current population at 95 (Freedman 89).

Endangered Species--Counts   Card 1

    The bald eagle became the national symbol in
1782, and there were nesting pairs in all the
lower 48 states. The current bald eagle population has been estimated at 5,000 in the lower 48
states. As of 1975, only 627 nests remained
active, and they produced approximately 500
young.

Graham, "Will the Bald Eagle Survive?" 99

Endangered Species--Counts

    "In 1948, the wild whooping crane population
was up by just two from a decade earlier--to 31.
The count sank to 21 in the winter of 1951-52,
Card 2 then rose gradually to an encouraging 74 in 1978-
79. Last spring there were six yearlings to join
the flight north. . . . The wild whooping crane
count now stands at 76, an improvement deriving
in large measure from protective practices at
Arkansas."

Wilson and Hayden, "Where Oil and Wildlife Mix"
37-38

Endangered Species--Counts

    "Whooping cranes, the largest cranes inhabit-
Card 3 ing North America, are on the U.S. endangered
species list. The big birds' population dwindled
to 14 in the late 1930s but is now estimated at
95."

Freedman, "Whooping Cranes" 89

WRITING PRACTICE 8   Combine closely related material from different note cards in a finished *sample paragraph*. Prepare three note cards that all bear on the same limited point. Turn to sources that you have used for one of the previous exercises, or to sources related to your own current research paper project. Use the material on your cards in a sample paragraph that introduces the material clearly and helpfully to your reader. Hand in the note cards with your finished paragraph. (Include page references in parentheses.)

---

44   FIRST DRAFT AND REVISION

OVERVIEW Even while you are collecting material, you will be ordering and shaping it so that you can channel it into a first draft.

PLANNING Often the nature of the subject or its history will suggest a tentative working plan. Writing about bilingual education, you are likely to operate tentatively with a rough pro-and-con sorting. On the con side, you may accumulate material from articles titled "In Defense of the Mother Tongue" or "Bilingual Classes? In U.S. But Few Other Nations." On the pro side, you may gather material from articles titled "Progress in Bilingual Education" or "Bilingualism: The Accent Is on Youth." As you proceed, you will be pushing from such tentative groupings toward an outline for your paper.

DRAFTING Once you have settled on a working outline, you use it as a guide in organizing and shuffling your notes. When your notes are in the right order, you can start writing your first draft. As you push ahead, keep in mind the needs you have to meet:

■   Make the reader see your *plan* and guide the reader's attention in the right direction. You need to raise the issue or dramatize the topic; you need an early preview or early hints of your general strategy; you need to mark major turning points.

- Show that your conclusions are not just *one person's opinion.* Throughout, you need to satisfy the reader who asks, "Who said this? What is the source of this information? What do the experts say? Is there another side?"

- *Integrate* the material from your notes in your text. This means that you have to select, adapt, and splice together material from your sources in such a way that there will be a smooth, natural flow.

REVISING When you revise your first draft, you can look at what you have done from the point of view of the reader. Do not limit yourself to final editing for better sentences, clear punctuation, or the right word. Adjust your plan as necessary. If necessary, shift important background information to an earlier part of your paper. Revise your strategy if you decide to leave the more controversial parts of a proposal till later in your discussion.

44a | DEVELOPING AN OUTLINE

Go from tentative groupings to a definite outline.

Early in your collecting of material, begin to set up tentative major categories. Remember the following advice:

(1) Group together notes that contain related material. Assign tentative common headings to groups of notes that deal with the same part of a larger issue. For a paper on prison reform, you might decide that your major groupings should include "Old-style penitentiaries," "Rehabilitation," "Experiments — U.S.," and "Experiments — Abroad."

(2) Work toward a unifying thesis. Ask yourself, "What is this paper as a whole going to tell the reader?" Try to sum up in one sentence the overall conclusion that your research has led you to.

Present this sentence as your thesis early in your paper — preferably at the end of an effective but short introduction:

The Isolated Americans

THESIS: The failure of Americans to learn foreign languages is producing a growing isolation of our country from the rest of the world.

(3) Work out a clear overall plan for your paper. Suppose you are writing about the threatened survival of the American bald eagle. You may decide early to group your note cards under major headings like the following:

Population counts
Dangers from pesticides
Dangers from sheep ranchers
Conservation measures

Here is a more detailed outline:

Saving the Bald Eagle

THESIS: The bald eagle will become extinct unless we come to understand and respect the special needs of this endangered species.

   I.   The history of the bald eagle
  II.   Dangers to the bald eagle
        A.   Pesticides used by farmers
        B.   Poisoned bait, traps, and bullets used by ranchers
        C.   Technological dangers
 III.   Steps toward improvement
        A.   New eagle refuge
        B.   Stricter control of poisons
        C.   Better power line structures

WRITING WORKSHOP 9 Prepare a *trial outline* for discussion in a small group or in class. Present it as an informal working outline, subject to refining and revision.

| WRITING THE FIRST DRAFT |

Funnel the material from your notes into a rough first draft.

Keep the following guidelines in mind to help you produce a strong first draft:

(1) Start with a strong overview. Do not just sketch out a "let's-see-what-we-find" program. Focus the readers' attention and arouse their interest by a more definite preview. Pinpoint the issue; sum up key findings; summarize the pro and con.

TOO OPEN:	Surrogate motherhood is an area filled with successes and problems. Some people believe in the surrogate program and others condemn the practice. Here we will explore some of the seemingly good and bad aspects of the program.
FOCUSED:	Conflicting voices on the use of animal experiments in medical research leave us unsure of which side to take. Our hearts tell us to listen to often-inflated news reports of cruelty and abuse. Our brains tell us that if it weren't for research involving other living creatures, many of the lifesaving techniques that are common today would not exist.

(2) Avoid the "dumped" quotation. Do not just spring a quotation on the reader. Prepare the ground; sum up who says what and why.

DUMPED:	Susan Jacoby is a "First Amendment junkie."
REVISED:	Susan Jacoby, who has written widely on women's issues, disagrees with the feminists on the issue of pornography. She is first and foremost a journalist who believes in free speech and the protection of the First Amendment. She is unequivocally a "First Amendment junkie."

(3) Bundle related quotations effectively. Add a lead sentence that shows what a set of quotations is supposed to prove:

> **Infertility, now affecting one in five couples, has many causes**. J. H. Guenero, writing in *Science News*, identifies familiar medical problems: failure to ovulate, inflammatory disorders, blockage of the fallopian tubes. Hilary Rose, a professor of Social Policy at Bradford University, points to modern birth control methods as a more recent culprit. The prolonged use of the pill, damage due to badly fitted coils, and poorly performed abortions all help explain the rising incidence of infertility.

(4) Look out for weak links. Avoid lame transitions using *also* or *another*. Help the reader who wonders, "Why is this in here at this point?"

WEAK: Another expert on the dinosaur puzzle is Janice Rotha, who writes in the *American Scientist*. . . .

BETTER: An expert who disagrees strongly with the sudden-extinction theory is Janice Rotha. She writes in the *American Scientist*. . . .

WRITING WORKSHOP 10   Prepare a first draft of your paper. Your instructor may ask you to submit it for suggestions for revision or for peer review.

44c | REVISING THE FIRST DRAFT

Allow time for revision of your first draft.

The first draft of your research paper gives you the opportunity to check what you have and to see if it will work. After a day or two, you will be ready to look at your draft with the reader's eye. Consult the following checklist as a guide to revision:

(1) Spell out fully what you have learned. What is obvious to you may not be obvious to your reader. Can you identify a sentence or a passage that sums up what you are trying to prove? Does a strong **thesis** appear in a strategic position — at the beginning or at the end?

(2) Strengthen support for key points. For example, in reading your first draft on the subject of the "Graying of America," you may decide that your statistics on forced retirement are too skimpy and dated. Revision is your chance to bring in updated information or to use a recognized authority to bolster your point.

(3) Reorganize if necessary. Check the flow of your paper and rechannel it as needed. Suppose you are writing your paper on the conflict between ideal and reality faced by many career women today. In your first draft, you have followed this outline:

The New Woman

   I.   The media image of the New Woman
  II.   Unresolved conflicts
      A.   The homemaker stereotype
      B.   "Femininity" versus being a professional
      C.   Career and motherhood
 III.   The realities of the workplace
      A.   Predominantly female occupations
      B.   Disparity in pay
 IV.   The price of progress
      A.   Health problems and stress
      B.   Difficult personal relationships

On second thought, your Part II delves too early into material colored by personal grievances, so you decide to start with a "let's-look-at-the-cold-facts" approach. In your second draft, you reverse the order of Parts II and III. You also plug in some material from the history of women's work to add perspective:

The New Woman

I. The media image of the New Woman
II. The working woman then
III. The working woman now
    A. Predominantly female occupations
    B. Disparity in pay
IV. Unresolved conflicts
    A. The homemaker stereotype
    B. "Femininity" versus being a professional
    C. Career and motherhood
V. The price of progress
    A. Health problems and stress
    B. Difficult personal relationships

(4) Integrate quoted material better. Should you do more to get your reader ready for a quotation, explaining the what and the why? Should there be a better mix of sentence-length quotations and brief quoted phrases, worked more organically into your text?

(5) Strengthen coherence. Give your readers a reason to keep on reading as they move from point to point. Revise weak links like the following:

WEAK LINK: **Another** point to consider is . . .
               We might **also** look at . . .

REVISED: A **similar, more recent** argument is that . . .
               People **outside the profession** usually look at the problem from a different perspective . . .

(6) Check for clear attribution. Can the reader tell throughout where your information came from or whose judgment you have trusted?

WRITING PRACTICE 11 Write a final outline that reflects your revision of your first draft. Observe the format of a formal outline.

IDENTIFYING YOUR SOURCES

OVERVIEW Effective **documentation** enables your reader to search out an article or book you have used and turn to the right page. The style of documentation shown in this section was recently developed by the Modern Language Association (MLA). It is similar to the style of documentation recommended by the American Psychological Association (APA) for research in the social sciences. Three principles underlie the provisos of the MLA style:

- Identify your sources briefly in your text.
- Give page references in your text, including the author's name and sometimes a shortened title as needed.
- Give a complete description of each source in a final alphabetical listing of "Works Cited."

45a PARENTHETICAL DOCUMENTATION (MLA) *doc*

Put page reference and needed identification in parentheses.

Identify your source not only when you *quote directly* but also when you *paraphrase* or *summarize*. In addition, show the source of all facts, figures, or ideas that are the result of someone else's effort or inspiration. Study the following possibilities:

1. SIMPLE PAGE REFERENCE You will often identify the author or the publication or both in your running text. You will then use your parenthetical reference to point the reader to the right page. Put page number (or page numbers) in parentheses after a closing quotation mark but before a final period:

```
For Gwendolyn Brooks, the "biggest news" about the
events in Little Rock was that the people there "are
like people everywhere" (332).
```

2. IDENTIFICATION BY AUTHOR Include author's last name with the page reference if author and work do not appear in your text (and if you cite only *one* source by this author):

> The familiar arguments in favor of bilingual educa-
> tion have recently been challenged by an outstanding
> Hispanic author (Rodriguez 32, 37-39).

3. IDENTIFICATION BY TITLE Include a shortened form of the title if you are going to use *more than one* source by the same author. Underline (italicize) the title of a book or whole publication; enclose the title of an article or part of a publication in quotation marks.

> Alex Comfort has frequently told us that the blunt-
> ing of abilities in the aged results at least in
> part from "put-downs, boredom, and exasperation"
> ("Old Age" 45); the changes we see in old people,
> according to him, "are not biological effects of ag-
> ing" (Good Age 11).

Note: If you shorten a title, keep the *first word* (other than *The, A,* or *An*) the same in the shortened title, so that your readers can find the source in alphabetical order in your list of "Works Cited."

4. IDENTIFICATION BY AUTHOR AND TITLE Include au-
thor's name and a short title if you use more than one source by an author not identified in your text. Put a comma between author and title, *no* comma between title and page number.

> The traditional stories that the Arabs brought with
> them into medieval Spain were always fairly short
> (Grunebaum, Medieval Islam 294, 305-10).

5. REFERENCE WITHIN A SENTENCE Put page reference and identification *where needed* for clarity part way through a sentence:

```
As Mahoney (14) had predicted, recent surveys show
that many who are forced to retire would prefer to
continue working (Bensel 132).
```

6. MORE THAN ONE AUTHOR Include names of several authors with page reference if you have not specified authors in your text. If there are more than three, give name of first author and then put et al. (unitalicized), Latin for "and others."

```
Tests and more tests have often been a substitute
for adequate funding for our schools (Hirsenrath and
Briggers 198).  When not clamoring for more tests
for students, legislators clamor for tests designed
to check "if the teachers know anything themselves"
(Rathjens et al. 112).
```

7. REFERENCE WITH BLOCK QUOTATION Although a parenthetical reference usually comes before a comma or a period, put it *after* final punctuation that concludes a block quotation. (Leave two spaces before the parenthesis.)

```
            alone.  Few of them show signs of mental
            deterioration or senility, and only a small
            proportion become mentally ill.  (114)
```

8. REFERENCE TO ONE OF SEVERAL VOLUMES Use an Arabic numeral followed by a *colon* for one volume of a work if in your "Works Cited" you list several volumes:

```
According to Trevelyan, the isolationist movement in
America and the pacifist movement in Britain between
them "handed the world over to its fate" (3: 301).
```

435

9. REFERENCE TO A PREFACE Use lowercase Roman numerals if you find them used in a book for the preface or other introductory material:

> In his preface to The Great Mother, Erich Neumann
> refers to the "onesidedly patriarchal development of
> the male intellectual consciousness" (xliii).

10. REFERENCE TO A LITERARY CLASSIC Use Arabic numerals separated by periods for such divisions of literary works as act, scene, and line (*Hamlet* 3.2.73–76). However, some authors prefer the more traditional use of capital and lowercase Roman numerals (*Hamlet* III.ii.73–76).

> In Shakespeare's Tempest, Gonzalo, who would prefer
> to "die a dry death," fits this archetype (1.1.66).

11. REFERENCE TO THE BIBLE Use Arabic numerals for chapter and verse (Luke 2.1), although some authors prefer to use a traditional style (Luke ii.1).

12. QUOTATION AT SECOND HAND Show that you are quoting not from the original source but at second hand. Your list of "Works Cited" will list only the secondhand source. (But quote from and cite the original source if you can.)

> William Archer reported in a letter to his brother
> Charles that the actor playing Pastor Manders never
> really entered "into the skin of the character"
> (qtd. in Ibsen 135).

13. REFERENCE TO NONPRINT MATERIALS When you refer to an interview, a radio or television program, or a movie, make sure your text highlights the name of the interviewer, person being

ABBREVIATIONS IN SCHOLARLY WRITING

©	copyright (© 1981 by John W. Gardner)
c. or ca.	Latin *circa*, "approximately"; used for approximate dates and figures (c. 1952)
et al.	Latin *et alii*, "and others"; used in references to books by several authors (G. S. Harrison et al.)
f., ff.	"and the following page (or pages)"
Ibid.	an abbreviation of Latin *ibidem*, "in the same place." (When used by itself, without a page reference, it means "in the last publication cited, on the same page." When used with a page reference, it means "in the last publication cited, on the page indicated.")
n.d.	"no date," date of publication unknown
op. cit.	short for *opere citato*, "in the work already cited"
passim	Latin for "throughout"; "in various places in the work under discussion" (See pp. 54–56 et passim.)
rev.	"review" or "revised"
rpt.	"reprint"; a reprinting of a book or article

interviewed, director or producer, or scriptwriter whose name appears in alphabetical order in your list of "Works Cited." Sometimes you may name a production or movie in parentheses to direct your reader to the right entry:

> In an interview in 1988, Silveira discussed the roots of his work in Aztec and Inca art.

> A news special by a local station fanned the long-smoldering controversy into bright flames (Poisoned Earth).

WORKS CITED — GENERAL
GUIDELINES (MLA)   *doc*

Code information accurately for your list of works
cited.

At the end of your research paper, you will furnish an alphabetical listing of your sources. This listing, titled "Works Cited," guides
the reader to the sources you have drawn on during your search. It
will often be more than a **bibliography** (a "book list" or list of printed
materials) and include nonprint sources. Start your page with the
centered heading "Works Cited." Then type your first entry, with the
first line *not* indented, but with the *second line* and additional lines
indented five spaces. Remember:

(1) Put the last name of the author first. This order applies
only to the first author listed when a book has several authors.

```
Brooks, Gwendolyn.  The World of Gwendolyn Brooks.
     New York: Harper, 1971.
Himstreet, William C., and Wayne Murlin Baty.  Busi-
     ness Communications: Principles and Methods.
     7th ed.  Boston: Kent, 1984.
```

If *no name of author or editor* is known to you, list the publication
alphabetically by the first letter of the title, not counting *The, A,* or
An.

(2) Show major breaks by periods. Separate the name of the
author or editor from what follows by a period. Set off the facts of
publication for a book from what precedes and what follows by periods. (Leave *two* spaces after periods separating blocks of
information.)

Silverberg, Robert, ed. Science Fiction Hall of
    Fame. London: Sphere Books, 1972.

(3) Underline (italicize) the title of a complete publication; enclose the title of a part in quotation marks. Underlining (when your typewriter has no italics) tells the printer to use italicized print. Italicize titles of books, collections, newspapers, or magazines: *A Brief Guide to Lean Cuisine*. Put in quotation marks titles of articles, reports, stories, or poems that were *part* of a larger publication: "How to Deep-Freeze Bait." *Angler's Monthly*.

(4) Include complete page numbers for an article. Give the inclusive page numbers for articles in periodicals or for parts of a collection. (If part of an article spills over onto later pages not consecutively numbered, use a plus sign to show that there is more later.)

Miller, JoAnn. "The Sandwich Generation." Working
    Mother Jan. 1987: 47–48.
Kaplan, Janice. "Politics of Sports." Vogue July
    1984: 219+.

Note: When a periodical uses continuous page numbering through several issues of an annual volume, include the *volume number* as an Arabic numeral. Use a colon before the inclusive page numbers: *PMLA* 96 (1981): 351–62.

(5) If you list several publications by the same author, do not repeat the author's name. In the second and later entries, use a line made of three hyphens instead:

Comfort, Alex. A Good Age. New York: Simon, 1976.
---. "Old Age: Facts and Fancies." Saturday Evening
    Post Mar. 1977: 45.

45c | WORKS CITED — MLA DIRECTORY *doc*

Study model entries for books, articles, and nonprint sources.

In the following directory, each sample entry for your final list of "Works Cited" comes with a sample reference for parenthetical documentation. Remember that most of the time you will identify author and source in your running text ("Isaac Asimov says in *The Age of Robots* . . ."), so that often your parenthetical references will give *page numbers* only. The sample references in this directory show what you have to do if your text has *not* already identified author or source.

A. Books (and other whole publications)

1. STANDARD ENTRY FOR A BOOK Put last name of author first. Underline (italicize) the title. Include place of publication, name of publisher, and date of publication. (Leave *two* spaces after periods.)

```
Schell, Jonathan.  The Fate of the Earth.  New York:
     Knopf, 1982.
```

SAMPLE REFERENCE: (Schell 89)

Note: In the current style, identification of publishers is often heavily abbreviated: *NAL* for New American Library, *Harcourt* for Harcourt Brace Jovanovich, Inc. Other examples:

(Oxford University Press)	New York: Oxford UP, 1990
(Academy for Educational Development)	Washington: Acad. for Educ. Dev., 1983

2. BOOK WITH SUBTITLE Use a colon to separate title and subtitle. Underline (italicize) both the title and subtitle of the book.

```
Rodriguez, Richard.  Hunger of Memory: The Education
     of Richard Rodriguez.  Boston: Godine, 1982.
```

SAMPLE REFERENCE: (Rodriguez 82-83)

3. BOOK BY TWO OR THREE AUTHORS For the first author, put last name first. Then give full names of coauthors in normal order. With three authors, note the commas between authors' names.

> Gilbert, Sandra M. and Susan Guber. <u>The Madwoman in</u>
>   <u>the Attic: The Woman Writer and the Nineteenth-</u>
>   <u>Century Literary Imagination</u>. New Haven: Yale
>   UP, 1979.
> Wresch, William, Donald Pattow, and James Gifford.
>   <u>Writing for the Twenty-First Century: Computers</u>
>   <u>and Research Writing</u>. New York: McGraw, 1988.

SAMPLE REFERENCES: (Gilbert and Guber 114)
                        (Wresch, Pattow, and Gifford 67)

4. BOOK BY MORE THAN THREE AUTHORS Give the first
author's name, followed by a comma and the abbreviation *et al.* (Latin
for "and others"). Do *not* put a period after *et*, and do not underline
or italicize.

> Stewart, Marie M., et al. <u>Business English and Com-</u>
>   <u>munication</u>. 5th ed. New York: McGraw, 1978.

SAMPLE REFERENCE: (Stewart et al. 34)

5. LATER EDITION OF A BOOK If you have used a book revised or brought up to date by the author, identify the new edition the
way it is labeled on its title page. After the title of the book, put *2nd
ed.* for second edition or *rev. ed.* for revised edition.

> Zettl, Herbert. <u>Television Production Handbook</u>.
>   4th ed. Belmont: Wadsworth, 1984.

SAMPLE REFERENCE: (Zettl 39)

6. REPRINTING OR REISSUE OF A BOOK If a work has been
republished unchanged (perhaps as a paperback reprint), include the
date of the original edition before full publishing data for the reprinting. If new material (like an introduction) has been added, include a
note to that effect.

> Wharton, Edith. <u>The House of Mirth</u>. 1905. Introd.
>   Cynthia Griffin Wolf. New York: Penguin, 1986.

SAMPLE REFERENCE: (Wharton 7)

7. BOOK WITH EDITOR'S NAME FIRST If an editor has assembled or arranged the materials in the book, use *ed.* after the editor's name or *eds.* if there are several editors.

```
Griffin, Alice, ed.  Rebels and Lovers: Shake-
     speare's Young Heroes and Heroines.  New York:
     New York UP, 1976.
Foster, Carol D., Nancy R. Jacobs, and Mark A. Sie-
     gel, eds.  Capital Punishment: Cruel and Unu-
     sual?  4th ed.  Plano: Instructional Aides,
     1984.
```

SAMPLE REFERENCES: (Griffin 17)
                   (Foster, Jacobs, and Siegel 86)

8. BOOK WITH EDITOR'S NAME LATER If an editor has edited the work of a single author, put the original author's name first if you focus on the *author's* work. Add *ed.* (for "edited by") and the editor's or several editors' names after the title. (Do not use *eds.*) However, put the editor's name first and the author's name later (after *By*) if the editor's work is particularly important to your project.

```
Mencken, H. L.  The Vintage Mencken.  Ed. Alistair
     Cooke.  New York: Vintage, 1956.
Cooke, Alistair, ed.  The Vintage Mencken.  By H. L.
     Mencken.  New York: Vintage, 1956.
```

SAMPLE REFERENCES: Identify by person mentioned first.
                   (Mencken 98)   (Cooke 4)

9. BOOK WITH TRANSLATOR'S NAME Put *Trans.* followed by the translator's name (or translators' names) after the title. But put the translator's name first if the translator's work is particularly significant to your project.

```
Lorenz, Konrad.  On Aggression.  Trans. Marjorie
     Kerr Wilson.  New York: Harcourt, 1966.
```

```
Kerr, Marjorie, trans.  On Aggression.  By Konrad
     Lorenz.  New York: Harcourt, 1966.
```

SAMPLE REFERENCES: Identify by person mentioned first.
     (Lorenz 34)   (Kerr 13)

10. SPECIAL IMPRINT A line of paperback books, for instance, is often published and promoted separately by a publishing house. Put the name of the line of books first, joined by a hyphen to the publisher's name: *Laurel Leaf-Dell, Mentor-NAL*.

```
Hsu, Kai-yu, ed. and trans.  Twentieth-Century
     Chinese Poetry.  Garden City: Anchor-Doubleday,
     1964.
```

SAMPLE REFERENCE: (Hsu 45)

11. UNSPECIFIED OR INSTITUTIONAL AUTHORSHIP Reports prepared by an organization and major reference books may list a group as the author or not specify authorship:

```
Carnegie Council on Policy Studies in Higher Educa-
     tion.  Giving Youth a Better Chance: Options
     for Education, Work, and Service.  San Fran-
     cisco: Jossey, 1980.
Literary Market Place: The Directory of American
     Book Publishing.  1984 ed.  New York: Bowker,
     1983.
```

SAMPLE REFERENCES: (Carnegie Council 29)
     (Literary Market 178)

12. WORK WITH SEVERAL VOLUMES If you have used *one* volume of a multivolume work, add the abbreviation *Vol.* followed by an Arabic numeral for the number of the volume: Vol. 3. (You may add the total number of volumes and inclusive dates at the end.) If the separate volumes have their own titles, include the volume title as well as the title of the whole multivolume work.

Woolf, Virginia. <u>The Diary of Virginia Woolf</u>. Ed.
  Anne Olivier Bell. New York: Harcourt, 1977.
  Vol. 1.
Churchill, Winston S. <u>The Age of Revolution</u>. New
  York: Dodd, 1957. Vol. 3 of <u>A History of the</u>
  <u>English-Speaking Peoples</u>. 4 vols. 1956—58.

SAMPLE REFERENCES: (Woolf 67) (Churchill 115—16)

If you have used *more than one* volume, list the whole multivolume
work, giving the total number of volumes: 3 vols.

Trevelyan, G. M. <u>History of England</u>. 3rd ed.
  3 vols. Garden City: Anchor-Doubleday, 1952.

SAMPLE REFERENCES: Include volume number as well as page number(s).
  (3: 156) (Trevelyan 3: 156)

13. PART OF COLLECTION OR ANTHOLOGY Identify the
article or other short piece (poem, short story) and the collection of
which it is a part. Put the part title in quotation marks; underline
(italicize) the title of the whole. Then go on to publishing data for the
collection. Conclude with inclusive page numbers for the part.

Rogers, Carl R. "Two Divergent Trends." <u>Existen-</u>
  <u>tial Psychology</u>. Ed. Rollo May. New York:
  Random, 1969. 87—92.

SAMPLE REFERENCE: (Rogers 87)

14. ENCYCLOPEDIA ENTRY Put titles of entries in quotation
marks. Page numbers and facts of publication may be unnecessary for
entries appearing in alphabetical order in well-known encyclopedias
or other reference books. Date or number of the edition used, however, should be included because of the frequent revisions of major
encyclopedias. (Include author's name for signed entries. If only initials are given, you may find the full name in an index or guide.)

Politis, M. J. "Greek Music." <u>Encyclopedia Ameri-</u>
<u>cana</u>. 1956 ed.

"Aging." <u>Encyclopaedia Britannica: Macropaedia</u>.
1983.

"Graham, Martha." <u>Who's Who of American Women</u>.
14th ed. 1985-86.

SAMPLE REFERENCES: No page numbers are needed for alphabetical
entries.
(Politis) ("Aging") ("Graham")

15. INTRODUCTION, FOREWORD, OR AFTERWORD If you
cite introductory material or an afterword by someone *other than the
author* of the book, start with the contributor's name, followed by the
generic description (*un*italicized, *not* in quotation marks): Introduction. Preface. Foreword. Afterword. Sometimes the introductory material has separate page numbers, given as lowercase Roman
numerals: v-ix or ii-xvi.

Bellow, Saul. Foreword. <u>The Closing of the Ameri-</u>
<u>can Mind</u>. By Allan Bloom. New York: Simon,
1987. 11-18.

DeMott, Robert. Introduction. <u>Working Days: The</u>
<u>Journals of</u> The Grapes of Wrath <u>1938-1941</u>. By
John Steinbeck. Ed. Robert DeMott. New York:
Viking, 1989. xxi-lvii.

16. GOVERNMENT PUBLICATION References to entries in
the *Congressional Record* require only the date and page numbers. For
other government publications, identify the government and the appropriate branch or subdivision. Use appropriate abbreviations like
S. Res. for Senate Resolution, *H. Rept.* for House Report, and *GPO*
for Government Printing Office.

<u>Cong. Rec.</u> 7 Feb. 1973: 3831-51.

California. Dept. of Viticulture. <u>Grape Harvesting</u>.
Sacramento: State Printing Office, 1990.

United States. Cong. Senate. Subcommittee on Con-
stitutional Amendments of the Committee on the

Judiciary. Hearings on the "Equal Rights"
    Amendment. 91st Cong., 2nd sess. S. Res. 61.
    Washington: GPO, 1970.

SAMPLE REFERENCE: (California. Dept. of Viticulture 18—20)

17. PAMPHLET OR BROCHURE Treat a pamphlet or brochure the way you would a book, but note that often author (and sometimes place or date) will not be specified.

Worried Sick About Cholesterol? Boston: Inst. for
    Better Living, 1991.

SAMPLE REFERENCE: (Worried Sick 12)

18. PART OF A SERIES If the front matter of a book shows it was published as part of a series, include the name of the series (unitalicized, no quotation marks) before the publishing data.

Rose, Mike. Writer's Block: The Cognitive Dimen-
    sion. Studies in Writing and Rhetoric. Car-
    bondale: Southern Illinois UP, 1984.

SAMPLE REFERENCE: (Rose 78)

19. BIBLE OR LITERARY CLASSIC Specify the edition you have used, especially if different versions of the text are important, as with different Bible translations or different editions of a Shakespeare play. Put the editor's name first if you want to highlight the editor's contribution.

The Holy Bible. Revised Standard Version. 2nd ed.
    Nashville: Nelson, 1971.
Hubler, Edward, ed. The Tragedy of Hamlet. By Wil-
    liam Shakespeare. New York: NAL, 1963.

SAMPLE REFERENCES: For chapter and verse: (Job 2.8)
            For act and scene: (Hamlet 3.2) or
            (Hamlet III.ii)

Note: Even when using specific page numbers for an edition you have used, you can help your reader find the passage in a different edition by adding the number of the chapter or of act and scene after a semicolon: (34; ch. 2).

20. QUOTATION AT SECOND HAND List only the work where the quotation appeared:

> Ibsen, Henrik. <u>Ghosts</u>. Ed. Kai Jurgensen and Rob-
> ert Schenkkan. New York: Avon, 1965.

SAMPLE REFERENCE: (qtd. in Ibsen 48)

21. TITLE WITHIN A TITLE Sometimes, an italicized (underlined) book title includes the name of another book. Shift back to roman (*not* underlined) for the title-within-a-title: *A Guide to James Joyce's* Ulysses.

B. Articles in periodicals

22. STANDARD ENTRY FOR MAGAZINE ARTICLE Start with the last name of the author. Put the title of the *article* in quotation marks; underline (italicize) the name of the *magazine*. Go on to the date (or month), separated from the *complete page numbers* by a colon. Abbreviate most months: Nov. 1990: 23–31.

> Hammer, Joshua. "Cashing In on Vietnam." <u>Newsweek</u>
> 16 Jan. 1989: 38–39.
> Weinberg, Steven. "The Decay of the Proton." <u>Sci-
> entific American</u> June 1981: 64–75.

SAMPLE REFERENCES: (Hammer 78)   (Weinberg 69)

Note: If an article is interrupted and continued later in the publication, use a plus sign to show that there is more later after the initial pages: 28 Feb. 1990: 38–41 + .

23. NEWSPAPER ARTICLE If necessary, specify the edition of the newspaper—early or late, east or west: *Wall Street Journal* 14 July 1989, eastern ed.: A3. Sections of a newspaper are often identified by letters (B34) or by numbers (late ed., sec. 3: 7 +):

> Hechinger, Fred. "How Free Should High School Papers Be?" New York Times 5 July 1989, western ed.: B7.

SAMPLE REFERENCE: No page number necessary for one-page article.
> (Hechinger)

Note: Leave off the article *The* in the names of newspapers like *The Wall Street Journal* or *The New York Times* when you include them in your list of "Works Cited."

24. ARTICLE BY SEVERAL AUTHORS Give the full names of coauthors. If there are more than three, put *et al.* (Latin for "and others") after the name of the first author instead.

> Gale, Noel H., and Zofia Stos-Gale. "Lead and Silver in the Ancient Aegean." Scientific American June 1981: 176–77.
> Martz, Larry et al. "A Tide of Drug Killings." Newsweek 16 Jan. 1989: 44–45.

SAMPLE REFERENCES: (Gale and Stos-Gale 176)
> (Martz et al. 45)

25. UNSIGNED OR ANONYMOUS ARTICLE If the author of an article remains unnamed, begin your entry with the title.

> "Environmentalists See Threats to Rivers." New York Times 15 July 1981, late ed., sec. 1: 8.

SAMPLE REFERENCE: ("Environmentalists")

26. ARTICLE WITH SUBTITLE Have a colon separate title and subtitle. Enclose both in the same set of quotation marks.

```
Schmidt, Sarah.  "From Ghetto to University: The
        Jewish Experience in the Public School."  Amer-
        ican Educator Spring 1978: 23-25.
```

SAMPLE REFERENCE: (Schmidt 25)

27. ARTICLE WITH VOLUME NUMBER For scholarly or professional journals, you will typically include the *volume number*, followed by the year in parentheses. (Usually page numbers are *consecutive* for the whole volume covering the issues for a year — the second issue will start with page 90 or page 137, for instance.)

```
Santley, Robert S.  "The Political Economy of the
        Aztec Empire."  Journal of Anthropological Re-
        search 41 (1985): 327-37.
```

SAMPLE REFERENCE: (Santley 327)

28. ARTICLE WITH NUMBER OF VOLUME AND ISSUE If page numbers are not continuous for the whole volume (each new issue starts with page 1), you may have to include the *number of the issue*. Add it after the volume number, separating the two numbers by a period (no space): 13.4.

```
Winks, Robin W.  "The Sinister Oriental Thriller:
        Fiction and the Asian Scene."  Journal of Popu-
        lar Culture 19.2 (1985): 49-61.
```

If there is *no volume number* but only the number of the issue, treat it as if it were the volume number:

```
Bowering, George.  "Baseball and the Canadian Imagi-
        nation."  Canadian Literature 108 (1986): 115-
        24.
```

SAMPLE REFERENCES: (Winks 51-53)   (Bowering 117)

29. SIGNED OR UNSIGNED EDITORIAL After the title, add the right label: Editorial (*un*italicized, *not* in quotation marks). If the editorial is unsigned, begin with the title.

```
Whitcroft, Jeremiah.  "Talking to Strangers."
     Editorial.  Plainsville Courier 13 Sept. 1989: 7.
"A Frown on the Interface."  Editorial.  Software
     News 3 Sept. 1988: 3-4.
```

SAMPLE REFERENCES: (Whitcroft) ("Frown" 4)

30. LETTER TO THE EDITOR After the name of the author, add the right label: Letter (*un*italicized, *not* in quotation marks).

```
Vinaver, Martha.  Letter.  Los Angeles Times 14 July
     1989, part II: 6.
```

SAMPLE REFERENCE: (Vinaver)

31. TITLED OR UNTITLED REVIEW Use the abbreviation *rev.* before the title of the work being reviewed. For unsigned reviews, start with the title of the review (if any) or the description of the review.

```
Harlan, Arvin C.  Rev. of A Short Guide to German
     Humor, by Frederick Hagen.  Oakland Tribune 12
     Dec. 1988: 89-90.
Rev. of The Penguin Books of Women Poets, ed. Carol
     Cosman, Joan Keefe, and Kathleen Weaver.  Arts
     and Books Forum May 1990: 17-19.
```

SAMPLE REFERENCES: (Harlan 89) (Rev. of Women Poets 17)

32. COMPUTER SERVICE For material obtained from a computer service, add the name of the system and access number or file and item number for the article you have used.

> Schomer, Howard. "South Africa: Beyond Fair Employ-
>   ment." <u>Harvard Business Review</u> May—June 1983:
>   145+. Dialog file 122, item 119425 833160.

SAMPLE REFERENCE: (Schomer 145)

33. INFORMATION SERVICE Information services like ERIC
provide both bibliographic listings and actual printouts of the documents themselves. If the material had been previously published else-
where, provide standard publishing information, followed by
identification of the service and an item number. If the material had
not been previously published, cite it as a complete publication published by the service:

> Kurth, Ruth J. and Linda J. Stromberg. <u>Using Word
>   Processing in Composition Instruction</u>. ERIC,
>   1984. ED 251 850.

SAMPLE REFERENCE: (Kurth 3)

C. Nonprint sources

34. PERSONAL INTERVIEW Start with the name of the per-
son you interviewed. Use the right label — *un*italicized, *not* in quotation marks.

> Silveira, Gene. Personal Interview. 23 Oct. 1990.
> Duong, Tran. Telephone Interview. 16 Jan. 1991.

SAMPLE REFERENCE: (Duong) No parenthetical reference is necessary if
your text names the person you interviewed.

35. BROADCAST OR PUBLISHED INTERVIEW Identify the
person interviewed and label the material as an interview.

> Asimov, Isaac. Interview. <u>Science Watch</u>. With
>   Dorothy Brett. KFOM, San Bruno. 19 Mar. 1986.

If an interview appeared in print, identify it as an interview, and then give standard publishing information about the printed source.

```
Asimov, Isaac.  Interview.  Scientists Talk About
     Science.  By Anne Harrison and Webster Freid.
     Los Angeles: Acme, 1987.  94-101.
```

SAMPLE REFERENCE: (Asimov)   For printed source: (Asimov 98)

36. PERSONAL LETTER For a letter you have received, name the letter writer and label the material as a letter. Give the date. For a published letter, use the name of the *recipient* as the title and then give full publishing data, with inclusive page numbers.

```
Chavez, Roderigo.  Letter to the author.  15 Jan.
     1990.
Hemingway, Ernest.  "To Lillian Ross."  28 July
     1948.  Ernest Hemingway: Selected Letters,
     1917-1961.  Ed. Carlos Baker.  New York: Scrib-
     ner's, 1981.  646-49.
```

37. TALK OR LECTURE Name the speaker and provide an appropriate label: Lecture. Keynote Speech. Address (*un*italicized, *no* quotation marks). If the talk had a title, use the title (in quotation marks) instead.

```
Freitag, Marilyn.  Keynote Speech.  Opening General
     Sess. New World Forum.  Atlanta, Apr. 7, 1988.
Jacobi, Jean.  "Television News: News from Nowhere."
     Valley Lecture Series.  Santa Clara, 29 Oct.
     1990.
```

SAMPLE REFERENCE: (Freitag)   No parenthetical reference is necessary if your text names the speaker.

38. PRINTED SPEECH If you had access to a printed version of a speech, add full publishing data to the usual information about a talk.

```
Partlet, Basil.  "Yuppies and the Art of Cooking."
        Western Chefs' Forum.  Phoenix, 19 Aug. 1989.
        Rpt. West Coast Review Spring 1990: 76-82.
```

SAMPLE REFERENCE: (Partlet 77)

39. TELEVISION OR RADIO PROGRAM Underline (italicize) the title of a program. The title may be preceded by the name of a specific episode (in quotation marks) and followed by the name of the series (unitalicized, no quotation marks): "The Young Stravinsky." *The Great Composers*. Musical Masterpieces. Identify network (if any), station, and city (with the last two separated by a comma: KPFA, Berkeley). Pull a name out in front to highlight a person's contribution.

```
The Poisoned Earth.  Narr. Sylvia Garth.  Writ. and
        prod. Pat Fisher.  WXRV, Seattle.  23 Oct.
        1988.
Rostow, Jacob, dir.  "The Last Bridge."  A Forgotten
        War.  With Eric Seibert, Joan Ash, and Fred
        Minton.  KMBC, Sacramento.  12 Dec. 1987.
```

SAMPLE REFERENCE: (Poisoned Earth) No parenthetical reference is necessary if your text names the program.

40. MOVIE Underline (italicize) the title. Identify the director and the production company, and give the date. Include further information as you wish about performers, scriptwriters, and other contributors. Pull a name out in front to highlight a person's contribution.

```
It's a Wonderful Life.  Dir. Frank Capra.  With
        James Stewart, Donna Reed, Lionel Barrymore,
        and Thomas Mitchell.  RKO, 1946.
Zeffirelli, Franco, dir.  Romeo and Juliet.  By Wil-
        liam Shakespeare.  With Olivia Hussey, Leonard
        Whiting, and Michael York.  Paramount, 1968.
        138 min.
```

SAMPLE REFERENCE: (Zeffirelli)

41. VIDEOTAPES AND OTHER VISUALS Label the medium: Videocassette. Filmstrip. Slide program (*un*italicized, *not* put in quotation marks).

> Creation vs. Evolution: Battle of the Classrooms.
> Videocassette. Dir. Ryall Wilson. PBS Video,
> 1982. 58 min.

SAMPLE REFERENCE: (Creation)

42. COMPUTER SOFTWARE Basic information includes writer of the program (if known), title of the program or material, distributor or publisher, and date. Because of frequent updatings of computer software, you may have to specify the version: Vers. 1.4. In addition, you may need to tell your readers what equipment and how much memory are required (in kilobytes: 128K).

> Crighton, Irene. Think/Write. Vers. 1.2. Computer
> Software. Celex, 1989. Apple IIe, 128K, disk.

SAMPLE REFERENCE: (Crighton)

43. AUDIO RECORDING Specify label of the recording company, followed by order number and date. (Use *n.d.* for "no date" if date is unknown.) Identify references to jacket notes or the like.

> Holiday, Billie. The Essential Billie Holiday: Car-
> negie Hall Concert. Audiocassette. Verve,
> UCV2600, 1969.
> Rifkin, Joshua. Jacket Notes. Renaissance Vocal
> Music. Nonesuch, H-71097, n.d.

SAMPLE REFERENCE: (Rifkin)

45d | USING FOOTNOTES/ENDNOTES   *doc* |

Know how to use endnotes for additional information.

In much traditional scholarly writing, footnotes (later usually **endnotes**) have been used to identify sources. Such notes are usually numbered consecutively. A raised footnote number appears outside whatever punctuation goes with the sentence or paragraph, as in this example.[2] At the bottom of the page (or on a separate page at the end of a paper or article), the note itself appears. It starts with the raised number, is indented like a paragraph, and ends with a period or other end punctuation:

> [2] Robin Northcroft, <u>A Short Guide to Fine British Cooking</u> (New York: Culinary Arts, 1989), p. 85.

Even though you are using a system of documentation that does not identify sources in footnotes, you may want to use notes for the kind of backup that can help satisfy an interested reader. For instance, your text may have mentioned the recent outpouring of books with titles like *Aging: Continuity and Change* or *Aging and Society*. For the interested reader, you may decide to provide a more extended listing in a note:

> [3] Books on aging from the publication list of a single publisher include <u>The Social Forces in Later Life</u>, <u>Social Problems of the Aging</u>, <u>Biology of Aging</u>, <u>Human Services for Older Adults</u>, <u>Families in Later Life</u>, <u>The Later Years</u>, <u>Working with the Elderly</u>, <u>Late Adulthood</u>, and <u>Aging: Politics and Policies</u>, among others.

Put such notes on a separate page headed "Notes" at the end of your paper before your "Works Cited."

As you study the sample research paper, do justice to three major dimensions:

LARGER ELEMENTS   Make sure you see how the author tackles her subject, guides the reader, and maintains the reader's interest. For instance, in the early pages, study the way she introduces her subject and leads up to her thesis. Study the "then-and-now" contrast that provides the basic historical perspective for the paper.

USING SOURCES   How has the author used and identified her sources? How does she introduce quoted material? What is the mix of short direct quotation, paraphrase, and longer block quotations?

DOCUMENTATION   Study the author's use of parenthetical references and her final list of "Works Cited." Where did she have to deal with special problems? How did she handle unusual or unconventional sources?

A Note on Format: Your paper does not need a separate title page. The first page starts with the **author block** (author, instructor, course, and date). Note *double-spacing* throughout, including author block, block quotations, and list of "Works Cited."

Running heads give the student writer's last name followed by the number of the page (plain numeral — no punctuation or abbreviation). A double space separates the running head from the top line on the page.

The **title** is *not* italicized (underlined), put in quotation marks, or typed as all capitals. (Use italics or quotation marks only if your title quotes someone else's title: *Star Trek* and the Myth of Innocence.)

A separate **outline**, when required by the instructor, is double-spaced throughout and follows conventional outline format (see **2d**).

Barbara Meier Gatten

Professor Lamont

English 2A

April 9, 1991

*outline if required by
instructor*

Women in Sports

THESIS: The revolution in women's athletics has
          changed both what women expect of them-
          selves and what we expect of athletics.

   I. Today's highly visible women athletes
  II. Progress toward equality in sports
     A. Challenging traditional restrictions
     B. Making progress: The 50s and 60s
       1. The Sputnik effect
       2. The spirit of political activism
     C. Breakthroughs: The 70s
       1. Commercial sponsorship
       2. Title IX and its aftermath
     D. Turning point: The Los Angeles Olympics
 III. Sports and the changing self-image of women
     A. Fitness: body and mind
     B. Testing the limits
     C. Increased self-esteem
     D. Sports and life
  IV. Women's athletics and traditional sports
     A. Competition vs. participation
     B. Downplaying violence
   V. A new concept of sport

↑
½″
↓
Gatten 1

Barbara Meier Gatten
Professor Lamont
English 2A
April 9, 1991

author block

Women in Sports:
Pushing the Limits

The gym was packed. Each time the home
team scored, there was a roar, followed by a
deathly quiet that magnified the slap of a hand
on the ball or the squeak of rubber on wood. When
the final buzzer sounded, signaling victory for
the home team and a trip to the state playoffs,
the gym went wild. Classmates and friends rushed
out onto the floor, lifting the players up in the
air. A few years ago, this scene could have
meant only one thing: the men's basketball playoffs. Tonight, it was the women's volleyball
sectionals.

Twenty years ago, such a scene would have
been unlikely. Then women who enjoyed sports had
two choices: They could join the Girls' Athletic
Association (GAA) and play intramurals, or they
could participate vicariously as cheerleaders on
the sidelines. Today, in addition to the highly
publicized women tennis players, runners, ice

skaters, and volleyball players, there are
women cyclists, swimmers, squash players, rowing
crews, mountain climbers, fencers, soccer play-
ers--and a rugby team called "The Gentle Women
of Aspen." What has happened? The revolution
in women's athletics has changed both what women
expect of themselves and what we expect of
athletics.   **thesis** *with preview*

For many years, progress toward equality of
the sexes in sports was slow. Women were free
to participate in genteel games like tennis or
golf as long as they did not perspire too freely
or appear too intent on winning. From the beginning, women athletes had to reckon with the
traditional ideal of the ladylike woman, who
could not appear tough or assertive. Outstanding athletes like the swimmer Esther Williams or
the ice skater Sonja Henie were praised for
their beauty and grace rather than for their
athletic achievement. In 1936, the editor of
Sportsman magazine wrote, "As swimmers and div-
ers, girls are as beautiful and adroit as they
are ineffective and unpleasing on the track"
(qtd. in Hart 66). Janice Kaplan claims in her
book Women and Sports that as recently as the
60s practically the only sport at which a woman
could hope to make money was ice skating, since
"ice shows were always looking for pretty girls
who could stand up on skates" (54). Writing in

paragraph integrating
several sources

Gatten 3

1971, Marie Hart, in an article titled "Sport:
Women Sit in the Back of the Bus," concluded that
"the emphasis in periodicals is still largely on
women as attractive objects rather than as
skilled and effective athletes" (66). It was not
until the 80s that a swimmer who had just won her
third Olympic gold medal could say: "Once the
Marilyn Monroe look was really in. Now it's the
lean, muscular, runner look" (qtd. in O'Reilly,
"Out of the Tunnel" 73).   *quoted at second hand*

In the 1950s and 1960s, real opportunities
for women in sports were slowly beginning to open
up, partly as the result of political pressures.
Phyllis Bailey, Assistant Director of Athletics
at Ohio State University, described a kind of
athletic "Sputnik effect":

> The international scene of the 1950s and
> 60s had put pressure on the government
> to take women's college sports more se-
> riously. The Olympics had become a po-
> litical battlefield, and our men were
> getting medals, but our women weren't.
> We had to do something to protect our
> standing in the world and get American
> women on a par with others. (qtd. in
> Kaplan, Women in Sports 59)

*block quotation (no
quotation marks — double
indentation)*

Look at how the author introduces quotations and other material from sources in the opening pages of the paper. Look at how she accomplishes one or more of the following purposes:

- identify the source
- establish the authority or the credentials of the source
- signal the point or the relevance of a quotation or other material

Study examples like the following:

> In 1936, the editor of <u>Sportsman</u> magazine wrote, . . .
>
> Janice Kaplan claims in her book <u>Women and Sports</u> that as recently as the 60s . . .
>
> Phyllis Bailey, Assistant Director of Athletics at Ohio State University, described a kind of athletic "Sputnik effect": . . .
>
> In this area, according to George R. LaNoue, former head of the Task Force on Higher Education of the U.S. Equal Employment Opportunity Commission, "the treatment of women athletes . . ."
>
> Linda Schreiber writes about how running helped to increase her energy and change her outlook, how she experienced the sharpened physical and mental edge of being in shape: . . .

*part paraphrase, part
quotation in account of a key event*   Gatten 4

At the same time, the climate of political
activism of the 60s and growing agitation for individual rights encouraged women to knock on
doors previously closed. In 1967, Kathrine
Switzer crashed the then male-only Boston Marathon. She filled out the entrant's application
as K. Switzer and then "was nearly shouldered off
the course by officials when they noticed she
was, in fact, female." The attempted ouster and
resulting controversy "infuriated Switzer and
galvanized her into action to change the system,"
making her a major force in the movement that led
to the inclusion of the first women's marathon in
the 1984 Olympics (Ullyot 44, 50—51).

The major breakthroughs for women's sports
occurred in the 70s. First, a few major companies
gingerly invested in women's pro sports and soon
realized that they had discovered a gold mine.
Colgate-Palmolive became the controlling dollar
behind women's golf, skiing, and tennis. The company decided to put its advertising money into the
women's pro circuit instead of afternoon soap operas, and the gamble paid off. Another company
to place a lucky bet was Phillip Morris, the to-
bacco company. The Virginia Slims tennis tour put
women's tennis on the map. The effect of the
Slims tour with its lucrative prize money was to

As the paper unfolds, keep an eye on the writer's use of her sources:

- What kind of sources does she turn to? Do they seem easily accessible or from out-of-the-way places?
- Do the sources represent a *range* of authorities?
- What are their *credentials?* Do they seem qualified, and do they merit attention?
- Does the writer seem *biased* in selecting sources — is there a predictable point of view?
- Which of the quoted sources seem most *relevant* or useful? Which least?
- Do any of the *quotations* seem especially eloquent or memorable? Why?
- Are any of the *facts and figures* surprising or startling? Why? Do any of them seem incomplete or bewildering? Why?

establish for the first time the role model of
the well-paid, well-respected female athlete. By
the early 1980s, Martina Navratilova, a top
player on the Virginia Slims circuit, could win
over two million dollars in tournament action in
one year, not counting the income from endorse-
ments (Sherman 194).

     While women were gaining in the profes-
sional arena, a landmark event changed women's
athletics in academia. In 1972, Congress passed
the Education Amendments Act. Chapter IX of the
Act barred an institution from receiving federal
funds if it practiced any form of sex discrimination. The heated controversies about how to
implement the law "focused on the relative facilities and funds available to male and female athletes." In this area, according to George R.
LaNoue, former head of the Task Force on Higher
Education of the U.S. Equal Employment Opportunity Commission, "the treatment of women athletes
by universities was often shabby at best" (28).

     The net effect of the new law was to pro-
mote sudden growth in women's athletics. Headlines like "Big Ten Begins Women's Program"
began to sprout in sports publications. According to Kaplan, before Title IX, colleges
spent an estimated 2 percent of their athletic
budgets on women's sports; by 1984, the figure
was close to 20 percent. Before, there were

summary of statistics

465

Gatten 6

virtually no athletic scholarships for univer-
sity-bound women; by 1984, there were more than
ten thousand ("Politics" 219). Robert Sullivan,
writing in <u>Sports Illustrated</u>, said:

> There were 32,000 females participat-
> ing in college athletics in 1972, the
> year the law was enacted; by 1983 the
> total had increased to 150,000. . . .
> From 1974 to 1981 the number of col-
> leges granting athletic scholarships
> to women increased from 60 to 500,
> while expenditures on women's programs
> by NCAA schools soared from $4 million
> to $116 million. This greater commit-
> ment to women's athletics resulted in
> vastly improved performances by fe-
> males not just in basketball, but also
> in track and field, swimming, and most
> other sports. (9)

*excerpted
block
quotation*

In 1984, a Supreme Court ruling took some
of the teeth out of Chapter IX, stipulating that
Title IX should be regarded as "program specific." In other words, it would ban sex discrimination only in a specific program (such as
math or science) that was receiving federal
funds, not in the institution as a whole. Since
little federal aid goes directly into sports programs, discriminatory athletic departments no
longer endangered federal aid for a college

or university as a whole. Nevertheless, according
to Sullivan, "having been forced to beef up women's
programs by Title IX," most schools now claimed to
be "morally committed" to parity for women's athletics (9). Pete Hamill, widely read columnist
for The New York Post and The New York Daily News,
said that Title IX "gave women solid coaching and
structured competition" and that "there now is no
going back" (19).[1]   *endnote will mention dissenting view*

  For many women, the twenty-third Olympic
Games in Los Angeles marked a turning point in
the quest for recognition for female athletes.
During the 1984 Olympics, 2,500 female athletes
from 140 nations competed in 76 events. In the
words of Cheryl Mosher,

      Although a far cry from the number of

      events open to male Olympians, it was

      a quantum leap from the first modern

block   Olympics, which denied participation

quotation to women--and a bigger jump from an-

for key   cient times when even female specta-

event   tors were hurled from the nearest

      cliff. (82)

  Like other observers, Jane O'Reilly, writing in Time magazine, saw the "dazzling accomplishments" of U.S. women at the 1984 Games
as the result of the advances triggered by
Title IX. She said that the U.S. Olympic
women's basketball team, which she called

Study the way material from these cards has been integrated into the finished paper.

Women in 1984 Olympics

Card 1

"Title IX became effective only in 1975, and enforcement has been sketchy. But the threat of losing federal funds was enough to raise the number of women in collegiate athletic programs from 16,000 in 1972 to more than 150,000 today. . . . The U.S. Olympic women's basketball team, probably the best female team ever assembled anywhere, is a direct result of the scholarships created by Title IX. As Olympic Basketball Player Miller says: 'Without Title IX, I'd be nowhere.'"

O'Reilly, "Out of the Tunnel" 73

Women in 1984 Olympics

Card 2

"The dazzling accomplishments of U.S. women at this year's Games were the direct result of changes in personal attitude and public policy brought about by two inseparable revolutions: the women's movement and the growth of women's sports."

O'Reilly, "Out of the Tunnel" 73

Women in 1984 Olympics

Numbers: 2,500 female athletes from 140 nations in 76 events

Card 3

"Although a far cry from the number of events open to male Olympians, it was a quantum leap from the first modern Olympics, which denied participation to women--and a bigger jump from ancient times when even female spectators were hurled from the nearest cliff."

Mosher, "Women in Motion" 82

Gatten 8

"probably the best female team ever assembled anywhere," was a "direct result" of the scholarships and the support created by the law ("Out of
the Tunnel" 73).   ***turning point:*** *major transition*

    What have the recent advances in women's
sports done for the self-image of women? When the
doors to free participation in sports swing open,
so do other doors, many of them psychological.
The grass roots movement towards greater fitness
among women affects both body and mind. In Marathon Mom, Linda Schreiber writes about how running
helped to increase her energy and change her outlook, how she experienced the sharpened physical
and mental edge of being in shape: *author and book identified*

> The more I ran, the easier hauling
> groceries and carrying babies became.
> I found I had more pep, needed less
> sleep. Running also seemed to allow
> me to see things in a more mellow per-
> spective. . . . I didn't feel so nar-
> row and confined, because my day had
> at least included a run. Somehow I
> didn't feel so "small" and events at
> home so petty. (8)

    Beyond the joy of simple fitness, there is
for many the added dimension of testing limits,
of having the opportunity to "push back the enve-

lope," in test pilot jargon.   Looking back over
the Los Angeles Olympics, Jane O'Reilly said,
"These women tested their limits, and having a
chance to do that is what sports and feminism are
all about" ("Out of the Tunnel" 73).   Every athlete has the experience of pushing at the barrier
of his or her own limitations, and many experience the satisfaction felt when the barrier
yields to persistent effort.   A case in point is
long-distance running for women: Women runners
were always assumed to lack endurance.   The 1928
Olympics were the first games where women were
allowed to run anything longer than a sprint.
Eleven women that year entered an 800-meter race.
Officials predicted disaster and were correct.
Five women dropped out, five collapsed at the
finish line, and the strongest collapsed in the
dressing room afterwards.   Kaplan believes that
these women failed because they were expected to
fail: "None of them had ever trained for long
distances, and they were psyched out by the adum-
brations of doom and the ambulance waiting at the
finish line" (37).   *extended account of case in point*

      Ironically, today women are thought to ex-
ceed men in their physical potential for endurance because of a superior ability to metabolize
fat.[2] According to an article in Science Digest,
statistical projections based on available sports
                              endnote will provide detail

Gatten 10

records show that "women may equal men in certain events, most notably the marathon, in the next few decades" (Torrey 91).

The experience of overcoming physical and mental barriers in sports is giving many women increased confidence and self-esteem. Women athletes are talking about their efforts and achievements with a newfound pride. In a recent interview, a woman who trains young riders for competition in equestrian events said:

> Equestrian competition is one of the few events in which men and women compete on an equal basis. Men used to dominate the sport because they were
> *material* trained in the military and because of
> *from* a common misconception that the sport
> *interview* was only for men. Now women are taking top positions in every area. Maybe this will be one sport where women will prove better than men. (Costello)

This increased sense of self-worth is not limited to sports that require money and leisure and may seem the province of the privileged few. As the director of International Running Circuit, sponsored by Avon Cosmetics, marathon runner Kathrine Switzer has organized races for women from Japan, Brazil, Malaysia, and Thailand, dis-

Gatten 11

regarding warnings that women running in the
streets would precipitate chaos. In Sao Paulo,
Brazil, 10,000 women ran a race, 2,000 with no
shoes. Switzer said afterwards, "Some had nothing else in their lives, but they took part and
were changed" (qtd. in O'Reilly, "The Year of
Getting Tough" 292).

Much testimony from women athletes indicates that self-confidence and determination
carry over from athletics into other areas of
life. Sally Voss, all-American golfer, said that
the pressures she encountered in her work as an
anesthesiologist were easier to deal with because
of her experiences in athletic competition: "Having been exposed to intense athletic competition,
I am better able to assess difficult situations
and react in a rational and even manner." Sally
Ride, first American woman in space, said, "Athletics teaches endurance and the value of pursuing
beyond one's perceived limits to achieve higher
levels of ability" ("A Winning Combination"
1–2).   *brochure with no author given*

The fact that women are participating in
sports in unprecedented numbers is obviously
having a strong impact on women. In turn, what
impact, if any, is this flood of female participants having on sports themselves? Although
the extent of actual change is difficult to
assess, women's athletics is challenging

turning point: *major transition*

Gatten 12

two features of traditional sports: excessive
competition and violence. Many women would agree
with Betty Lehan Harragan, a management consultant, that "women have to learn about competition
and developing a winning attitude" (qtd. in Kaplan, Women in Sports 112). But they would also
agree that excessive emphasis on competition is
one of the main things wrong with sports, leading
to such abuses as "the ridiculous salaries of the
pros (and some college players!), the rah-rah
chauvinism, and the corruption of recruiting"
(Chapin vii—viii).   *quoted from a preface*

Women's sports have traditionally laid
stress on participation. Because athletic programs for women tended to be recreational and
low-budget, the "everyone-can-play" ethic pre-
vailed. Today, dazzled by the rewards of increased money and prestige, women's athletics is
in danger of losing sight of the ideal of sport-
for-all. Competition systematically narrows the
field of participants to only those who are good
enough to compete. When there are limited recreational facilities or team berths, some get to
play and others become spectators. If the only
thing that counts is being Number One, then
only a select few battle it out while the
many watch. Recruiting and training of top
performers become the overriding priorities.

BACKGROUND AND COMMENTARY

In the revision of her first draft, the author faced a familiar problem for writers of research papers: In her first draft, she had used an excessive number of block quotations, giving the paper too much of a stitched-together effect. In her revision, she made a special effort to excerpt and integrate quoted material more. Read the third and last major part of the paper, and answer the following questions:

- Which paragraphs excerpt and integrate material from *several sources*?
- Where and how does the author use *partial quotations* and sentence-length quotations as part of her running text?
- Where does she use *block quotations*, and why? Is the more extended quotation justified by an important point, by an eloquent personal statement, or by helpful authentic detail?
- What is the proportion of quoted or paraphrased material and *interpretation* or discussion by the author?
- How effective or adequate are the *transitions* that take the reader from paragraph to paragraph?

From the beginning of the current expansion of women's sports, there have been voices warning against an imitation of the "male model." George R. LaNoue, in an article in Change, said in 1976:

> Among the leaders of women's athletics there is strong opposition to turning women's sports into an imitation of men's. They do not want to engage in wide-spread off-campus recruiting. They would prefer to remain teachers instead of becoming win-at-any-cost sports promoters. (30)

Sports sociologist Stephen Figler said in Sport and Play in American Life that funding mandated by Title IX was leading to hasty expansion, "fostering the development of the same faulty mechanism that drives men's school athletics" (289). Figler quoted Katherine Ley, a faculty member of the United States Sports Academy, as saying, "as much of a boon as equal opportunity legislation has been," it "derailed the early attempts of women to devise an improved athletic model" (285).   *partial quotation*

Nevertheless, the search for the "improved model" continues, and the rallying cry of "Sport for all!" continues to be heard. Kaplan writes:

> The desire to have sports available to women does not have to translate into programs with the same questionable

Gatten 14

> priorities as the men's, where millions
> are poured into money-raising games
> that few can play but many watch. It's
> time to raise a generation of partici-
> pants, not another generation of fans.
> (<u>Women in Sports</u> 167)

She commends some of the smaller schools
that have opted for cuts in big-budget sports
like football in favor of more even distribution
to sports like volleyball, basketball, and tennis. Figler has suggested the broadening of in-
tercollegiate competition by the creation of
parallel, independent teams for those not skilled
enough to make varsity teams. As he explained in
a recent interview:

> The element that gives collegiate
> sports its excitement is competition
> between schools--that's why intramurals
> don't really fill the need. A better
> idea would be a kind of extramural pro-
> gram in which a team had a budget, a
> schedule, and a coach, all funded by
> either state money, tuition, student
> fees, or some combination. Often P.E.
> departments have good former coaches on
> their staffs because they didn't like
> certain aspects of big collegiate
> sports--these people would be ideal for
> a program of this type.

*from
telephone
interview*

Gatten 15

Excessive competition and glory-for-the-few is not the only idea being challenged by the women's sport movement. Another area of traditional athletics to come under attack is the notion that violence is an inescapable element of sport. Traditional male sports often seem motivated by "an inherent aggressiveness in man stemming from the Darwinian struggle for existence," with sports serving "as substitutes for actual fighting, mock struggles that satisfied the urge to conquer" (Nash 181). Some of the most popular men's sports--football, ice hockey, boxing--are extremely violent. Don Atyeo says in Blood and Guts: Violence in Sports about football: "Each year it kills on average twenty-eight players and maims thousands more. It leaves everyone who reaches its higher levels with some form of lasting injury." He quotes a former player for the Los Angeles Rams as saying that people who play for any length of time "carry the scars for the rest of their lives." These may not "be showing on the outside, but they'll have knees that are worn out, shoulders that don't work right, fingers that point in a different direction" (219–20). Part of the code of the male athlete has been that one must take the pain to prove his manliness. As Kathryn Lance says in A Woman's Guide to Spectator Sports, the idea of playing with pain, of "giving everything, including the integrity of one's body," to the team or club "is so extreme that players will enter a game anesthetized to the point where they can bear the pain of possibly severe injuries" (13).

The growth of women's sports, if not eliminating violence in sport, is at least helping to temper it. Women's sports are not burdened with the tradition of violence linked to the idea of sport as a proving ground for sexual identity. This is not to say that the risk of pain and injury are not part of the challenge of sports for many women athletes. Ann Roiphe, reminiscing about field hockey, her favorite game when a young girl, says:

> I remember a girl named Karen with blood pouring down her face and onto a white middy blouse and a dark accusing hole where her front teeth had been. It is blurred in my mind whose stick was responsible, but I was close enough to feel guilt and fear and the excitement of both those emotions. It never occurred to me that a simple child's game, a ball playing, might not be worth a lifetime of false teeth. (14)

from printed interview

Gatten 17

Increasingly, women are competing in tests of endurance that were once male-only events. In
1985, Libby Riddles became the first woman to win
the Iditerod, a 1,000-mile dogsled race from An-
chorage to Nome, Alaska. Riddles won by driving
her dogs through a howling blizzard that no other
contestant would challenge. This race "pits the
wits of a cold, sleep-starved musher against
the vagaries of weather, trail, and dogs. More
than speed and experience, it takes audacity"
(O'Hara 40).   *author not identified in text*

        While women are increasingly facing up to
tests of courage and endurance, at least some men
in the world of sports seem ready to turn away
from the image of the violent, aggressive man as
the male ideal. Former football heroes such as
O. J. Simpson and Al Cowlings are telling youngsters to play tennis instead of football because
tennis will benefit them longer and because they
will not have to spend their lives suffering from
football knees (Schmerler 8).

        Women's sports are helping society move away
from the glorification of violence as media time
is increasingly devoted to women's sports like
tennis and golf. Both the airing of women's athletics and increased participation in sports by
women are creating a wider audience of female
spectators, which in turn creates greater demand
on the networks for coverage of women's events.

In conclusion, the struggle for the acceptance of women's sports is not a battle between men and women. The real enemies of sport for women are the same as they are for men: the danger of being a mere passive spectator, the philosophy that winning is the only thing, and finally the idea of violence as a normal, inescapable part of sport. What is needed is a new concept of sport that sees the purpose of sport as lifelong enjoyment and pleasure, increased fitness for life, and a feeling of well-being and joy.

Gatten 19

Works Cited

Atyeo, Don. <u>Blood and Guts: Violence in Sports</u>.
     New York: Paddington, 1979.
"Big Ten Begins Women's Program." <u>Coaching Wom-
     en's Athletics</u> Oct. 1981: 20.
Chapin, Henry B., ed. <u>Sports in Literature</u>. New
     York: McKay, 1976.
Costello, Arlene. Personal Interview. 6 Jan.
     1990.
Figler, Stephen K. <u>Sport and Play in American
     Life</u>. Philadelphia: Saunders, 1981.
---. Telephone Interview. 8 Feb. 1990.
Hamill, Pete. "Women Athletes: Faster, Higher,
     Better." <u>Cosmopolitan</u> Nov. 1985: 19+.
Hart, Marie. "Sport: Women Sit in the Back of
     the Bus." <u>Psychology Today</u> Oct. 1971: 64–
     66.
Kaplan, Janice. "Politics of Sports." <u>Vogue</u>
     July 1984: 219+.
---. <u>Women and Sports</u>. New York: Viking, 1979.
Lance, Kathryn. <u>A Woman's Guide to Spectator
     Sports</u>. New York: A & W, 1980.
LaNoue, George R. "Athletics and Equality: How
     to Comply with Title IX Without Tearing Down
     the Stadium." <u>Change</u> Nov. 1976: 27–30+.
Mosher, Cheryl. "Women in Motion." <u>Women's
     Sport and Fitness</u> May 1985: 82.
Nash, Roderick. "Heroes." <u>American Oblique:
     Writing About the American Experience</u>.

Gatten 20

Ed. Joseph F. Trimmer and Robert R. Kettler. Boston: Houghton, 1976. 180–88.

O'Hara, Doug. "Libby Riddles Beat a Blizzard to Become Top Musher." <u>Christian Science Monitor</u> 28 Mar. 1985: 1+.

O'Reilly, Jane. "Out of the Tunnel into History." <u>Time</u> 20 Aug. 1984: 73.

---. "The Year of Getting Tough." <u>Vogue</u> Nov. 1984: 290–92.

Roiphe, Ann. Interview. <u>Ms.</u> June 1982: 14.

Schmerler, Cindy. "Splitting Ends." <u>World Tennis</u> May 1985: 8.

Schreiber, Linda and JoAnne Stang. <u>Marathon Mom</u>. Boston: Houghton, 1980.

Sherman, William. "The World of Tennis's Top Women." <u>Tennis News</u> May 1983: 194–97+.

Sullivan, Robert. "A Law That Needs New Muscle." <u>Sports Illustrated</u> 4 Mar. 1985: 9.

Torrey, Lee. "How Science Creates Winners." <u>Science Digest</u> Aug. 1984: 33–37+.

Uhlir, G. Ann. "Athletics and the University: The Post-Woman's Era." <u>Academe</u> July–Aug. 1987: 25–29.

Ullyot, Joan. "Forcing the Pace." <u>Runner's World</u> Jan. 1986: 43–51.

"A Winning Combination." Cardinal Club Brochure. Stanford, CA: Stanford U Dept. of Athletics, 1986.

OVERVIEW Many publications in the social sciences follow the APA style of documentation, outlined in the publication manual of the American Psychological Association. You will encounter this style (with some variations) in periodicals in areas like psychology, linguistics, or education. For identification of sources in the text of a paper, this style uses the **author-and-date** method. The date of publication appears with the parenthetical page reference: (Garcia, 1985, p. 103), or (1985, p. 103) if the author has been named in your text. Often, the APA style identifies an authority and the publication date of research *without* a page reference; interested readers are expected to familiarize themselves with the relevant research and consider its findings in context: (Garcia, 1985).

47a | PARENTHETICAL IDENTIFICATION: APA *doc*

Know the major variations of parenthetical identification in the APA style.

Study the following possibilities. Note use of commas, of *p.* or *pp.* for "page" or "pages," of the symbol & for *and*, and of similar distinctive features.

1. AUTHOR AND DATE ONLY:

The term <u>anorexia nervosa</u> stands for a condition of emaciation resulting from self-inflicted starvation (Huebner, 1982).

2. DATE ONLY — author's name in your own text:

As defined by Huebner, <u>anorexia nervosa</u> is a condition of emaciation resulting from self-inflicted starvation (1982).

3. PAGE REFERENCE — for direct quotation or specific reference:

Anorexia nervosa is "not really true loss of appetite" but "a condition of emaciation resulting from self-inflicted starvation" (Huebner, 1982, p. 143).

4. WORK BY SEVERAL AUTHORS — use *et al.* only in second or later reference: (Filmore et al., 1984).

Much advertising leads young women to believe that weight control equals beauty and success (Filmore, Suarez, & Thomas, 1984, p. 128).

5. SAME AUTHOR — for several publications in same year, use *a, b, c,* and so on, in order of publication:

Gamarken has conducted several similar experiments (1978, 1981a, 1981b).

6. REFERENCE TO SEVERAL SOURCES — list in alphabetical order, divided by semicolons:

Statistical estimates concerning the occurrence of the condition have varied widely (Gutierrez & Piso, 1982; Huffman, 1981).

7. Unknown or Unlisted Author — identify source by shortened title:

```
The influence of the media is pervasive and more
often than not harmful ("Cultural Expectations,"
1985).
```

Study model bibliography entries for the APA style.

Use the heading "References" for your final alphabetical listing of works cited or consulted. The APA style provides essentially the same bibliographical information as the MLA style. However, note the author-and-date sequence at the beginning of the entry. Watch for differences in the use of capitals, quotation marks, parentheses, and the like. (The following entries are adapted from *Researching and Writing: An Interdisciplinary Approach*, by Christine A. Hult.)

1. Book with Single Author Use initial instead of author's first name. Capitalize only the first word of title or subtitle (but capitalize proper names that are part of a title as you would in ordinary prose).

```
Bruch, H. (1973).  Eating disorders: Obesity, an-
     orexia nervosa, and the person within.  New
     York: Basic Books.
```

2. Book with Two or More Authors Put last name first for each of several authors. Use the symbol & (ampersand) instead of the word *and*.

```
Minuchin, S., Rosman, B., & Baker, L. (1978).  Psy-
    chosomatic families: Anorexia nervosa in con-
    text.  Cambridge, MA: Harvard U. Press.
```

3. MAGAZINE OR NEWSPAPER ARTICLE Do not put titles of articles in quotation marks; do not use italics (or underlining). If there is no volume number, use *p.* or *pp.* for "page" or "pages." If an article is concluded later in the issue, use a semicolon between the two sets of page numbers.

```
Miller, G. (1969, December).  On turning psychology
    over to the unwashed.  Psychology Today, pp.
    53-54; 66-74.
```

4. ARTICLE WITH VOLUME NUMBER Underline (italicize) the volume number for a periodical, with inclusive page numbers following after a comma: *6*, 152–69. If the number of the issue is needed, put it in parentheses between the volume number and the page numbers: *6*(3), 152–69.

```
Holmi, K. (1978).  Anorexia nervosa: Recent investi-
    gations.  Annual Review of Medicine, 29, 137-
    48.
Steinhausen, H. & Glenville, K. (1983).  Follow-up
    studies of anorexia nervosa: A review of re-
    search findings.  Psychological Medicine: Ab-
    stracts in English, 13(2), 239-45.
```

5. UNSIGNED MAGAZINE OR NEWSPAPER ARTICLE Alphabetize by the first word of the title, not counting *The, A*, or *An*.

```
The blood business.  (1972, September 11).  Time,
    pp. 47-48.
```

6. EDITED BOOK OR NEW EDITION Put abbreviation for "editor" (*Ed.* or *Eds.*) or for number of edition in parentheses.

Hartman, F. (Ed.). (1973). <u>World in crisis: Read-</u>
<u>ings in international relations</u> (4th ed.). New
York: Macmillan.

7. SEVERAL WORKS BY SAME AUTHOR Repeat the author's name with each title; put works in chronological order.

Bruch, H. (1973). <u>Eating disorders: Obesity, an-</u>
<u>orexia nervosa, and the person within</u>. New
York: Basic Books.
Bruch, H. (1978). <u>The golden cage: The enigma of</u>
<u>anorexia nervosa</u>. Cambridge, MA: Harvard U.
Press.

8. PART OF A COLLECTION Reverse initial and last name only for author or editor of the part, not of the collection.

Cherns, A. (1982). Social research and its diffu-
sion. In B. Appleby (Ed.), <u>Papers on social</u>
<u>science utilisation</u>. Loughborough U. of Tech-
nology: Centre for Utilisation of Social Science Research.

9. ENCYCLOPEDIA ENTRY If the author of an entry is identified, include the name.

Anorexia nervosa. (1978). <u>Encyclopedia of Human</u>
<u>Behavior</u>.

10. NONPRINT MEDIA

Maas, J. B. (Producer), & Gluck, D. H. (Director).
(1979). <u>Deeper into hypnosis</u> [Film]. Engle-
wood Cliffs, NJ: Prentice-Hall.
Clark, K. B. (Speaker). (1976). <u>Problems of free-</u>
<u>dom and behavior modification</u> (Cassette Record-
ing No. 7612). Washington, DC: American
Psychological Association.

Brewer, J. (1979, October). Energy, information, and the control of heart rate. Paper presented at the Society for Psychophysiological Research, Cincinnati, OH.

Problems of Freedom. (1982, May 21). New York: NBC-TV. Hult, C. (1984, March). [Interview with Dr. Lauro Cavazos, President, Texas Tech University].

Society's Effect upon the Rise of Anorexia Victims

A second direct cause of anorexia is the expectation society has regarding beauty. Over the
years, society's ideal of a beautiful body has
changed. The current look is angular and lean.
Starved, emaciated models portray this image in
the media, and it is promoted through diet pills,
drinks, foods, weight-loss centers, and bulge-
hiding clothes (Garfinkle, Garner, Schwartz, &
Thompson, 1980). Adolescents, vulnerable to peer
pressure, see these norms and strive to conform.
The male is exposed to ideal beauty also, through
such models as Miss America or Playboy center-
folds appearing on television and in magazines.
These models tend to exaggerate parts of the body
(DeRosis, 1979). A number of researchers have
linked these sociocultural pressures to the apparent increase of anorexia victims. Dieting is
a "sociocultural epidemic" and fashion's ideal
may indirectly affect adolescent women who eventually believe that weight control is equal to
self-control and will surely lead to beauty and
success (Garfinkle et al., 1980).   *second reference
                                        uses et al.*

Survey

In order to discover whether or not the family
and cultural pressures that lead to anorexia in young

12

PRACTICAL PROSE FORMS

Often you will be aiming at a summary about *one third* or *one fourth* the length of the original. Remember the following guidelines:

(1) Make sure you grasp the main trend of thought. Identify key sentences: the thesis that sums up the main point of an essay (or section of an essay), the topic sentence that is developed in the rest of a paragraph. Look out for major turning points — a strategic *however* or *on the other hand* that signals an important step in an argument.

(2) Reduce explanations and examples to the essential minimum. Leave out phrases that merely restate or reinforce a point already made. Condense lengthy explanations; keep only the most important details, examples, or statistics.

(3) Use the most economical wording possible. Write "negotiate" for "conduct negotiations"; "surprisingly" for "it came as a surprise to many observers that. . . ."

(4) Beware of oversimplification. Preserve an essential *if, but,* or *unless*. Keep distinctions between *is, will,* or *might*. Keep words like *only, almost,* or *on the whole*.

The following versions of the same passage will help you reconstruct the process by which one writer produced a summary. Notice how the writer crossed out everything that merely repeated or expanded the main points:

WORKING VERSION:

~~There are~~ numerous ~~cases of~~ societies ~~in which the armies of the night~~ have ridden triumphantly over minorities in order to establish a powerful orthodoxy ~~which dictates official thought~~. Invariably, the ~~triumphant~~ ride is toward long-range disaster.

Spain dominated ~~Europe and the world~~ in the 16th century, but ~~in Spain orthodoxy came first, and~~ all divergence of opinion was ~~ruthlessly~~ suppressed. The result was that Spain ~~settled back into blankness and~~ did not share in the scientific, technological and commercial ferment ~~that bubbled up in other nations~~ of Western Europe. Spain remained an intellectual backwater ~~for centuries~~.

~~In the late~~ 17th century, France ~~in the name of orthodoxy revoked the Edict of Nantes and~~ drove out ~~many thousands of~~ Huguenots, who added their intellectual vigor to lands of refuge such as Great Britain, the Netherlands and Prussia, ~~while France was permanently weakened~~.

~~In more recent times,~~ Germany hounded out the Jewish scientists ~~of Europe~~. They arrived in the United States and contributed ~~immeasurably~~ to scientific advancement here, while Germany lost ~~so heavily that there is no telling how long it will take it to regain~~ its former scientific eminence. The Soviet Union, ~~in its fascination with Lysenke~~, destroyed its geneticists, and set back its biological sciences for decades. China, during the Cultural Revolution, turned against Western science and is still laboring to overcome the devastation ~~that resulted~~.   Isaac Asimov, "The 'Threat' of Creationism," *The New York Times*

SUMMARY:

Many societies have suppressed minorities to establish a powerful orthodoxy, with disastrous long-range results. Spain, a dominant power in the sixteenth century, suppressed all divergence of opinion; as a result, it did not share in the scientific, technological, and commercial progress of Western Europe. Seventeenth-century France lost the intellectual vigor of the Huguenots who took refuge in Great Britain, the Netherlands, and Prussia. Germany lost its scientific eminence when it drove out Jewish scientists who advanced science in the U.S. The destruction of the geneticists set back Soviet science; the revolution against Western science devastated science in China.

WRITING PRACTICE 1   Study the following passage about artificial intelligence. Then write a summary of about one third the original length. (You may want to compare your summary with those prepared by your classmates.)

Some of the debates about the potential of artificial intelligence are fueled by confusions between intelligence and other elements of human-ness. Philosophers such as Herbert Dreyfus in *What Computers Can't Do* suggest that computers will never be able to pass beyond certain critical limits. For example, they will never "understand" language the way a human being can. A computer program encountering words telling it that "John loved Jane" or that "John felt pain when Jane socked him in the nose" will confront significant limits to what it can comprehend. It may be taught rules of inference based on the meanings of these words or on typical patterns of human interaction so that it could follow or make sense of a story containing these words. It could show that it understood by asking questions about the story, answering questions, or proposing consistent statements that might follow.

On the other hand, according to this view of the limits of artificial intelligence, the computer would never comprehend such notions as being in love or physical pain. It would lack the immediate emotional and physical experience of being a human body and psyche and the years of experiences that we use to flesh out our understandings of communications from others.

The problem with these claims is that intelligence is being confounded with consciousness and human-ness. Artificial-intelligence programs some day will most likely be able to manipulate language and other information in ways that we would judge as intelligent understanding when manifested by other human beings. However, such programs will never be conscious in the way a human being is.

On the other hand, these limitations can be partially overcome. Human beings regularly use the abstraction of language to expand their base of experience. We can converse and make inferences about worlds of which we have no direct experience because we have learned about them through language. Examples are faraway lands and times and uncommon emotions that we don't comprehend in the same way as those who have directly experienced them.   Stephen Wilson, "An Introduction to Artificial Intelligence," *Cadre 84*

---

49   **WRITING BUSINESS LETTERS**

OVERVIEW   Here are some general guidelines for letters that will get attention and results:

(1) State your business early in the letter. Close to the beginning, bring the issue or the problem into focus. Are you asking for information? Do you want to clear up a mistake? Do you need documents?

(2) Provide essential information. Include essential data such as order or document numbers, dates, or locations. Make sure your readers can locate an item, incident, or situation in their records or files. Where appropriate, give a brief history of the problem or condition to fill your readers in or bring them up to date.

(3) Highlight separate points. When there are several parts to a request or several layers to a grievance, you may find that the first one or two points get attention while the others get lost. Highlight (perhaps number in order) the several related points that need attention.

(4) Spell out what action you expect or request. Make sure your readers understand how they are expected to act on what you are telling them. What do you want them to *do?*

(5) Remember that appearance counts. A hastily written letter with messy erasures and added scribblings will not inspire confidence. Why should our reader invest time and effort in our problem or need if we ourselves don't seem to care?

49a | USING A MODERN FORMAT *form*

Use a functional modern format.

Much modern correspondence uses the **block format**, which does away with paragraph indentation and aligns all elements of the letter flush left. Paragraph breaks are shown by double-spacing between paragraphs. Letters using the block format are easy to produce on the typewriter or word processor, and they have a simple uncluttered look.

In a **modified block format**, the date and often also the closing with the signature block will move out to the center of the page. And some writers continue to prefer traditional indentation — five spaces — for paragraphs. The following are major elements of the business letter:

LETTERHEAD Most firms or organizations have stationery with a printed letterhead. It usually includes address and zip code, often in addition to a company logo or slogan ("The Sunshine People"). You can then start your typing with the date of the letter and go on to the inside address.

RETURN ADDRESS When you are not using the letterhead of a firm or an organization, type your return address above the date, as follows. Place it on the right side of the page:

```
                        138 South Third Street
                        San Jose, California   95126
                        January 12, 1990



        Ms. Patricia Sobell
        Personnel Manager
        San Rafael Gazette
        2074 Washington Avenue
        San Rafael, CA   94903


        Dear Ms. Sobell:
```

INSIDE ADDRESS If you know the title of the person, include it — on the second line, or after a comma on the same line as the name.

```
Ms. Patricia Sobell            Ms. Jane Day, President
Personnel Manager              The Waxo Company
San Rafael Gazette             225 East Elm Street
2074 Washington Avenue         Walls, KS 76674
San Rafael, CA 94903
                               Dear Ms. Day:
Dear Ms. Sobell:
```

Use a courtesy title like *Mr.* or *Ms.* (the latter now widely replacing the traditional *Mrs.* and *Miss*). A woman may show her preference for one of the possible choices in the signature line of her own correspondence:

Sincerely,   Sincerely,

Kate Gordon   *Helen Freid*

(Mrs.) Kate Gordon   (Ms.) Helen Freid

GREETING Whenever you can, address your letter to an individual. Put a colon after the greeting:

```
Dear Dr. Morton:
Dear Professor Grimaldi:
(No Prof. here — use Prof. only with full name in addresses)
Dear Ms. Freedman:
Dear Mr. Scopaz:
```

Things get complicated when you address a firm or an office-holder not known to you by name. The traditional "Gentlemen:" and "Dear Sir:" are out, since the person reading your letter may be a woman. "Dear Sir or Madam:" avoids sexism but sounds very old-fashioned. Try naming the group or identifying the person by office or status:

```
Dear AT&T:
Dear Ombudsman:
Dear Colleague:
Dear Fellow Student:
Dear Reader:
```

The **simplified style** does without the salutation altogether (thus skirting the gender issue) and puts a **subject line** instead. It often also omits the complimentary close (*sincerely, cordially*).

SIMPLIFIED: The Jackson Manufacturing Company
                 1334 West Devonshire Road
                 Bolivar, MO 65613

                 SUBJECT: Water Rationing During July

BODY OF THE LETTER Lay out your message in a series of pointed paragraphs, with a good flow from point to point. Avoid long rambling paragraphs in which information gets lost. Double-space between paragraphs.

COMPLIMENTARY CLOSE AND SIGNATURE The traditional closing is a variation of *sincerely, sincerely yours, cordially,* or *yours truly,* followed by a comma. (This **complimentary close** is omitted in the simplified style.)

Leave four lines for your signature and then type your name. Include an official title or function if you are writing in an official capacity. Align the signature block with the *Sincerely.*

Sincerely,

Pat Gramat

Pat Gramat
Program Chair

NOTES If someone other than the author of the letter has typed it, the typist's initials appear a double space below the signature block, flush left. Other possible concluding notes include *Enclosure* (for instance, a chart, résumé, or offprint is attached) and *cc* to name people who have been copied (that is, sent a copy).

jw
Enclosures
cc: Chris Cremona

Study the following examples of business letters using the block format or the simplified style. Some of the sample materials in this section have been adapted from Walter Wells, *Communications in Business,* 5th ed. (Boston: Kent, 1988).

full block
format
BETTER BUSINESS COMMUNICATIONS
23875 South Campbell Avenue
Tucson, Arizona 85721

April 28, 1990

Dr. LaVerne Prescott, President
Modern Graphics
1987 Ocean View Drive
Los Angeles, CA 90025

Dear Dr. Prescott:

Thank you for your recent inquiry about the format of current business letters. This letter illustrates the full block format widely used in
business today. All major elements of the letter
begin at the left margin, including the first
word of each paragraph. The body of the letter
is single-spaced, with double spacing between
paragraphs.

This format is easily produced on a typewriter or
word processor. It has a simple and uncluttered
modern appearance. However, some businesses prefer a modified block format, with the date and
the signature block moved to the center of the
page.

Many businesses adopt an official letter format
and then expect everyone in the organization to
follow it. Please feel free to write or call
with any questions about the details of this
style.

Sincerely,

Greg Traverse

Greg Traverse
Customer Relations

simplified style **BETTER BUSINESS COMMUNICATIONS**

23875 South Campbell Avenue

Tucson, Arizona 85721

May 19, 1990

Dr. LaVerne Prescott, President
Modern Graphics
1987 Ocean View Drive
Los Angeles, CA 90025

SUBJECT: The Simplified Format for Business
Letters

As a follow-up to my letter of April 28, I'm
writing this letter to illustrate the simplified
format in action. The simplified format, with
its subject line in place of a salutation, makes
it easy for the reader to identify the subject.
But if that subject is negative, the writer may
want to find some phrasing that avoids a negative
impression.

Some teachers now teach the simplified format ex-
clusively. Others are holding out for one or the
other of the more traditional forms.

Please note that the complimentary close as well
as the initial salutation has been left out in
the simplified style.

Greg Traverse

Greg Traverse
Customer Relations

km

BUSINESS ENVELOPES Here are some examples of well-typed business envelopes. Remember: Accurate names and addresses are essential. Neatness counts.

```
Lawndale Pharmaceutical Company
170 Medena Road
Akron, Ohio 44321
                                                    SPECIAL DELIVERY


                     Dr. Joan Coulton
                     10372 White Oak Avenue
                     Granada Hills, CA 91344
```

```
United Bank of Iowa
1640 Medina Road
Des Moines, Iowa 50313


          Attention Ms. Pat Corveau

                     Schrader Lock Company
                     624 South First Avenue
                     Sioux Falls, SD  57104
```

```
San Marcos Resort,
Country Club & Colony
Chandler, Arizona 85224


                          Mr. Don Busche, President
          Confidential     Northridge Manufacturing Company
                          402 West Main Street
                          Northridge, Illinois  60162
```

49b | THE LETTER OF APPLICATION

Send letters of application that get results.

Remember the following advice:

(1) If you can, be specific about the position for which you apply. Mention the advertisement or the person that alerted you to the vacancy. (But do not mention leads that smack of the grapevine.)

(2) Find a way in. If possible, show some knowledge of the company or the institution. Show that the future employer already means something to you. For instance, mention an open house you attended at the company's research facility, a tour of a manufacturing plant, or a newspaper article about the company's plan for a new product or technique.

(3) Present your academic qualifications to advantage. Mention selected key courses that might relate to the employer's needs; stress what you learned.

(4) Stress previous experience. Make the most of part-time work. If appropriate, mention volunteer work, fund-raising efforts, campaign organizing, and the like. Stress what you learned from such experiences — for instance, learning to handle people's special needs by working with disabled students or learning to budget resources by being in charge of equipment in a youth camp.

(5) If you want to list references, first get permission from those whose names you want to use. Quietly drop from your list the names of teachers or former employers who show little enthusiasm when you tell them about your plans.

(6) Consider preparing a separate résumé. If the account of your qualifications is extensive, put it on a separate data sheet.

letter of application

892 N. Brendan Ave.
San Jose, CA 95113
November 17, 1990

Ms. Carla Gabriel, Editor
South Valley News
2239 Monterey Highway
Live Oak, CA 95032

Dear Ms. Gabriel:

In answer to your advertisement, I wish to apply
for the position as general reporter. I am a
journalism major and have worked for a student
daily and an urban newspaper. I have come to appreciate the effort and perseverance required in
newsgathering and in overcoming the obstacles in
its path.

On February 1, I will graduate from San Jose
State University. While getting a degree, I have
taken a broad range of courses, representing all
areas of editing and reporting. Also, I have
been a general reporter for the Spartan Daily for
two years. Last summer I worked for thirteen
weeks on the Santa Clara Journal, as an intern
sponsored by the Journalism Department of my
college.

My most satisfying assignment was a guest editorial for the Spartan Daily, in which I stressed
the role of the journalist in keeping the public
informed about community needs, crime, and health
hazards and in defending the right to know.

References are available on request. I will be
glad to come to your office for an interview. I
can be reached at (408) 294-4789.

Sincerely,

Pat Romeros

Pat Romeros

résumé   JEAN LAPORTE

Demmler Hall
Valhalla University
Kent, Ohio 26780
(613) 428-7600

Education

  B.S. in Industrial Engineering, Valhalla University, June 1989; top ten percent of class,
  with special course work in statistics, moti-
  vational psychology, business law, and
  communications
  Dean's Honor Roll 1987–1989
  U.S. Paint Company Scholarship 1987
  Member of Industrial Relations Club
  Secretary of the Student Council
  Attended Colfax College, Colfax, Indiana,
  1985–1986

Experience

  Station Manager, Arco Service Station, Cleve-
  land, Ohio, 1986–1987
  Staff Supervisor, Cleveland Summer Camp, Kiowa,
  Ohio, summer 1986; responsible for housing,
  activities scheduling, and occasional disci-
  pline of fourteen counselors and 110 campers
  Camp Counselor, Cleveland Summer Camp, Kiowa,
  Ohio, summers of 1983 and 1984

Personal Interests

  Politics, world affairs, camping, chess
  Junior chamber of commerce member and volunteer hospital worker

---

WRITING PRACTICE 2 Write a *letter of application* for a position in which you have at one time or another taken an interest. State the qualifications that you might have by the time you are ready to apply for the position in earnest.

---

50   WRITING ESSAY EXAMS

OVERVIEW Essay examinations require you to organize your thinking and marshal evidence in a limited time.

Remember the following guidelines:

(1) Get an overview of the exam. Know what you are expected to do, especially if the exam comes in several parts. Take in specific instructions: Are you being asked to *summarize* information? *compare* two procedures or historical events? *explain* a point of view and show why you agree or disagree? *define* and illustrate a key term?

(2) Budget your time. Set aside some time at the beginning to collect your thoughts, to organize your thinking. (Take some rough notes.) Allot the right share of time for different tasks. (Be sure to respond to the last part of a three-part or four-part question.) Save some time for last-minute proofreading.

(3) Work from a rough outline. If you can, have a clear three-point or four-point program in mind as you write. A well-worked-out plan will minimize backtrackings, afterthoughts, and lame repetition.

(4) Make strategic use of detail. Select a key example to illustrate a concept or to support a point. Include an apt quotation or a striking statistic to show your familiarity with the subject.

(5) Write legibly. The people grading essay examinations are only human, and they feel the pressure of time. By and large, they will prefer an answer that is short but well written to one that is scribbled and goes on and on.

| ANALYZING A PASSAGE |

Organize your reactions when analyzing a passage.

Suppose you are asked to explain a passage that the American poet Walt Whitman wrote about capital punishment. You are then asked whether you agree or disagree with the writer, and to show why. To help you focus your reading and organize your response, remember guidelines like the following:

(1) Sum up the author's central message. Early in your response, give an overview or preview that summarizes the main idea, including important distinctions or reservations:

> In this passage, Whitman does not say outright that he is for or against the death penalty. Instead, he attacks the system that *implements* the punishment — a system riddled by indecision and contradiction. Whitman feels that society should make a definite choice, for or against the death penalty, and then act firmly on that resolve.

(2) Organize your answer around major points. Try to mark off major steps in the argument, major segments in the author's train of thought:

> Whitman touches on at least three reasons why the contemporary practice concerning capital punishment is unsatisfactory. First, the application of the law is fitful and *inconsistent*. The law seems undecided whether to inflict capital punishment for murder, and the authorities often find ways to spare or pardon the offender. . . .
>
> Second, the application of the law often seems patently *unfair*. When an execution does take place, as often as not the condemned prisoner belongs to a racial minority. . . .
>
> Third, and above all, the authorities *procrastinate*. Any minor technicality can delay a case indefinitely. . . .

(3) Respond to the author's style. Quote striking or revealing phrases:

> Although Whitman does not state his own position on the justification of capital punishment outright, we can infer that he person-

ally favors it from several remarks he makes in the passage. With a sarcastic tone, he refers to "soft-hearted (and soft-headed) prison philanthropists" who sympathize with convicted criminals. He refers to "penny-a-liner journalists" who write melodramatically about the plight of convicted murderers. He criticizes judges and lawyers who bend the law to give "the condemned every chance of evading punishment."

(4) Take a stand. State your own position clearly and forcefully. Use precedent, parallels, or revealing contrast to clarify and bolster your own point of view:

> There are times when our anger makes us clamor for the death of an offender. But in our more thoughtful moments, we are likely to think differently. In Tolkien's *Lord of the Rings*, there is a passage that goes roughly as follows: "There are many who live who deserve to die. There are many who die who deserve to live. Can you give life? If not, do not be so quick to take it."

(5) Back up the stand you take. Fortify your position with reasons or examples:

> My main reason for opposing capital punishment is that it is too arbitrary and unpredictable. Too much hinges on the cleverness of lawyers and on the prejudices of juries. One recent study found that good-looking, personable defendants are more likely to be acquitted than those who look threatening, gloomy, or disturbed. To judge from this study, juries may well send a man to his death because he *looks* like a villain; they thus make a mistake that can never be made good.

SAMPLE TEST 3 *Instructions:* In the following passage from *Progress and Privilege*, William Tucker joins in the debate between advocates of progress and advocates of conservation. Where does he take his stand? What is his argument in this excerpt? Is it in any way new or different; does it shed new light on the issue? Where do you stand on the issue raised in this excerpt, and why?

> The fact is that, from a human perspective, nature, for all its diversity, is still not very stable. For most of nature, the laws of

survival still mean matching the ever-present possibilities for catastrophe against the inborn capabilities of organisms to reproduce fantastic numbers of offspring to continue the genetic line. Let me give an example. In 1963, scientists doing an oceanographic survey in the Indian Ocean came across a 4,000-square-mile area covered with dead fish. The number equaled about one quarter of the world's catch at the time. The fish had not died from human activity but were the victims of the inevitable nutrient cycles that govern most of the ocean environment. . . .

The unpleasant truth is that natural cycles, for all their diversity, are still enormously unstable. Genetic diversity can protect diversified forests from diseases, for example, but fires can still destroy whole forests. It is this uncertainty that evokes the widely used strategy of fantastic procreative abilities among plants and invertebrates.

As mammals, we have tried to overcome these unpredictabilities through a different strategy — by internalizing our environment and building self-correcting controls. That is why we do not need the heat of the sun, as reptiles do, to warm our blood and give us energy at the start of the day. Nor are we as devastated by dryness or changes in the weather. (Some insect populations have been shown to go through population explosions and crashes from temperature changes of only a few degrees.) By building internal controls, we have been able to stabilize the relationship between our internal and external environments.

The business of human progress, then, has been a *continuation* of this evolutionary line of development. Human progress has not been "growthmania" or "growth for growth's sake," as environmentalists often charge. It has been a deliberate effort to extend our control over the external environment so that we are not subject to the instabilities and unpredictabilities of nature's cycles.

Thus, we do not guarantee ourselves any kind of stability in human affairs by foregoing the effort to humanize the environment, and letting nature take its course. That only returns us to nature's unpredictabilities. What we *can* do is be very cautious about disrupting natural systems any more than is necessary, and conserve wildlife whenever possible. This does not have to be strict preservation, but only a matter of taking concern for wild systems where they still exist.

Make an essay examination show what you know.

Many tests, whether open-book or written without books or notes, ask you to show how well you know the material you have studied. Keep in mind guidelines like the following:

(1) Prepare for a writing test. Much of your preparation will be to *prestructure* the material that you might use in a paragraph or short essay. Identify key terms that could provide the focal point for explanation or discussion. Chart the main steps in a procedure or the key parts of an argument: *Photosynthesis* — what are the essential processes that make it work? *Alienation* — what does a character in a short story say and do to show his alienated condition? *Agrarianism* — where, when, and why did it originate?

(2) Memorize key supporting details. Imprint on your memory pointed definitions, striking examples, telling statistics, and short pointed quotations.

Modern civilization, what D. H. Lawrence calls "my accursed human education," has alienated us from our roots in the natural world.

According to Barbara Tuchman, dates are fundamental to the historian because they show order in time and thus make possible "an understanding of cause and effect."

(3) Check the exact wording of instructions. Assume the question in a history exam is "What do you consider the most important difference between the fall of Greece and the fall of Rome?" Do not simply put down everything you can remember about the fall of Greece and the fall of Rome. Focus on the key word in the instructions: *difference*. What *is* the difference? How can you line up material that will bring out this difference as clearly and convincingly as possible?

(4) Structure your answer. Especially in a paragraph-length response, try to come straight to the point — make your first sentence sum up your answer or your stand on the issue. Proceed to cover major parts of the problem or key reasons in a clear order — for instance, from simple to difficult or from unlikely to probable. (Avoid lame transitions like *also* or *another*.)

Study the following instructions for an essay exam on a literary subject and a student response that a teacher selected as a model:

INSTRUCTIONS: *A common type of character in much contemporary literature is the individual who is trapped by a trick of fate, by the environment, or by his or her own nature. Choose such a character from a short story you have recently read. Define the trap in which the character is caught. Describe any struggle on the part of the character to become free.*

ANSWER: Katherine Mansfield's Miss Brill finds herself trapped by her spinsterhood and the advancement of age. She is old, as the story tells us; she's as old as her out-of-date fox fur. She is alone, with no friends, relatives, or close neighbors. This is her trap. Like a bird that will create its own prison in its own territory, Miss Brill makes hers. She does not socialize, nor does she try to make something useful out of her life but rather preys like a parasite on other people's more interesting, colorful lives. In her own way, Miss Brill struggles to escape her prison. She daydreams. The world that she lives in is a fantasy world where all people are friendly and related. She "belongs" in this world, whereas in the other world, the real world, she actually belongs to no one.

Quite successfully, Miss Brill loses the real world for a time, but she cannot escape the real world entirely. The real world sticks its head in, in the form of a boy who says "Ah, go on with you now." So she goes home, more aware than ever of her prison's boundaries and helpless (by her own nature) to do anything else. She can only fly on home to the security and solitude of her cold, dark nest.

Note the following points about this answer:

- It responds directly to the *key term* or *key idea* in the assignment. The assignment asks about a character who is *trapped*.

This word and its synonyms keep echoing throughout the student's answer: *trapped, prison, boundaries.*

- The first sentence sums up the answer as a whole. It gives the brief, clear definition of the "trap" that the question asks for.

- The point about the character's trying to escape through daydreaming responds to the *second* part of the question. But note that this point is worked organically into the first paragraph. The student has planned this answer; there are no afterthoughts, no "Oh-I-forgot" effect.

WRITING WORKSHOP 4   Work with a group that shares an interest in one of the topics listed below. Find and study background material in a textbook or encyclopedia. Help set up a timed essay test on the topic chosen by your group. In writing your own short essay on the topic, start with a preview or overview. Trace clearly the major steps, arguments, or dimensions of the topic. Include some striking details or examples. After the test, share in a group critique of the results. Possible topics:

- evidence for the theory of evolution
- the Ptolemaic and the Copernican views of the solar system
- diet and heart disease
- the abolitionist movement
- the Mayan civilization
- causes of the Great Depression

INDEX

Note: Boldfaced numbers preceding page numbers refer to the numerical handbook key. Page numbers followed by (gl) refer to an entry in the Glossary of Usage.

INDEX

INDEX

INDEX

Additional Symbols

¶	New Paragraph
no ¶	No Paragraph Break
?/ *or* ;/	Use Mark Shown
^	Correct Omission
x	Correct Obvious Error

Guide to Charts and Lists

Guide to Revision

ab	abbreviation
adv	adverb
agr	agreement
ap	apostrophe
awk	awkward
ca	case
cap	capitalization
coh	coherence
coord	coordination
CS or /;	comma splice
d	diction
dev	development
div	dividing word
DM	dangling modifier
emp	emphasis
FP or //	faulty parallelism
frag	sentence fragment
FS	fused sentence
gl	glossary
gr	grammar
hy	hyphen
inc	incomplete
inf	informal
ital	italics
log	logic
MM	misplaced modifier
ms	manuscript
mx	mixed construction
NS	nonstandard
num	number
pass	passive
plan	plan
ref	reference
rep	repetition
sf	shift
sl	slang
sp	spelling
st	sentence structure
sx	sexism
trans	transition
var	variety
vb	verb
w	wordiness